Lecturing the Victorians

Lecturing the Victorians

Knowledge-Based Culture and Participatory Citizenship

Anne B. Rodrick

BLOOMSBURY ACADEMIC
LONDON • NEW YORK • OXFORD • NEW DELHI • SYDNEY

BLOOMSBURY ACADEMIC

Bloomsbury Publishing Plc, 50 Bedford Square, London, WC1B 3DP, UK
Bloomsbury Publishing Inc, 1359 Broadway, New York, NY 10018, USA
Bloomsbury Publishing Ireland, 29 Earlsfort Terrace, Dublin 2, D02 AY28, Ireland

BLOOMSBURY, BLOOMSBURY ACADEMIC and the Diana logo are trademarks of Bloomsbury Publishing Plc

First published in Great Britain 2024
This paperback edition published 2026

Copyright © Anne B. Rodrick, 2024

Anne B. Rodrick has asserted her right under the Copyright, Designs and Patents Act, 1988, to be identified as Author of this work.

For legal purposes the Acknowledgments on p. x constitute an extension of this copyright page.

Cover image: Royal Institution – Sir Roderick Murchison's Lecture on the Distribution of Gold Ore, 1850. Geological talk in London © The Print Collector / Alamy Stock Photo

All rights reserved. No part of this publication may be: i) reproduced or transmitted in any form, electronic or mechanical, including photocopying, recording or by means of any information storage or retrieval system without prior permission in writing from the publishers; or ii) used or reproduced in any way for the training, development or operation of artificial intelligence (AI) technologies, including generative AI technologies. The rights holders expressly reserve this publication from the text and data mining exception as per Article 4(3) of the Digital Single Market Directive (EU) 2019/790.

Bloomsbury Publishing Plc does not have any control over, or responsibility for, any third-party websites referred to or in this book. All internet addresses given in this book were correct at the time of going to press. The author and publisher regret any inconvenience caused if addresses have changed or sites have ceased to exist, but can accept no responsibility for any such changes.

A catalogue record for this book is available from the British Library.

A catalog record for this book is available from the Library of Congress.

ISBN: HB: 978-1-3502-8860-7
PB: 978-1-3502-8863-8
ePDF: 978-1-3502-8861-4
eBook: 978-1-3502-9947-4

Typeset by Newgen KnowledgeWorks Pvt. Ltd., Chennai, India

For product safety related questions contact productsafety@bloomsbury.com

To find out more about our authors and books visit www.bloomsbury.com and sign up for our newsletters.

To Jules and Birdie

Contents

List of Illustrations	viii
Acknowledgments	x
Introduction: The Development of Knowledge-Based Culture	1
1 "The Desire to Form a Little Lecture Union": Early Lecture Circuits	13
2 Shaping "Intelligent Public Opinion": The Development of Civic Institutions	45
3 "The General Literature and Thought of Our Country and Time": Mid-Century Lectures, Debates, and Discussions	73
4 Professionalizing the Popular Lecture	115
5 The Late-Victorian Popular Lecture	157
Conclusion	181
Notes	185
Select Bibliography	241
Index	261

Illustrations

Figures

1.1	Sites of lectures for Balfour, Dawson, and Grossmith, 1852–62	37
1.2	Titles of lectures delivered at reporting institutions by Clara Lucas Balfour, George Dawson, and George Grossmith, 1852/3–1861/2	39
3.1	Categories and subcategories of analysis	76
3.2	Lectures by reporting institutions in the *Journal*, 1850–72	78
3.3	Numbers of lectures by category	78
3.4	Subcategories of science lectures as a percentage of all science lectures	79
3.5	Subcategories within social science lectures, 1850–71	84
3.6	Lectures in two subcategories of current events, 1850–71	88
3.7	Lecturers in reports and lists, 1850–70	90
3.8	Lecturers listed in 1854, 1859, and 1862 by subject area	93
3.9	Subject categories for discussion and debate	105
4.1	Decline in reported lectures, 1878–1903, in YUMI institutions	119
4.2	Categories of sampled lecture/entertainment advertised in *ILG*, 1862–87	125
4.3	Sample of advertisements from July 1, 1884 issue of *ILG*	126
4.4	Selected programs in the *ILG*, 1866 and 1883	127
4.5	Decline in institutions affiliated with the Society of Arts, 1867–98	144
4.6	Lectures delivered by category, 1870–1900	144
4.7	Changes in lecture categories as a percentage of all lectures	145
4.8	Leeds Phil.-&-Lit., 1869–1900	147
4.9	Birmingham and Midland Institute, 1870–1901	148
4.10	Newcastle Lit.-&-Phil., 1869–95	148
4.11	London Sunday Lecture Society, 1869–90	151
4.12	Selected programming at institutions, January–May 1889	152
5.1	Advertisement by the Lecture Agency, Ltd., 1899	176

Tables

3.1	Lecture Categories by Number and Percentage of Total Lectures Delivered	77
5.1	Program of Lectures, Titles, and Fees for Halifax SLS, 1896–7 Season	170

5.2	Leeds Phil.-&-Lit. Lecture Program, 1899–1900	173
5.3	Midland Institute Monday Evening Lectures, 1899–1900 Season	174
5.4	Halifax Sunday Lecture Society, 1899–1900 Lecture Program	174
5.5	Bradford Mechanics' Institute Lecture Program, 1903–4	175

Acknowledgments

This was an undertaking of many years and could not have come to life without the resources of the Hathi Trust and the British Library or the comments and suggestions from colleagues at a decade of British and Victorian Studies conferences. Warm thanks go to Wofford College for research funding and sabbatical time; the wonderful Wofford College librarians, especially Emily Witsell; and my history department colleagues. Thanks also to Elizabeth Rodrick and Steve Brandwood for research assistance, and to my writers' group: Christine Dinkins, Laura Barbas Rhoden, Kimberly Hall, and Rachel Vanderhill. Much love and gratitude to friends and family: Trina Jones, Sally Hitchmough, Karen Goodchild, Donna Creedon, Jane Arrington, Jolene Satre, Dave Rodrick, Delia Beard, and Kathy Phillips; my daughters, Elizabeth and Julie; my sisters, Susan and Jane; and my grandson, Henry (because every book should have a baby). This was a two-dog project: thanks to Toby and Sadie.

Introduction

The Development of Knowledge-Based Culture

> As a valuable means of friendly intercourse between different classes of society, as affording an agreeable variety and imparting a lively interest to the lecture season, and as giving an opportunity to many highly gifted persons of charming and instructing their neighbours, amateur lectures are of vast importance.[1]

A season subscriber to the Bradford Mechanics' Institute, scanning the program of lecture offerings for 1860–1, would have found many "highly gifted persons" willing to charm and instruct. Among them were J. L. Burnet, vicar of Bradford, on "The Importance of Character"; exiled French socialist Louis Blanc on "The Mysterious Personages and Agencies of France, Toward the End of the Eighteenth Century"; William Lankester on "Animals Used by Man as Food"; local Baptist minister J. P. Chown on "Six Days in Rome"; writer and humorist George Grossmith on "Sketches by Boz" and "The Ludicrous in Life"; and the wildly popular Birmingham minister, George Dawson, on "John Calvin" and "William Cobbett." These men and others contributed to a season that offered science and morality, history and humor, and travel and political economy, launched by an opening soiree and prize-giving ceremony that combined the pleasures of sociability with the rewards of scholarship. Missing from the platform this year was Clara Lucas Balfour, one of the favorites of the institution, who had appeared with Dawson and Grossmith two seasons previously in what was regarded by many institution secretaries as the most coveted trifecta of "amateur" popular lecturers, guaranteed to attract a standing-room-only audience. The broad attractions of this lecture season appeared both unexceptional and customary to subscribers. Yet a mere decade earlier, the very existence of the popular lecture was under scrutiny as a dangerous waste of time, seducing serious men and women into idleness and complacency, providing only the smallest fragments of fact wrapped in a mantle of frivolity.

How did this most ubiquitous of Victorian cultural artifacts become unremarkable? This book explores the rise of the popular lecture in provincial England between about 1850 and about 1910, beginning with the earliest individual attempts to organize a lecture circuit and ending with the popular lecture as a consumer good, largely organized by the formal lecture agency. I focus both on the changing content of the popular lecture itself and on the ways in which educators, critics, politicians, and audiences perceived the multiple purposes of the lecture: its presence within a lecture season provided sociability, entertainment, and education for individual men and women, on the one hand, and status, identity, and local power for the institution and its governors and donors, on the other. Delivered in venues that ranged from the venerable mechanics' institute to the purpose-built regional culture center, the popular lecture was used by cities and towns outside London to shape their own civic identity as they provided both leisure and culture across lines of class and gender.[2] At the same time, participation in knowledge-based culture, defined below, empowered individual men and women to claim the rights and privileges of participatory citizenship.

Martin Hewitt has argued that "there are numerous obstacles … to a more general account of public lecturing and it is unclear to what extent a coherent single narrative of its history is feasible."[3] Lectures numbered in the thousands in villages, towns, and cities throughout the nineteenth century, and to treat them as a unitary, consistent cultural phenomenon is both impossible and wrongheaded. In fact, one of the challenges faced by scholars is the basic question, "What are we talking about when we say 'lecture culture?'" Hewitt has suggested that the "popular lecture" be defined as one "delivered under the auspices of associations of rational recreation or in recognized public spaces, and constituted by its newspaper coverage," while noting that this approach excludes much deliberately religious and political rhetoric.[4] This approach helps us embrace the variety of societies and associations that emerged in the second half of the nineteenth century to provide knowledge-based culture, especially in the provinces. It also helpfully cordons off the work of a number of hobby and leisure clubs, many of which moved steadily away from formal lectures, as well as civic service groups like the Union of Workers among Women and Children, which turned to lectures as part of their educational mission for working-class wives and mothers.[5] And while newspaper coverage of the popular lecture was thin and inconsistent while taxes on paper, ink, and postage remained in effect, after the repeal of the final paper duty in 1861 an expanded army of reporters enthusiastically embraced these vehicles of education and entertainment as fit subject matter for their readers, while the widespread deployment of scissors-and-paste journalism ensured broad reprinting across the provincial press for well-received speakers.[6]

Defining Knowledge-Based Culture

The genealogy of the English popular lecture will be explored in the following chapters, but here I want to introduce the ways in which this artifact and others like it were used by both the provincial locality and the individual resident. I focus on areas outside London where the choices for leisure and culture were relatively limited, in contrast to the capital, and thus where the popular lecture attracted broad attention. While London helped shape both early and late iterations of the popular lecture, its institutions were often grappling with the city's oversupply of lecture options, and thus their work was often guided by issues of economic competition and survival in ways that were peculiarly metropolitan. Further, London as the capital had no need to deploy knowledge-based culture as a municipal tool to claim authority and importance, while provincial cities and towns—seeking to both emulate and distance themselves from London—actively encouraged such culture as a marker of modernity. By mid-century, well before formal incorporation defined the political status of growing urban areas, city leaders and social critics generally agreed that commerce and industry should be tempered by judiciously selected instruments of culture, from libraries and reading rooms to concerts and lectures. Such offerings might, with great care, be made available not only to trustworthy middle-class men and their families but also to workers striving to rise. Clergyman and scholar Robert Vaughn claimed in his 1843 *The Age of Great Cities* that such spaces "have now raised a large portion of our people from their former state of ignorance and sensuality, to their present measure of acquaintance with letters and with the means of mental improvement."[7]

Early-nineteenth-century social critics, less sanguine than Vaughan about the inherent civilizing effects of literacy, had urged careful oversight of new working-class readers who might well retain a dangerous measure of sensuality, couching their fears in the worries about unsupervised idleness that persisted throughout the century. However, faced with the brutal realities of industrialization and urbanization, city leaders by mid-century were generally willing to identify the benefits of "discussion and mental progress" as markers of modernization. In 1844, Richard Cobden, MP, told his Manchester audience that "wealth will only be a tainted lustre, unless accompanied by civilization, and by the cultivation of the intellect."[8] Other Manchester leaders argued that their city embodied "moral, social, and political progress," based on Mancunian energies as "a go-ahead sort of people," while Liverpool's social institutions were "calculated to meet every form of bodily distress and every moral evil, which is capable of being mitigated by the action of benevolence."[9] Birmingham leaders claimed that its cultural offerings helped remove "the reproach that the word 'Brummagem' has too often conveyed from careless or malicious mouths."[10] Leeds, Bradford, and Newcastle made similar claims, often invoking the splendors of Rome, Venice, and other ancient cities in order to deflect charges of philistinism.[11]

Smaller towns were nearly as energetic as these larger cities in demonstrating their dedication to "mental and moral progress," a phrase regularly deployed in early nineteenth century to describe the autodidact's solitary pursuit of knowledge under difficulties. These provincial leaders stressed the ways in which their cities and towns were simultaneously paradigms of modernity as well as protectors of tradition, each adopting a relatively similar frame of "moral, social, and political progress" and then selecting a diversity of illustrative examples that marked them as unique. Placing this type of mental progress in the public sphere, adjacent to the physical symbols of modernization—halls, roads, parks, and civic centers—helped smaller cities and towns claim a space at the table of culture as well: a multipurpose town hall or dedicated library might be beyond their resources, but lectures and classes in an existing mechanics' institution would signal that town leaders were as dedicated to mental and moral progress as the regional centers of Birmingham, Manchester, and Leeds.[12]

This type of mental progress, available to create go-ahead Mancunians and benevolent Liverpudlians, formed the basis of what I refer to as "knowledge-based culture" in the second half of the nineteenth century. Using this neologism allows us to consider not only the popular lecture but also the related field of what has been labeled "argument culture," describing the culture of debate and discussion that flourished during this period.[13] This phrase also releases us from the class hierarchies embedded in the leisure/idleness divide that was instantiated in the idea of "rational recreation" and that colored many nineteenth-century discussions of working-class self-improvement, such as those by James Hudson and James Hole in the 1850s.[14] As I show below, while Hudson, Hole, and many of their peers argued that the early attempts at informal adult education embedded in "rational recreation" had uniformly "failed to reach the audience for which they were intended," many other social critics and educationists moved quickly away from this focus on failure and instead reimagined the grand social project of knowledge-based culture.

Exactly what constituted this grand project? In 1860, reflecting on the growth of mechanics' institutes, literary societies, and the like, Society of Arts member Harry Chester described in detail the pattern institute that he predicted would soon be found in every town across the kingdom. It would do the work of both education and recreation, bringing order out of the chaotic jumble of small clubs and competing societies, and would acknowledge the responsibilities and opportunities of a locality's active citizens as well as the hobbies and interests of its more passive members. Importantly, it would "include all grades of society":

> There should be of course a comfortable reading room, and a circulating library from which books may be taken to be read at home. There must be lectures to instruct and amuse, and concerts to delight and soften. There ought to be open committees of social science to elicit and diffuse useful information concerning health, education, and other common points of political, social, and domestic economy; there ought to be a museum, not of miscellaneous objects, like a pawnbroker's shop, but a well arranged and carefully and fully labelled collection, illustrating the natural history, the trade, and the antiquities of objects of art and industry. Classes for the discussion of suitable subjects under the guidance of a competent moderator; readings of Shakespeare and other standard authors; innocent amusements, such as chess and draughts, fencing and single-stick for indoors; and for out-of-doors gardening, cricketing, leaping, swimming, boating, and other manly and invigorating games; tea parties of course and excursions occasionally; and (I should say) tea and coffee, and their edible accompaniments, every evening, if it be possible to provide them. Care must of course be taken that the amusement may not inconvenience the readers. Above all, and the foundation of all success, all real utility, there must be classes for systematic instruction under competent paid teachers.[15]

Chester's description of an ideal society, which summarized and distilled the clamorous mid-century debates over leisure and culture, reconsidered the early Victorian model of adult self-improvement—heroic, lonely, and often unfocused—and in its place envisioned spaces that combined physical comforts of masculinized domesticity with intellectual commitments to a new kind of useful knowledge. Eclectic cabinets of natural history specimens, formerly associated with the earliest learned societies but by 1860 regarded as "miscellaneous" rather than coherent, were to be replaced by collections curated to tell stories of progress and wonder that would be accessible to any visitor. The working-class autodidact, attempting to master whatever knowledge he could grab hold of in his solitary and limited free time, would give way to the mutually supportive debaters, discussants, and careful readers who relied not only upon trained teachers and ably managed libraries but also upon experts providing access to modern knowledge in a modern world, and who could balance the efforts of "brain-work" with manly exercise. All of this would take place in physical spaces that were conducive both to study and to organized leisure pursuits, and where the labor of providing coffee, tea, and comestibles was rendered invisible. The haphazard would give way to the purposeful; the wasteful would give way to the efficient; the exclusive would be opened up to inclusivity. Thus was the early-nineteenth-century vision of rational recreation updated and modernized for "all grades" of the Victorian man—and occasionally the Victorian woman. Knowledge-based culture was a shared pursuit that was optimistic, expansive, flexible, and robust.

As we will see in the following chapters, this model inspired the creation of hundreds of individual institutes. Their successes and failures were at least as dependent upon interlocking pressures of local interests as on broad national trends. At the same time, however, the shared commitment to knowledge-based culture allows us to see connections across space and time, minimizing to some degree the particularism embraced by individual cities and towns. While individual civic institutions claimed to carefully curate their offerings to reflect the specific interests of their locality, the reality was that programs across geographical space were remarkably similar, shaped by and helping to shape the mélange of science and social science, arts and literature, and current events that bound educated and half-educated men and women loosely together. Certainly, the emphasis on the local was frequently mentioned: it helped shape an early and unyielding commitment to organizational autonomy within provincial institutions, and also encouraged the late-century elevation of local talent as part of a holistic interpretation of the provision of knowledge-based culture. However, as we shall see in the following chapters, the content of this culture followed generally similar guidelines across space and status.

Knowledge-based culture was rooted specifically in the decades between 1850 and 1910, when difficult conversations about education, suffrage, and empire could be balanced by the conviction that intellectual and moral progress, pursued by an interested public and underwritten by subscribers, patrons, and consumers, was embedded in Victorian notions of citizenship. The spread of knowledge-based culture was, by 1850, emerging as a recognized badge of modernity equal in importance to the production of new knowledge in the elite learned societies. A good lecture season, tightly constructed to attract the most popular speakers and reflecting the specific interests of its subscribers, was one crucial way to demonstrate this, especially when such a lecture season was embedded within programming that also highlighted local resources and talent. Knowledge-based culture was local and national, individual and social, inclusive and disciplined, voluntary and embedded in civic activism. It served as a messy social glue that held together an increasingly inconsistent bundle of needs and demands, and it would inevitably erode under the pressures of changing notions of citizenship and governance. By the eve of the Great War, knowledge-based culture was a national commodity rather than a resonant form of community identity.

Citizenship and Cultural Competence

In the decades after 1850, however, this social glue was especially important to men and women in the middle and lower middle classes who lacked other entry points into provincial society. They had no direct political voice, as it would be decades before most adults would be permitted even the local franchise. Indeed, the cultural institutions, lectures, and debates under scrutiny in this study invite us to consider anew the ways in which cultural competence was interpreted as a model of nineteenth-century citizenship that was only partially embodied in political belonging. Scholarship on the scope and meaning of British citizenship has exploded over the past decade, especially in examinations of the modern welfare state and contemporary policy debates over immigration. Many of these works gesture briefly to the nineteenth century to acknowledge the roots of modern discourses over power and belonging. Yet, Victorian citizenship was not merely a precursor to the ideas that shaped the twentieth century, and as a concept it requires careful attention in order to be a useful tool in nineteenth-century history. Do we begin from a notion of citizenship as a legal status based upon rights enshrined in a constitution or a set of legal precedents? Do we refer to the political rights of direct representation, or to the qualifications necessary to serve in public office? Do we mean "social citizenship," that is, the notion undergirding the modern welfare state that men and women have legitimate expectations not only of personal autonomy but also of access to general services like unadulterated food, clean water, and education for their children? Does such social citizenship lead in a straight line to political representation, or vice versa?[16] Can these terms sufficiently encompass the complexities of identity and exclusion in the nineteenth century?

In a recent essay, Matthew Grant suggests that we consider "registers" of citizenship as we examine the postcolonial world, and further that we examine these registers from the perspectives of both status and practice:

> In post-war Britain, we can see that citizenship has been historicized within three broad registers. First, historians often see citizenship as a narrowly politico-legal framework, analyzing the legal, political and social rights of the population, but also the obligations expected in return. Secondly, historians see citizenship as resulting from "Belonging" to a constructed national community, and investigate both how belonging has been a key marker, or gateway, to citizenship status, and the ways in which concepts of national community have been constructed (not to mention the consequences for those deemed "outside" that community). Thirdly, historians have also focused on what we can call differentiated aspects of citizenship, particularly on the creation of "good citizens" and on debates about how citizenship can be enhanced or improved, often with a particular emphasis on voluntary action or engagement.[17]

These three registers generally map onto three broadly defined areas: legal/political rights (along with their associated expectations of basic government services), community ties, and civic engagement. Citizenship as a *status* encompasses all three of these registers, Grant argues; one might hold a passport, be registered to vote, or receive public assistance as part of a menu of legal and political rights; live within a defined neighborhood as part of a network of community ties; and meet eligibility requirements for public office as one mode of civic engagement. Citizenship as a *practice* also embraces all three of these registers, whether positively or negatively. Positive practices of citizenship might range from suffrage to volunteer work, while negative practices might include the active avoidance of pursuits that could flag immigration or work status. Both status and practice intertwine, and all three registers—legal/political, community belonging, and civic engagement—inflect status and practice.

This paradigm of "registers of citizenship" has obvious and urgent resonance in the twenty-first century, but it can be fruitfully deployed for the nineteenth century as well. In fact, with some modifications, it may help us sort out some of the many overlapping ways in which citizenship is used to describe activities and attitudes over the course of municipal development and modernization in our period.[18] Citizenship as a status in this period was legal and political, but not always simultaneously. Women as a group lacked political status, of course, but married women also notoriously lacked any autonomous legal status for much of the century. Citizenship as a practice could be equally exclusive: for working-class men, legal citizenship—defined most basically as a recognition of such legal rights as to enter into contracts, inherit money or property, or be recognized in a court of law—existed, while political citizenship was a goal only slowly and partially realized over the course of the century.

Because the legal/political register of citizenship—both as a status and as a practice—was so contradictory and limited in the Victorian period, it is difficult to apply this register consistently to men and women of the nineteenth century. Similarly, the range of social rights contingent upon legal and political status was so narrow that "social citizenship" in the modern context is anachronistic when applied backward to the Victorian and Edwardian eras. Social citizenship is a twentieth-century artifact that simultaneously grows out of and makes invisible a nineteenth-century focus on the moral ties between citizen and state. And it is this moral component that encourages us to explore the second and third registers of citizenship outlined by Grant: community belonging and civic engagement. Much of the language used by nineteenth-century writers on citizenship clustered around the interaction between these two registers. As a number of scholars have shown, Victorian social critics from John Stuart Mill to T. H. Green, inspired by the Greek notion of the *polis*, found it relatively easy to equate "citizen" with some version of "engaged community member," rather than reserving the label for those who could participate politically.[19] As early as the 1840s, Mill was famously wrestling with the ways in which "the participation of the private citizen ... in public functions" could best permit even the least among many "to feel himself one of the public."[20]

This emphasis on civic engagement as an expression of participatory citizenship within a local community was an important through line in Victorian society. Decades after Mill, T. H. Green would argue that civic participation was indispensable to the fullest development of both individual humans and collective human society: "only citizenship makes the moral man; ... only citizenship gives that self respect which is the true basis of respect for others, and without which there is no lasting social order or real morality."[21] In fact, by the end of the nineteenth century, many writers would insist upon the need to rediscover and to reinvigorate the personal connections not only between subject and empire but also between individual and municipality. In each realm, "citizenship" was used to signify both status and practice, both membership and engagement. Thus, in 1893 textbook author and University Extension lecturer Oscar Browning explained that "every Englishman is a citizen in several different ways. He is a citizen of the town or the county district to which he belongs; he is a citizen of England, as a Scotsman he is a citizen of Scotland and an Irishman of Ireland; he is a citizen of the United Kingdom, and he is also a citizen of the great British Empire. He has different duties in each of these capacities—they begin with him at home, and they gradually widen until they embrace the circuit of the world."[22] Similarly, Percy Matheson, in an 1897 essay tracing the meanings of the word back to the ancient world, argued that the "citizenship" of Demosthenes and Plato was built upon the intimate relationship of man to polity, and that this intimacy was essential to good citizenship: "The very vastness of the [Roman] Empire meant loss of civic unity and loss of civic character," he argued, and the British Empire, still intact, was a modern iteration of that enormous and impersonal entity. Matheson argued that one could only reconcile the apparent incommensurability of the individual and the empire by remembering that "every man counts; ... no man can say that his action or inaction is indifferent to the community in which he lives. ... If one is swallowed up in a million, let us remember, on the other hand, what a tremendous human force a million means, if only every unit is alive with devotion and endeavor, if all are actual citizens, and not merely ciphers in a census." Thus, if all are participatory members of a community, however small or vast, all may claim the prestige as well as the responsibilities of citizenship. The key to a more productive understanding of being in the world, he argued, was to remember that "there is not one of us who has not power in his [sic] measure to contribute to the commonwealth by the devotion of personal service and by the force of personal opinion and character and conduct."[23]

This emphasis on the personal relationship between citizen and community, and the imperative that this relationship result in active contributions to some aspect of civic life, was not novel to the late-Victorian social critics who sought to persuade readers that they each had duties and opportunities within an apparently vast society. Instead, it had deep roots in early and mid-Victorian culture, expressed perhaps most famously in Samuel Smiles's 1859 *Self-Help*. Smiles's work articulated not a simple paean to individual self-interest but rather a complex imprecation to "*be* and *do*," to pursue self-culture in whatever form possible, and then to become an "artisan of civilization," shaping the health of the community through participation in some civic space that could range from the tiny chapel-based debating society to the municipal reorganization of housing and sanitation.[24] This participatory citizenship was theoretically open to all, across lines of class and, slowly but increasingly, of gender; it embraced vast spaces of intellectual interest and practical activism within the growing city, celebrating the local as a space in which individual virtue could signal civic competence. Those mid-century men who entered wholeheartedly into this pursuit of both self-education and civic culture, especially from the lower middle and upper working classes, regarded themselves as a caste, a self-appointed community toiling in the vineyards of the Lord, and they were generally viewed by the local elite as participating in a kind of citizenship that conjoined individual aspiration and civic improvement in a period where the demand for voluntary effort was both vast and rewarding.[25] Women entered this space about a generation after this caste of men had done so, discovering after 1867 that the combination of party politics and increasingly professionalized municipal governance had bifurcated citizenship into suffrage, on the one hand, and voluntary civic participation, on the other. Men could vote, but most below the middle class were increasingly viewed as unnecessary to the development of good civic health. Women, especially in the middle classes, continued to be excluded from the national franchise but were encouraged to pursue maternalist civic interests and to enter the voluntary public sphere that operated as an adjunct to the expanding work of the municipality. Their efforts to reorient the conversation back to a generally participatory "*be* and *do*" were often frustrated by rhetoric that privileged the economically competent male worker at the expense of the culturally competent woman. Indeed, it appeared to many active middle-class women that the vote, especially on the national level, had become, in Frances Power Cobbe's 1877 plaint, "the typical act of citizenship" and had supplanted the "*be* and *do*" that had encouraged and ennobled such a variety of activisms.[26] Despite this frustration, as Helen Meller has shown, middle-class women continued to seek out new opportunities for "displaying citizenship."[27] In a period of shifting expectations, and as the precursor to the idea of "social rights" for every citizen that would guarantee health, education, and well-being, voluntaryism continued to provide an acknowledged site for participatory citizenship.

By focusing on voluntaryism as a marker of both identity and belonging—the two registers of status and practice—Victorian participatory citizenship elevated the individual within the local and focused on the associational within the municipal. Urban residents might exercise a civic voice via cultural events that included debates, club memberships, and participation in *conversaziones* and public meetings, knowing that this voice would in turn influence choices made by city leaders. These civic voices were amplified by the local press: individual societies depended upon advertisements as well as celebratory reports of *conversaziones* and lecturers, while lecturers needed good reviews and advance ticket sales. Press coverage of these speakers was fundamental to cementing the community ties that undergirded provincial reputation, and the nineteenth-century practice of "scissors-and-paste" journalism bound local efforts into a national web of knowledge-based culture.

The Evolution of Lecture Culture up to the Great War

This book is intended as a first exploration of lecture culture in England and how it intersected with issues of civic identity, citizenship, and cultural competence. In the pages that follow, much of this exploration will come not only through the records of these societies and institutions, but also through the popular press, as these lectures were reported in numerous forms and in countless newspapers across the kingdom. Indeed, these lectures themselves formed one part of an ecosystem of popular culture, and in examining the journalistic representations of Victorian lecturing, we can also begin to see how content spilled across boundaries of form, with "serious" public lectures for the middle classes, "discussion clubs" for working men, and Sunday evening lectures for "the people" all grappling with such contemporary questions as "Shall We Bury or Cremate Our Dead?"[28]

The following chapters proceed chronologically. Chapters 1, 2, and 3 explore the emergence and stabilization of lecture culture. Chapter 1 will explore the early decades of lecturing and the ways in which the successful American lyceum model challenged English educators and social critics to formalize and centralize this crucial vehicle for cultural competence. This period, from about 1850 to about 1870, will highlight the shifting ways in which civic leaders and educators understood the nature and purposes of lecture culture, from its roots in amateur science to its location within mechanics' institutes, literary and philosophical societies, and other private bodies. The early, ineffective attempts of the Society of Arts to establish a national agency that could provide "appropriate" lecturers and subject matter to these nominally private institutions will allow us to trace the fraught conversations over the purposes of higher education and the ways in which class and caste might limit access to culture.

Chapter 2 will trace the emergence of intentionally civic societies—that is, institutions publicly dedicated to the cultural improvement of the town or city—during this same period. It is in these spaces that we can see how knowledge-based culture was differentiated from earlier models of rational recreation in its implied links to civic engagement. Late Georgian and early Victorian rational recreation had been sufficiently expansive to incorporate the elite learned society or the carefully-policed Sunday school or gardening club, all sites focused on the experience of the individual and his or her conscious pursuit of improvement. Knowledge-based culture, in contrast, was increasingly assumed to be located in spaces available to all who chose to participate, across lines of class and gender, where social interaction and the consumption of established knowledge were combined in an often-unspoken imperative to demonstrate cultural competence both to and in the world. These mid-century institutions, from the smaller mechanics' institutes to the old-established literary societies to the new purpose-built regional centers, all participated in the conviction that both knowledge and culture were integral to participatory citizenship, and that such citizenship was theoretically open to all. In Chapter 2, we will see how both existing and new societies and institutions interpreted these imperatives in order to best suit the needs and demands of their local contexts, adopting programs that located the popular lecture within a broader provision of soirées, conversaziones, concerts, and classes. We will also explore the gaps between aspiration and reality, as committee members and subscribers worked through a platonic model of inclusivity that often did not match up with ingrained prejudices of status, class, and locality.

Chapter 3 will look in detail at the content of this knowledge-based culture. Using data gathered from society and institution reports, newspapers, and the unexplored riches of the *Journal of the Society of Arts*, and augmenting that data with the many books and pamphlets dispensing guidance and practical hints to lecturers, discussion societies, and institutions, this chapter will present an ecosystem of popular knowledge between 1850 and 1870. What were the shared assumptions that governed the programming of elite literary-&-philosophical societies (hereafter "lit.-&-phils"), middle-class debating societies, local civic institutions, and other sites of knowledge-based culture? How did topics circulate among committees, individuals, and audiences? In short, what were the Victorians talking about?

Chapters 4 and 5 move into the period after 1870, as the landscape of knowledge-based culture began to buckle under pressure from educators, entertainers, and subscribers. In Chapter 4, we will focus on two developments: first, the tireless efforts of editor and lecturer Joseph Simpson to professionalize the practices of the popular lecture through the pages of his *Institute, and Lecturers' Gazette*, and second, the development of new physical and temporal spaces for the popular lecture pioneered by the Sunday Lecture Society (SLS). Founded in 1869 by Thomas Huxley and others "to provide for the delivery on Sundays in the Metropolis, and to encourage the delivery elsewhere, of Lectures on Science—physical, intellectual, and moral—History, Philosophy, and Art; especially in their bearing on the improvement and social well-being of mankind,"[29] the SLS was pitched to an ideal imagined audience of educated men and women from the middle and artisan classes who understood "improvement" within the model of participatory citizenship. The ways in which provincial cities and towns adopted this model, and how they located their own "kindred societies" alongside existing spaces for knowledge-based culture, illustrate the range of interpretations placed upon the "well-being of mankind."

Chapter 5 explores the ways in which late-century popular lecture culture, by now a settled part of civic society, began to spill over into new spaces and functions. These spaces included the suburban institute, which generally augmented serious offerings in science, history, and art with music, travelogues, and performances by popular entertainers, such as the light-opera performer known simply as "Snazelle,"[30] as well as the growing number of University Extension centers, where the popular lecture provided the foundation for courses of tutorials and examinations. Many lecturers appeared on the dockets of both civic and educational institutions, often delivering identical or only lightly edited versions of their lectures to audiences divided by class but united by interest. This chapter will also examine how the formation of the Workers' Education Association in 1903 purposively and decisively divided the popular lecture from twentieth-century webs of popular adult education.

The sheer volume of lectures delivered during this period calls for some editorial decisions here, at the beginning of this book. As noted above, following Hewitt, lectures delivered in churches and chapels, as well as within and for political organizations, have been eliminated from this study. Many of the lecturers themselves have faded into complete obscurity. For the speakers who can be recuperated, I have included brief identifiers in the text and in the notes; thus, art history lecturer Whitworth Wallis is identified as the director of the Birmingham Museum and Art Gallery, while Arthur Diosy is noted as the founder of the Japan Society of London. Fuller biographical notes have been supplied for the men and women especially important to knowledge-based culture as a set of aspirations and institutions, and who may be harder for readers to trace.

The trajectory from 1850 to 1914 can be informally likened to a transition from the serious science lecture to a focus on comfortable cultural enrichment and thence to a restoration of class-based boundaries of access and participation. This monograph, with its data-rich exploration of the content and structures of knowledge-based culture, will add significantly to our understanding of how this important aspect of Victorian culture was inseparable from changing ideals of citizenship and participation.

1

"The Desire to Form a Little Lecture Union"

Early Lecture Circuits

The Society of Arts would do well to have a list of lecturers whom they could recommend to country societies, who would then be relieved of some difficulty in the choice of proper men.[1]

In 1869, the American *Putnam's Magazine* published an essay entitled "How They Manage Their Lectures in England." The short answer was "very badly indeed." According to this anonymous columnist, the English system was vastly inferior to the American lyceum system, which was by the postbellum period well established as a national web of culture.[2] American audiences paid for lectures, American lecturers demanded fair payment, and this cash nexus permitted "first-rate men" to make a living via "this really noble and thaumaturgic agency for the public culture."[3] In England, by contrast, lecturers were expected to lecture *gratis* or for minimal fees; such men, noted the columnist, tended to be "the gentry and the aristocracy" who were conservative by nature and delivered lectures that were "improving" but dull, while avoiding any energizing or controversial topics that could attract large audiences. Thus, "a curse of pettiness shrivels the whole scheme," leaving the system "lean, scant, miserly" and—worst of all—built upon "neutrality—the most contemptible word in the English language." Inevitably, claimed the writer, English audiences "soon come to loathe what are called instructive lectures, and they clamor for musicians and buffoons."[4]

This slashing critique was certainly overdrawn. Thousands of lectures were delivered every year at a variety of institutions throughout the kingdom. What England lacked was a parallel to the American lyceum system, an organized web of more than 5,000 institutions bundled into a "commercial circuit."[5] Within the American system, lecture culture "was at once a formative class practice, a market transaction, an instrument of reform, and a marker of civic identity" that evolved rapidly from the primarily local to a highly efficient bureaucracy booking lecture stars across the young nation.[6] By mid-century on both sides of the Atlantic, the popular lecture—described in 1860 as "almost a necessity in modern civilization"[7]—was generally defined as a formal talk by a paid speaker, given to a nonspecialized audience of ticket-holders that routinely crossed lines of class and gender, and often delivered in a recognizably public space. In England, however, the lack of a kingdom-wide system or circuit intensified the aura of ephemerality already surrounding the popular lecture, especially for those observers not intimately involved with a local institution or society striving to establish its own robust programs of culture. English lecture culture was never wrestled into a coherent or programmatic model, nor was the English lecture circuit ever standardized in the same way as the American circuit. Early lecture culture was instead disconnected and unorganized, and English lecturers operated autonomously and independently. By the time the American system had entered into its highly bureaucratized "star phase" in the 1850s and 1860s, however, many English institutions had realized that a centralized lecture system might standardize the provision of lectures and make them more affordable.

This chapter examines the often fractious conversations around the first broad attempt "to form a little lecture union"[8] under the aegis of the Society of Arts, as well as the competing and eventually overwhelming imperative to preserve local autonomy. Representatives of several hundred institutions used the Society's meetings and publications to spar over the nature of the popular lecture, its relationships to education and entertainment, and its place within institutions struggling to adopt new models of civic culture. The decades of the 1850s and 1860s saw particularly lively debates about the interplay between adult education and respectable leisure, with societies, athenaeums, institutes, and clubs defining and redefining lecture culture in the provinces, attempting and sometimes failing to reconcile their founding principles with the changing needs of their subscribers and the neighborhoods they served.

These vigorous arguments can be traced in the pages of the *Journal of the Society of Arts*. Founded in 1754, the Society of Arts was formed for "the Encouragement of Arts, Manufactures and Commerce" throughout the UK, offering advice and support to local philosophical societies and highlighting problems and developments of scientific and technological interest in its *Transactions*.[9] Nearly a century later, in order to facilitate this encouragement in a modern world transformed by industry, the Society founded the Union of Institutions "to increase the efficiency of the metropolitan and provincial mechanics' institutes" in promoting education for workingmen (and, less commonly, women).[10] The establishment of the Union included the launch of a new weekly *Journal* to replace the century-old *Transactions*. This new periodical not only continued the *Transactions*' practice of reporting and parsing developments in the arts of science and commerce, it also specifically invited letters, essays, and institutional annual reports that addressed the purposes of higher education, the meanings of "mechanic" and "artisan," the utility of lectures as supplements to formal classes in the sciences, and the increasing attractions of entertaining rather than strictly educational offerings. The pages of the *Journal* provided a forum for advocates who sought to persuade the Society to formalize a lecture web that would supply these affiliate societies with speakers appropriately vetted by and, in some cases, outfitted and compensated by the Society of Arts itself. The *Journal* also printed correspondence and institute reports that interrogated the centrality of the lecture to both working-class adult education and the broader scope of middle-class culture. Indeed, much of the early correspondence and reporting in these pages exposed multiple fractures within the very idea of the lecture. Should it be "popular," attracting an intentionally wide audience, or merely "public," maintaining an air of exclusivity by limiting admission to well-to-do society members and their guests? Should it be part of a multi-lecture course within a set curriculum? Must it focus on work-related instruction? Ought it to be accompanied by demonstrations or visual aids? Could it be entertaining as well as educational? Why did it cost so much? What *was* a lecture, anyway?

The Early Science Lecture: Performing Cultural Competence

All of these questions can be traced back to the emergence of lecture culture in Britain with the development of the science lecture in the late 1790s and early 1800s. Private associations dedicated to the amateur but enthusiastic pursuit of scientific knowledge emerged across the kingdom in this period, often coalescing around an individual member's personal collection of specimens or implements and growing to include not only small museum spaces, informal talks by members, and a general air of "clubbability," but also more formal addresses by specialists.[11] The science lecture dominated the intellectual world of the emerging middle classes for much of the Romantic and early Victorian periods, decades before it was reshaped as a tool of respectable education for the working classes.[12] University lecturers, physicians, inventors, and other men of science lectured first to amateur societies in London and other urban centers; then, as they found that they could augment their income or even, in increasing numbers, make a living solely by presenting lectures on scientific and technological phenomena, they began to travel throughout the country. "Science," born of a highly respectable partnership between natural history and theology, had by the late eighteenth century become a recognized marker of middle-class status.

The culture of the science lecture, as it developed within the emerging middle classes of the late 1700s and early 1800s, was shaped by multiple pressures. The earnest and serious pursuit of scientific knowledge helped define middle-class leisure, especially in the provinces, where cities and towns lacked London's cultural riches. The associational life that nurtured this pursuit provided a masculine conversational space in which to signal intellectual competence, while the social practices such as soirées and *conversaziones* that emerged around these associations engaged women as guests as well as organizers, thus recognizing feminine claims to inclusion.[13] Because these associational activities were recognized across the kingdom, they also provided tools with which men and women could demonstrate cultural competence even in small provincial towns.

In addition, while the pursuit of scientific knowledge incorporated its adherents into a "republican scientific community"[14] that could handily demonstrate middle-class status, such knowledge was neither overtly political nor completely class-based. As Howard Wach has shown in the case of Manchester, "science" could be curated and controlled in ways that excluded divisions rooted in party politics or religious enthusiasm, "the twin afflictions of sectarian strife," or in class antagonism.[15] Further, scientific inquisitiveness did not necessarily demand disciplinary rigor nor lead inexorably to specialization, but instead often helped inform what R. J. Morris has referred to as a general middle-class culture of "collectors and borrowers"[16] and what one president of the Manchester Lit.-&-Phil. would describe retrospectively as "the *dilettante* element."[17] Finally, this pursuit of knowledge did not necessitate a break with older forms of natural theology, although the policing of boundaries over "appropriate" discussion content could occasionally be difficult to enforce.[18] Thus, early science lecture culture appealed to a range of audiences, eventually becoming so familiar that novelists like Elizabeth Gaskell and Charles Dickens, a generation apart, would create beloved minor characters around the comedic possibilities of scientific intelligence.[19]

By the 1820s and 1830s, science lecturers met a growing demand for scientific but specifically non-rigorous generalism with a potent mix of demonstrations, illustrations, slides, and other techniques of showmanship. These moments of spectacle grew rapidly over the years, as audiences increasingly expected entertainment as well as intellectual stimulation.[20] As a result, audience composition for science lectures inevitably branched off from serious and well-prepared members of private associations to embrace as well a public defined primarily by disposable income and curiosity. This middle-class public was broadly if not deeply educated, passably interested in current questions of science and technological innovation, and committed to the presentation of knowledge *qua* knowledge, even if in highly colored and entertaining forms. It was also willing to pay a reasonable price for the opportunity to perform this kind of cultural competence, which was based on the consumption rather than the production of knowledge.

The science lecture was born in London but spread rapidly throughout the kingdom. The associationally grounded life of science in London was "chaotic" in the early decades of the nineteenth century, but J. N. Hays argues that it had become "more highly structured and institutionalized" by the 1830s.[21] One result was that the itinerant science lecturer—and his counterpart, the "practical" man "who carried on a trade or business and occasionally lectured on it"[22]—became more fully identified with the provinces than with the capital. It was increasingly possible to make a living outside of London as a science lecturer, although the per-lecture fees in the provinces rarely reached the same dizzying levels as the seven or eight guineas that could be charged in London.[23] Simon Naylor, examining the associational world of the natural sciences in Cornwall, argues that early lecture networks linked these private science associations across local, provincial, and national lines, so that itinerant lecturers could move from a club in Ireland to an association in Scotland to a lecture hall in the north of England and find an "immediate familiarity" with both the place and the audience.[24] Itinerant lecturers appeared on platforms across the kingdom under the auspices of literary and philosophical institutes and local science societies.[25] These lit.-&-phils. and other similar societies were nominally private, but regularly relied upon lecture ticket sales and a public audience both to offset other costs and, just as importantly, to demonstrate cultural credibility, not only to local men and women but also to peer institutions and rival urban centers across the country. This web of lecturing helped shape urban culture in part around "subscriber science," defined by Diarmud Finnegan as "a collective and voluntary interest in science as a social and intellectual pursuit suitable for citizens in an age of reform."[26] And in this age of reform, the world was watching: as Enda Leaney notes, "High turnouts reflected well on towns while poor attendances received public censure from newspaper proprietors."[27] Thus, although these early lectures were, strictly speaking, private affairs, they were perceived of, written about, and attended as cultural offerings to a larger public.

Many itinerant science lecturers straddled the line between these popular public offerings and more demanding educational lecture courses focused around specialized knowledge and new technologies and aimed at students and practitioners in medicine, chemistry, and other fields. Such courses were usually located within a private association: the Newcastle Lit.-&-Phil., for example, launched its first season of lectures in 1793 with a complete course on comparative anatomy, followed by "a syllabus of nineteen lectures on the Philosophy of Natural History, ... to be illustrated and confirmed by experiments where the subjects may require them," while in 1835 the Manchester Athenaeum offered a course of twelve lectures on geology.[28] Science lecturers moved with ease between specialist and generalist spaces, thereby connecting lecture audiences to a web of listeners and helping to reinforce the place of "science" within popular culture. A similar ease characterized men whose reading in theology augmented their education in the sciences, allowing them to present the wonders of science within the context of the broader wonders of creation, so that, as Leaney has argued, many lecturers "could deliver what amounted to scientific sermons."[29] Thus, in the early decades of the nineteenth century, geologists, physicians, chemists, botanists, and others carved out significant lecture circuits in the provinces, where scientific and technological innovations couched in the context of natural theology attracted eager audiences.

The high point of the independent itinerant science lecturer came slightly before mid-century; after about 1870, generally speaking, the autonomous amateur speaker in the sciences would be eclipsed by the professionally trained university man, on the one hand, and the permanent exhibit hall, on the other.[30] Between 1840 and 1860, however, these lecture practices shaped public culture in several important ways. First, the growth of a science-based lecture culture as a kingdom-wide pursuit normalized the lecture as a space in which some part of the public gathered and paid to listen to a speaker expound on a specific topic, in a way that was recognizably different from the experience of a Sunday sermon. Second, the broad umbrella of "science" permitted lecturers and lecture organizers to explore topics only peripherally related to difficult or arcane subjects, thus appealing to those who were most keenly attuned to the social and mental pleasures of pursuing not-too-difficult knowledge in a public hall surrounded by friends and neighbors. The flexibility of the science lecture, in turn, afforded new opportunities for itinerant lecturers to support themselves outside of London. And finally, the purported neutrality of the sciences appeared to render these lectures politically and theologically tame; they were safe not only for men of status but also, in more entertaining iterations, for their wives and daughters. Taken altogether, then, the science lecture as an artifact could be tailored to serious as well as general audiences, and could be deployed both for academically rigorous study and for entertaining sociability.

Science, Sociability, and Self-Help: The Mid-Century Mechanics' Institutions as Sites of Culture

Importantly, these characteristics shaped the science lecture into a genre that appealed powerfully not only to the provincial middle classes but also to the maturing mechanics' institute movement, from which the popular lecture would emerge as an indispensable component of civic culture. Mechanics' institutions originated in Glasgow, Edinburgh, and London in the early 1820s, then spread rapidly across England and Scotland.[31] Their founding documents generally articulated a commitment to continuing education for workers engaged in industry. The Manchester Mechanics' Institution in 1824 was typical in delimiting its practical goals: "It is not intended to teach the trade of the Machine-maker, the Dyer, the Carpenter, the Mason, or any other particular business, but there is no Art which does not depend, more or less, on scientific principles, and to teach what these are, and to point out their practical application, will form the chief objects of this Institution."[32] Early mechanics' institutes generally did not assert claims to "the betterment of mankind," a phrase which would echo throughout the speeches and reports produced by many subsequent associations, including the Sunday Lecture Society and its offshoots examined in Chapter 4. Instead, "practical applications" of "branches of science" would be elucidated through lecture courses and evening classes as well as the establishment of reading rooms and libraries.

As Thomas Kelly has shown, these earliest institutions drew intentionally upon the organizational models of a number of London literary and philosophical societies and emulated their deployment of lectures and lecturers as fundamental educational tools.[33] By about 1840, despite the economic contractions of the mid-1820s, these institutions were a fixture throughout the kingdom. In the first history of the movement, published in 1851, James W. Hudson estimated that there were over seven hundred "Literary and Mechanics' Institutes" in England, Wales, Scotland, and Ireland.[34] The 1851 census, published in 1854, put the number of such institutions at 1,057, while noting that many were more accurately described as mutual improvement societies "established in connection with Sunday schools" or "professional institutions, for the benefit of the members of particular professions."[35] Many of them came together to form regional unions in order to share resources, including libraries and classroom equipment; the largest and most well-known of these unions was the Yorkshire Union of Mechanics' Institutes (YUMI), founded in 1838 in Leeds and claiming 109 affiliates by 1850.[36] Other local and regional unions followed, including the Lancashire and Cheshire Union, based around Manchester, and similar unions for institutes in the west, north, and midlands.[37] When the Society of Arts founded its own Union of Institutions in 1852, it would welcome these regional unions into membership alongside hundreds of stand-alone institutes.

Hudson's 1851 study, like the 1851 census, differentiated the category of "Literary and Mechanics' Institutes" from such other purveyors of adult education as Sunday schools, temperance clubs, and stand-alone circulating libraries.[38] Yet this broad umbrella sheltered a wide variety of institutions linked only loosely by some commitment to knowledge-based culture for adults, a commitment that ranged from basic instruction in literacy and numeracy to courses of advanced science lectures and from curated museum spaces to *conversaziones*. The disparate titles adopted by these institutions were a testament to the disparate nature of their offerings: a very large majority called themselves "Mechanics' Institutions" (or "Institutes"), but a large minority were self-labeled as "Literary and Scientific Institutes," with smaller numbers adopting the titles of "Literary, Scientific, and Mechanics' Institute," "Athenaeum," "Polytechnic," "Lyceum," "Literary and Mechanics' Institute," "Reading Room" or some offshoot of "Society for the Diffusion of Useful Knowledge."[39] The inclusion of "literary" in these self-chosen labels signaled a level of aspirational affinity with the lit.-&-phils. and other learned societies, an affinity reinforced by the lecture programming, reading rooms, and other benefits offered to members.

Hudson himself attempted to offer some clarification between, for example, the lyceum or athenaeum for the young middle-class man and the polytechnic for the pursuer of advanced coursework in the sciences, but his focus on the commonalities of all of these institutions—that is, their commitment to the purposeful provision of knowledge-based culture during leisure hours—both reproduced and reinforced in print one of the problems that he and his contemporaries encountered in talking and writing about these institutions. The earliest mechanics' institutions had generally been founded only to provide science instruction to local workingmen. Yet membership was never exclusive to one class. Janet Flexner, examining the first decade of the London Mechanics' Institution (established 1823), found that the proportion of "operatives"—defined inclusively to take in workingmen at any skill level—ranged from 72 percent to 68 percent of the total membership of some 1,100 men.[40] Thus, almost one-third of the members were not from "the class for which they were intended." As late as 1870, the percentage of workingmen in any mechanics' institution could range from 7 percent (at Nottingham) to nearly 70 percent (at Huddersfield).[41]

Both Hudson and James Hole, the YUMI honorary secretary whose 1853 *Essay* built on Hudson's work, acknowledged the variety within these institutions and, indeed, lauded much of the work done in broadening access to both education and culture.[42] They also shared a conviction that these societies had uniformly failed to achieve their founding goal: to provide science instruction to operatives. Hudson acknowledged "the universal complaint that Mechanics' Institutions are attended by persons of a higher rank than those for whom they were designed," while Hole, more optimistically, argued that "if clerks and shopkeepers had not joined the Institutes, the operative would have no more participated in their benefits than he does now, perhaps much less, since, in many cases, there would have been no such place open to him at all."[43] Hudson argued that in almost every case, all of these societies—mechanics' institute, literary society, library, athenaeum, society for the diffusion of useful knowledge—had become middle-class venues, defined and limited by patronage and class. While "we may congratulate ourselves at the useful operations of 'the Mechanics' and other middle-class Institutions," those useful operations—reading rooms, lecture seasons, circulating libraries, and evening classes—had been effectively appropriated by "men of middle age, principals of firms, professional men, managing and confidential clerks, factors, brokers, agents, and wholesale shopkeepers," and did not "supply the chief wants of the actual working population" or even of aspiring young men who were not yet old enough for formal membership.[44] As for the lit.-&-phils., especially in the provinces, they had become "imbecile" and were characterized primarily by "an aversion to amalgamate with the more popular and really useful Institutions."[45] Hudson's excoriations were tempered with examples of success—for instance, he commended Liverpool for its "many temples dedicated to the improvement of mankind," Nottingham for "the active thirst for information, so strikingly apparent in every department of human knowledge," and Preston for its "public spirit"—but he argued that, in general, these institutions had become "social necessities" rather than educational venues.[46] They reinforced claims to cultural competence within the middle classes instead of providing useful instruction for workers, and in the process drained off precious patronage that ought to go to programs specifically and exclusively devoted to working-class adult education.

Hole, a decade younger than Hudson and markedly less pessimistic, linked the changing nature of these institutions both to the large-scale social and economic upheavals of the 1830s and to small-scale pressures on individual workingmen. He noted, in the first instance, that the "great political excitement" that had attended the Reform Bill "is always unfavourable to the interests of such Institutions, especially among people like our own, with whom politics, in important epochs, possess an absorbing interest."[47] The strictures against political discussion in these societies pushed members away, he argued, and after 1832 institute committees made strategic choices to instead attract members with soirees, exhibitions, light reading, and music. This second generation of membership differed from the first in experience and expectation, and Hole argued that "in catering to the taste for amusement, [institutions] had formidable rivals in the singing saloons and similar places."[48] The result was inevitable: institutions lowered their membership fees and increased their "amusements," bleeding off funding for programs of science instruction and failing to attract either the serious operative or the professional teacher or lecturer. Compounding this redirection of resources, Hole argued, workers stayed away for other reasons: "want of early instruction," "later hours of employment" especially in the summer, shame-inducing levels of poverty, or those irksome prohibitions against political and religious debate. "All these causes have been, and still are, operative; but all are, happily, in the way of rapid removal," he observed, predicting a renewal of interest and effectiveness if the government would simply do its job and provide sufficient funding for adult education.[49] In this he broke from Hudson, who was a committed voluntaryist in education and was deeply suspicious of government grants or other avenues of officious interference. Both men, however, shared an unshakable commitment to the spread of working-class education, whether through private or public means, and the patchwork of inadequate resources for this cause—so essential in enabling the march of civilization and industry—rendered every other service provided by these institutions, including the lecture programming already in place in many of them, irrelevant to the only real task at hand.

Debates over the successes and failures of these institutions, thus already well-established, punctuated the first decade of the *Journal*, with individual members and patrons offering their own experiences as a model for what was, essentially, an aggregation of institutions only loosely linked by a commitment to culture. The noisy focus on "a freer intercourse of classes" was especially prominent in the early 1850s, and other concerns were temporarily eclipsed by suggestions that ranged from the deliberate mixing of "a colony of mechanics" with agricultural laborers, on the one hand, to the rejection of patronage and the restriction of institution management to workingmen, on the other.[50] The latter plan had been instituted in Carlisle, noted *Leeds Mercury* editor and proprietor Edward Baines, where "a rule was laid down that no person should be a member of the council who did not live by weekly wages. The consequence of this was immense. At once the rooms were filled."[51] Other critics challenged committees, patrons, and the public to reexamine their foundational assumptions about such societies, arguing not only that most mechanics and operatives did work that required neither scientific nor technological knowledge, but also that the widespread assertion that factory hands "naturally" preferred instruction in the sciences to all other subjects was in and of itself based upon biases rooted in class and exacerbated by ignorance. W. H. J. Traice, then secretary of the Leeds Mechanics' Institute and Literary Society and later the secretary to the Institutions in Union, noted acerbically that "we, of the North, have, it is intimated, an ostrich craving for the hard realities of science, and really ought to be forced to take a little literature and *belles lettres*, to save us from 'vulgar utilitarianism'; but the people of the South are supposed to have a liking for the 'desultory dissertations despised at Oldham.' "[52]

The arguments over the appropriate beneficiaries of the mechanics' institutions were complicated in two important ways, both of which can be traced through the subsequent debates over the place and purpose of the popular lecture. First, to a degree largely invisible to urban critics, mechanics' institutions and other similar societies in smaller towns often found themselves the only physical space in which any type of sociable popular culture could be offered. Unlike the large towns of Manchester or Leeds, where multiple societies could cater to and compete for specific audiences through their carefully delineated offerings, less populated areas could not support multiple societies that might each focus on a single component of the complex provision of culture. Indeed, in many locales, neighboring villages and towns might even have to share a single lecture hall, juggling details of scheduling, cleaning, and rental for often inadequate facilities.[53] By default, then, the original conceptualization of an institution devoted exclusively to the scientific and technological instruction of workingmen was swamped by the competing needs of men and women across lines of class and space. As we will see in detail in Chapter 2, this confusion of purpose echoed throughout the annual reports of institutions as committees and secretaries strove to accommodate the reality that many localities could manage only one healthy institute or lyceum or society, which would have to be expanded beyond its original brief to supply the needs of a more complex membership.

Second, and inevitably, committees and patrons faced problems posed by a lack of basic education for workers and, increasingly, by the need for appropriate middle-class education for both young men and young women. The former group might well be eager but was often grossly underprepared for courses and lectures in the sciences and other fields; early institutes had "introduced an ardent mind into a wilderness of knowledge, without a guide, without even a clue," noted Lord Ashburton, speaking at the 1856 annual meeting of the Society of Arts.[54] As for the sons and daughters of the middle classes, by the second half of the century they were frequently turning to such culture institutions for the lectures and entertainments that would provide the polish essential to their looming responsibilities as citizens and leaders. Serving both groups together appeared increasingly sensible and desirable: Sir John Pakington, delivering the presidential address in September 1862, commended the Birmingham and Midland Institute for offering "a range of study by which the middle classes and skilled artizans of this great city have the means of moral and intellectual improvement placed within their reach."[55] The governing committee of the Leeds Mechanics' Institute and Literary Society similarly justified its fundraising for a new building as calculated "not indeed to neglect in any degree the advancement in knowledge of the mechanic, but to superadd to it, and to carry on concurrently with it, the mental recreation and instruction of the middle class."[56] Such goals could easily be at cross-purposes, however, and for the generally middle-class men presiding over the fortunes of these hundreds of institutions, finding a way forward that was both culturally and financially successful involved false starts and wasted resources as well as innovations and imaginative programming.

The General Union of Literary, Scientific, and Mechanics' Institutes

The issues raised by early critics of the mechanics' institutes, and explored by modern scholars, were not exclusive to the question of working-class education and culture. The debates over audience and programming shared by mechanics' institutes, athenaeums, literary institutes, and other culture institutions—even the elite lit.-&-phils.—centered around one issue: if there was no single model of a successful society, then there could be no single model of successful programming. When the Society of Arts, guided by longtime member Harry Chester, launched the General Union of Literary, Scientific, and Mechanics' Institutes in 1852, this conundrum was already uppermost in the minds of many affiliate institute secretaries and directors. These secretaries and directors represented more than 90,000 members of some 225 institutions "in all parts of the Empire," including the Indian subcontinent and Australia.[57] This membership in itself represented the voices of slightly less than a quarter of the 1,051 institutions enumerated in the 1851 census and about one-third of those counted by Hudson in his *History*, but the members ranged from very large to quite small, from the old-established Newcastle Lit.-&-Phil. to the infant Bury Athenaeum, and thus provide a significant source of information about the shared aspirations and concerns of mid-century culture institutions. In 1852, these affiliates were already sanguine about their dedication to "the chief objects" for which they were established. By mid-century, many had adapted their founding statements to incorporate not only the scientific instruction that had defined the earliest mechanics' institutes but also broader statements of purpose that could accommodate a more flexible model of cultural competence. The Leeds Mechanics' Institution, for example, noted that its educational mission embraced both "the provision of a constant and increasing supply of Books and Periodical literature for all classes of readers, combined with the delivery of a sessional series of Lectures, embracing a very wide range of Literary and Scientific subjects" and a "systematic or orderly" curriculum of classes necessary for "the instruction and proper discipline of the mind."[58] The much younger Kelvedon Literary Institution was urged to a "greater diffusion of useful and scientific knowledge" in order to compete effectively with "foreigners,"[59] while the thirteen-year-old Basingstoke Mechanics' Institution claimed it would "improve the social, moral, and intellectual conditions of all classes within its influence, and … lead the minds of all its members … to the Divine Authority of all the wonders with which this earth abounds."[60] The Newcastle Lit.-&-Phil., founded in 1793 as an elite learned society and labeled "the cheapest literary institution in Great Britain,"[61] had within fifty years shifted its mission to a broader understanding of cultural competence and was providing dozens of "miscellaneous lectures by gentlemen from a distance" annually.[62] Traice, in his mid-century handbook for new and growing institutions, warned that a rigid emphasis on science instruction at the expense of literary education would result in "boorishness of manner" among those who had "missed some of the highest and purest sources of enjoyment and mental culture."[63] The period from 1850 to 1870 was a ferment of experimentation and change as committees and governors responded to an almost overwhelming collision of pressures.

The *Journal*, as an instrument of the Society of Arts, never swerved from its editorial mission to report and reflect the interests, activities, and concerns of society members. The Society's own annual reports, reprinted verbatim in the *Journal* each November, remained resolutely within the bounds of imperial economic and industrial progress, and the balance of each issue explored in minute detail such real-world problems as the relative values of coal and coke, the utilization of night soil, the quality of American cotton, or the development of standards of musical pitch. Presidential addresses inevitably dwelt more intensively on science and technical education than on the overall challenges of providing knowledge-based culture. However, in its founding role as a repository of institute reports and proceedings in the 1850s and 1860s, the *Journal* reproduced the variety of ways in which affiliates strove to achieve the financial and social health that would permit them to provide such culture. Its first volumes were especially characterized by lively discussions about how best to provide the menu of "subjects calculated for general discourse" eventually published by Society of Arts member Hugo Reid: "History, not forgetting the history going on at the present time; Biography, particularly of recent celebrities; Anecdotes and curious traits of human nature; Remarkable Crimes and Trials; Adventures; Voyages and Travels; Manners and Customs of Different Nations; Antiquities; Geography; Curious Facts in Physical Science; Natural History; Commerce and Manufactures; Inventions; Statistics; and, above all, a knowledge of the Lives, Works, Opinions, and Sayings of Great Men of all ages."[64] This list, exhaustive in the 1860s but regarded as quaintly old-fashioned by 1890, sketched out the appropriate content of knowledge-based culture for men and women across class lines, but did not suggest how best to deliver such content to those who were separated in reality by education, interests, time, and money, leaving that instead to the individual institution.[65] As a result, within the reproductions of lecture seasons and affiliate reports included in the *Journal*, we can track the development of two related realms of civic culture, realms that would by the mid-1860s be established as "industrial" spaces for the instruction of working-class men and women, and "general" spaces for the education and entertainment of their middle-class counterparts. The popular lecture was the adhesive connecting these two categories of culture.

Defining the Popular Lecture: A Decade of Disagreement

As we will see in the following chapter, affiliate institutions wrestled with a number of practical challenges that built on the foundational questions of mission and purpose.

If the provision of knowledge-based culture was increasingly seen as indispensable to civic maturity, how was that culture to be delivered? The early years of institute reports, correspondence, and proceedings of annual meetings spoke about the relationships among "lectures," "education," "entertainment," and "science" in ways that were often internally contradictory. The maiden issue of the *Journal* included, on the one hand, critiques of "common-place and inferior lectures" that were "things of dull and prosy routine," and on the other, praise for "useful and beneficial" lectures that were "very numerously attended."[66]

Early criticisms of the use of lectures centered on several specific areas. First, there was the confusion attendant upon using "lecture" to denote both the serious lecture provided as a centerpiece of or an adjunct to classroom learning and the more general entertaining offering that was detached from any curriculum. By 1852, lengthy courses of subject-specific lectures that provided some rough equivalent of a semester of teaching, such as the twelve-lecture course on geology that had launched the Manchester Athenaeum in 1835, were increasingly anomalous within the overall programming of these institutes. Instead, institutes turned their attention to single lectures, variously labeled "miscellaneous," "occasional," "general," "amateur," "desultory," and even "perambulating,"[67] and focused on how best to secure "good and cheap lecturers." Both the technical scientific addresses for the educated amateur and the more general curricula of basic chemistry or botany were, by mid-century, too intentionally specialized to appeal to a popular audience. The former were increasingly relegated to the audiences of the learned societies devoted to the production of new knowledge; the latter formed the focus of general debates over the provision of primary and secondary education in the decades before the 1870 Education Act. Instead, program committees labored to assemble seasons of lectures pitched to the level of the broadly curious, intellectually able adult eager to gain new insights that would permit the display of cultural competence outlined by Hugo Reid and many others.

Moving away from the language of knowledge production that remained rooted in the culture of the learned-society science lecture, and toward the language of knowledge-based culture found in these hundreds of Union affiliates, was not always easy. "Courses" conveyed an aura of intention and seriousness that could help institutes claim space in the public sphere: for example, "E.W." described one lecture list as "a four months' course" even though the offerings were widely disparate in topic and speaker, while "G.H." referred to the Society's "list of short courses" as the foundation of his institute's general nonscientific programming.[68] Despite the lingering attachment to the gravitas conveyed by the phrase "course of lectures" rather than "lecture program," however, correspondents within the pages of the *Journal* rapidly established a consensus that "lecture" itself, as used within the context of their institutions, referred generally to the stand-alone, intellectually accessible offering for a public of working-class and middle-class men and women. Thus, programs of lectures, even when they were advertised as a "series" or "course," were increasingly a buffet of delights: for example, in 1854–5 the Mechanics' Institute at Poole announced that its forthcoming "series" included lectures on "American Orators and Oratory," "Astronomy and Christianity," and "Canada, as a Field for Emigration," in addition to musical interludes.[69]

Although the single general-interest popular lecture rapidly and by default became a staple of programming for many institutes, there were several related issues debated almost endlessly in the first two years of the *Journal*. One especially knotty problem was just how to locate the single lecture within competing discourses of education and entertainment. Did giving up the word "courses" imply that institutes were abandoning their educational responsibilities? This implication was especially strong where secretaries and program committees faced the hard truth that science lectures had ceased to be the ultimate goal of the institutes, even while they acknowledged that highly specialized or technical offerings were incapable of attracting and holding subscribers. By 1855, the Society of Arts acknowledged that such "difficult" subjects were an almost complete failure within the lecture season: "Scientific lectures, as they are called, or talk about physical phenomena, or abstract researches in pure science, are of very little educational value. They are useful because they amuse; they are pernicious because they beguile those who habitually listen to them into a loose sort of notion that they know something of science."[70] The complexities of advanced chemistry and physics were outside the interest of many middle-class subscribers and ranged far beyond the reach of the haphazardly educated operative or artisan, no matter how intrinsically intelligent or curious: "the [science] lecturer, too often soaring to the height of his longest range, gets beyond the reach of the mental vision of a popular and half youthful audience, and then science is dry and unattractive."[71] Making science comprehensible to a popular audience meant, in essence, infusing it with the magic of flashy experiments or the familiarity of the domestic object, as in Michael Faraday's enormously popular "Chemical History of a Candle" and other lectures on "domestic philosophy."[72] The undiluted power of pure science was already, by mid-century, increasingly reserved for specialists.

Some affiliates sought to preserve the scientific lecture but to alter its rigid concordance with working-class interests. Traice, in the same 1853 column in which he mocked the clichéd geographical division of literary and scientific interests, argued that the conflation of "mechanic" or "artisan" with "higher education in science" was an artificial relationship that should not be preserved out of some misplaced and outmoded sense of fitness: "In the midst of a manufacturing population, the bulk of the members of an Institution have no direct connection with actual manufactures; and moreover, ... the more intellectual of the artizan class are very apt to devote themselves to literary studies, while the cultivation of science is pursued by those unconnected with mechanical or manufacturing operations."[73] In essence, he argued, the association of "worker" with "science" and "gentleman" with "literature" should be flipped within these institutions, as more and more men and women who worked for wages were attracted to literature, music, and other aspects of the liberal arts, while focused scientific lectures were increasingly confined to the halls of the elite learned society. Denying working people access to what would become, in the twentieth century, "the humanities" degraded whole groups of people and would drive many potential members away from these institutions altogether. Thus, Traice urged institute secretaries and governing committees to stop trying to reverse and instead simply accept as inevitable the move away from pure science in the stand-alone lecture program, arguing instead that a mixed economy of educational and entertaining lectures was, in fact, the clearest path to fulfilling their founding commitments to working men and women.

"Capacities Spiritual, Intellectual, and Physical": Redefining Instruction and Education

These contradictory tendencies—continuing to valorize the science-loving "artizan" of the 1820s and 1830s while simultaneously trying to reach the messy, class-crossing, and intellectually disparate audiences of the 1850s—could also be traced within the fractures that separated "instruction" and "education" in the discourses of mid-century educators, patrons, and institute secretaries. The labels were often used indiscriminately, but over the first decades of the century, "instruction" came to imply a hierarchical relationship built on struggle and toil; it was most often a label applied to a basic acquisition of knowledge by children of all classes or by adolescents and young adults in the working classes, including those in early mechanics' institute classes or adult Sunday school classes.[74] By mid-century, educationists—the growing number of those theorizing about education, even when they did not deliver it themselves—were increasingly wrestling with the assumptions about class and age embedded in this hierarchy, both as part of their own professionalizing efforts and as they sought to expand the scope of their work to incorporate as many potential students as possible. Much of the discourse within the pages of the *Journal* in the 1850s was concerned with working-class men and women, while the educational needs of the middle classes—especially those older boys and younger men preparing for professional life—would occupy most of this space in the 1860s. Across both decades, the attempts to redefine education and instruction into fields deserving of professional attention pushed educationists into language that incorporated and augmented emerging ideas of participatory citizenship.

Thus, Reid argued in 1853 that "instruction"—which was necessarily of "an incomplete character" and was characterized by "miscellaneous information … acquired previous to fourteen years of age"—was the precursor to actual "intellectual training" that called upon "higher powers of mind," without which an individual man or woman remained "mentally but a half-formed being."[75] Instruction was quite literally an elementary endeavor without which no man or woman could pursue the "intellectual education" that would permit them to "value the lectures which were given in various Institutions."[76] And if "instruction" was redefined away from class and instead linked to youth, it then followed that "education" was the province of the adult: A. J. Scott, then principal of Owens College, Manchester, argued in 1854 that education was pursued by "men with manly aspirations."[77] The man with no such aspirations remained immature, even animalistic: he was "(figuratively speaking) no more than a pig."[78]

This changing language of instruction and education was linked deliberately to contemporary discourses over citizenship. In the long run up to the 1867 Reform Act, these intertwined arguments focused not on Robert Lowe's epigrammatic "we must educate our future masters," but rather, in Scott's words, on how to "enable a person to perform the duties of any office which may devolve upon him as a citizen of a free state."[79] Instead of rhetorically reinforcing the hierarchies of class, these debates often explored the promises of an emerging democracy. The description of the working man as a fungible and obedient unit within a system of political economy, so prominent in the 1830s and 1840s, gave way after 1850 to questions of how best to prepare that same man for participatory citizenship. Those involved in the provision of knowledge-based culture adopted as their foundation the claim that the working classes were as "naturally possessed of intellectual capacities" as their middle-class counterparts,[80] and focused on how best to encourage "the general strengthening of all the powers of the mind, so that, when applied to any subject of enquiry, ... they [these powers] may be prepared to grapple with it in the most successful manner."[81]

We can trace uneasy echoes of concern within these debates, many of which focused on how to square the idealized claim that the desire for education was the "original appetite in the human soul"[82] with the persistent realities of class antagonism and gender inequality. The "human soul" was neuter in terms of both class and gender, but the human person was not. Thus, the project of breathing life into the participatory citizen was a difficult one rhetorically. The solution, however temporary, had several strands. First, the citizen was reimagined not simply as an independent individual but also, simultaneously, as part of a larger social body defined by obligations as well as opportunities. The autonomous self-educator had never been wholly self-sufficient, and by the 1850s Samuel Smiles was not the only writer urging self-improvers to adopt some form of "*be* and *do*." Within the expanding world of knowledge-based culture, such persons were increasingly imagined as fully integrated into a community of service and exerting "a mighty effect ... on society" through the power of their educated understanding.[83] This effect was energetic and effortful: "real intellectual education" included "the cultivation of the capacity and disposition for intellectual action."[84]

Second, such action linked both education and citizenship. "The man who felt no compulsion to further to the utmost of his power the course of education, was undeserving the name of citizen or patriot," argued the president of the Huddersfield Mechanics' Institution in 1855.[85] Education, claimed these speakers, would transform individuals into "better citizens and better men."[86] However, this effect was simultaneously subtly demasculinized. The adult man who cultivated and disposed was active, but his activity was directed toward "greater and more intelligent self-restraint."[87] His participation in knowledge-based culture required the energy of a "progressive spirit," but it also instilled a womanly "love for the beautiful" and "sympathetic hope for the coming age."[88] Indeed, "his firm moral culture, his self-sacrifice in the attainment of knowledge—what an agreeable companion, what a useful citizen, what a kind heart such a man possessed."[89] Beauty, morality, self-sacrifice, companionability, usefulness, kindness: these were familiar signals of Victorian femininity, here used to demarcate all those who rejected the putative characteristics of the working-class rough. The adoption of this language thus placed the participatory citizen into a space that was, in the language of solicitor and lecturer J. P. Dodd, "contiguous" to both the working and middle classes, associated with both the active power of the man and the passive influence of the woman, producing a "person" as neuter as the human soul itself and with infinite capacity for good.[90]

Third, knowledge-based culture was perceived as a quasi-religious pursuit. One institute president in 1857 characterized intellect as "part of the soul's inalienable property" rather than as some type of movable "furniture."[91] In 1858, the Vicar of

Leeds, president of the city's Phil-&-Lit., argued that "the whole man ought to be subjected to it [development into citizenship], the body by soberness, temperance, and chastity, the soul by the immediate office of religion, and the intellect by those exercises which, in addition to reading, were afforded by philosophical and literary institutions."[92] By 1860, at the midpoint of this period of growth, Chester could state without challenge that "education is the development and training of the human being in all his capacities, spiritual, intellectual, and physical."[93]

Finally, although the intertwined capacities of spiritual, intellectual, and physical growth were still only partially delineated, "education" was increasingly seen as fitting adults not only to find their place as citizens within a community but also to make an interesting world inside their own heads. Lord Ashburton, presiding over the Union's 1856 annual dinner, argued that the role of the institution was "to devote at once our utmost efforts to the solution of the question, What is the pack of knowledge which each man should carry with him into the world? His wants are boundless; his means of carriage are small; life is short; school-time is shorter; knowledge is infinite—what shall his pack of knowledge be?"[94] That "pack of knowledge"—an awkward phrase that was not adopted by later speakers—gestured toward the radical idea that literature, history, philosophy, music, and the like all had value well beyond mere instruction and should be available to all.

Education as Entertainment? Principles versus Practicality

If instruction was by definition a basic foundation for education, and education was increasingly seen as the "pack of knowledge" that fitted an adult for both work *and* leisure, how would mixed programs of popular lectures serve these dual purposes without descending into "mere" entertainment? This fear haunted many affiliates in the first years of the Union. While a number of secretaries and directors argued that serious lectures were often found to be "a profitless affair," thinly attended,[95] many more complained that "the amusing and the imaginative had been allowed to take the place of the useful and real."[96] Institute secretary J. C. Buckmaster, writing in 1854, lamented that "during the past fourteen years the character of Institutions has entirely changed, the word, 'lecture' is changed to the more attractive word 'entertainment'; and light literature takes the place of more solid and useful reading. The educational character of Institutions is almost lost."[97] Others saw these entertaining bits of "education" as essentially misleading, an *amuse bouche* for the mind: "Lectures, by whomsoever delivered, are ... but of little use only so far as they induce those who hear them to study the subjects at home. ... I believe that it is in this way only that they are capable of doing much good."[98] The president of a new institute in Sydney, Australia, was especially strong in condemning this approach: "Globules of instruction dissolved in tumblers of amusement, were like delicate comfits to a hungry man; they tantalized without satisfying the appetite; they enfeebled the powers until they rejected solid meat, whilst the light food they craved yielded no nourishment."[99]

Many warned that purely entertaining lectures were useful only for manipulating an audience's feelings, not stimulating its intellect.[100] Union affiliates regarded as especially troublesome the advice to mask the hard work of intellectual engagement with humor and theatrics. The Working Men's Educational Union, for example, founded in the same year as the Union of Institutions to train lecturers, and striving to place its own speakers in many of the institutes joined together under the Society's umbrella, urged its volunteers to adopt "striking titles" to "attract a crowded house," and to hold the attention of the audience with "playful references" and "merriment," delivered in "a lively style of speaking."[101] This more entertaining approach cloaked serious matter, especially in the sciences, in the garb of "Natural Magic Chemically Explained," "Mesmerism and Phrenology," and "Practicability of Aerial Navigation" rather than prosaically focused offerings like "The Manufacture of Iron," "Extinct Animals of the Ancient World," or "Jet and Its Manufacture."[102] Yet it appeared fundamentally dishonest to many: "What would be thought of lectures being delivered in a literary institution … on 'spectral illusions,' when a lecture on optics would have been much better?" asked the representative from the Sudbury Mechanics' Institution at the 1853 annual meeting of the Society.[103]

Several institutions, including the Oldham Mechanics' Institute, considered suspending lectures altogether on the grounds that they were "desultory, unproductive, and expensive."[104] Others argued that only the unconnected "general" lectures were a problem: "They had had several lectures, and very excellent lectures too, but he thought they were not such as they should have. They had had a lecture on Indian missions, then one on Oliver Cromwell, then another on missions, followed by one on Queen Anne. That appeared to be very absurd."[105] Such a move opened the institute to ridicule, as one correspondent noted: " 'Mechanics' Institutions,' says the *Times*, 'which began with the idea of teaching science to artizans, are now places for the exhibition of dissolving views, and the delivery of lectures on or by popular novelists.' To a large extent, this sweeping censure is no doubt well deserved."[106] Similar critiques came from within the Union itself: Reid argued in 1853 that mechanics' institutions had declined into places where young men "frittered away" their time, ultimately abandoning their undisciplined and half-formed instincts for self-culture and instead joining "the crowd of triflers."[107] Others argued that such institutions simply could not provide culture, and any programming in that direction was not only absurd but valueless: "For his own part, he had never met with a thoroughly cultivated man who had received any benefit from lectures," claimed a member at the 1855 annual conference of the Society of Arts, concluding that "the lecture system was utterly useless."[108] His criticisms echoed the laments of the anonymous author of "Mechanics' Institutions" in the 1850 *Chambers' Papers for the People*, surveying the 1,000 lectures "recently delivered" at 43 literary, philosophical, and mechanics' institutes. He noted with dismay that "there were scarcely two lectures to each subject. If any man were gravely to propose to narrate the 'History of the Last Fifty Years' in about an hour, or give an account of the 'Nature of Man' in a brief essay, or impart sound ideas of 'Mental Philosophy' in one lecture, or instruct people in the 'Philosophy of Life' between eight and nine o'clock on a winter's night, he would be laughed at as a visionary, if not denounced as a charlatan. And yet each of these subjects had one lecture appropriated to it out of the number mentioned above, and the feelings of the audience were at the conclusion expressed in a 'vote of thanks to the lecturer, passed by acclamation.'"[109]

Similar critiques came from institutes large and small, scattered throughout the kingdom. Smaller, more isolated societies were just as likely to resist any move away from the serious to the entertaining as their larger, more cosmopolitan counterparts. But by the mid-1850s, institutes had to choose. Did they continue to interpret the lecture as primarily scientific and fundamentally serious, the pursuit of knowledge under difficulties as part of a formal intellectual agenda? This path would force institutes to pass over the tempting offerings of "Curiosities in Natural History" or "The Chemistry of the Breakfast Table" as "too popular." Or did they choose to design lecture seasons that incorporated literary, musical, and other topics appealing to a broader constituency? Most institutions eventually chose the latter path, striving to provide programming that was simultaneously popular and respectable, that would facilitate both participatory citizenship—Dodd's "duties which may devolve upon a citizen of a free state"—and the construction of a well-furnished mind—the "pack of knowledge" described by Lord Ashburton. By 1863, Traice argued that every individual should have access to "the luxury of intellectual exercise and recreation," a combination presented most attractively in a good popular lecture "which may be listened to by people in all ranks of society, and nearly all ages."[110]

These philosophical questions were themselves a luxury for many mid-century institutions, for whom the work of simply keeping the doors open and the balance sheet in the black crowded out any broader ruminations about the provision of culture. When Traice assumed the duties of agent and secretary to the Institutes in Union shortly after its formation, and began a long career of regular lectures at and advisory visits to hundreds of affiliates each year, he counseled members to continue to redefine their programming away from a narrow understanding of "instruction" and toward a vision of education that was both intellectual and entertaining. "Lectures of an amusing character" would attract enthusiastic audiences, and the judicious construction of a lively program that included "occasional miscellaneous concerts" and similar offerings would "keep the Institute in the public mind ... which is indispensable to the success of its educational efforts."[111] Many institutes took his advice, and quickly came to defend the tendency to present "good lectures ... in a pleasant and amusing, as well as in an instructive manner," arguing that serious young men could still gain significant intellectual capital through entertaining lectures that also guaranteed financial capital for the institution.[112] Seriousness was in the mind of the beholder, and a good lecture season that combined "history and biography, invention and discovery, music, poetry, and topics purely, or partly imaginative" as well as science should equally attract the self-improving artisan and the man of substance, as well as their possibly more frivolous wives and adolescent daughters.[113] In fact, counseled YUMI secretary Barnett Blake in 1858, a good season of mixed popular lectures "may prove a very valuable aid to most Institutions, and promote not only the pecuniary resources but the efficient working of the other departments by exciting a taste for mental cultivation."[114] Thus, the Derby Working Men's Institute programming in 1854 featured the very popular Clara Lucas Balfour speaking on "Female English Poets of the Present Century" and Spencer Hall—almost as coveted a speaker as Balfour—on "Phrenology and Physiology."[115] The

Newcastle Lit.-&-Phil.'s programming for 1856 included lectures on "The Field Sports of Scotland," "The Arctic Regions," "The Manufacture of Glass and Iron," "The Music of Various Nations," "Marine Zoology," "Poetic Literature," and "The Origin of the Names of Places, Rivers, and Mountains," by speakers that included nationally known figures such as Philip Gosse and John Henry Pepper.[116] These purveyors of mental cultivation lent a sheen of undeniable respectability to institutions up and down the social scale, while at the same time helping bind them into a loosely unified national conversation of knowledge-based culture.

Organizing the Popular Lecture Circuit: Demands and Resistance

The general appreciation of the value of the popular lecture led inexorably to demands that the Society of Arts assist with the organization of lecture programs. Ironically, the Society itself had contemplated such assistance even before the establishment of the Union of Institutions, approaching such luminaries and members as Charles Lyell, Edwin Lankester, Lyon Playfair, Robert Airy, and Charles Babbage to provide lectures in programs that would be coordinated by the Union. As A. D. Garner has shown, while most of those contacted "expressed sympathy with the Society's aims," they uniformly declined the honor, some because they were too busy and others because they felt that the Society's plans were "premature" and "ill-conceived."[117] Indeed, many of these men would energetically participate in the London-based SLS and travel as well to the SLS's "kindred societies" across the kingdom during the 1860s and 1870s, as we will see in Chapter 4. But in 1852, they perceived the organizing committee for the Union as too sparsely populated with men of science, and thus "we do not feel justified in recognizing its authority to the extent required."[118] An innovative attempt that same year to create "a band of Missionary Lecturers, itinerant apostles of science," from within the ranks of Oxbridge faculty, was rejected by the very men "of not inferior mental power and scientific attainment" invited to join this intellectual Band of Hope on the grounds of both time and money.[119] At the same time, as Garner shows, institutions themselves evinced only lukewarm enthusiasm for lectures by the giants of science, in part because of the financial outlay that would be required.

This reluctance to commit financially to the most prominent of scientific speakers did not mean that institutions dismissed out of hand the idea of structured lecture programming. Such structure, albeit relatively weak, was familiar to the members of the YUMI and other unions, and in the decade before the Union of Institutions was established, some secretaries of stand-alone institutes had also made informal overtures to their counterparts nearby in order to coordinate schedules and negotiate reduced fees by sharing lecturers. However, as "E.W." noted in 1852, "brother Secretaries frequently decline to answer such letters, although by this plan each might often reduce the cost of Lectures one-third or more." He urged the Society to assume the "parental duty" of "recommending to its affiliated Institutions a more kindly and fraternal spirit."[120] Most "brother Secretaries" thought that the Society should, at the very least, publish a list of available lecturers with information on location, price, and areas of expertise—distinctly not limited to speakers in the sciences—and the Society agreed to provide such a list, drawn from recommendations by member institutes. This resolution was imperfectly successful, as many quickly pointed out: the same "jealousy" that had led individual secretaries to ignore requests for joint scheduling by their peer institutions made many reluctant to supply a list of local lecturers who might be poached by others.[121] The schedule of lecturers for the spring session of 1853, distributed in late 1852, was immediately criticized as both too late and too brief to be helpful for most secretaries. "A Working Man" placed the blame for this inadequacy on affiliate institutes, noting that only 66 of 285 affiliate secretaries had bothered to send in any names. "Your Society cannot help us if we will not stir a finger to help ourselves," he admonished his fellow members.[122] Subsequent lists, in which the Society listed gratuitous and paid lecturers separately, became gradually much more complete, featuring hundreds of lecturers and their topics and fees; these lists will form the basis for the analyses in Chapter 3.

But affiliate institutes wanted more than names. They also specifically sought endorsements from or accreditation by the Society. Most secretaries before 1853 could rely only on newspaper reports, "which were frequently very fallacious," sometimes hiring bad lecturers who did such harm to an overall season that "it required three or four months ... before the members were in a disposition to go and hear another stranger."[123] Endorsements would help institutes secure "first-class lecturers instead of mere quacks."[124] Robert Dalgliesh of the Leek (Staffordshire) Mechanics' Institution suggested a highly structured vetting system, with the Society's annual meetings providing space in which members could vote on the lecturers to be endorsed: "A judicious selection might thus be hoped for, and a place on the list of lecturers for the Society of Arts would then be considered, what it certainly is not now, an honour and a distinction."[125] The Society resisted the idea of endorsements, echoing the adjuration of "A Working Man" that affiliates needed to rely upon their own judgment and not expect the Society to do their work for them. In late 1855, it reiterated that the list was a list merely, and did not constitute any recommendation whatsoever. This reminder was part of a larger refusal to accept blame for the problems experienced by the Pembroke Dock Mechanics' Institute. That committee, "having seen Mr. Charles F. Partington's name and address in the Society's List of Lecturers, where he describes himself as a lecturer to the Royal Panopticon," secured his services for two lectures. Partington failed to appear but instead sent "his son or nephew, a young gentleman" with "a stammering indistinct utterance and incorrect pronunciation" who delivered "a dull prosy outline of the history of the Crimea," and then unsuccessfully "attempted to illustrate, with the aid of a few explosive chemicals, the principle of the Russian infernal machines."[126] A few weeks later, a correspondent from Bilston wrote that they, too, had "experienced disappointment with regard to the lectures of Mr. Partington," who had performed to "universal dissatisfaction."[127] At the annual meeting following these disappointments, the Society proclaimed that "Institutions will therefore distinctly understand that the present list is not to be taken in any sense as a selected or recommended one."[128]

This reluctance to help police a lecture circuit was even more apparent when the Society was urged to establish a system in which it would coordinate schedules, supply lecturers and lecturing equipment, and pay speakers out of an annual fee assessed on participating institutes. The YUMI and other unions each had a designated agent—usually the union secretary, such as Barnett Blake of the YUMI—whose duties included delivering lectures to member societies upon request, and the Union of Institutions adopted a similar strategy with Secretary Traice. However, even the most industrious individual could not visit, much less deliver lectures to, the hundreds of institutes within the Union each year. A pool of vetted and organized speakers who could be adapted to the needs of the individual institute, therefore, appealed to many secretaries who found it difficult to fill a season and who lobbied for what was essentially a version of the American lyceum model. The Society considered for several years the many proposals to develop such a system for the entire Union, but in late 1855, then chairman Rev. James Booth argued that it was simply "impossible to lay down beforehand an organized system of sending forth from the Society a selected staff of approved lecturers—men for whom the Society would not hesitate to be responsible—who, at a moderate charge to each, should proceed from Institution to Institution to deliver lectures day by day during their progress. This would be a practicable system, but the Institutions show but little disposition to support it" through subscriptions or even, at a minimum, through an attempt to coordinate requests for speakers.[129] He reiterated this some six months later: the Society "could not undertake to do everything in behalf of the Institutions; they must have some freedom of action amongst themselves," and "he very much questioned whether the Institutions would be disposed to enter into such an arrangement for the purpose of being supplied by them with lecturers."[130] Institutes founded to promote self-improvement must, in effect, exercise those faculties themselves, or they would be undone by their own "supineness."[131]

The Society, then, would neither force nor cajole member institutes into a system that only some of them claimed to want. There were hundreds of institutions, with no single model of successful programming. Walter Royton, already a popular author and lecturer, summed up the problem thus: "We have Quaker towns, Roman Catholic towns, Unitarian towns, Independent towns, Puseyite towns, Wesleyan towns, High Church, and Low Church towns, Total Abstinence towns, Peace towns and War towns; and especial care ought to be taken to avoid wounding the prejudices of any class of persons in any of these towns. Now, how could the Society of Arts guarantee this? It would, as I have said, be utterly impossible."[132] While the Union refused to vet speakers or to supervise programming, its officers constantly urged Union members to coordinate local or regional schedules, especially for science lecturers, which might permit them each to pay only £2–£3 or even less per lecture. Even this was a bridge too far: many committees admitted that they were unwilling to yoke their own programs to the needs and schedules of their neighbors, and would prefer to muddle along constructing the seasons that they felt best served their membership.

"Literary Sappers and Miners" and the Reliance on Gratuitous Lecturers

While the preference for local autonomy became only more pronounced over time, especially as the Society itself moved away from any interventions in or even sage advice regarding the popular lecture, affiliate institutions grappled with several chronic problems surrounding lecture programming. Perhaps the most pressing of these was the financial challenge of filling a season that, by mid-decade, had expanded to anywhere between eight and twenty lectures over the course of the mostly standardized November–April season that had been adopted from the American model. Professional lecturers were expensive: "Experience proves that London lecturers … will never come within the reach of the great mass of Institutions. Most Institutions with which I am acquainted cannot, consistently with their permanent interests, afford more than from £1 to £1.10s per lecture," argued one correspondent.[133] Lecturers in science charged fees at least three or four times that amount. Even unpaid science lecturers could be out of reach financially, as smaller institutes learned the hard way that trying to secure a volunteer to help carry the weight of the science program was actually very costly: "Mercator" wrote that after contracting with a "gratuitous" science lecturer, "the young Institute had to purchase everything necessary, and many things unnecessary. In truth it seemed as though a laboratory had to be formed; and in the end it was found that the amount paid for two or three lectures on chemistry would have procured the delivery of entire courses on several subjects by the most experienced teachers."[134] Maintaining a lecture season—increasingly a mark of a cultured community, large or small—demanded innovative financial planning; and that innovation in turn often required committee secretaries to beat the bushes for volunteer lecturers, referred to humorously as "a (literary and scientific) corps of sappers and miners."[135] Voluntaryism was not in itself shameful, as the American perspective in *Putnam's* had implied; it was historically and culturally embedded in the English landscape in spaces from politics and education to medicine and charity, and was virtually encrusted with tradition. However, many of the rising men who served on the committees of local institutions and societies worried that such encrustation could cripple the growth of the robust, modern, and forward-looking town. Would not an old-fashioned reliance on gratuitous lecturers "tend to foster a spirit of pauperism and dependence, unhappily too prevalent already"?[136] Was easy access to volunteer lecturers promoting the spread of knowledge-based culture, or diluting it? Society member William Hughes, already a well-known geographer and educator and among the more popular lecturers at mid-century, argued that "the facility with which gratuitous lectures are obtainable by many Institutions has been productive of disservice to the whole system of public lecturing," in much the same way that a Union-wide system of coordination and endorsement might weaken individual committees who did not want to undertake the difficult work of assembling a locally-appropriate lecture season.[137]

Hole, in his 1853 *History*, took a more realistic approach, arguing that "gratuitous lectures … neither should nor can be dispensed with."[138] Most secretaries and governing bodies agreed. It was nearly impossible to deliver a mixed season of education and entertainment—to suspend the "globules of instruction" in the "tumblers of amusement"—without the services of unpaid lecturers. Such unpaid men and women were especially crucial to the well-rounded program that was only partially built upon the science lecture: "It is so much easier to find men competent to take up literary than scientific subjects, that the former constitutes the chief part of these unprofessional lectures," noted Traice that same year.[139] As more and more institutes sought to balance science with literature, music, and other broadly appealing topics, the "unprofessional" lecturers became increasingly indispensable, with committees often filling a season with twice the number of unpaid as paid lecturers.

Hole had advised in his essay that institutions continue to balance professional, albeit expensive, science lecturers with unpaid speakers in other topics, arguing that "the remedy [for incoherent programming] consists in diminishing, *not discontinuing entirely*, the number of miscellaneous lectures, and adding to each winter session, one or two complete courses on those branches of science."[140] However, he was increasingly alone in his belief that courses of expensive, professionally delivered science lectures were essential to good programming. Although some local institutes continued to plead poverty and ask for help in securing popular men of science in order to keep costs down, they regularly rejected specific measures that might permit them each to pay reduced fees for prestigious lecturers who could fit them into complicated professional schedules. Many instead shared the perspective of Chester, who in 1853 argued from his experience at the Highgate Literary and Scientific Society that "in point of quality I do not hesitate to say that the unpaid lectures have been at least equal to the others."[141] Indeed, gratuitous lectures in the arts and humanities, delivered by amateur speakers, were "more calculated to benefit Institutions such as ours, than those given by professional lecturers, who are generally too fond of using hard words and technical phrases, which a rustic audience cannot understand," wrote Frederick Parker, the secretary of the Baker-street and High Peak Institute in Derbyshire, in 1854.[142] Hole had argued that such simplified offerings were suited only to "small towns and villages" where the levels of interest and education were relatively low: in such places, he argued, "a familiar lecture by an amateur pleases better than one by a scientific man, unless the latter possesses the rare qualification of conveying his information in the simplest manner."[143] Parker, Chester, and others argued instead that the issue was not lack of intellect or lack of scientific knowledge, but rather that audiences mixed by gender and age overwhelmingly preferred the "tumblers of amusement" in which instruction could most easily be dissolved.

The nearly universal tendency to use interchangeably such labels as "gratuitous," "amateur," "nonprofessional," and "free" masked important distinctions. The gratuitous speaker was one who accepted no fee, although he or she usually expected the host society to meet travel expenses. Gratuitous speakers were almost always "amateur," that is, without advanced training in the sciences or indeed in any specific subject; in the first decades of the popular lecture, many such speakers were local men, often of substance, who offered their services as a way to show paternalistic support for the extension of knowledge-based culture. As we will see in Chapter 3, a significant minority of these local speakers were clergy, whose university training was readily deployable in spaces outside the pulpit.

While gratuitous lecturers were almost always "amateurs," that is, without specialized training, many amateurs were not gratuitous. The "literary sappers and miners" could be relatively well paid and fully booked, season after season, by institutes who appreciated their ability to connect emotionally with subscribers and paid ticket-holders even if they lacked the national scientific reputation of a Charles Lyell or a Robert Airey. They helped expand the breadth of knowledge-based culture, speaking on subjects of general or popular interest: history, literature, music, travel, theology, and even science in its most domestically entertaining forms. As they proved their worth, more and more organizing committees leaned heavily on "literary" speakers in order to guarantee large and paying audiences with as little monetary investment as possible.

The "Big Three" of Mid-Century Lecturing: Clara Lucas Balfour, George Grossmith, and George Dawson

In marked contrast to the American system, however, even the most popular amateur lecturers were forced to book their own schedules without the help of institute secretaries operating in cooperation, as the brief examples of three of the most sought-after amateur lecturers from this period—Clara Lucas Balfour, George Grossmith, and George Dawson—illustrate in Figures 1.1 and 1.2.

Clara Lucas Balfour (1808–1878) began her public speaking career as a temperance lecturer and soon became immensely popular in other venues as well.[144] With a large family dependent upon her income, she charged and collected fees that were comparable to those of her male counterparts, generally about £5 per lecture but "subject to occasional deduction to small or struggling institutions."[145] Her work in 1854, reconstituted from private family papers by Janet Cunliffe-Jones, illustrates an exhausting and exhaustive schedule of travel and speaking, from Plymouth and Devonport (unreachable by railway) in the southwest to the West Riding of Yorkshire in a space of twelve months. She delivered sixteen discrete lectures on subjects ranging from "Youthful Poets of the Present Century" to "The Domestic History of the Bonaparte Family," often giving between fifteen and twenty lectures each month. Only 7 of these 1854 lectures were delivered at member institutes reporting back to the Union, although 24 member institutes reported lectures by Balfour between 1852 and 1862, reminding us that the English lecture circuit stretched far beyond the reach of the Union.

During that same decade, George Grossmith (1820–1880) lectured at least forty-two times at reporting affiliate institutions, with his most popular titles including "A Humorous Lecture on Lecturing," "English Notions of American Character," and humorous readings of many of Dickens's novels.[146] His listing in the 1854 "List of Lecturers" stipulated that he was available only to "such Institutions as are accessible by railway the same afternoon," although he occasionally ventured as far afield as the Bradford Mechanics' Institute. By the 1862 season, however, he reported that he was "now enabled to accept engagements in any part of England, and, at certain periods of the year, in Scotland and Ireland also." Like Balfour, many of his engagements were not at reporting Union affiliates: in 1862, his entry in the Union's list included 59 cities and towns as well as "400 other provincial Literary and Mechanics' Institutions," while the total number of institutions reporting lectures was less than 100. Also like Balfour, his fee by 1862 was £5 per lecture, with a reduction for "small or embarrassed societies."[147] The lament of the anonymous lecturer of 1853, above, that most institutions could not afford to pay even the common £1 or £1.10s per lecture, appears to have disappeared by the early 1860s, as the weakest institutions died and their more robust counterparts moved into more stable financial positions.

Clara Lucas Balfour

Alton Mechanics' Institution
Basingstoke Mechanics' Institute
Bedford Literary and Scientific Institution
Bradford Mechanics' Institute
Chelmsford Literary and Mechanics' Institution
Cheltenham Literary and Philosophical Institution
Croydon Literary and Scientific Institution
Derby Working Men's Institute
Devonport Mechanics' Institute
Dover Museum and Philosophical Institution
Ebbw Vale Literary and Scientific Institution
Edinburgh Philosophical Institution
Faversham Mutual Improvement Society and Faversham Institute
Hackney Literary and Scientific Institution
Halifax Mechanics' Institution
Hastings Mechanics' Institute
Lewes Mechanics' Institution
Louth Mechanics Institution
Plymouth Mechanics' Institute
Reading Literary, Scientific and Mechanics' Institution
Redhill Institution
Royston Institute
Sherborne Literary Institution
Whitchurch Mechanics' Institution

George Dawson

Banbury Mechanics' Institute
Barnsley Mechanics' Institute and Literary Society
Bedford Literary and Scientific Institution
Birmingham and Midland Institute
Birmingham Polytechnic Institution
Bradford Mechanics' Institute
Chelmsford Literary and Mechanics' Institution
Croydon Literary and Scientific Institution
Darlington Mechanics' Institution
Gosport and Alverstoke Literary and Scientific Institution
Hackney Literary and Scientific Institution
Hastings Mechanics' Institute
Hitchin Mechanics' Institution
Lewes Institution
Lewes Mechanics' Institution
Loughborough Literary and Philosophical Society
Newport Athenaeum and Mechanics' Institute
Nottingham Mechanics' Institution

Poole Mechanics' Institute
Portsmith and Portsea Athenaeum and Mechanics' Institute
Redhill Institution
Royston Mechanics' Institute
Tunbridge Literary and Scientific Society
Wakefield Mechanics' Institution

George Grossmith

Alton Mechanics' Institution
Banbury Mechanics' Institute
Barnsley Mechanics' Institute and Literary Society
Bradford Mechanics' Institute
Brighton Mechanics' Institution
Bury St. Edmunds' Athenaeum
Coventry Institute
Croydon Literary and Scientific Institution
Dover Museum and Philosophical Institution
Dunmow Literary and Scientific Institution
Lewes Institution
Newbury Literary Institution
Newport Athenaeum and Mechanics' Institute
Nottingham Mechanics' Institution
Redhill Institution
Royston Mechanics' Institute
Saffron Walden Literary and Scientific Institution
Sevenoaks Literary and Scientific Institution

Figure 1.1 Sites of lectures for Balfour, Dawson, and Grossmith, 1852–62.

Source: *Journal of the Society of Arts*, Vols. 1–10.

Like Grossmith and Balfour, George Dawson (1821–1876)—easily the most beloved of popular lecturers during this period—also delivered some forty-five lectures to reporting institutions in the first decade of the Union; he traveled across the country (and eventually across the Atlantic), and by 1862 was so sought after during the usual November–April season that he refused all engagements in the summer months. Dawson offered lectures "Historical, Biographical, and Literary," with an established and eclectic set of offerings ranging from "Old Books," "The Style and Characteristics of English Glee Writing," and "Crime and Its Remedies" to biographical sketches on Bunyan, Wellington and Napoleon, George Fox, Alfred the Great, Beau Brummell, and Martin Luther. While Grossmith and Balfour were highly regarded lecturers who could reliably pack a room, George Dawson was in a category all his own. One memoirist described his powers in almost supernatural terms: "The intelligent public went to hear, and were amused and instructed; chaffed out of any prejudices they had, their ears were delighted, their souls lifted up, and the lecturer ended by carrying them away body and soul with him."[148] In a similar vein, journalist W. E. Adams

1852/3

Clara Lucas Balfour
- The Structure and Function of Plants
- On Home Influence and Early Impressions
- The Female Characters of Shakespeare
- On Contrasts and Parallels in the Lives of Celebrated Women, at the Times of the Great Revolutions in England, America, and France
- The Moral and Intellectual Influence of Woman on Society
- The Life of Cowper (with musical accompaniment)

George Dawson
- Wellington and Napoleon: A Parallel and a Contrast
- Old Books

George Grossmith
- English Notions of American Character
- The Ludicrous in Life

1853/4

Balfour
- The Memorable Youthful Poets of the Present Century
- The Uses of Poetry, and the Mission of the Poet
- On Botany
- On Female Characters as Delineated by English Poets
- On the Study of Biography

Dawson
- No titles listed

Grossmith
- English Notions of American Character
- The Recent Writings of Charles Dickens

1854/5

Balfour
- On the Moral and Intellectual Influence of Woman on Society
- Memorable Youthful Poets of the Present Century
- Female English Poets of the Present Century

Dawson
- Alfred the Great
- Crime and Its Remedies

Grossmith
- Humorous Characteristics

1855/6

Balfour
- The Seasons and Their Relations
- On Celebrated Women, Living at Times of Great Revolutions, in England, America, and France
- Female Character, as Delineated by English Poets

Dawson
- Admiral Blake

Life and Times of George Fox, the Founder of the Society of Friends
Beau Brummell
John Bunyan
Some Passages of Russian History
Grossmith
David Copperfield
Martin Chuzzlewit

1856/7
Balfour
Poets of the People
Dawson
Popular Proverbs, Their Wisdom or Want of It
George Fox
Admiral Sir J. Drake
Martin Luther: His Private Life and Character
Peter the Great
The Style and Characteristics of English Glee Writing
Old Books: Their Uses, Beauties, and Peculiarities
The Life of John Calvin
Hamlet
On the Wild Flowers of the Neighbourhood
Grossmith
English Notions of American Character
Humorous Characteristics
Lecturing
The Ludicrous in Life
Nicholas Nickleby
Pickings from Pickwick

1857/8
Balfour
Charlotte Bronte
On the Remarkable Women of the Nineteenth Century
Celebrated Women of England, America, and France
Dawson
On Daniel Defoe
John Bunyan
Beau Brummell
Martin Luther
The Origin, Character, and Doings of the Anglo-Saxons
On the Sayings and Doings of the Anglo-Saxons
The Improvers of Shakespeare: Their Principles, Practices, and Failures
Grossmith
David Copperfield

    Lectures on Lecturing
    Nicholas Nickleby
    On Pickwick
    A Humorous Lecture on Lecturing
    English Notions of American Character

1858/9
Balfour
    Charlotte Bronte
    The Domestic History of the Bonaparte Family

Dawson
    Good Queen Bess

Grossmith
    Wit and Humour
    Humorous Characteristics
    Martin Chuzzlewit

1859/60
Balfour
    On the Moral and Intellectual Influence of Woman on Society

Dawson
    Popular Proverbs

Grossmith
    A Humorous Lecture on Lecturing

1860/1
Balfour
    The Buonaparte Family
    Charlotte Bronte

Dawson
    John Calvin
    William Cobbett
    On Popular Proverbs, Their Wisdom, or Want of It
    On Hamlet
    Sayings and Doings of the Anglo-Saxons

Grossmith
    Sketches by Boz
    The Ludicrous in Life
    On Wit and Humour

1861/2
Balfour
    Charlotte Bronte
    George Stephenson

Dawson
    Daniel Defoe
    The Origin, Character, and Doings of the Anglo-Saxons
    Ill-used Men

The Life and Works of Thomas Hood

Grossmith

Adam Bede

English Notions of American Character

Wit and Humour

Figure 1.2 Titles of lectures delivered at reporting institutions by Clara Lucas Balfour, George Dawson, and George Grossmith, 1852/3–1861/2.

Source: *Journal of the Society of Arts*, Vols. 1–10. Note: This table lists only discrete titles for each year. In some cases, the same lecture was given more than once during the season.

recalled hearing Dawson several times at the Cheltenham Philosophical Institution during his youth: "of his 'raucous voice,' his sarcastic humour, his conversational style, and his general appearance—I retain the clearest recollection. I do not think any lecturer of my time in the matter of quiet ease and entertaining power ever quite came up to Dawson's standard."[149]

In contrast to literary and "miscellaneous" lecturers like Balfour, Grossmith, and Dawson, even the science lecturers most frequently reported in the first decade of the *Journal* were significantly less important to building a good programming season. Geographer William Hughes gave fifteen lectures to Dawson's forty-five, many of them some iteration of "Volcanoes and Earthquakes," but also including a popular offering entitled "Australia: The El Dorado of the 19th Century," while Edwin Lankester gave eleven, including a four-week series on the physiology of circulation, digestion, respiration, and the nervous system. Lankester, who had a busy medical and research practice, charged only £3 per lecture, and limited his geographical reach to within 100 miles of Leeds; Hughes, professor of geography at King's College and Queen's College, London, declined altogether to be included in the Society of Art's 1862 List of Lecturers, although he continued to lecture at affiliate institutions and became a fixture for the Sunday Lecture Society. Credentialed science lecturers, even when they charged lower fees than the well-established "amateurs" in literature and history, were difficult to secure and were increasingly regarded as an add-on to an established season. In the next chapter, we will examine in greater detail the trends and specifics of the emerging ecosystem of knowledge-based culture that developed within these institutions, both during the heyday of the Union and after it had ceased to focus on the provision of lectures.

The Endurance of Lecture Culture

The enthusiasm with which the Society of Arts launched both the Union of Institutions and the weekly *Journal* attested to the centrality of the lecture in mid-century culture. Lectures, both pedagogic and entertaining, permitted men and women to come together and publicly demonstrate their interest in the forces shaping their world. They were an instrument of change that would fit the workingman for the "good times coming" and provide middle-class families with vetted spaces for the performance of cultural competence.[150] The *Journal* served as a compendium of lecture offerings in its first decade, uniting affiliate institutes through the "Proceedings of Institutions" columns that ran every week. Gradually, however, the nature of these proceedings shifted; instead of speakers and titles, augmented by annual reports and the recounting of particularly successful platform offerings—G. J. French's 1858 lecture on "Stained Glass Windows" at the Bolton Mechanics' Institute occupied three closely printed columns of the *Journal*[151]—editors increasingly minimized information on lectures and lecturers to focus more broadly upon the examination system developed by the Society of Arts. By the early 1860s, as we shall see in the following chapter, lecture seasons were discussed within the pages of the *Journal* almost wholly within the overall context of broader programming that included penny readings, book clubs, flower shows, day schools, and gardening clubs. The handwringing over appropriate lecture content had been replaced by discussions over whether to request annual examinations in Latin or how best to structure evening elementary classes in composition and penmanship. In 1869–70, only one lonely and decidedly brief report of institute programming appeared, advertising the anticipated set of art history lectures of G. G. Zerffi at the Birkbeck Literary and Scientific Institution.[152] By the early 1870s, "Proceedings" columns had disappeared altogether, and in 1875, the annual meeting of representatives of Institutions in Union with the Society of Arts was itself dissolved, to be replaced by a series of conferences on Adult Education and Domestic Economy.[153] Institutes were on their own, to sink or swim depending on their ability to respond flexibly to the various pressures of membership, local politics, social change, and finance. Traice ascribed the failures of some institutes not to battles over patronage or deference, but rather to the dangers of societies conforming to a "stereotyped" model that failed to adapt "to the peculiarities of a locality."[154] Those peculiarities—temperance, shopkeepers, beautiful picnic areas—were the strength of a society, he implied, and local members would neglect them at their peril. Localism was the key to survival. The attempts to form a broad, structured lecture circuit had failed, although the lecture season itself had become a fixed expectation of the provincial citizen. While individual institutions were bound loosely in a common understanding of participatory citizenship that was rooted in knowledge-based culture, those bonds did not include shared programming resources. Instead, each society found itself in a frequently confusing marketplace of talent, and those that could not compete would not survive.

2

Shaping "Intelligent Public Opinion"
The Development of Civic Institutions

Literary and Scientific Institutions are a feature of the transition of society towards higher civilization.[1]

How did institutions large and small, left to succeed or fail without the organizing support of the Society of Arts, aim to hit the mark set by Harry Chester in his description of knowledge-based culture? Even as the Society transferred its own attentions to the promises of national examinations—noted at the 1856 Annual Dinner as "the great event of this Session"[2]—and the Union of Institutions gradually ceased to provide formal resources of experience and advice for lecture committees, individual institutions continued to turn to their peers for encouragement and support. Urban and rural, large and small, they increasingly perceived "the power of knowledge" as essential both to "the general tone of society" and "the moral dignity of [the] country,"[3] linking the elite and the popular in a common pursuit of active progress. In 1856, the vice president of the Manchester Athenaeum, John Ashton Nicholls, rehearsed with ease the manifold responsibilities assumed by his listeners: "We are … citizens of a great community, towards which we owe many and serious duties, which it behoves [sic] us fully to comprehend. … We have now a state of civilization unparalleled since the world began, which has brought with it social difficulties which we must endeavour to surmount. The old distinctions have passed away," ushering in an age of participatory citizenship marked by "the influence of our intelligent public opinion."[4] Five years later, Sir John Pakington, speaking at the Birmingham and Midland Institute, could remind his audience of sympathetic listeners that "the system of government under which we live involves us all in serious responsibilities, and the more enlightened are the people the greater is our security for those responsibilities being faithfully fulfilled." Further, he explained, these responsibilities were not limited by class: "the skilled artisan is a man of scientific education and cultivated intellect, fitted to take his place among the most intelligent of his fellow-citizens."[5]

This language, framing citizenship in enlightenment and education, was intimately familiar to audiences up and down the social scale by the middle decades of the century. The institutions and societies responsible for spreading this enlightened education, including both members of the voluntaryist army of culture providers as well as the many critics of that voluntaryist system, took seriously the charge to shape "intelligent public opinion." In this chapter, we will look at how these civic bodies developed during the period from 1850 to 1870, when societies large and small committed their energies and resources to knowledge-based culture. How did they define their missions? What impediments to success stood in their way? How were commitments to both education and entertainment shaped by the pressures for economic survival? What elements appeared essential to the nurturing of "intelligent public opinion," and how did space and place influence the varieties of programming that formed a loose nexus of culture across the kingdom? The overall shape of this web of institutions will provide the context for the popular lecture, the heart of their collective mission, which will be examined in detail in the following chapter.

Money and Management: Organizing the Culture Institution

The rapid growth of literary societies, mechanics' institutions, and the like at midcentury was due to a number of interlocking factors. At a national level, Parliament intervened via the Scientific Societies Act of 1843, which exempted institutions and societies offering literary or scientific education from local rates and led directly to "the formation of young institutions" and the expansion of existing bodies.[6] The act was revised in 1845 to clarify its application to all societies "instituted for purposes of Science, Literature, or the Fine Arts," provided they were supported by voluntary contributions and did not distribute dividends.[7] They were held to strict standards: in 1851 the Manchester Athenaeum lost its rate exemption despite its argument that "science and literature might very properly be followed by coffee and light dancing," while the Society of Arts itself suffered a similar fate twenty years later because it provided housing for its porters and other servants.[8] In 1854, the Literary and Scientific Institutions Act simplified gifts and grants of land by individuals for the establishment of new institutions, and another flurry of building followed.[9] These acts of Parliament affirmed a national commitment to knowledge-based culture, so long as its provision was local, voluntary, and earned no profit.

Most of the institutions participating in the Union spent the 1850s and 1860s wrestling not only with questions about the purposes of the popular lecture but also with organizational issues that would permit them to build the lecture programming analyzed in Chapter 3. Their discussions covered subscription fees and ticket prices, hospitality for uncompensated lecturers, scheduling and advertising, the pros and cons of penny lectures, and the need for "a really efficient secretary," the absence of which would be inevitably harmful or even fatal to an institute.[10] All were urged to secure the most attractive accommodations possible, and their annual reports frequently included self-congratulatory notes about new buildings; the Ipswich Mechanics' Institution, for example, celebrated its refurbished space by admitting that before renovations "more than one professional lecturer had spoken of it as the worst hall in England for a man to speak or make himself heard in," while the Redditch Literary and Scientific Institution announced plans for a purpose-built space "in the Palladian style."[11] Gifts and legacies from private donors were frequently mentioned: the York Institute announced "a legacy of nineteen guineas," while the Chatham, Rochester, Strood, and Brompton Mechanics' Institution reported that "its most pressing want, that of a suitable public lecture hall, [had] been supplied by private enterprise." Support from elite circles was especially highlighted, as in the case of donations totaling twenty guineas from the royal family for the annual fête at the Windsor and Eton Literary, Scientific, and Mechanics' Institution.[12] Institutions that refused to share lecture programming could still be persuaded to work with other local societies to leverage resources: for example, the Darlington Mechanics' Institution received a gift of £400 from a Miss Pease specifically for a building to be shared with the local Temperance Society, "to contain a library, reading-room, class-rooms, large lecture-hall, and ante-rooms, together with accommodation for a person to reside on the premises. The cost is estimated at £1,500." Within months her fellow townswoman, Mrs. Barclay, would donate £300, illustrating one significant way in which middle-class women could both contribute to and gain public recognition for such involvement.[13] These material efforts fit neatly into the wave of modernizing noted by Hewitt and others, as new or renovated institutes became one of the many built expressions of culture at mid-century and were recognized as such by the societies and institutions themselves. The Boston Athenaeum, for example, argued that "in many towns beautiful and commodious edifices have been erected, devoted to Science, Arts, and Literature,—an ornament to the place, an honour to the subscribers, and a blessing to the people," and claimed that its current fundraising campaign was thus essential to the cultural profile of the town.[14]

While the 1843 and 1854 Acts prompted periods of optimistic growth, the *Journal* also chronicled waves of retrenchment as legal relief from property rates proved insufficient to support ambitious and unrealistic programming. Committees might easily misjudge the audiences, programming, fees, and staffing that could be supported by their locality: for example, the Cheltenham Literary and Philosophical Institution and Athenaeum lamented in 1856 that, due to financial difficulties, "the attempt to support it as a reading-room has failed, and it is now proposed to confine it to the original objects of its founders—as a Lecture-room, Museum, and Library of Reference."[15] The Newport Athenaeum and Mechanics' Institute, having declared its fundraising campaign a failure, was forced in 1857 to trim its programming while it retired old debts and continued to search for more affordable accommodations.[16] The Hartlepool Mechanics' Institution and the Hartlepool Workingman's Literary Institute were amalgamated in 1859 after it "became evident that two such institutions were more than the borough could support with any degree of energy," with safeguards in place to guarantee that workingmen were equally represented on the board of the new institute.[17] In 1860, the Lockwood Mechanics' Institution chairman stressed that the failure to build a promised new lecture hall was due not to mismanagement by the committee but rather to "the difficulties met with by the collectors amongst those who had been solicited for subscriptions," while in the following year the Avenham Institution for the Diffusion of Knowledge in Preston had to abandon plans to purchase an adjoining plot of land in the face of chronic mortgage debt.[18]

The dangers of overreach were constantly on the horizon, and not just in smaller localities: the Manchester Athenaeum, famous for its "monster soirees" in the 1840s, was rescued the following decade from near bankruptcy only through the imposition of extraordinary measures of fiscal discipline that included reducing annual subscription fees from 40s. to 24s., ending the monster soirees, and subletting its spaces to other organizations, including the city's Court of Bankruptcy.[19] Even the venerable London Mechanics' Institution avoided bankruptcy and liquidation in part through the generous donations of societies like the Liverpool Institute, whose members presented a gift of £50 to the London Mechanics' Institution in 1858.[20] The Lord Mayor of London, speaking at the annual meeting of the Crosby Hall Evening Classes that same year, noted that a continued debt of some £500 "had very much crippled the efficacy and usefulness" of the institution, a situation shared by societies around the country: "He knew that many of them were struggling for existence, and very few could be said to be out of debt."[21] London institutions were dogged by exceptionally high rents, a problem that would also cripple the SLS, but throughout the provinces many institutions were forced to introduce new, specifically popular entertainments to raise money for building funds or mortgage debt, combining more traditional exhibitions of local minerals, fossils, or manufactured goods with bazaars, concerts, and theatrical recitations at annual fêtes. These events were marketed as particularly attractive, as when the Beechin Mechanics' Institute advertised half-price admission to "the musical concert given by the Hungarian band, and to the entertainment of natural magic of Signor Bosco" as part of an overall push to attract new subscribers in 1855.[22] The Blackburn Literary, Scientific, and Mechanics' Institution used the proceeds of *The Dumfries Album*, published in 1856, to help fund a new lecture hall, while as late as 1862 the Bacup Mechanics' Institute lamented that it was compelled to rent its meeting spaces and classrooms to other organizations to defray new building costs.[23] As we saw in Chapter 1, YUMI secretary Barnett Blake had argued in 1858 that a good season of mixed popular lectures "may prove a very valuable aid to most Institutions" by underwriting the costs of serious classes and teachers; many institutions discovered as well that a variety of popular entertainments provided the financial support necessary for the good popular lecture programming that would excite "a taste for mental cultivation."[24]

Reading Rooms and "Light Literature" as Part of Knowledge-Based Culture

The concerns raised by the overall drift of programming away from the serious and toward the entertaining were most apparent in the discussions over libraries and reading rooms. "A limited Library is like a bank restricted in specie, unable to honour the various claims upon it," wrote George Jacob Holyoake in 1854, and societies provided specific and granular detail about that specie, enumerating numbers and types of books and newspapers, annual circulation figures, funds spent on repair and restoration, gifts of new volumes, and the like.[25] Organizers were advised that "39 feet of available linear space at tables, reading stands, &c., will be ample provision" for most institutions in smaller towns, while larger institutions were advised to have "two reading-rooms, first and second class, with payments accordingly," in addition to a lending library.[26] The Radcliffe and Pilkington Lyceum and Mutual Improvement

Society reported in 1852 that its classroom space had been almost entirely underused but "the reading-room had been generally well attended."[27] The 22-year-old Chester Mechanics' Institution, with an average quarterly membership of about 250, noted proudly in 1857 that it had purchased, "on very easy terms, the whole of the library and fixtures of the 'City Library'; the Mechanics' Institution thus becoming the only public repository of literature in the city; the whole constituting a collection of about 16,000 volumes."[28] Surcharges for libraries and reading rooms were common: the Much Wenlock Agricultural Reading Society doubled its annual reading room fees and raised its annual library fees in 1854 to 10s. for the former and 6s. for the latter, while proposing a separate workingmen's reading room at an extra 2s. per year, and the Royston Mechanics' Institution levied a surcharge of 2s. per year to all subscribers who used its reading room.[29] Similar surcharges were also often levied for access to the volumes of patent listings provided via subscription by the new British Patent Office's library, established in 1852.

Discussions over what to include in libraries and reading rooms echoed the same conundrum posed to lecture committees: what was the appropriate ratio of entertainment to serious intellectual content? Debates over reading material fed into debates over lecture content, and vice versa, within the mid-century ecosystem of knowledge-based culture. Library agents and society secretaries, especially in smaller institutions, struggled to balance members' idealized capacities for self-governance with the reality of all-too-available cheap fiction. On the one hand, "the better class of light literature should form a part of the library, as affording a wholesome relaxation."[30] On the other, how might librarians appropriately curate and supervise "mere fiction, whose professed and whose only end was to amuse" and which could easily incorporate ideas that were "pernicious," "immoral," or "evil"?[31] B. F. Duppa's 1839 *Manual for Mechanics' Institutions* had suggested that only about 10 percent of a library's holdings ought to fall under the heading of "poetry and fiction." Prefiguring mid-century discussions of lecture content, he warned that "the unceasing seeking after such reading is very distinct from, and is rarely found in combination with, a love of knowledge and a desire of improvement."[32] Traice's *Hand-book for Mechanics' Institutions*, published two decades later, was much less proscriptive but still imbued with concern over "works of Imagination," which he argued should be chosen only "with great circumspection." His list of recommended works of "miscellaneous literature" included poetry by Burns and Byron, novels by Eliot and Scott, and the various periodicals published by Robert Chambers.[33]

Many institution secretaries and governors felt that they should make available only those works "which have been raised to the shelves of the library by the common consent of all men, … for all generations, and for all time."[34] Complete freedom was potentially dangerous, especially for younger members: "if a society is to receive young people of the ages of thirteen and upwards," wrote Faversham Mutual Improvement Society president Frederick Monk, "and if the subscription is so small as to enable all classes to avail themselves of the advantages offered (and I maintain this is the most useful of all kinds of Literary Institutes), then there should be the exclusion of those books which are usually classified as 'works of fiction.'"[35] The Bradford Mechanics' Institution noted that the fiction that accounted for some one-third of its holdings was "neither refused nor transformed into leading objects, but introduced so far, and so far only, as [it] could be rendered subservient" to the more serious aims of the library.[36] The Bingley Institute reassured its supporters that it "scrupulously avoid[ed] all that was of a baneful or poisonous nature,"[37] while the Carlyle Mechanics' Institution announced in 1855 that it had banned all publications from the Minerva Press School, notorious as a publisher of gothic fiction and famously mocked as the producer of trashy novels in Jane Austen's *Northanger Abbey*: "This class of literature had been quickly crushed."[38] Blake urged institutions a year later to continue to weed out works of "diluted twaddle" and "milk-and-water sentimentality," which lacked the "mental vigor" desired by serious men.[39] These concerns over appropriate reading material for male subscribers reflected the concurrent debate over the public libraries being established across the country: library historian Edward Edwards argued in 1859 that a good public library "must offer to all men, not only the practical science, the temporary excitements, and the prevalent opinions of the passing day, but the wisdom of preceding generations; the treasures of a remote antiquity; the hopes and the evidences of the World to come."[40] Fiction, except in the form of novels that had reached some unarticulated but widely agreed upon status as "literature," was largely relegated to the margins of such discussions, at libraries and within other institutions of knowledge-based culture. Instead, committee reports expressed the consistent hope that subscribers would choose intellectual heft over ephemeral froth.

Over the course of the decade, library committees within these institutions became more optimistic about the ability of members to choose wisely. By 1858, the Nottingham Mechanics' Institution reported that they had changed their regulations so that "free access to the books is now allowed."[41] Institutions whose subscribers could demonstrate their trustworthiness through the payment of the extra premiums were eager to classify their more entertaining holdings as "the more valuable and permanent parts of Literature,"[42] or even simply as "novels," rather than "fiction," and to underscore their institutional subscriptions to well-known lending libraries as a badge of sophistication. Mudie's, Booth's, and the London Library Company could be trusted to supply "the latest contributions to general literature," already curated through the demands of the middle-class reading public, "with obvious advantage to the convenience of members."[43]

Libraries were linked to but separate from reading rooms, where institutions provided increasingly broad access to a variety of periodicals, hoping to increase the revenues that might support other aspects of knowledge-based culture. The Halifax Mechanics' Institution reported in 1852 that about one-third of its members paid the additional surcharge for access to "six daily London papers, twenty-two weekly and other local papers, five quarterly reviews, [and] eighteen magazines and serials," while the Macclesfield Society for Acquiring Useful Knowledge subscribed to fifteen daily and nineteen weekly newspapers. A few years later, the chair of the Halifax institution's annual meeting "urged the importance of the constant perusal of the daily press, saying that he believed it was perfectly necessary that in a free country like this all the intelligent portion of the community should have access to papers of every description and advocating all classes of opinion."[44] Many societies started with very limited hours of availability but increased access to accommodate demand; some, like the Newington Working Men's Association, kept a running tab of the number of discrete visits made to the reading room, noting that its 435 members visited the reading room more than 12,000 times in 1860.[45] Many reading rooms also provided "telegraphic intelligence" up to three times a day, although some, like the Bury Athenaeum, discontinued this intelligence when it became clear that the costs were prohibitive.[46] The adoption of these extras was occasionally linked directly to concerns over membership numbers: the Manchester Athenaeum, hoping to stanch an alarming (although ultimately temporary) loss in membership, added daily telegraphic intelligence with the advent of the Crimean War, with one member noting that "the Czar had contributed something to their funds this year."[47]

The addition of this service at the Manchester Athenaeum, whose self-identity rested on "the importance of literature to men of business,"[48] prompted several members to chastise the directors for reallocating funds that would have normally gone to the purchase of books, privileging ephemeral news coverage over "general literature" and more serious reading. A small but noisy contretemps—one member, a Mr. Currie, mocked the Crimean coverage as "flashy maps, bedaubed with parti-coloured shawl-pins"[49]—highlighted the ongoing tension between the library as a place of quiet, steady, and presumably intellectual improvement, to which carefully curated novels now contributed, and the reading room as a space for the rapid consumption of news and ephemera. Which should be the core of knowledge-based culture? Currie had charged that the directors were neglecting "legitimate educational and literary functions" to pander to "the resultless [sic] excitements of the day."[50] In response, secretary James Hudson argued that "nine-tenths of the members of the institution entered on account of the news-room," and they wanted the latest news.[51] Propelled by subscriber demand, the athenaeum, like societies large and small, moved inexorably to the provision of these "excitements."

The decision to incorporate journals and miscellanies, like the decision to provide novels and "light reading," had been debated for several decades, but over time, warnings that periodicals could be purveyors of "dogmatical opinion," fallacy, and ignorance to the undiscriminating novice were replaced by warnings that failure to provide such materials was a dereliction of duty.[52] Thus, in 1851 the Duke of Argyll could warn his listeners at the Glasgow Athenaeum that newspapers imparted only "floating information" and "ready-made opinions ... without the discipline of thought."[53] Similarly, in 1858, Chancellor Barton, president of the Church of England Religious and General Literary Association (Carlisle), "urged upon the members that while the establishment of the news-room was an advantageous part of the system of the Institution, the mere reading of periodical publications was not their main object. ... Standing alone, it might be found a very unsafe source of intelligence, and a closer—not an expander of the mind. He did not say, then, that they should not read the newspapers, but that they should not let them be their sole or even their principal reading."[54] Just as the uncurated library could be dangerous to junior members, the uncurated newsroom could also be a threat, especially to the working men who were the prime objects of this group's attention.

Just two years later, however, Chester argued that newspapers and journals were generally considered the mark of a cultured reader and that "if a man never reads [newspapers], he is unfit for the duties, and therefore for the privileges, of citizenship."[55] Neatly pivoting such reading away from the haphazard and undisciplined adoption of untested opinion to the careful consideration of contemporary problems, Chester helped normalize newspaper reading as a necessary pursuit of knowledge-based culture within participatory citizenship, across class lines. Even while he concurred in the adoption of "strict rules to prevent the institution from being troubled by theological or political controversies"—those noisy arguments disruptive of the carefully cultivated atmosphere that embraced "all grades" of members—he cordoned off individual reading. "Of course these rules must not be so framed as to exclude newspapers," he stated, "nor books treating of theology and politics."[56] Two decades of institutional development had helped transform active class animus into muted friction, and Chester was cheerfully optimistic about its eventual extinction through the operation of the societies that opened their doors but also superintended their members. He could thus link newspapers to "books treating of theology and politics," while asserting that those men who chose membership in these societies would exercise such self-control as to avoid controversy.

Curating Recreation

New buildings had to be filled, and libraries and reading rooms in and of themselves could not guarantee sufficient subscription income. Affiliate institutions after 1850 had to respond decisively to the demands for programming that moved beyond instruction and education into "recreation." This was not the "rational recreation" long associated with the systematic, disciplined, and generically moral leisure activities of "respectable" workers, but rather a calculated appeal to members' "feelings and tastes."[57] Committees increasingly recognized that those men who might join an institute had legitimate preferences for certain kinds of programming, and that institution governors were not promoting moral turpitude by curating certain types of leisure. Societies that depended on members from the working classes—even if this dependence was not exclusive or absolute—faced new competition in the establishment of the Working Men's Clubs movement in 1862, although founder Henry Solly and several others argued that "the workmen who entered the clubs were altogether a different class from those who recruited the classes in the Mechanics' Institutions."[58] At the same time, institutions for the middle and lower middle classes were also reevaluating their programming. Participants at the 1860 Warminster Conference on Adult Education lamented that many athenaeums now largely ignored the established commercial man who sought "a place rather for profitable business than the promotion of literature, science, or the fine arts exclusively." Instead, they catered for the partially educated young men of the lower middle classes, who tended to eschew "close study" and instead focus on "essentially popular" lectures, musical entertainments, and social gatherings.[59] By 1861, Barnett Blake, evaluating both the reenergized athenaeum movement and the nascent workingmen's club movement, advised Union affiliates to consider "a judicious system of recreation" that would allow them to compete for membership with less intellectually and, he implied, less culturally rigorous institutions while continuing to provide alternatives to casinos, pubs, and music halls.[60] Two years later, the governing committee of the four-year-old South Staffordshire Association for Promoting Adult Education argued that "such subjects as entertainments and systematic recreation … came very properly within the scope of the society's operations," alongside "the establishment of free libraries, local museums, and so forth."[61] By 1864, four years after Chester's articulation of the paradigmatic society, and in response to the ways in which consumer demand was helping reshape ideas of culture and respectability, Union affiliates as a whole were willing to formalize their commitment to carefully curated "recreation" in a resolution at the 13th annual meeting of the Institutions in Union:

> [Resolved.] That the social character of Institutes may be materially promoted by the addition of a room for conversation, indoor games (such as chess), and greater freedom than is ordinarily allowed in a reading-room, by encouraging athletic games, and by occasional excursions for recreation, and social gatherings for conversation, short readings, music, microscopic and photographic exhibitions, and similar entertainments, on which occasions suitable refreshments might be provided.[62]

The ways in which institutes implemented this resolution over the next decade varied widely. Some institutes increased spaces for gardening, cricket and bowls, choral societies and classes in tonic sol fa, games of chess and draughts, and regular fêtes. Others repurposed classrooms as smoking rooms, instituted discussion and essay classes in which "the custom to exclude controversial theology and party politics" might be relaxed, or formed debating clubs embedded within the larger institution "to extend its usefulness."[63] Spaces for coffee as well as smoking were noted as part of "the 'Club' feature of such institutions."[64] A few, determined to reflect some mythic model of ancient England, instituted athletic competitions with generous prizes: for example, the Much Wenlock Agricultural Reading Society in 1854 reported "rustic sports and trials of strength and skill," including the "old English sports" of wheelbarrow racing, football, and hurdles; by 1859, it awarded a variety of prizes, including £5 for "tilting at the ring on ponies" and £4 to "Best Ode, with a Chorus, to the Victor in the Tilting Match, capable of being adapted to Music."[65] Classes in gymnastics, fencing, dueling, and drill also became increasingly popular in rural societies, especially those in agricultural counties. These aspects of "the physical training of the population" often helped boost subscriber rolls, and the Union itself eventually urged its affiliates to organize "friendly contests" with challenge cups and other recognitions.[66]

These leisure pursuits, when they were adopted, aimed at the paradigm described by Chester but were generally treated in formal annual reports as secondary to the classes, lectures, and reading rooms that had by now shaped culture institutions for two decades. Affiliates might note the success or failure of a cricket club or a gymnastic class, but generally placed these items adjacent to rather than within more traditionally serious offerings. For example, the Haley-hill Working Men's College in Halifax reported in 1862 both that "we have improved our cricket ground, and rendered our bowling green one of the first in this part of the country" and that "the literary and scientific society in connection with the college still continues in a prosperous state."[67] Some societies appointed separate governing committees for their recreational programs: the Hull Young People's Christian and Literary Institute noted that its cricket club, "under the management of a separate Committee, was vigorously carried on during the summer, and proved no inconsiderable adjunct to the Institute."[68] Similarly, those institutions with museums offered museum-only subscriptions and reduced admission rates on certain days each year, sometimes opening the grounds for free. These secondary offerings provided recreation that was at least loosely conjoined to knowledge-based culture, permitting many institutions to remain committed to their founding ideals while cultivating dependable income streams. While both members themselves and the general public might value these recreational spaces more highly than the formal lecture theaters and classroom spaces, officers and committee members consistently presented the sporting grounds and singing clubs as subsidiary to their primary mission. As had happened in the move to open up even the most venerable mechanics' institutions to membership outside the working classes, the rhetorical stance that "the cultivation of the mental is not inconsistent with the enjoyment of the recreative"[69] was emphatically a response to changing social and economic pressures and cloaked the inescapable imperative to change or die.

Rewriting the Failure Paradigm

By 1860, Chester's description of the paradigmatic institution reflected a widely accepted set of aspirational guidelines for culture providers. However, the muted class friction he had deliberately downplayed was a matter of continued concern for educationists, teachers, patrons, lecturers, and committee members. One consistent thread in the reports and correspondence of this period led inexorably back to the fears that, after all was said and done, mechanics' institutions and literary societies after 1850 really were part of the failure to reach the working classes that Hudson, Hole, and others had articulated. Hudson offered as quintessential examples of this failure both the Manchester Athenaeum and the Manchester Mechanics' Institution, which he berated for having been "led into unhealthy excitement by weekly lectures, frequent concerts, ventriloquism, and Shaksperian [sic] readings."[70] The Athenaeum in particular, he fumed, had turned its face "towards light and meretricious subjects" in books and lecture programming, failing to support all classes except those in French, German, Spanish, and Italian, which charged "a small extra fee" but "which are not numerously attended."[71] The successes of the gymnastic club and subsocieties for chess, music, essay and discussion, and elocution and dramatic reading—whose "proneness to amateur stage representation" Hudson condemned—testified to the complete abandonment of any serious intellectual intent by these institutions.[72]

Despite Hudson's criticisms, hundreds of affiliate institutions would come to rely upon these ancillary programs as essential not only to fiscal health but also to the needs of the modern civic body. Indeed, committees and governors rapidly moved to characterize these programs away from a paradigm of failure and instead to present them as much-needed solutions to problems of adult education and civic culture, often arguing that they were doing more good locally than any strictly working-class institution might have done, because they were providing education *and* recreation, learning *and* leisure, credentials *and* culture. Educational programming, while important, was less crucial than "promoting a friendly intercourse amongst the inhabitants of the town by means of classes, a library, reading rooms, lectures and entertainments, &c."[73] Indeed, in making this claim, the Croydon Literary and Scientific Institute argued that "to apply the purely educational test in ascertaining the measure of usefulness of all institutions, appears to the committee to be a mistake." This usefulness, so integral to a broad aspirational model of citizenship, was rooted in a model of stability that rejected the rigid economic and social divisions of the revolutionary 1840s and instead embraced a carefully crafted inclusivity based on the appreciation of knowledge-based culture. In 1854, the Macclesfield Society for Acquiring Useful Knowledge celebrated its nineteen years of existence as "the centre of news and business, as well as the leading channel of learning and useful knowledge in the town" by recapping its work in offering classes for "our industrious artizans" and their families, alongside concerts, lecture programming, books and periodicals, and telegraphic intelligence "for our mercantile members."[74] The Leeds Mechanics' Institute and Literary Society described its membership as "the union of different classes," which was both "one of the most valuable features of the Institution, and one of the main causes of its success."[75] The Literary, Scientific, and Mechanics' Institution in Reading claimed in its 1857 annual report that "the Institution ... occupies a place in the town which it could not relinquish without occasioning a blank which would sensibly be felt, if not regretted, by all. It is considered that not only the members, but the inhabitants of the town generally, are indebted to its agency for the means of intellectual improvement and recreation to an extent which few, if any, towns of similar circumstances enjoy."[76] The Earl of Carlisle, addressing a prize-giving ceremony that same year in Manchester, commended his listeners and noted that "the friends and members of all such institutions would show great wisdom in promoting such a spirit of good fellowship, and in maintaining as much *esprit de corps* as possible," employing a phrase that would become especially important in the last decades of the century.[77]

This "spirit of good fellowship" was often regarded as sufficient not only to defuse class tensions but even to erase them altogether: the pursuit of knowledge-based culture was understood to culminate almost inevitably in broad participatory citizenship. Baines, speaking at the Ripon Mechanics' Institution and Literary Society, described these institutions as "so plastic as to be capable of adapting themselves to the largest cities and towns, and almost to the smallest villages," in which "the fusion of classes and not their isolation ... the harmonious union and reciprocal action of the whole" could be achieved. Class division remained as an economic fact while class cohesion emerged as a cultural fact, theoretically transforming antagonism into a common pursuit of civic-mindedness. Similar magic erased political partisanship even as it left political parties intact: in 1864, the inaugural report of the reconstituted Bingley Mechanics' Institute noted that its membership, built as it was "on the broadest possible basis, ... stands safe against the accusation of being subject to any class or party interest."[78] The committee responsible for the renewed life and health of this institute deliberately retained a name fraught with allusions to a narrow membership and then immediately took pains to explain away those class valences: "the name Mechanics' Institute hardly conveys a proper notion of the actual composition of a society like ours," noted the chair in his inaugural address. "The members in this Institution belong to all classes of society, from the gentry of the neighborhood and the master manufacturers down through the various grades of tradesmen and shopkeepers, shopmen, overlookers, clerks, farm labourers, combers, weavers, and spinners."[79]

The project of reframing and muting class divisions could be slow and uneven: the Committee of the Sudbury Literary Institute noted in 1852 that "the lecturer, *although a working man*, appeared fully to understand the subject,"[80] neatly communicating that its lecture programming was crafted to appeal to a broad audience while simultaneously reminding readers of this annual report that class still mattered. The editor of the *Monthly Literary and Scientific Lecturer* (1850-3) collected lectures delivered at a variety of institutions, curating them for "shopkeepers' assistants, clerks, and other young men, whose intellectual culture was somewhat in advance of that of the mechanics and artisans."[81] The Tunbridge Literary and Scientific Institute deliberately highlighted the "respectable" nature of the working-class audience at a lecture by George Dawson. Chester himself alluded to the need for "innocent amusements" and "the occupation of dangerous leisure" when planning for "the association of different classes," while the annual report of the Wirksworth Mechanics' Institution underscored the "patient and attentive" audience at a lecture on "Binocular Vision," where the lecturer, delivering a quintessentially class-based example of what Enda Leaney has described as a "scientific sermon," stressed that "the great operations of nature" reflected "the wonders with which the goodness of God has on every hand surrounded them."[82] Speeches lauding a commitment to knowledge-based culture that transcended class divisions could be awkward and unpersuasive: Oliver Heywood's 1868 address to the members of the Manchester Mechanics' Institution revisited its founding commitment to the self-education of the operative by noting that "with regard to the desire for self-improvement, let him say how he enjoyed it himself," while the Duke of Argyll, speaking to the YUMI in 1864, reminisced that "there was a sense in which he had always felt that he was the son of a mechanic, for it so happened that his father was for many years much devoted to mechanical pursuits," and the Duke himself had passed "some of the happiest years of his childhood" in a workshop.[83]

Indeed, for every committee, president, or locality boasting about community cohesion, there were localities confronting the realities of continued class division rehearsed by one columnist in the 1863 *London Quarterly Review*: "The mechanic and artisan class do not readily mix with the poor, nor even with the lower orders of unskilled labourers; and the benefit of both will, we believe, rarely be attained by the same undertaking."[84] Londoner Benjamin Shaw "very much doubted whether the clerks and book-keepers in the south would be found to associate with the working men in the same Institution,"[85] but the problem was not geographically specific. The Sheffield Athenaeum and the Sheffield Mechanics' Institution, for example, had collaborated in 1847-8 on a new space and then fell out over the allocation of square footage to each institution and the reluctance of athenaeum members to enter the building by the same door as the operatives who attended the mechanics' institution.[86] Less than a decade later, the Highgate Institute—in contrast to the Bingley Mechanics' Institute above—"preferred that the word 'mechanics' should not be introduced," because its membership was more heavily drawn from "the class of clerks and book-keepers" than "those engaged in manual operations."[87] Reid, proposing a plan for "approximating Mechanics' Institutions into People's Colleges," met with entrenched resistance: "Mr. W. Beckett, MP, said, it appeared to him that Mr. Reid's plan contemplated the mixing of classes, while he believed such institutions were originally only concerned with the industrious class."[88]

Those skeptical of the inevitability of "class fusion" were reluctant to fall back on the old failure paradigms of Hudson and Hole, however. Instead, these critics reallocated responsibility for continued class tensions away from institution committees and patrons, on the one hand, or students and readers, on the other. They placed their frustrations at the feet of those who refused to take advantage of the buffet of cultural offerings available for a minimal subscription fee. These individuals were the willfully ignorant, who were perceived as choosing not to participate in this ideal of citizenship: "the committee regret that so few, comparatively, of the working-classes take advantage of the privileges of the Institution, which are so numerous and applicable, that whoever is now without a good secular education must in after years, when the want is found, lay the blame upon his own shoulders."[89] This allocation of blame was especially common in institutions sponsored or overseen by specific interests—railway and mining companies, religious organizations, and others—whose reports often expressed disappointment that "so many of the Company's servants still stood aloof from the Institution."[90] These remarks also echoed those found in the records of smaller mutual improvement societies scattered throughout the working and lower middle classes, whose members frequently noted that many of their social peers deliberately refused to join. These society members, confidently a part of the mid-Victorian caste of self-improvers, ascribed this resistance to attitude: the nonjoiners, they said, were simply reluctant to be policed out of rowdy behavior. Others, however, argued that the problem was rooted in the spatial and temporal geographies of work and leisure: institutions were generally "established as near the centre of the town as possible," but by the 1850s, as factories and offices sprang up in the emerging suburbs, many potential members could not comfortably or easily undertake the necessary walk of a mile or two into town "after his ten or twelve hours' toil." This distance was more "deteriorative" to the success of many institutions than any love of rowdiness, and apparently much more difficult for committees and long-standing members to appreciate.[91]

"That Youth, Tender in Age"

Concerns over class and caste were new iterations of old worries. A fresher source of anxiety within many of these institutions had to do with generational change. The broad appeal of knowledge-based culture was widely regarded both by providers and by spectators as having "saved the character of many an apprenticed youth, removed from the parental restraints, by superseding the billiard-room, theatre, and casino."[92] The Carlisle Church of England Religious and General Literary Association in 1856 urged its existing members to focus their recruitment efforts "especially among young men,"[93] who were generally understood to be both singularly susceptible to evil influences and peculiarly important to England's future prosperity. This cohort was identified by age—thirteen to eighteen—rather than specifically by class, incorporating both "young members of middle-class families, who seek to gain instruction without absorbing effort, and to be amused without encountering the presence of vice," and the youth of the working classes who required "an agreeable, yet effective, bracing up to do battle with indolence and self-indulgence, impurity, and foppish display."[94] Left to their own devices, younger members from both classes would simply cluster within "societies or sections of the Institution in which young men can display the little they have learned," rather than pursue serious learning.[95]

Perhaps the most melodramatic portrayal of this population had been delivered in 1844, when president Benjamin Disraeli, speaking at the annual soiree of the Manchester Athenaeum, rose to new heights of hyperbole:

> When for a moment we conceive ... the position of a youth perhaps of very tender years, sent, as has frequently been the case, from a distant district, to form his fortunes in this great metropolis of labour and of science; when we think of that youth, tender in age, with no domestic hearth to soothe, to stimulate, to counsel, or to control—when we picture him to ourselves, after a day of indefatigable toil, left to his lonely evenings and his meagre lodgings, without a friend, without a counsellor, falling into dissipation from sheer want of distraction, and perhaps involved in vice before he is conscious of the fatal net that is involving him,— what a contrast to his position does it offer when we picture him to ourselves entering, with a feeling of self-consciousness which supports and sustains him after his daily toil, into a great establishment, where every thing that can satisfy curiosity, that can form taste, that can elevate the soul, that can lead to noble thoughts and honourable intentions,—surround him! ... [This institution is] a great harbor of refuge, I would say a great harbor of intellectual refuge and social propriety.—(Cheers).[96]

Disraeli's powers of evocative rhetoric were unique, but the trope of the dangerously autonomous adolescent, so promising as a future worker and leader and so susceptible to the seductions of dissipation, emerged at mid-century as a common way to recast the paradigm of failure. Hope previously vested in the workingman had only inconsistently been realized and could more appropriately be focused upon the young: the committee of one 1852 institution, "while lamenting the indifference and carelessness of the adult labouring population of the neighborhood, for whose especial benefit it was designed, expresses the belief that, in the younger members, they have a pledge of future prosperity," while another deliberately highlighted its work in "promoting the comfort and intellectual advancement of youth" rather than of adult working men.[97]

The "youth" who were to be courted were expected to mature under the sheltering surveillance of the institution, where they would eventually contribute both their full subscription fees and their energies on boards and committees, but one of the chronic sources of concern for a number of societies was the irritation and even outright contempt expressed by younger men for their elders, whose ideas of culture and leisure did not keep pace with the modern world. The arguments over Crimean telegraphic coverage in the Manchester Athenaeum, above, were only peripherally related to maps and pins. Mr. Currie's lengthy diatribe focused on what he charged were two decades of poor management: "I ask my fellow members ... to try and get directors with the proper qualifications," who would restore the Athenaeum to a space where young men "could exhilarate their spirits by reading or intellectual converse," which would not only fit them to be better conductors of business but also "enabl[e] them to take a part in the moral and intellectual progress of this populous community."[98]

The clashes between the silverbacks on governing committees and their younger and more inexperienced counterparts were troublingly frequent in these middle decades. Young members—including that vexing junior cohort of late adolescence but extending upwards to include young men in their twenties—saw older directors as staid and reactionary; the directors, for their part, saw the younger members as "very uncertain and fickle," obstinately refusing to grow into their roles as culturally competent citizens. "When the directors had made efforts to make the institution a literary one, or to bring it in contact with literary institutions of the highest standing," noted the Athenaeum president, "they had been defeated by the coldness of the parties who they were told were so anxious that it should be made available for those purposes."[99] These parties—not the small group of self-described eager learners represented by Mr. Currie, but a larger group whose main concern was the best placement of the billiard table—subscribed to the notion that "it was a sufficient guarantee of a man's respectability in the Athenaeum that he was a member of the Athenaeum."[100]

Disraeli in 1844 had told his audience, "You have dis-enthroned Force, and placed on her high seat Intelligence. ... And the necessary consequence of this great revolution is, that it has become the duty and the delight equally of every citizen to cultivate his faculties."[101] Subsequent speakers, presidents, and members—at the Athenaeum and in similar institutions across the kingdom—would continue to frame the importance of cultivating this particular kind of citizenship. No boy was too young for such duty and delight. Participation in culture—whether through lectures, elocutionary exercises, or simply attendance at annual meetings—was a mark of maturity that could be assumed by even the most tender youth with the most meager of resources. Neither age nor income should be the defining characteristics of citizenship. However, to the dismay of officers and board members across the kingdom, the "considerable and important class [of] young men engaged in ... commercial pursuits"[102] did not eagerly shoulder these responsibilities, as defined by their elders; not only did they absent themselves from the expression of citizenship represented by the annual meeting, they also frequently preferred cricket, chess, amateur theatricals, and music to lectures and language classes. They dropped their memberships in large numbers during the summers, and often did not return to the nurturing classrooms and lecture halls of the society in the fall.[103] And they did not hesitate to express their feelings, rather than their citizenship, in the pages of annual reports submitted to local newspapers, which gleefully reprinted "rather sharp recriminations," "remarks of a somewhat personal character," and "attacks" by younger members on their elders.[104]

Examples of this intergenerational conflict were most common in larger, older institutions. At the Manchester Mechanics' Institute, the "cozy family party" of directors regarded the student members as persistently obstreperous, especially during a lengthy power struggle in 1866–8 over control of the curriculum. In this case, students found support in the *Manchester Guardian*, whose editors were happy to remind the board "that they are possessed of a public trust for the moral, as well as the intellectual, well-being of their members."[105] Other forms of youthful disrespect at institutes across the kingdom included defacing library books, breaking windows, and blandly disregarding limits on topics for discussion and debate.[106] Working-class adults might simply ignore programming that directors believed was in their best interest; junior members were more vocal in flouting rules that they regarded as outmoded or stodgy. Governors and elected committee members of larger and multipurpose institutions had to exercise a certain degree of restraint to maintain membership levels.

Two Models of Growth and Change

It is clear that the broad web of mechanics' and other institutions had not ceased their activities after 1850; instead, England saw an explosion of these societies and witnessed their growth along a general trajectory of expansion and realignment. Almost every Union affiliate reporting within the *Journal* followed a loose but identifiable pattern: taking advantage of changes in tax law to purchase and build; securing funding streams through the provision of add-on services that were often recreational in nature, such as cricket grounds or chess clubs; accommodating the realities of "ephemeral" reading through novels and periodicals; wrangling tensions between unreliable and noisy junior members and executive directors who put fiscal health before faddish popularity; emphasizing their roles in establishing and securing community stability by tailoring programming to local and regional needs; and framing their work in a language of citizenship and culture that retained traces of class antagonism but also strove for inclusivity.

Despite its general applicability, however, this pattern did not guarantee success. Many of these institutes faded into obscurity rather quickly, and success or failure was only loosely linked to size. Small societies were dangerously member-dependent, but also often more flexible in response to subscribers' needs and demands: Alan Woods's comparative work on institutions in Acrington, Blackpool, and Darwen shows how only Darwen, responding to pressure by members to open up the society to classes, lectures, and books in theology and politics, became "in every sense the people's own."[107] Larger institutions were not self-evidently vulnerable to the same issues that crippled and eventually closed so many smaller institutions: they had broader and more stable pools of potential members, they enjoyed fiscal resources that would permit at least some innovative programming, and they attracted and paid well-known lecturers, performers, and teachers. In many ways, they embodied Chester's paradigm and as such they regarded themselves, and were regarded by others, as part of the civic brand of the municipality. However, the arc of development in these larger areas fractured civic culture institutions into two major categories. The first, largely coterminous with the membership of the YUMI and similar unions, would in the period after about 1860 expand rapidly to provide a range of classes and other offerings specifically to workingmen and women, in programming that led relatively directly to the development of industrial schools and workingmen's colleges.[108] This trajectory was apparent long before the passage of the Technical Instruction Acts of 1889 and 1891. As early as 1854, the secretary of the Huddersfield Mechanics' Institution reported that "lectures had not been frequent, the directorate desiring to interrupt the nightly routine of classes as little as possible," and that as a result, according to its president, "the Huddersfield Mechanics' Institution was the only ... 'People's College' he knew."[109] The Worcestershire Union of Educational Institutes was founded in 1858 to respond to "an increased desire on the part of managers to make such Institutions not only ostensibly but in reality Working Men's Colleges, not only mainly places for intellectual recreation, but direct educational establishments."[110]

This new division, between "intellectual recreation" and serious "direct" education, pushed the fraught conversations of the 1850s and 1860s firmly into the next decades, where the understanding of knowledge-based culture would be mapped onto an emerging and incomplete division between "general" programming for the middle classes and "industrial" offerings for the working classes. By 1860, at the annual meeting of the YUMI, a platform of worthies led by Lord Ashburton applauded the emphasis on serious coursework and generally concurred that, "as a rule," popular lectures "on matters of local history, on travels, and on popular books ... should be shortened" in order not to interfere with classes.[111] Despite Blake's tireless work delivering literary, topical, or humorous lectures to member institutions—the seventy-two lecture engagements on his 1860 schedule, for example, included "Sam Slick the Clockmaker," "The Life of the Late George Stephenson," and "Our Indian Empire"—more and more YUMI affiliates were self-identifying not as literary but increasingly as "industrial" educational institutions "calculated to promote the intellectual advancement of the working-classes of the town."[112] By 1860, one reporter characterized the annual meeting of the YUMI as "a kind of educational and social science conference,"[113] tying the Union directly to the work of the young National Association for the Provision of Social Sciences (NAPSS) rather than to the broader conception of knowledge-based culture that had been so widespread just a few years earlier and that was now beginning to be linked more exclusively to the "general" programming for middle-class families.

This reorientation in existing mechanics' institutions, and the significant establishment of new mechanics' institutions after 1860, was prompted by several converging factors: the benefits of the examination and credentialing systems offered by the Society of Arts and other groups; the interest sparked by the 1867 international exhibition and renewed national worries over "taste" and competition from continental craftsmen; and the establishment of state-funded primary schools after 1870, which relieved many institutions of their investment in elementary classes and permitted them to move rapidly into secondary and technical education with courses that were tied to skilled jobs in chemistry, engineering, and other technical fields.[114] The passage of the 1870 Education Act in particular permitted mechanics' institutions to be "gradually made what they were intended to be—centres of education, in which youths and working men may follow the course of study which taste or interest marks out, and thus prepare themselves for discharging with greater efficiency the duties of their respective occupations."[115] By 1877, a speaker at the annual YUMI meeting asserted that "the continual struggle for existence among the rival [curricular] classes, resulting in an unjustifiable waste of power both educationally and financially," had ended, and that member institutions were "carrying education systematically forward from the primary schools."[116]

As John Laurent shows, these institutes did not reject knowledge-based culture, but they tended to frame their offerings through a reworked understanding of class-based education. Popular lecture programming, for example, might continue, but it was presented as a clear adjunct to classroom work: the Keighley Institute's 1872 annual report noted that lectures on "history, literature, voyages and travels" and other popular topics were provided not as a season-long package for subscribers but instead were "given to working men in the great lecture hall at a charge of threepence each.'"[117] These workingmen were seeking education that would, as Society chairman of council Rev. James Booth had argued in 1856, aid in their "temporal advancement,"[118] and the lectures on these more popular topics were relegated to leisure and to such limited space and funding as these institutions could spare from their responsibilities as "centres of technical education for the industrial population."[119]

The second category of institutes and societies continued to emphasize the specific cultural needs of the locality, including those general popular lectures that were regarded as increasingly less important in the first category of institutions. These institutions situated themselves as the primary local purveyors of knowledge-based culture, emphasizing both education and entertainment and usually crossing class lines. Some were purpose-built, absorbing the energies and potential subscribers of earlier failed institutions; others found their missions subtly changing as they sought to position themselves as regional rather than local centers of culture. On the one hand, they all generally strove to instill in their mixed audiences a common appreciation of the best contemporary popular lecturers, musical and theatrical entertainments, and curated sociability; on the other, they also struggled to maintain adult-education classes and to expand their curricula to meet the needs for youth and "ladies." Often, their subscribers showed a definite preference for the former over the latter. The Hastings Mechanics' Institution, for example, noted in its thirty-fourth annual report that its mission, "to lead on the members to the cultivation of an elevated taste," led naturally to active lecture and musical programming as well as to such innovations as an annual regatta, but that classes designed to feed into the Society of Arts examinations were met with "much apathy." At the same time, its governing committee stressed that they refused to introduce "changes that would have made the Society more attractive to the thoughtless and the gay."[120] Hastings, a small and prosperous community just outside of London, grew increasingly dependent upon programming made "more attractive" to its middle-class members even as it remained rhetorically committed to "the spread of education," and its annual reports throughout the 1850s and 1860s reflected an internal struggle over mission and purpose. Hastings was far from alone in wrestling with these tensions. As we will see later, there was no single path for these multipurpose institutions. However, like the recognizable route to higher education pursued by YUMI members and other mechanics' institutes, they generally followed a course that both emphasized inclusivity and failed to provide clear answers to the thorny questions of class, caste, and cultural access that accompanied unanticipated levels of popular success.

Utility and Patriotism: The Examples of Leeds

The division of knowledge-based culture into "industrial" and "general" programs, one for the working and lower middle classes and the other for their social superiors, was reflected in the changing fortunes of two Leeds institutes, the elite Phil.-&-Lit. (founded 1819) and the popular Leeds Mechanics' Institution (LMI, founded 1824). The former, founded as a private institution dedicated to "the conversational diffusion of knowledge," which would offer "a relief to the severe and dry study of science," had a somewhat rocky beginning; the short-lived *Leeds Monthly Magazine* in 1829 mocked its "dilettanti members" delivering "plagiarized papers" and "pure, unadulterated nonsense" in front of audiences of adoring mothers and sisters.[121] It soon found its feet as a serious producer of knowledge, however, and remained almost wholly inward-turning until its museum introduced penny admissions in 1852 after receiving a gift of the remains of a hippopotamus found near the city.[122] In 1853, a popular program of Juvenile Lectures at Christmas began. Taken altogether, the Phil.-&-Lit. at mid-century was a successful model of an institution that served the local patriciate, emphasizing the cultural needs of wealthy families in the town and suburbs while preserving an elitist conception of knowledge production. The LMI, in contrast, was deliberately inclusive in nature. It claimed the provision of popular lectures as part of its brief, along with a day school to provide "a sound commercial English education" for young "clerks, assistants or workmen," carefully calculated "to draw from them all that is evil and to engage them in virtuous and honourable pursuits."[123] Its lecture program in 1850 was described by one speaker as a veritable "Pantheon of intellect," one which attracted the loyalty of "dignitaries of the Church; mechanics from the loom; members of parliament; authors of no mean repute; ministers of religion of all creeds; professors from universities; advocates at the bar; doctors of medicine and of law; and if last, certainly not least, a Privy Councillor and a Peer of the realm."[124]

Lofty claims notwithstanding, neither institution pitched its ambitions too high, despite expanding subscriber lists: in 1858 the vice president of the Phil.-&-Lit., John Hope Shaw, commended the Society as "solid and steady ... he would not say brilliant, for they did not aim at brilliancy,"[125] while Lord Stanley, in the chair of the annual meeting of the LMI, remarked just a few years later that "we did not suppose that they [culture institutions] would effect marvels," would effect marvels. We did not suppose that they would put down drunkenness or crime; but he thought it would be a help to many, a pleasure to more."[126] The LMI, as a public and popular institute, argued that it had an appropriately "aggressive and forward character" that allowed it "to lead the public mind, rather than to wait for impulses from without, to interpret the intellectual signs of the time, and to originate and sustain those efforts by which alone the demands indicated by those signs may be met and satisfied."[127] However, the difficulties of providing both services for established businessmen and their sociable families, on the one hand, and for rising "youth" seeking to climb a career ladder, on the other, was the source of subdued but chronic tension. As YUMI secretary, Hole reported that "Leeds boasted that it contained the largest Institute in the kingdom, having now about 2,200 members; but, in practical utility, it fell far below Institutions making much less pretensions. He was frequently written to for information as to the best method of conducting an Institute, but he and his fellow secretary, Mr. Dixon, never referred to Leeds as a model, but to Huddersfield."[128] Younger members appeared to agree: while the governors of the LMI described a lecture season as "agreeably varied in character, embracing a wide range of interesting topics in history, philosophy, science and art, general literature (including the drama), and also in music," the rising young men of the institute argued that the season was insipid, "remarking that there was almost an entire absence of sterling scientific lectures." The governing committee focused on "newspapers, the electric telegraph, and novels," rather than "practical utility" and sufficient course offerings.[129]

"Practical utility" would slowly come to govern the LMI's mature years. A decade-long fundraising effort for a new building, which would open in 1868, promised and delivered a variety of programs and services increasingly found in institutes devoted primarily to formal education, from elementary and advanced evening classes to Society of Arts examinations and day schools for children and "ladies." This expansion of educational services signaled an unplanned transition away from the role as the center of knowledge-based culture in the town. The library's holdings shifted away from the serious novels and treatises of a solid commitment to knowledge-based culture, instead embracing works of fiction "of an ephemeral character"; by 1868, such ephemera accounted for some two-thirds of books issued from the library. Popular lectures, which continued to be presented, rapidly ceased to be mentioned in the annual reports. Even the phrase "literary society" was dropped from the title of the reconfigured LMI.[130] By 1870, it was no longer the sole nor even the primary provider of such culture: its work had bifurcated, so that the educational mission of the institute was increasingly separated from cultural programming that now tended strongly to the purely entertaining, as the space of more serious knowledge-based culture was filled, somewhat unexpectedly, by the Leeds Phil.-&-Lit.

The Phil.-&-Lit., whose carefully curated museum had become one of the most popular centerpieces of the city, also found itself at a turning point in the late 1850s. Rooms were too small, members too reluctant to produce and read their own papers, families increasingly demanding not just the enormously popular juvenile Christmas lectures but also an array of other cultural resources. Institute directors puzzled over how to retain a sense of exclusivity while courting much-needed popular support: how could the Phil.-&-Lit. continue to cloak its subscribers in the mantle of the patriciate while also rapidly increasing its membership base? The solution was twofold: first, permanently reimagine the institution as the center of the entire region rather than simply one urban area, and second, temporarily redefine the notion of membership as "patriotism" in order to establish a broader base of emotional and financial support. A fundraising campaign launched in 1860 emphasized that the Society's "property and effects" were owned by "the Public," held in trust "for the advancement of Science, Literature, or Art, in the town of Leeds."[131] The Society and Museum "have now become, in fact, a Public Institution," noted the governors, who articulated their fundraising efforts as "a patriotic duty."[132] Each annual report for half a dozen years repeated the council's confident trust in "those patriotic citizens" whose "patriotic bequests" would help "raise the character of the West Riding of Yorkshire and its great capital."[133] This choice of language was unique among culture institutions; the word "patriotism" as a fundraising tool was generally limited to campaigns associated in some way with empire or war, such as the Patriotic Fund that had raised subscriptions for disabled Crimean War veterans, while "patriotism" as an ideal would eventually be cemented into the curricula of late-Victorian elementary schools.[134] In this case, however, it was successfully applied to a local, elite, and peaceful endeavor: the town's wealthy were encouraged not to support the provision of education for the workingmen and women of Leeds, a task now shouldered by the LMI, but rather to enact a patriotism that reflected the city's importance to the region, the kingdom, and even the empire. That importance had been represented by the museum when it first opened its doors to the public in 1821; now it was embedded in every fundraising effort and annual report between 1860 and 1866. By 1862, membership had nearly tripled and every donation to the Phil.-&-Lit., whether to the fundraising campaign or to the museum or library, was announced as a "patriotic example" of "patriotic interest." By 1866, thanks to "the public spirit of their townsmen," the Phil.-&-Lit had discharged its debts and could now boast "a Building alike honourable to the town, and inferior to that of no provincial Institution of the kind."[135]

The success of the reimagined Phil.-&-Lit. was due not only to this effusion of patriotism—a word that ceased to figure in most of the institution's materials after 1867—but also to the innovations of Honorary Secretary Peter O'Callaghan, elected in 1857. O'Callaghan introduced popular lectures—that is, open to the general public rather than limited to season subscribers and their families—into the annual programming and further broadened access to the museum, where "specimens of Yak, Moose Deer, and even the coveted Gorilla"[136] had transformed it into a kingdom-wide exemplar of its kind. He himself delivered popular lectures to large public audiences, appearing alongside such notables as balloonist James Glaisher and "famous Naval Architect" John Scott Russell. This expansion into the world of the popular lecture was measurably successful: by 1868, the number of general subscribers to the Phil.-&-Lit. was up to 646.[137]

These successes were lauded, but they also prompted a somewhat melancholy review of the Society's history and future prospects. By 1870, it was clear that the original goal of the Phil.-&-Lit.—to produce new knowledge, especially in the sciences—had never really been achieved. Membership had been mostly "miscellaneous" and inattentive to "technical details." The Phil.-&-Lit. now had the opportunity to popularize and disseminate existing knowledge, rather than to produce anything new; it could in this way minister to "a growing popular want" through its lecture programming and, simultaneously, increase "the desire for scientific knowledge among all the classes of the community" through the museum and its innovative new programming in local schools.[138] Founder Edward Baines, speaking at the fiftieth anniversary dinner in 1870, looked resolutely ahead, describing the Phil.-&.Lit. as "one of the most successful of the Philosophical Societies which exist out of London," characterized by "a free, catholic, liberal, and generous spirit" of impartiality. Its work bore witness to the importance of knowledge-based culture to the entire region:

It has promoted the intellectual development of the inhabitants; it has promoted their enlarged knowledge and refined taste; it has stimulated the studies of the young; it has led many men to devote themselves to the pursuit of science and art and literature, who otherwise might have devoted themselves to less elevating pursuits; it has allayed party and sectarian prejudices, it has promoted social harmony; it has contributed to promote the education of all classes; it has proved a parent institution, having a large offspring of institutions of a similar kind though not of the same name; it has contributed to the improvement, to the embellishment, to the prosperity of the town of Leeds; and I conscientiously believe that it has borne a fair share and proportion in the mighty advance of science and art and literature which has taken place in this and in other countries.[139]

Other city leaders concurred, noting that the Society's future responsibilities were vast: it would "mould that almost noblest type of humanity, the English gentleman," form "the rallying point for all the literary and scientific taste of the town," and "do away with quackery in education."[140] Such language, familiar to the world of knowledge-based culture, was calmly reassuring in its self-assessment, especially compared with the rather self-deprecating remarks by John Hope Shaw and Lord Stanley a dozen years earlier.

The Birmingham and Midland Institute and the Hybrid Lecture

In Birmingham, the division into "general" and "industrial" culture developed within a single, purpose-built center, the Birmingham and Midland Institute, where hybrid spaces launched hybrid lecture programs. Mid-century Birmingham, one of the triad of English "second cities" that also included Leeds and Manchester, appeared to many to symbolize the failure of knowledge-based culture, occupying ground littered with the corpses of more than a dozen voluntary cultural societies and having seen its electors reject in 1852 the Free Libraries and Museums Act.[141] In 1853, however, the Midland Institute was founded "to promote Literature, Science, and the Arts, by Lectures and Discussions, a Library, a Museum, a Laboratory and Apparatus, and the publication of Transactions."[142] Other enticements were to include an art gallery, collections of mining records and patents, and two newsrooms, along with the usual annual soirees and the occasional picnic or concert. The Midland's organizing committee had been determined to provide knowledge-based culture for both the working classes, in its Industrial Department, and the middle classes, in its General Department, and thus become "a great Educational Institution of an essentially public character."[143]

The Industrial Department took over the work generally performed in mechanics' and polytechnic institutions, including elementary and advanced evening classes in mathematics and the sciences. Within two years, it added classes in literature, history, and the arts. Early enrollment figures showed that students choosing higher mathematics, literature, and history consistently outweighed those in the sciences, and that "artisans" preferred nonscience to science classes by a ratio of about 3 to 1.[144]

The governors in the first decade of the Midland struggled with the failure paradigm articulated by Hudson and Hole, worrying that the Industrial Department had "failed to reach the class for which it was intended" and instead had embraced clerks, schoolmasters, literary-minded artisans, and young women. Over time, the response of the governors was to adopt the language of caste already in use in a variety of societies and institutions, coming to regard the Midland student as a member of "our excelsior class" rather than an "average" worker.[145] As Midland students accumulated the prizes offered by the Society of Arts and other examining bodies—the Midland joined the Union of Institutions in 1856—this language of caste became more entrenched.

The General Department, on the other hand, was regarded as a success from its infancy. Subscriptions of £1.1s annually—that golden guinea that signified respectability—gave members access to the newsroom and reading room, the museum, the entire season of Monday evening popular lectures, the annual inaugural address, and the annual soiree.[146] The first lecture program began in February 1855, with courses on geology and "The Animal Kingdom." Within three years, the Midland moved away from courses and into the "miscellaneous" lectures that were by now characteristic of popular lecture culture, attracting both subscribers and nonsubscribers in such numbers that by the 1870s many members would complain they could not get into the theater. With classes, lectures, and a museum, the Midland claimed it was "the centre around which all the Educational institutions which addressed themselves to the public at large might cluster," leasing space to other local societies, including the Natural History Association and the Birmingham and Edgbaston Debating Society.[147]

In 1865, the General Department added day classes for "Ladies" in English language, literature, history, French, geometry, and physiology. Evening classes in the industrial department already covered many of these subject areas for working-class and lower-middle-class men and women. The day classes in literature and history, which consisted of lectures rather than rote memorization, proved so popular that the council announced late in the year that all General Department subscribers could attend, at no extra cost, and that nonsubscribers could also attend for 6d. per lecture. The teachers of these two classes changed over time but were consistently recruited from among the most well-attended of local speakers, including Sam Timmins, Sebastian Evans, and the especially beloved George Dawson. They attracted up to ninety students and members of the public to each lecture.[148]

It was these hybrid lectures—rooted in the classroom but open to a culture-hungry public—that signaled a new wave of local debate over the purposes of knowledge-based culture. Much of this debate was shaped anonymously by John Alfred Langford, Birmingham's quintessential Victorian autodidact, who in 1860 joined the staff of the *Birmingham Gazette* as the local editor responsible for content on arts, culture, and education.[149] Langford was already well-known as a man who had "pursued knowledge under difficulties," a path especially associated with Birmingham. Through a series of unsigned but highly characteristic articles as well as carefully curated correspondence, Langford pushed the Midland into contemporary debates about the relationships between education, culture, and citizenship. Editorials and letters were specific and bossy: the institute was urged to clean its windows, remove the mud from its pavement, improve its classroom ventilation, increase its teaching staff, admit Industrial Department students to the Monday evening popular lectures at the reduced price of 6d. each, and decorate the panels of the new art gallery with "a series of portraits of Birmingham or Warwickshire men."[150] One editorial lamented "how little the town uses this admirable Institute," while another criticized the upcoming lectures on "the Socialistic Schemes of St. Simon and Fourier" by Dr. Hodgson as "not being very promising for popular lectures to the class of persons who frequent the Midland Institute."[151] Correspondents were thorough in their critiques: "Ego" testified that the "primitive" seating arrangements drove him away "in perfect disgust," while "J. C." and "F. D." both advocated for the establishment of an Elocution Class and Debating Society, and "A Member from the First" called for reforms in both management and curriculum, arguing that "the burgesses did not grant the land in order to provide finishing education for people who can well afford to pay for it elsewhere."[152]

Langford explored in detail the decisions of the governing council and the responses of the public. He was especially focused on the fortunes of the men and women below the solid middle classes who were united in a love of learning and hungry for substantial courses and lectures in the arts and humanities. This was the class of artisans who preferred music and literature to chemistry and physics; it was also the class that Langford himself both exemplified and advocated for. He was not shy about arguing that these students should "unite their efforts with those of the constituted authorities towards furthering the best interest of the Institute, and extending its benefits," so that in the near future "this important College will at last assume its rightful position," and enter upon a "noble" career "of even higher advantage to the general community" than conceived by the founders.[153]

By 1865, at the same time that the Manchester Mechanics' Institution was facing the difficult transition to a workingman's college and the Leeds Phil.-&-Lit. was moving from exclusivity to a more popular orientation, these editorials expanded to explore the pedagogy explicitly necessary for the needs of Birmingham and for people like Langford himself. A series of lengthy disquisitions in the *Daily Gazette* between May 1865 and January 1866 linked together the instructional lecture, the popular lecture, and the traditional practices of the classroom. The first piece asserted that "in nearly all our public schools, new methods of teaching, new ideas on the subject of education, have as yet made scarcely any impression on the old routine. ... Explanation, exposition, illustration, if given at all, are reduced to a minimum, and the entire process of teaching and learning reduced as nearly as possible to a merely mechanical performance."[154] Langford's focus on "nearly all our public schools" was a rhetorical strategy to elevate the discussion of learning beyond debates over the classes for workingmen in mechanics' institutions or the primary-school offerings in the "payment by results" institutions. Rhetorically, he tied his local arguments to the ongoing national critiques of the classics-based Oxbridge system, where, in the words of an 1850 critic, "a person ignorant upon every [point]" of history, science, language, and literature "may carry with him, from the University of Oxford, the very highest testimonials of proficiency."[155] Langford was advocating for a particular relationship between the adult learner and the adult teacher, framing his advice in what he called "real education ... the collision of mind with mind," and addressing the particular needs of Birmingham, "where so many have risen from the ranks, where so many more who have not risen are anxiously seeking means by which to rise, where almost every citizen takes a strong interest in political affairs, where the average of intelligence is higher and the average of book-learning lower than in almost any other large town."[156]

For Langford, the key was not to limit "the collision of mind with mind" to a small economic or social elite but to address that broad group of participatory citizens characterized by high intelligence and low book learning. Langford himself had "toiled upward," acquiring knowledge under difficulties, and he spoke disparagingly of those who continued to believe that an understanding of culture—which by the 1860s was framed as the history, literature, and current events considered fundamental to citizenship—could be acquired by the lonely individual in his meager spare time. Such a man or woman needed a boost, and that boost should not be limited to the Monday evening lectures for guinea subscribers. "Without some knowledge acquired from other quarters, he [the adult student] can no more decide whether CROMWELL was a hero or humbug or both, than he can recover from the usually accepted authorities whether GEORGE III was the best of monarchs, or an immoral imbecile," Langford argued, echoing the assertions of Sir John Pakington four years earlier that "the man who has studied the history of this country is the least likely to undervalue our institutions."[157] Langford concurred: without the familiarity that came from reading biography, literature, and history, one could not fully rise. To hasten this familiarity, Langford argued, it was necessary to innovate, and especially to break down the barriers between classroom instruction and cultural education.

He offered specific advice. "In looking down the list of lectures given in the Industrial Department," he wrote in a May 1865 editorial, "it will be seen that while some are of a purely elementary character, others are on subjects with which many even well-educated people are only superficially acquainted." Such superficial acquaintance, especially for subjects in English literature and history, could be easily deepened through "lectures, properly so called," which could "with just as much ease be delivered to a large audience as a small one." The council, he urged, should move the classes in literature and history to the large lecture theater, admit the public at the doors for the payment of a small fee, and avoid at all costs the practice of calling roll or taking attendance, practices that offended "English Feelings." In this way, the Midland would establish lectures "intermediate in character between those delivered on Monday evenings, and those in the Industrial Department," and thereby "consult the interests of the 'average Englishman.'"[158]

This innovation would, in practical application, turn these industrial classes in literature and history into popular lectures offered at an alternative time to Monday evenings; they would become spaces in which the ladies of the General Department would mingle with the increasing number of young women in the Industrial Department, optimizing a gendered model of "class fusion"; and they would appeal as well to grown men who would never voluntarily enter a history classroom but who could with ease and comfort attend a quasi-public popular talk delivered by speakers like George Dawson, whose fame and skill made such lectures a social privilege rather than an instructional burden. By placing these courses in the General Department but continuing to offer them to industrial students, Langford advised, the Midland governors would accomplish four important goals: they would bridge the still existing class gap, increase the institution's income, deepen the knowledge of the average Brummagen in the subjects that John Alfred Langford himself regarded as indispensable to modern citizenship and that he would begin to teach at the Midland in 1868, and model for the country true intellectual education rather than mere instruction. Within four months of this final editorial, the governing council announced that the ladies' classes in literature and history would be treated in just this way: open to the public for a small fee, dispensing with attendance rolls, and providing cultural instruction in the humanities, broadly conceived. Langford, in the *Gazette*, announced this course of action even before the newspaper published the Midland's own annual report, noting that this was a change "that we have long advocated ... to the advantage of the pupils, the teachers, and the public."[159]

Langford was keenly aware of the contemporary arguments that popular lectures were no substitute for deep classroom learning. "It is certainly not the vocation of the Midland Institute to turn out a generation of smatterers," he wrote, "and but few will deny that a full and thorough understanding of even a single play of Shakspere [sic] is a more desirable thing than superficial acquaintance with most of the great names in literature." However, he contended, most classroom instruction in literature, history, and the arts was merely "a careless perusal of extracts in a class-book." In contrast, he argued, a good popular lecture was "education," not "instruction" or even merely "entertainment." The changing nature of society and citizenship, as well as the wider access to instruments of culture, made it imperative that institutions like the Midland take a bolder attitude to what he called "thorough knowledge." Indeed, he offered, "the attendance on these [hybrid] lectures may be such as to vindicate the Birmingham community from the charge of apathy to educational progress."[160]

This series of editorials essentially rehearsed and updated the arguments that had characterized hand-wringing about science in the mechanics' institutions: just as scientific knowledge was indispensable to the culture of both the operative and the skilled artisan in the 1830s, so literary knowledge was indispensable to the culture of both the industrial student and the general subscriber in the 1860s. Literary, historical, and artistic knowledge, for Langford, held society together; his only real scientific interest was in geology, which he described as "not science at all" but rather as "the past and present history of the globe, as revealed by other sciences." In his final editorial he noted approvingly that, since the Midland had adopted and adapted his suggestions, "the Institute is at last fast rising into popular favour."[161]

Langford's relationship with the Midland continued for almost another decade; he left the *Gazette* shortly after these editorials and became one of the popular teachers of the same English literature classes he highlighted as the key to the Midland's future. While he treated with some disdain the ongoing debates over examinations and credentialing—two things he had absolutely no interest in—he helped reinforce the links between education in the humanities and a model of citizenship based on aspiration and participation rather than on wages and suffrage. He was a man of his time, and indeed within another generation, as we will see in Chapter 4, men like Langford would be mocked as needing to "continue to settle annually the vexed question of Oliver Cromwell's claim to the admiration of posterity, or periodically determine if King Charles the First was the Blessed Martyr the Book of Common Prayer used to call him"[162]—indeed as "a generation of smatterers." But his series of editorials brought into the general public's notice important questions about what education actually meant at mid-century, and who might be granted the keys to that kingdom.

"We Must Cultivate Intellect as We Cultivate Corn": The Ecosystems of Popular Knowledge, 1850–70

While each of these institutions had its own character and mission, in the provision of lectures and discussions they fit neatly into an overall map of knowledge-based culture for the mid-century. In the following chapter, the first efforts toward drawing that map will build on data about lectures and lecturers, as well as the other intellectual work produced in discussion and debating societies. Examining the records printed in the *Journal* as well as the separate annual reports and newspaper coverage of these institutions will yield important information about what mid-Victorians talked about. Placing these data in conversation with the advice given by educators, committee members, and social critics to lecturers, audiences, Union affiliates, debaters, and mutual improvers will provide a comprehensive look at the rich world of mid-Victorian knowledge-based culture. Such culture was necessarily expansive. Society of Arts president James Booth, praising the work of the Union in 1856, rapturously enumerated the imperial adventures that demanded the continuing efforts of his listeners:

> The fact is, we English are actually too few in number for the gigantic work we have undertaken. Here at home are our own vast commerce and manufactures to be managed and controlled. What amount of intellect is expended on the trade of Manchester alone? Then we have Australia to colonise and reclaim, the fertile regions of New Zealand to civilize. The Chinese difficulty is looming on us through the lurid mist which rests on the soil of India soaked and reeking with English blood. The truth is, we must cultivate intellect as we cultivate corn, and for the same reason, that the spontaneous production of nature does not afford an adequate supply.[163]

Union affiliates could assist in the cultivation of the intellect. Whether abroad in the empire or closer to home, more and more programming claimed to focus on "the well-being of mankind" through the incorporation of lectures in the humanities, current affairs, contemporary questions of health and hygiene, and the discussions of those evergreen questions about Cromwell, Charles I, and the talents of Shakespeare. Knowledge-based culture, whether it sought to "educate and amuse" or "delight and soften," could be a confusing welter of choices. How committees sought to make these choices purposeful, efficient, and inclusive will be the focus of the following chapter.

3

"The General Literature and Thought of Our Country and Time"

Mid-Century Lectures, Debates, and Discussions

Our Lecture Course may be regarded from its varied character as the viva voce *exposition ... of the general literature and thought of our country and time.*[1]

When president Edward Baines, speaking at the annual meeting in 1853, exhorted the YUMI to continue its important work in lectures, reading rooms, social meetings, "and the like," he told his listeners that "these things should be so diffused in our large towns, as to become a part of the daily social life of the nation."[2] Over the course of two decades, between 1850 and 1870, Baines and countless others witnessed the fulfillment of this exhortation. Institutions large and small had rooted themselves in their localities and helped shape an ecosystem of knowledge-based culture that ranged from the large public institutions to the small, often almost invisible, spaces of mutual improvement and debate. This ecosystem was fed not only by lecturers and the lectured but also by educationists, politicians, and committee directors, on the one hand, and journalists, editors, and periodical readers on the other; by upper-middle-class debaters and working-class discussants; by young men imbued with a sense of economic and social confidence and, to a small but no longer trivial extent, by middle-class wives and daughters motivated by desires for consequence, influence, and the pleasures of knowledge. While these constituents and constituencies differed by status, class, and interest, contemporaries did not hesitate to group them into the single cohort of the "educated populations" described in 1855 by F. W. Naylor, who as a group were becoming "more and more sensible of their literary wants."[3] The institutions ministering to these literary wants were themselves seen not as completely autonomous entities but as parts of a loose corporate body bound by their common efforts in "render[ing] good service to the cause of literature."[4] The efforts to delineate these "literary wants"—as well as the concurrent desires for history, science, the arts, and current events—and guide them into sanctioned channels produced thousands of pages of reports, statistics, and handbooks. Through these data, we can begin to answer the question: what did the mid-Victorians talk about?

The following pages rely on data culled from a number of sources. First, of course, are the "Proceedings" of the *Journal of the Society of Arts*. The men and women who submitted their names for inclusion in the *Journal's* "List of Lecturers" in 1854 and 1862, as well as to the 1859 edition of the short-lived *Literary and Educational Year-book*, are also included, along with their self-identified subjects of expertise. Annual reports for the larger institutions in Birmingham, Leeds, and Manchester provide more thorough compilations of lecturers than the "Proceedings" columns after about 1856. Other sources of data include newspaper coverage of lecturers, especially in the larger cities; reports of programming reproduced in the popular journal, the *British Controversialist*, over this twenty-year period; and a variety of handbooks for lecturers, compilations of lectures curated and cheaply printed for purchase, and individual lectures printed as stand-alone pamphlets. Drawing from these data, we can recuperate the titles and, occasionally, the content of lectures delivered; information about lecturers promoting their own services; and lists of debate and discussion topics from the reports of elite and middlebrow debating societies, on the one hand, and discussion and mutual improvement societies run primarily by young men in early adulthood, on the other. While there are lacunae in these data—more ephemeral societies that submitted summary reports and left no formal records can be glimpsed only incompletely in the pages of these sources—they provide sufficient evidence to sketch out the topics that formed the intellectual diet of mid-Victorian men and women in the middle and working classes and to give us a picture of the "*viva voce* exposition" of the period.

Categorizing Knowledge

Classifying and assessing these data—nearly 4,000 individual lectures, 1,000 individual lecturers, and over 900 debate and discussion topics over the period from 1850 to 1870—produces a number of challenges. The earliest assessments of knowledge-based culture divided offerings into the three categories of literature, science, and fine arts. Hudson and Hole both found that in the 1830s and 1840s, lectures at major institutions declined in science and rose in literature and fine arts, supporting their observations that institutes had moved sharply away from their founding principles.[5] Science lectures as a percentage of the whole dropped from 62 percent to 39 percent at the Manchester Mechanics' Institute and from 49 percent to 20 percent at the Manchester Athenaeum between 1835 and 1850, while science lectures at YUMI member institutions dropped from 30 percent to 23 percent in the following decade.[6] Applying this tripartite division to lectures reported in the *Journal* also shows a preference for non-science lectures: of the 1,800 lectures listed for the decade 1852–1862, for example, 22 percent were scientific, 52 percent were literary, and 7 percent were musical.

The imminent demise of the science lecture appeared to be reflected in several mid-century collections of lectures, pocket-sized compendia designed to be read and reread. In the *Monthly Literary and Scientific Lecturer*, verbatim or carefully abridged lectures were reprinted from "Lectures Delivered in Mechanics' Institutions, Athenaeums, Literary and Philosophical Societies, Schools of Design, Etc." The first volume, in 1850, reflected the general lingering emphasis on "courses" of scientific lectures, with a series of four lectures on "Rain and Wind, and the Causes which Produce Them; Being an Investigation of the Hadleyan Theory of Wind, and the Huttonian Theory of Rain" by

Manchester Alderman Thomas Hopkins; six lectures on "Curiosities of Natural History" by Thomas Rymer Jones; and another six by John Phillips on "The General Truths of Geology." A similar emphasis on "courses" also guided the choice of non-science lectures in this volume, with a three-lecture series on "The History of Commerce" by Thomas Hogg and four offerings on "The Troubadours—Their History and Poetry," by J. McDougall. The emphasis on courses of lectures rather than stand-alone offerings linked this editor to the faction of educators and critics who remained convinced that, as the Chambers article had lamented, no good could come of shallow single lectures delivered by "charlatans" rather than serious men. Indeed, the curation of courses or series of lectures rather than single lectures was a defining feature of this short-lived journal, but by the final volume in 1853, these series were much more likely to be focused on literary and historical subjects than scientific ones: "A Course of Four Lectures on 'The Science of Botany,' by the Late John Just, Esq." was more than balanced by a course of five lectures on "The German Literature of the 19th Century" by Gottfried Kinkel, a course of three lectures on "The History of Ecclesiastical Music," by W. H. Monk, and pairs of lectures each, on patents by Benjamin Fothergill and "Literature and Poetry" by a Professor Scott. Of the 59 lectures reproduced in the 1850 volume, 33 (56 percent) were on science topics; by 1853, only 14 of the 46 lectures (30 percent) were on science topics.[7]

The apparent decline of the physical and biological sciences was only temporary. Lectures on the sciences and applied sciences were subjects that were especially amenable to exciting illustrations with magic lanterns and homemade volcanic eruptions, and could attract families as well as the serious amateur man of science. They were simultaneously, however, increasingly inaccessible in print; the physics and chemistry became more arcane, the prose more specialized, the sketches and pictures less exciting or helpful. Thus, printed volumes of lectures abandoned many science topics in favor of literature and history: by 1864, for example, the twenty-six stand-alone lectures in *Pitman's Popular Lecturer* series included only one lecture each in geography and astronomy, two on the steam engine, and a balance that were focused on topics biographical, literary, or gently moral in nature, from "Charles James Napier" and "Two Stephensons" to "Remarks on Reading" and "Poetry and Religious Feeling." Current events were represented by lectures on "Slavery and Freedom," "The American War," and "A Day with the Iguanodon," a continued source of interest since the opening of the Crystal Palace.[8] The popularity of these printed collections helped support the unfounded worry that "science" was in decline.

The tripartite categorization scheme used in so many reports and collections reveals only the most shallow of information about what was actually under discussion and how these topics shifted over time. A more complex set of categories and subcategories allows us to account for two major mid-century developments: first, the steady growth of specialization, including but not limited to the sciences, which made it difficult to neatly divide topics into only three discrete categories, and second, the claims of listeners, debaters, and discussants to seriously examine not only established knowledge but also the events and ideas shaping their contemporary world, "those questions which now so absorbed the thinking part of the community."[9] Many educators conceded, in the words of lawyer and lecturer George Higinbotham, that "a well-arranged map of knowledge" would merely restrict "the limits of human study" and quash what one young debater

Physical sciences	Biology (including anatomy, zoology, physiology); chemistry; paleontology; geography; geology; physics; meteorology; applied science/technology
Social sciences	History and biography; mathematics; linguistics; economics; government; ethnography and anthropology; education; archaeology; laws of health and sanitation; national progress
Mental sciences	Psychology; psychiatry; mesmerism; spiritualism; phrenology; physiognomy
Literature	Literature, poetry, and drama; general fiction; performances and readings from any field of literature; oratory
Fine arts	Music; art and architecture; photography; performances from any field of fine arts
Philosophy and religion	World philosophies; world religions
Domestic morality	General morality and advice on how to live; observations on family; unsectarian Christianity; self-improvement
Humor	Humor for the sake of humor; lectures and debates on humorous subjects or authors
Current events	Contemporary events and issues; travel; foreign affairs, foreign policy and empire; local studies
Miscellaneous	Lectures and discussions listed in sources (with or without a lecturer) but without a specific title

Figure 3.1 Categories and subcategories of analysis.

called the "outgush and flow-forth of ... mental life" that made "a noble and wise man, giv[ing] a true and genuine selfhood to us."[10] The system used in this current analysis, as shown in Figure 3.1, attempts to combine growth and specialization, on the one hand, and an expanding horizon of interest, on the other.

These ten categories and their subgroups have guided the general analysis that follows. Following a broad visual overview, this chapter uses a series of snapshots of specific lecture seasons, institutions, and subject matter to analyze changes in knowledge-based culture as the experimental 1850s gave way to the more established and confident 1860s.

General Trends, 1850–70: Visualizing Lectures

The total number of individual named lectures reported by institutions—via the *Journal*, annual reports, and various periodicals—was 3,648. This number excludes courses of lectures, not only in the sciences but also in other areas; these were infrequent, but included two courses of twenty-five untitled lectures on music, by William Rea, and on English language and literature, by Robert Spence Watson, both at the Newcastle Lit.-&-Phil. in 1868/9. These data also bleed slightly past 1870 into 1872 in order to accommodate the final few lectures reported in the *Journal*. Lectures delivered as part of the SLS, beginning in 1869, are not included in this analysis and will be addressed in the following chapters. Applying the categorization model outlined above, and focusing

Table 3.1 Lecture Categories by Number and Percentage of Total Lectures Delivered

	Science	Social sciences	Literature	Arts	Philosophy/religion	Mental science	Domestic morality	Humor	Current events	Untitled	Totals
1850	0 (0%)	5 (13%)	17 (43.5%)	1 (3%)	3 (7.5%)	3 (7.5%)	8 (20.5%)	0 (0%)	2 (5%)	0 (0%)	39
1851	12 (19)	18 (29)	13 (21)	9 (14.5)	1 (1.5)	1 (1.5)	4 (6.5)	0 (0)	2 (3)	2 (3)	62
1852	33 (25)	31 (23)	31 (23)	20 (15)	0 (0)	0 (0)	10 (7.5)	1 (1)	5 (4)	1 (1)	132
1853	70 (25.5)	64 (23)	31 (11)	30 (11)	16 (6)	7 (2.5)	28 (10)	4 (1.5)	23 (8)	2 (.5)	275
1854	59 (29)	43 (21)	25 (12)	15 (7)	6 (3)	1 (.5)	6 (3)	7 (3)	22 (11)	22 (11)	206
1855	48 (23)	45 (21)	27 (13)	15 (7)	8 (4)	3 (1)	13 (6)	3 (1)	19 (9)	32 (15)	213
1856	76 (27)	48 (17)	38 (14)	15 (5)	11 (4)	3 (1)	16 (6)	4 (1)	24 (8)	45 (16)	280
1857	74 (20)	97 (27)	47 (13)	51 (14)	15 (4)	2 (1)	20 (5)	9 (2)	42 (12)	8 (2)	365
1858	51 (19)	62 (23)	34 (13)	37 (14)	7 (2)	2 (1)	22 (8)	6 (2)	40 (15)	7 (2)	268
1859	36 (23)	38 (24)	23 (15)	17 (11)	3 (2)	0 (0)	7 (4)	2 (1)	13 (8)	17 (11)	156
1860	40 (30)	28 (21)	24 (18)	11 (8)	4 (3)	0 (0)	7 (5)	2 (1)	17 (13)	0 (0)	133
1861	71 (25)	61 (22)	31 (11)	28 (10)	4 (1)	1 (.5)	23 (8)	7 (2.5)	47 (17)	9 (3)	282
1862	77 (26)	63 (21)	24 (8)	49 (17)	8 (3)	5 (1.5)	19 (6)	13 (4)	31 (10.5)	7 (2)	296
1863	40 (32)	21 (17)	14 (11)	17 (14)	1 (.5)	2 (1.5)	7 (6)	4 (3)	14 (11)	4 (3)	124
1864	82 (44)	46 (25)	15 (8)	21 (11)	0 (0)	1 (.5)	6 (3)	4 (2)	9 (5)	1 (.5)	185
1865	39 (28)	42 (30)	22 (16)	18 (13)	5 (4)	0 (0)	4 (3)	1 (1)	7 (5)	0 (0)	138
1866	37 (37)	20 (20)	10 (10)	9 (9)	2 (2)	3 (3)	3 (3)	2 (2)	13 (13)	0 (0)	99
1867	44 (48)	20 (22)	7 (8)	8 (9)	1 (1)	3 (3)	0 (0)	1 (1)	8 (9)	0 (0)	92
1868	31 (38)	16 (20)	6 (7)	6 (7)	11 (13.5)	0 (0)	0 (0)	0 (0)	7 (9)	4 (5)	81
1869	36 (37)	15 (15.5)	13 (13.5)	15 (15.5)	4 (4)	0 (0)	1 (1)	0 (0)	13 (13)	0 (0)	97
1870	26 (33)	29 (37)	6 (8)	5 (6)	2 (2.5)	0 (0)	4 (5)	2 (2.5)	5 (6)	0 (0)	79
1871	11 (25)	12 (27)	7 (16)	5 (11)	0 (0)	0 (0)	2 (5)	1 (2)	6 (14)	0 (0)	44
Totals	993 (26%)	824 (23%)	465 (13%)	402 (11%)	112 (3%)	37 (1%)	210 (6%)	73 (2%)	369 (10%)	161 (4%)	3646

Source: *Journal of the Society of Arts*, Vols. 1–22.

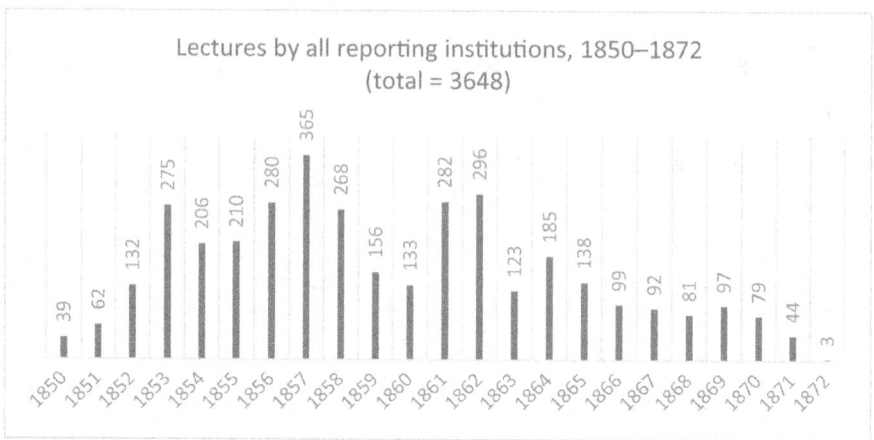

Figure 3.2 Lectures by reporting institutions in the *Journal*, 1850–72.

Source: *Journal of the Society of Arts*, Vols. 1–22.

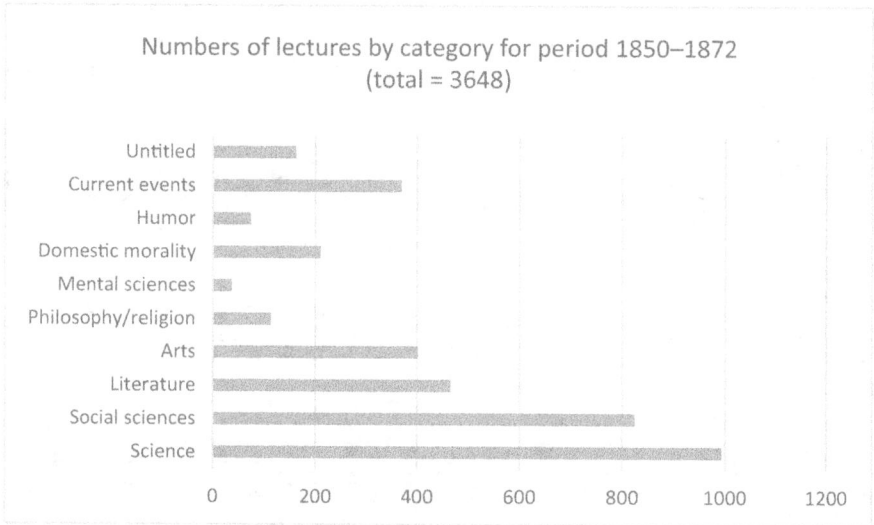

Figure 3.3 Numbers of lectures by category.

Source: *Journal of the Society of Arts*, Vols. 1–22.

on the ten major categories in Table 3.1, above, we can see how each year's offerings attempted to present "the general literature and thought of our country and time."

Figure 3.2 shows the distribution over time of reported lectures in the *Journal*. The overall trend line clearly reflects the editorial decision to move away from lectures to focus on examinations and other issues important to its member institutions.

Figure 3.3 provides a visualization of the total numbers in each category over time. Figure 3.4 shows the trends over time in the top five categories of lectures (science, social science, literature, arts, and current events).

Changes in the Popular Science Lecture

While the general numbers reported by Hudson and Hole for the 1830s and 1840s show a notable drop in the overall numbers of science lectures during these two decades, by the mid-1850s "science" as a focus had rebounded and remained steadily in the first or second place of lecture topics for these two decades. It was surpassed by lectures in the social sciences in only three years: 1857 (74 science, 89 social sciences), 1859 (36 and 38), and 1865 (39 and 42). The persistent popularity of science lectures, like the persistent attractions of the mechanics' institutions generally, represents a stabilization after the relatively chaotic period of the late 1840s. The apparent staggering decline in the importance of "sciences" reported by Hudson and Hole was instead a combination of two interrelated factors: first, the move away from series or courses of lectures and toward stand-alone science lectures, and second, the disaggregation of sciences into subfields that were more easily presented as stand-alone lectures for a mixed audience. Figure 3.4 shows the breadth of the sciences during this period.

Within subcategories, it is possible to make some preliminary judgments about content and level of difficulty based on the lecturer and the title of the lecture: for example, W. R.

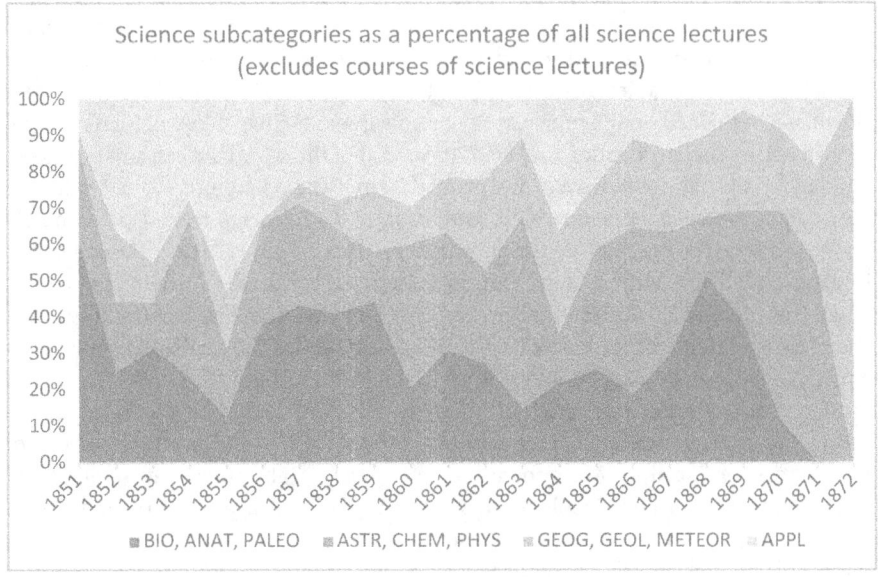

Figure 3.4 Subcategories of science lectures as a percentage of all science lectures.
Source: *Journal of the Society of Arts*, Vols. 1–22.

Selway's lecture on "The Wonders of Vision" (St. Leonard's-on-Sea Mechanics' Institution, 1851/2) and Dr. Grierson's "Our Bodies, and How We Live" (Annan Mechanics' Institute, 1856/7) were less focused or specialized than Michael Foster's lectures on "The Involuntary Movements of Animals" (Midland Institute and the Newcastle Lit.-&.-Phil., five total in 1868/9) or Edwin Lankester's lectures on aspects of physiology (Midland Institute, eight total in 1861/2 and 1862/3). Similarly, the Rev. A. B. Alexander's only reported lecture, on "Ants and Bees" (Farnham Young Men's Association, 1863/4), was self-evidently less specialized than W. Mitchell's "The Habits and Instincts of the Hive Bee" (Croydon Literary and Scientific Institution, 1856/7) or Sir John Lubbock's "The Metamorphoses of Insects" (Midland Institute, 1865/6). It represented—like the other lectures in this list—the specific listeners catered for by the institution.

"The Chemistry of the Breakfast Table": Many Audiences, Many Approaches

We can see efforts both to make "hard" science more approachable and to reach specific audiences, as the ever-popular "Chemistry of the Breakfast Table" illustrates. Lectures on this topic (delivered variously by Albert James Bernays at the Newcastle Lit.-&-Phil. in 1869/70, Robert Gardner at the Sherborne Literary Society and the Nottingham Mechanics' Institution in 1852/3 and 1864/5, respectively, and Mr. Mason at the Alton Mechanics' Institution in 1860/1) inspired such similar titles as "The Chemistry of the Kitchen" (R. E. Scott, Brompton Church of England Young Men's Society, 1860/1) and "The Chemistry of Common Life" (S. R. Atkinson, Salisbury Literary and Scientific Institution, 1859/60; J. F. Johnston, Leeds Phil.-&-Lit., 1854/5; William Marriott, Huddersfield Mechanics' Institution, 1855/6; and Dex Bean, Mossley Mechanics' Institute, 1863/4). A similar lecture, "The Chemistry of a Breakfast," remained on the program of the Bow Baptists Chapel Young Men's Mutual Improvement Society, London, in 1869/70. Several of these lectures can still be traced, although many did not survive in any printed form. Bernays' lecture, for example, was reprinted in *Household Chemistry, Or, Rudiments of the Science in Everyday Life*, nearly two decades before his 1870 lecture appearance; in the columns of the printed lecture, he explained "I have written chiefly for the young, and for those who, although people of general education, witness in the processes of daily life, some of the most important chemical operations in themselves, and all that is done for their subsistence, without either knowing or heeding those great laws by which the Author of the Universe has produced and sustains His creation."[11] Bernays's lecture dealt with water, sugar, tea, bread, and eggs, presenting each item both domestically—"And first let us speak of tea"—and scientifically—"More than one half of the weight of tea leaves consists of woody fibre; a substance insoluble in water, and without a particle of nutriment." In contrast, John Ryan's lecture on this subject placed the various components of a middle-class breakfast table within the context of empire, noting "the beautiful wares of China," "the aromatic coffee-berry from Mocha," "the sugar-cane of the West Indian colonies," and "the lustrous silver, dug from the bowels of some distant land," all "spread upon the snow-white damask of our own land."[12] These two lectures remind us that common topics were treated in a variety of ways by individual lecturers, and also how the knotty issues of "instruction" and "education" remained problematic during this period. The London-based Bernays also delivered short series of more specialized lectures on organic chemistry, the history of chemistry, and the properties of heat, all at the Newcastle Lit.-&-Phil. where he was engaged for twenty-three lectures between 1864 and 1871. His continued popularity at Newcastle and elsewhere—his biographer in 1892 noted that he "gave over a thousand free public lectures during his lifetime"— underscores his ability to meet the expectations of a "much-lectured people" that both courted families and continued to attract serious listeners sufficiently educated to understand "The Unitary System of Chemistry, or the New Notation," a three-part lecture at Newcastle in 1866/7.[13] Similarly, Ryan's emphasis on the luxurious trappings of the table—the white linen, the mahogany wood, the delicate porcelain—enticed an audience accustomed to such domestic furniture, who then listened not only to "the tedious methods of bleaching linen" but also to the more melodramatic descriptions of how burning wood produced carbonic acid, the same product as "the impure air emanating from animal lungs" that not only transformed "crowded and confined places like the Blackhole [sic] in Calcutta" into "scenes of death" but that, as a gas, could also be described as "the demon which leaps from the brazier of burning charcoal to smother its sleeping and unconscious victim; or to answer, too readily, the call of the despairing suicide."[14]

Like the chemistry of food, many other apparently narrow subjects were served by multiple lecturers, especially within the subcategory of "applied science," and many of these lectures themselves could straddle more than one category. John Bennett gave eleven lectures on some form of watchmaking, from "The Birth, Parentage, and Education of a Watch" to "Women and Watchwork, with a view to the introduction of Female Employment" between 1855 and 1862, speaking at institutions in Chelmsford, Hackney, Royston, London, Leeds, Plymouth, and Banbury. A Mr. Fowler spoke on "Clocks and Watches—Their History and Inventors" (Redhill Institute, 1857/8) and R. McGuire delivered his own lecture on "The Construction of a Watch" (Brompton Church of England Young Men's Society, 1860/1), while Mr. Miles spoke on "The History and Mechanism of Clocks and Watches" (Thame Mutual Improvement Society, 1851/2) and J. G. Allison introduced basic physics with his "The Pendulum and Its Application to Horology" (Newcastle Lit.-&-Phil., 1868/9). Similarly, lectures on the telegraph were timely and therefore both numerous and variable: they accounted for forty separate entries over this twenty-year period, from "The Electric Telegraph," delivered by half a dozen different speakers, to Robert Dodwell's "Two Hours in a Telegraph Office, illustrated by apparatus" (Bacup Mechanics' Institution, 1864/5) and the Rev. Thomas Hincks's more technical "A Description of the Telegraphic Plateau in the North Atlantic," (Leeds Phil.-&-Lit., 1857/8).

Literature and the Arts

The emphases on biography and literature in *Pitman's Popular Lecturer and Reader* were echoed in the lectures delivered at affiliate institutions during these decades. Within "Literature," lectures on Shakespeare, the Romantic poets, Cowper, Chaucer,

Hood, and Jerrold were most popular. Many an "Evening with the British Poets" shared programming space with the hundreds of literary biographies delivered by Dawson, Balfour, and dozens of lesser-known men and women: Shakespearean scholar Charles Cowden Clarke, for example, delivered some forty-five literary lectures during this period, ranging from "The Comic Writers of England" and "The Genius of Moliere" to "Subordinate Characters in Shakespeare" and "On Shakespeare's Numskulls."[15] Balfour's reported lectures included dozens on women poets and women writers as well as general lectures on British poetry. Increasing numbers of evenings devoted to literary readings rather than formal lectures permitted more women to appear on the platform, often to perform readings from Shakespeare or from various poets. Actress Isabella Glyn, described posthumously as a "tragedian of the Kemble school,"[16] gave Shakespearean readings in Leeds, Newcastle, Bradford, and Croydon during this period, while Fanny Kemble, who after the dissolution of her marriage often performed under the name of Mrs. Butler, delivered Shakespearean readings from Brighton to Leeds.[17] This broad category encompassed occasional lectures on the art of oratory or on the examples of past great orators, such as "The Influence of Oratory on the Minds and Actions of Men, as It Appears in Various Periods of History," delivered by George Bankes, MP (Corfe Castle Mutual Improvement Society, 1852/3) and the Rev. J. C. Fishbourne's "On the Genius and Oratory of Lord Brougham" (Hastings Mechanics' Institute, 1857/8). Lectures on phonetics and linguistics included John Deakin Heaton's "Some Recent Observations on the Physiology of Language" (Leeds Phil.-&-Lit., 1868/9) and Unitarian minister Edward Higginson's "The Phonetic Orthography, Theoretically and Practically Viewed" (Leeds Phil.-&-Lit., 1851/2), as well as the Rev. A. J. D. D'Orsey's "Study of the English Language" (Midland Institute, 1862/3) and "How the English Language Was Formed" (Nottingham Mechanics' Institution, 1864/5).

As was the case with "Literature," the broad category of "Fine Arts" (music, art, photography) increasingly embraced performance, both vocal and instrumental. Robert Ellis, harpist to the Prince of Wales, appeared on platforms in Newport, Croydon, Barnsley, and Dover, often accompanied by vocalist Annie Cox; Frederick Chatterton, harpist to the Duchess of Gloucester, appeared more than a dozen times to deliver performances and lectures on the history of the instrument. Musical performances, like literary readings, also permitted women to take the platform in small but increasing numbers, either as vocal accompanists or as performers in their own right: these latter included Julia Bleadon (Chelmsford Literary and Mechanics' Institution, 1858/9; Gosport and Alverstoke Literary and Scientific Institution Society, 1859/60; Croydon Literary and Scientific Institution, 1860/1); Grace Egerton (who offered "Sketches of Odd People" with her husband, George Case, and performed at Croydon and Newport in 1861/2 and 1862/3); and the Scottish singer Lizzy Stuart (who delivered "Musical Performances" at Banbury, Ebbw Vale, and Croydon in 1857/8, 1859/60, and 1860/1). Elizabeth and Mary Mascall, who would enjoy great popularity into the 1870s, were in 1861/2 listed only as accompanists for Joseph Edwards Carpenter, whose "the Road, the River, and the Rail, with 12 Original Songs, Ballads, and Duets" (Brighton Mechanics' Institution, 1856/7; Newport Athenaeum and Mechanics' Institute, 1857/8) was noted in the 1862 "List of Lecturers" as having been performed 530 times.

Domestic Morality

The category of "Domestic Morality" was a topical descriptor unused at the time, but helpful today in examining a broad range of important mid-century subjects. Chief among these, unsurprisingly, was the topic of self-improvement, especially in the mechanics' institutions. This period witnessed, albeit in slowly declining numbers, instructive offerings on "Books and Study" (W. E. Baxter, MP, Brechin Mechanics' Institute, 1855/6), "The Triumphs of Self-Education: illustrated by Examples" (the Rev. J. Baker, Leeds Young Men's Association, 1861/2), and "Intellectual Improvement" (Dr. H. Barber, Ulverton Lecture and Scientific Association, 1863/4). Barnett Blake, acting the traveling agent and lecturer for the YUMI, gave a number of these lectures, including "On the Advantages of the Study of Science and Literature" (Leeds Mechanics' Institute, 1855/6). This category also includes generally moral lectures such as "On the Distinctions in Society Worth Having, and How To Obtain Them" (the Rev. R. Ainslie, Chester Mechanics' Institution, 1856/7), "On the Beautiful in Nature and in Morals" (the Rev. G. Mather, Barnsley Mechanics' Institute and Literary Society, 1861/2), and the Rev. S. M. All's "On Moral Power" (Newland Young Men's Mutual Improvement Society, 1859/60); many other lectures focused on some version of "Failures and Successes in Life," or "Great Men and Little Men," as well as unsectarian but generally Christian offerings like "The Insect World: A Testimony of God" (the Rev. J. D. Brocklehurst, Leeds Young Men's Association, 1861/2). Lectures on women's roles, the importance of family, and the comforts of a well-regulated home all fit under this umbrella as well, providing ample space for Balfour's "Home Influences," and "On the Moral and Intellectual Influence of Woman on Society," as well as lectures by Georgiana Bennett ("Women," and "An Hour with the Poets," both at the Birmingham Polytechnic Institute in 1850/1 and 1852/3) and James Kay Applebee ("The Three Graces of Womanhood," Newport Athenaeum and Mechanics' Institute, 1861/2). A pedantic thread of moral improvement, often couched in the same subtly demasculinized terms as the versions of "citizenship" explored in Chapter 1, wound through all but the most elite institutions during these two decades.

Questions of Contemporary Interest: Social Sciences and Current Events

Two additional broad categories, "Social Sciences" and "Current Events," each incorporated a number of topics that had no home in the tripartite division of science, literature, and music, and each increased in importance over this period and into the next. "Social Sciences" included not only the traditional areas of history, biography, and political economy, but also education, archaeology, "laws of health," and a variety of lectures that can be grouped together under the subheading of "national progress." Figure 3.5 shows the distribution of the largest subcategories—biography, history, economics, and national progress/laws of health—and their relative importance between 1850 and 1871. The much smaller subfields of education, archaeology, and all other social sciences are grouped together as "other."

Unsurprisingly, within this category lectures on history and biography were the most numerous throughout the period. Lectures on the fifteenth and sixteenth

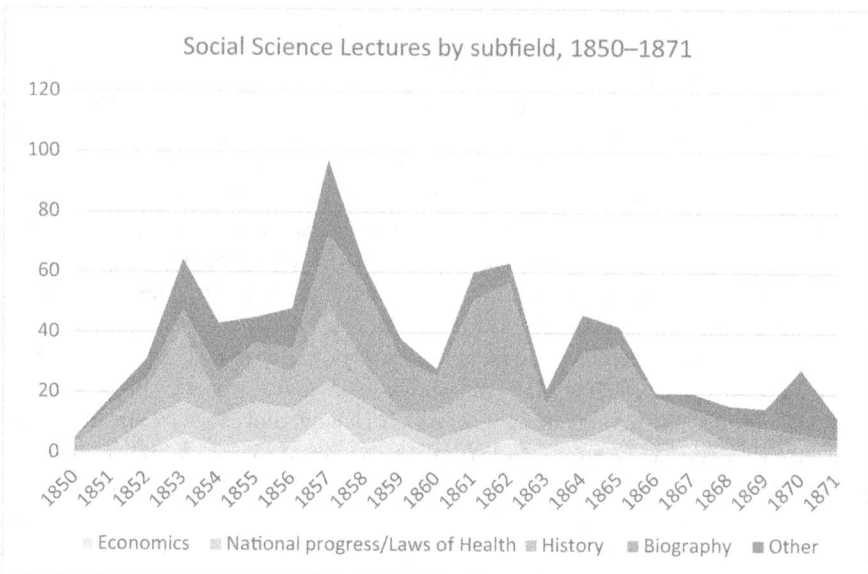

Figure 3.5 Subcategories within social science lectures, 1850–71.
Source: Journal of the Society of Arts, Vols. 1–22.

centuries were especially popular, forming a kind of national myth that could rally audiences in shared feelings of pride and patriotism: George Dawson's two-lecture series on "Good Queen Bess"—"the most thorough-paced English*man* the land has ever produced" (Bradford Mechanics' Institute, 1858/9)—was a prime example of how a skilled lecturer could avoid the pitfalls of antiquarianism and deliver instead a resounding reminder of triumph over imperial and religious peril. Among the many offerings on early modern England (and, much less frequently, Scotland) were Balfour's lectures on "Henry VIII" (Wakefield Mechanics' Institution, 1864/5), "Henry VIII and His Queens" (Newport Athenaeum and Mechanics' Institute, 1862/3), and "England in the 16th Century" (Croydon Literary and Scientific Institution, 1861/2); historian James Anthony Froude's series of three on "The Times of the Reformation" (Newcastle Lit.-&-Phil., 1866/7); the Rev. Alfred Barry's "The Tudor Period and Its Recent Historians" (Leeds Phil.-&-Lit., 1860/1); the Rev. T. D. C. Morse's "Life and Times of Cardinal Wolsey" (Salisbury Literary and Scientific Institution, 1863/4); D. C. Moss's "Cardinal Wolsey" (Ulverston Lecture and Scientific Association, 1863/4); Mr. Sumpter's "The Life and Times of Mary, Queen of Scots" (Barnet Institute, 1855/6); and Joshua Toulmin Smith's pair of lectures on "Illustrations of the Early Manners, Customs, Language, and History of England, Derived from the Public Records of the State" (Midland Institute, 1864/5). Henry Vincent delivered several multi-lecture series on the Protestant Reformation, as well as a series of eight lectures on Oliver Cromwell and on the English Commonwealth. Cromwell was also the chosen subject of many other lecturers, including the Rev. A. Anderson, assessing "The Character of Oliver

Cromwell, as a Warrior, a Statesman, and a Christian" (Sudbury Literary Institution, 1852/3), W. C. Beck, "Oliver Cromwell" (Hastings Mechanics' Institute, 1866/7); W. N. Froy, "Life and Character of Oliver Cromwell" (Barking Mutual Improvement Society, 1853/4; Redhill Institution, 1856/7). More prolific than all of these speakers, however, was historian J. C. Daniel, who delivered some thirty-five lectures on this era at institutions in Croydon, Royston, Darlington, Chelmsford, Newcastle, and other locations in the eight-year period of 1857–65.

As we saw above with the "chemistry of the breakfast table" lectures, titles alone cannot clearly convey the approach and content of apparently similar lectures. George Dawson's biographical and historical lectures are a case in point. "On the Origin, Character, and Doings of the Anglo-Saxons," which he delivered at five reporting institutions between 1851 and 1862 (Birmingham Polytechnic Institution, Redhill Institution, Plymouth and Portsea Athenaeum and Mechanics' Institute, Bedford Literary and Scientific Institute, and Nottingham Mechanics' Institution), was a stream-of-consciousness ramble through early history, full of description and humor but always coming back to the present day, where Dawson located the best of "Saxon, *plus* Dane, *plus* Norman" in the modern Englishman. Peppering his lecture with brief observations about jury trials, contemporary proposals to amend the poor laws, the dourness of Puritanism, and the extent of the Victorian empire, he sketched out the ways in which his provincial audiences were profoundly important to the overall health of the country. "London is not everything," he argued. "London is too large to be united; it is more like a number of small towns, without unity; the man in the west is not known in the east. The interest of one has nothing to do in common with the other. London is certainly a mighty city, but it is not all in all; it wants help from the country. This is as it should be, and shows good, healthy, circulation; an evenness of political power."[18] The actual "doings" of the Anglo-Saxons had only a small part in this very popular lecture.

A similarly titled lecture, "Manners and Customs of the Ancient Britons and Anglo-Saxons," delivered by historian George Harris at the Midland Institute during the 1857/8 season, took an entirely different tack; as part of Harris's larger work on English history, the lecture was much more scholarly in nature, beginning in the fifth century and moving steadily toward the Norman conquest. "At the time when they invaded Britain the Saxons were as rude and uncivilised as any of the other barbarian nations," Harris told his audience before outlining developments in the arts, military strategies, religious practices, roadbuilding, and agriculture. Whereas Dawson had harrumphed his way through certain long-standing myths about the period—"That Alfred first started trial by jury, is nonsense"—Harris rehearsed carefully the known history of jury trials and trials by ordeal, concluding that, for the trial by jury, "the precise period of its establishment in this country does not appear to have been very clearly ascertained" despite Blackstone's massive researches into English common law.[19] A third approach to this subject, institute president Horace Martin's "On the Saxon Conquest of England" (Battle Mechanics' Institution, 1852/3), has disappeared from the historical record; the institution's report described it briefly as "chiefly taken from a recent French author, many of whose ideas, it was believed, were new and of an interesting character."[20]

Biographical subjects were also almost always historical rather than contemporary; in addition to "Good Queen Bess" and other English and Scottish royalty, there were numerous lectures on Wellington, Macaulay, Milton, Galileo, and Locke. Following on Samuel Smiles's best-selling 1857 biography of George Stephenson, the engineer was the subject of seven reported lectures. Balfour delivered a biographical lecture on Stephenson at the Hastings Mechanics' Institute (1861/2) and also used Stephenson as a model of self-improvement in several of her novels. Other lecturers on Stephenson included Martin C. Wykeham (Bromley Literary Institute, 1860/1); the Rev. H. H. Carlisle (Gosport and Alverstoke Literary and Scientific Institution, 1859/60); the Rev. T. G. Hatchard (Farnham Young Men's Association, 1860/1); the Rev. J. Steer (Croydon Literary and Scientific Institution 1858/9); and even Basil Young, who usually delivered light and fizzy musical entertainments but was one of the first to jump on the Stephenson bandwagon (Banbury Mechanics' Institute, 1857/8.)

Other popular topics ranged from local history to lectures on the ancient world, both of which straddled history and archaeology. The former could take the form of "Rare Old Chester" (J. B. Marsh, Darlington Mechanics' Institute, 1857/8, and Blackburn Literary, Scientific, and Mechanics' Institution, 1859/60) and "Young Bingley" (the Rev. Mr. Heron, Bingley Mechanics' Institute, 1864/5). The latter focused primarily on Assyria and Egypt, prompted by ongoing archaeological discoveries in the middle east; there were some two dozen stand-alone lectures on the digs and their artifacts during this period, including a dozen individual offerings on Nineveh and its ruins as well as a thirteen-lecture course entitled "On the Dead Sea and Cities of the Plain" (the Rev. W. J. Butler, Nottingham Institute, 1854/5).[21]

The subcategories of "national progress" and "laws of health," defined here to exclude the lectures on foreign affairs, government, and empire which were folded into the subcategory of "current events," were a small but consistent subset of lectures during the 1850s, peaking at fourteen in 1858 and declining sharply thereafter. Lectures on the laws of health ranged from specific discourses on food supply, water and sewage, and housing reform, on the one hand, to more general lectures such as "The Physical Condition of the People, in Its Bearing upon Their Social and Moral Welfare" (Robert Bickersteth, Bishop of Ripon, at the Leeds Phil.-&-Lit., 1859/60). While some lecturers delivered the same talk to different audiences—during the 1854/5 season Robert Scott Burn offered his lecture, "On Sanitary Science as Applied to Home Construction and Convenience," to the elite Leeds Phil.-&-Lit and the less exclusive institutions in Peterborough and Stamford—subject matter was often tailored to listeners, as we have already seen in the areas of science and social science. For example, the substance of the Rev. F. Skinner's "Physiology Applied to Health and Education, Shewing How To Have a Sound Mind in a Sound Body" (Blackburn Literary, Scientific, and Mechanics' Institution, 1856/57) was reimagined as "The Importance of Sanitary and Economic Science as Part of General Education" by political economist William Ballantyne Hodgson (Midland Institute, 1857/8). Similarly, within the overall arc of "national progress," lectures on prison reform could take the shape of biographical treatments of John Howard, five of which were reported in the 1850s, or more general approaches, such as "On Reformatory and Retributory Punishments," "On the Mode of Treating Discharged Criminals, and on the Ticket of Leave System," and "Some Attempts to

Discover a System of Reformation for Adult Criminals," all delivered by Leeds MP Robert Hall during the 1855/6 season—the first two at the Leeds Mechanics' Institute and the last at the Leeds Phil.-&-Lit.

General lectures on national progress peppered the first decade of these reported lecture seasons. These included E. Ward Jackson, "On the Moral, Social, and Physical Condition of the People of This Country during the Past Fifty Years" (Darlington Mechanics' Institute, 1851/2); R. Monckton Milnes, MP, "The Laws of the Progress of Society, as Illustrated by Present Condition of Mankind" (Leeds Phil.-&-Lit., 1853/4); the Rev. William Sinclair, "The State and Prospects of England Considered in Connection with the National Character" (Leeds Phil.-&-Lit., 1858/9); the Rev. J. D. Snow, "The Present Time" (Alton Mechanics' Institution, 1857/8); R. W. Blencoe, "On Some of the Moral and Physical Changes That Have Taken Place in the English People" (Lewes Mechanics' Institution, 1856/7); and Henry Vincent, "Our Young Men and Women: Their Present Position and Future Prospects" and "The Progressive Tendencies of Society in Great Britain" (both at the South Eastern Railway Mechanics' Institute, Ashford, 1857/8). After 1859, this set of topics subsided into a few specialized lectures each year on the military, newspaper standards, savings banks, and educational innovations; the general "state of the kingdom" lectures declined altogether with the exception of two on "Modern Society," delivered by journalist and novelist Edmund Yates at the Croydon Literary and Scientific Institution in 1861/2 and the Nottingham Mechanics' Institution in 1864/5. These areas of interest would reemerge after the 1870s, reflecting a shift in attitudes toward adult education, suffrage, municipal improvement, and systems of health and medicine. They are important even in their relatively small numbers, however, because they form one of the areas where we will most easily be able to trace connections with the debate and discussion societies examined below.

Similarly, the category of "current events" forms another link across lectures, debates, and discussions. Within reported lectures, this subject area includes the two subcategories of travel and adventure, on the one hand, and foreign affairs, foreign policy, and empire, on the other. (Because lectures on contemporary events were extremely rare, they have been dropped out of the following analysis; they will, however, figure prominently in the analysis of discussion and debate topics in this period, and in lecture offerings after 1870.) Figure 3.6 shows the distribution of these lectures.

The travel lecture was a persistent feature within these decades, and served a variety of functions. These lectures were described as particularly well-suited to the attentions of the fatigued working man: instead of science or literature, "some accounts of foreign travel would interest a great deal more, and in the course of that they might introduce a good deal of useful information."[22] Many travel lectures simply recounted leisure trips abroad, such as W. Duncan's "Rambles on the Rhine" (Kingston Mechanics' Institute, 1857/8), Mr. Avery's "Travels through Spain" (Redditch Literary and Scientific Institute, 1851/2), or W. Wyke Smith's "Poland" (Barnet Institute, 1855/6). Such trips were often recounted not only with "dissolving views" but also titled as "impressions," "recollections," or "reminiscences," reinforcing the ephemerality of such trips and also, simultaneously, the privileges of income and leisure that were the invisible foundation of such offerings. Former MP Edward Aldham Leatham's "Recent Trip to the East" (Wakefield Mechanics" Institution, 1856/7) was publicized as an informal "talking

Figure 3.6 Lectures in two subcategories of current events, 1850–71.

Source: *Journal of the Society of Arts*, Vols. 1–22.

lecture," in a way that no unpolished amateur would attempt. Similarly, Dr. John Anthony's "Impressions of Three Visits to Palestine" (Midland Institute, 1862/3), J. W. Atkinson's "A Ramble through Some of the Sublime Passes in Central Asia" (Leeds Mechanics' Institute, 1862/3), and F. E. Baines's "Westward Ho!" (Barnet Institute, 1861/2) all reinforced the subtle ways in which travel might remain merely aspirational for a great number of listeners, while the Rev. J. F. Bateman's "Notes of a Visit to Canada and the Atlantic Cities of the Union" (South Eastern Railway Mechanics' Institute [Ashford], 1857/8) and the Rev. Thomas Bacon's "Rough Notes on a Tour in Norway" (Basingstoke Mechanics' Institute, 1856/7)—which eventually became the completed lecture "On Norway" (Farnham Young Men's Association, 1860/1)—also underscored the gap between those who could casually recount enviable travel anecdotes and those who could only listen and learn.

Descriptions of the world abroad were not always casual. Many were imbued with the gravity appropriate to their subjects. "An Account of the Manners, Habits, and Religion of the Natives of New Zealand" (the Rev. F. W. Chapman, Leeds Phil.-&-Lit., 1856/7) was serious despite its source in "personal observations," while "Jerusalem and its Environs" (the Rev. Thomas W. Aveling, Bedford Literary and Scientific Institution, 1854/5), "Abyssinia and the Abyssinians" (geographer Charles T. Beke, Midland Institute, 1867/8), and "Algeria—Its Manners, Customs, and Scenery" (Mr. H. Blackburn, Croydon Literary and Scientific Institution, 1856/7) promised holistic pictures of far-off lands. MP Frederick North's "The Plains of Italy" (Hastings Mechanics' Institute, 1860/1) was self-evidently more serious than the Rev. M. Mitchell's "Olives and Maccaroni [*sic*]" (Yarmouth Parochial Library and Museum, 1856/7). A large subset of these travel lectures was built on the continued fascination with the Arctic (14) and the Alps (9), both associated with risk and adventure. Regular offerings on the loss of explorer John Franklin and the subsequent expeditions through the 1850s to discover his fate and repatriate his remains ranged from Sir Edward Belcher's "The Nations Inhabiting the Arctic Regions of North America; Their Habits, Customs, Weapons, Implements, &c, &c." (Leeds Phil.-&-Lit., 1860/1) to the Rev. J. Coutt's "The Frozen Regions, and the Fate of Sir John Franklin, Captain Crozier, and Their Brave Companions" (Banbridge Young Men's Mutual Improvement Society, 1862/3) and "The Arctic Regions, an Hour's Entertainment for the Young" (Mr. Hick, Barnsley Mechanics' Institute and Literary Society, 1857/8). Alpine adventures were described by many amateur climbers, including Edward Baines in "An Alpine Panorama: Monte Rosa and the Matterhorn" (Leeds Phil.-&-Lit., 1856/7) and the Rev. Edwin Sydney, "A Visit to the Alps in 1860, Illustrated with Views and Photographs" (Bury St. Edmunds Athenaeum, 1860/1).

The lectures in foreign affairs, about 50 percent fewer than those in travel (111 compared to 232), were uniformly more serious and ranged from overviews of the various pieces of the formal and informal empire to discussions of policy, military power, and the prospects of the Australian gold fields. Some sought to contextualize recent events: for example, Col. Michael J. Rowlandson's "The Chain of Brahminical [*sic*] Caste" (Croydon Literary and Scientific Institution, 1856/7) set the stage for his subsequent lectures on "The British Rule in India" (Croydon, 1858/9) and "India and the Sepoy Mutiny" (Brompton Church of England Young Men's Society, 1860/1), while William Theobald's pair of lectures on "The Institutions of India" (Midland Institute, 1857/8), delivered during the fighting itself, attempted to provide some background for the rebellion. Some were extremely specific, such as the Rev. C. L. Smith's "Cutting a Ship Canal through the Isthmus Which Connects North with South America" (Dunmow Literary and Scientific Institution, 1852/3) and Claude G. Wheelhouse's "A Topographical Description of the Seat of War on the Danube and Black Sea" (Leeds Phil.-&-Lit., 1854/5), while P. H. Andre's "The American Revolution of 1861; Its Consequences to Liberty, Civilization, and Commerce; to the People of the Free Labour, Cotton, and Border Slave States, Great Britain, and British America. Illustrated by a Map of America" (Midland Institute, 1860/1) was as broadly comprehensive as its audience could manage. These topics, together accounting for a consistent 10 percent of all lectures during this period, allowed audiences to share in the experiences of physical daring, intelligent town planning, and measured scrutiny of the broad and complicated modern world that increasingly characterized "our culture and time."

On the Platform: The Lists of Lecturers, 1854–62

The Society of Arts issued their formal lists of lecturers irregularly, and here we will focus on the lists published in 1854 and 1862. The list published by the short-lived *Literary and Educational Year-Book* (*LEYB*) in 1859 will provide another source of information on the individuals who chose to have their names and lecture topics publicly available for committee secretaries and clubs (see Figure 3.7). However, the named lecturers recuperated from these data comprised only a portion of those

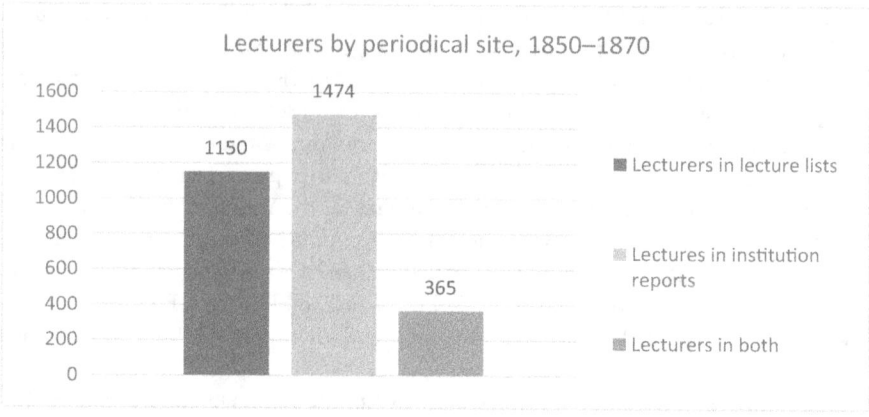

Figure 3.7 Lecturers in reports and lists, 1850–70.

Source: "Appendix: List of Lecturers," *Journal of the Society of Arts*, 1854, 1862; *Literary and Educational Year-Books, 1859.*

men and women on lecture platforms during this period. There were hundreds and thousands of speakers whose work never gained the attention of committees or editors; for example, of the twenty-six lectures listed in *Pitman's Popular Lecturer and Reader* in 1865, only three were by men who were included in the 1862 List of Lecturers and only one of those three—the Rev. H. Griffiths, "The Age of Great Reptiles" (Wakefield Mechanics' Institution, 1864/5)—also delivered a lecture at a Union affiliate. Of the 2,624 lecturers collected for this analysis, only 365—14 percent—were named in both the affiliate reports and in any of the lists of lecturers that appeared in 1854, 1859, and 1862.

There were several reasons lecturers might appear in the former and not in the latter. First, speakers with very limited availability, like explorer Paul Du Chaillu or political exile Louis Blanc, preferred to work within their own private networks of friends and supporters to secure speaking engagements. Second, many early-career entertainers and performers often appeared in rural institutes long before they were able to advertise nationally. Finally, many named in the "Proceedings" simply did not rise to the level of the national lecturer; they were local or regional men and women, they delivered lectures only to their own institution or to institutions in their locality, and they did not advertise their services to other institutions. This regional focus suggests that local talent remained crucially important during this period. Local men and women were not necessarily less able, less interesting, or even less available; several large civic institutions were as reliant on local talent as smaller and more rural institutions, in part because familiar local speakers often would appear for free and with little advance notice.

Most of the lecturers in these lists appear in more than one, often in all three. All three lists include descriptions of the subject matter each lecturer might present, although the *LEYB* was spare in its descriptions and tended to note general subject areas such as "Chemistry, Electricity, Experimental Philosophy" (Dr. George H. Bachhoffner), "Roman and English History and Literature, Generally" (the Rev. Charles McKensie), or "Historical, Biographical, and Literary Subjects" (George Dawson). In some cases, the *LEYB* included limited lists of titles: "Aspects of the Present Age; General Literature" (the Rev. George Gilfillan), "The Wonders of the Crystal Palace; Natural Magic; Common Things; &c." (C. F. Partington), or "The Indian Empire; The Triumphs of Enterprise; Modern Education; Elocution; &c." (J. H. Stocqueler). The *Journal*'s lists were much more expansive, in some cases listing over two dozen lecture titles and also, occasionally, titles under preparation (for example, Edmund Yates, noted above, alerted committee secretaries in 1862 that he had a new lecture in preparation, entitled "London out of Town.") The *LEYB* included no information about fees or travel except to note which lecturers would appear without charge; the *Journal* provided uneven levels of information on fees, travel expenses, and limits on distance in both the 1854 and the 1862 lists.

The 1862 list also included the names of other institutions that had hosted each lecturer, although, as we saw in Chapter 1, the Society vehemently refused to vet these speakers and did not include any positive or negative feedback with the listings of previous hosts. Thus, a committee seeking to engage musical performer John Edney could contact the secretaries of the sixty-six institutions he listed as references, while Robert H. Williamson's "Poetic Recitals" could be vetted only through "Masham, &c." and many local clergy, such as the Cheltenham County Gaol chaplain Rev. L. Aspinall-Dudley, had no references listed at all. The lists of reference institutions were extensive for paid lecturers, even for the most popular speakers like Dawson, Balfour, and Grossmith. They were significantly less extensive for gratis lecturers; journalist I. A. Bernard of the *Ulverston Mirror*, who spoke only in his own neighborhood and district, listed as references only a few local institutions. References for lecturers in literature, the arts, and the social sciences were generally much more extensive than those in the sciences, although even well-established science speakers like naturalist Edwin Lankester generally included a few names of institutions. In the early lists, a lecturer's own self-deprecations might be included: the 1854 list, for example, was peppered with warnings that the lecturer "does not lay himself out as a professional lecturer" or "is merely an amateur lecturer," cautions that appear neither in the 1859 nor the 1862 lists.

Many of the lecturers during this period were clergy, primarily Anglican but occasionally from other denominations: they comprised 232 of the 1,151 named lecturers in the three formal lists, and 242 of 1,062 in the lectures reported by affiliates, making up some one-fifth of the lecturers offering their services. Many of these clergy had no other title than "Rev.," likely indicating workaday ministers who gave occasional lectures as part of their parish responsibilities. Clergy had, by definition, some minimal ability to speak from a pulpit, and this lent them the verbal polish often lacking in young society members who might give a single lecture before subsiding gratefully into a sea of subscribers. They often, therefore, formed the core of a committee's bench of speakers in smaller societies.

For all speakers, including clergy, these compendia included honorifics and credentials from "Esq." and "MA" to "Dr.," "Prof.," and "LLD." Memberships in royal societies and other credentialing institutions were also listed. While the formal lists did not use "Mr." and therefore included 481 lecturers with no honorific, the affiliate reports had no hard-and-fast rule in this regard; thus, in the pages of the *Journal*, 176 men were labeled as "Mr." while 116 had no honorific whatsoever. The formal lists also gave additional information when it was provided, so that, for example, orator Charles John Plumptre, LLD, was listed as both a barrister-at-law and a teacher of elocution at Oxford. This was especially helpful for less well-known speakers: John Sanders Blockley was identified as "managing chemist," David Burnett as "Author of *Atheism, Unphilosophical* and *The Apocalypse an Unsealed Book*," a Mr. John Jones was noted to be the organizing agent for the South Staffordshire Association for the Promotion of Adult Education and Evening Schools, and Duncan Macmillan was identified as a ventriloquist.

Gratis lecturers, as we saw in Chapter 1, formed an important resource for these institutions, although many affiliates were inconsistent in reporting the numbers of lectures delivered for payment of expenses only or even for free. The "Proceedings" columns between 1852 and 1862 indicate some 16.5 percent of lectures were specifically labeled as gratis, but the number of actual uncompensated lectures was almost surely closer to 75 percent or 80 percent, based upon the acknowledgments within institute reports that "this department depended entirely on the gratuitous assistance of gentlemen resident in the neighbourhood." Some institutes or unions, such as the Halifax Mechanics' Institute and the two dozen affiliates of the Northern Union of Literary and Mechanics' Institutions, routinely noted that an entire season's offerings were delivered without payment. Even larger and more robust institutes, such as the Hastings Mechanics' Institute, depended upon volunteer lecturers for some 50 percent or more of any given season during this period, with the secretary arguing at its twenty-first annual meeting that the institute "need not be ashamed at the results it has been instrumental in producing in the lecture department."[23]

This dependence on uncompensated lecturers was slow to change. The YUMI, surveying its members in 1852, noted that out of 788 lectures delivered at the 80 member institutes that submitted reports, 645 lectures were gratis. In 1857, out of 710 lectures delivered at the 88 reporting member institutes, 586 were gratis. By 1864, the YUMI secretary reported, "The demands for gratuitous lecturers have somewhat decreased, while there has been an improvement in the employment of professional lecturers," so that of 407 lectures delivered in 60 reporting member institutes, 314 were uncompensated; thus, the percentage of gratis lectures dropped from about 82 percent in both 1852 and 1857 to 77 percent in 1864. Moving from the YUMI to the reporting affiliates as a whole, we see that gratis lecturers accounted for 57 percent of the 609 listed lecturers in 1859 and 48 percent of the 481 listed lecturers in 1862. Of these volunteer speakers, clergy accounted for 38 percent in 1859 (for a total of 132 listed lecturers, or 22 percent of the entire list) and 32 percent in 1862 (for a total of 74 listed lecturers, or 12 percent of the entire list). While the dependence upon the unpaid services of local clergy declined significantly during this time, they still formed an important core of speakers.

It is clear that a robust understanding of popular platform culture cannot be fully obtained from either the reports or the lists alone, although we can begin to draw some conclusions from these sources. Generally speaking, we can see that lecturers during this period shared certain characteristics: while the social status of those speaking ranged from the elite aristocrat and bishop to the obscure untitled institution member,

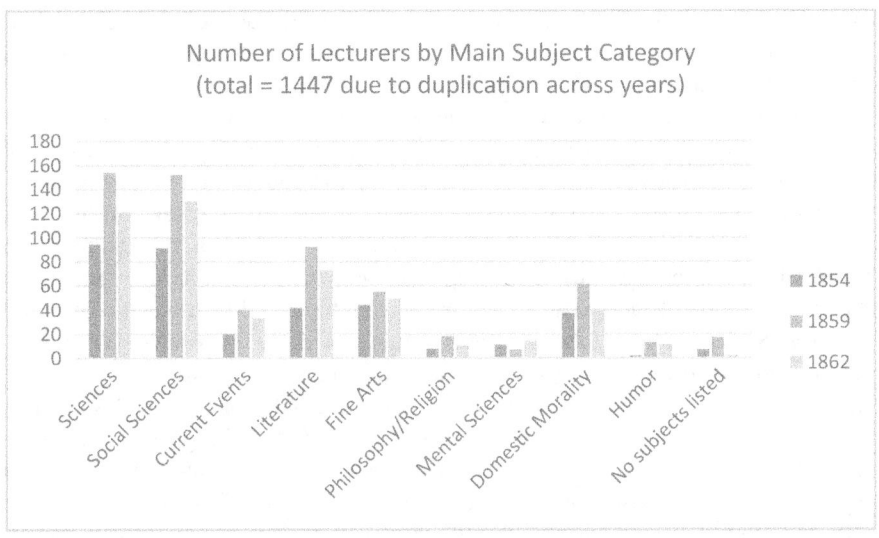

Figure 3.8 Lecturers listed in 1854, 1859, and 1862 by subject area.

Source: "Appendix: List of Lecturers," *Journal of the Society of Arts*, 1854, 1862; *Literary and Educational Year-Books*, 1859.

the percentage of unpaid "sappers and miners" remained quite high at mid-century; the number of clergy offering unpaid services was nearly double the number of clergy who sought remuneration; only a small fraction of platform speakers were women, who were generally associated with dramatic and musical performance rather than with formal lectures; and lecturers as a whole spoke primarily on topics in sciences, social sciences, and literature, and only rarely about current events, as we can see in Figure 3.8.

On the Platform: Critiquing Speakers and Subjects

The references included in the lists of lecturers were important guides for secretaries curating a season, but—as we saw with the disappointing progeny of Charles Partington in Chapter 1—institutes also could draw upon printed reports of lectures and audience responses as they crafted their programming. In the first years of the *Journal*, before examinations distracted the attentions of editors and correspondents, opinionated descriptions of lecturers and lectures were particularly common. For example, an 1852 lecture by royal harpist Frederick Chatterton, "On the Antiquity of the Harp," showed "deep research" and was "pointed and highly instructive,"[24] while, despite his standing within the Society and the Union, Hugo Reid's lecture on James Watt at the Chichester Literary Society and Mechanics' Institute was reported as "purely rudimentary" and lacking "experiments and working models in illustration of his remarks."[25] J. T. Topham's 1853 lecture "On the History and Utility of Poetry," which was reported over the course of two closely written columns, "showed the poetical in nature around us, insisted upon its utility, and with considerable warmth and energy compared and contrasted natural with artistic beauty."[26]

Editors and correspondents assessed delivery as well as content, often focusing on the elusive "manner" so crucial to a successful lecture in addition to the "matter" of the lecture itself. Science lecturer Michael Faraday had counseled his fellow speakers to "appear easy and collected, undaunted and unconcerned," to speak with the goal of "conveying ideas with ease ... and infusing them with clearness and readiness into the minds of the audience," using language that was "smooth and harmonious and at the same time simple and easy."[27] Ease and unconcern could be difficult to achieve, however: Society of Arts member Robert Hunt noted that it required a "peculiar aptitude" for the correct delivery of a popular lecture on science in order to avoid failure "from too exalted a tone" or "from too low and imperfect a demonstration."[28] A reporter for the *Manchester Guardian* was delightedly sarcastic in describing the spectroscopic entertainment of a Mr. Gompertz at the Manchester Mechanics' Institution: "the 'chorus of invisibles' made us wish that the vocalists were also inaudible."[29] Weak lecturers were critiqued as merely "men having hobbies," speaking only "the jargon of the subject."[30] One especially dull speaker in Newcastle, buried in the pages of his lecture, failed to notice that "after a weary hour and a half, only three auditors remained in the hall. ... So we gradually turned the gas lower and lower, and this brought him to a full stop some quarter of an hour after the regular time for closing the building had passed."[31]

However, a good lecturer was also commended in ways that helped lecture committees fill their seasons: Henry Vincent, for example, "gave his lectures with a moderation of tone pleasing to all political parties in the town."[32] The Newcastle Lit.-&-Phil.'s vice president John Clayton, a frequent speaker, was known for his "finished language, careful enunciation, and polished manners."[33] The Avesham Institution for the Diffusion of Knowledge reported that its 1861 season was characterized by subjects "treated in a style at once able and popular."[34] By the mid-1860s, inadvertently securing a disappointing speaker was less and less common: lecturers took their performative roles more seriously, and affiliates were more willing to signal to their peers the competence of individual platform speakers. Even as the *Journal* significantly cut its own coverage, the Society's lists of lecturers contained more extensive lists of references, and local newspapers had begun to critique rather than merely report these events. By the middle of the 1870s, as regional journalism rapidly expanded, coverage of lectures, institutional programming, and even annual meetings would become more descriptive, more opinionated, and more plentiful.

Building a Lecture Season: Six Snapshots, 1852–65

We have seen in Chapter 1 the unshakable resistance to collaboration among regional affiliate secretaries who claimed to "want to build a little lecture union." We have also seen here that reporting institutions relied only partially on the lists of lecturers that they continued to demand. How, then, did institutions build their seasons? There were certainly points of general agreement in terms of the most effective speakers.

The names of Dawson and Balfour, for example, were often linked together in the earliest columns of the *Journal*. Traice remarked on the public's "especial desire for lectures typified by those of George Dawson and Mrs. Balfour," rather than on science lectures; James Boorne, the honorary secretary of the Reading Literary, Scientific and Mechanics' Institution, commented at the Union's first annual meeting that "there were such lecturers as Mr. Dawson and Mrs. Balfour, who were popular at Reading, in different senses. One lecturer might be exceedingly popular, and yet not bring so much money into the exchequer as another who was not quite so popular; one might be popular with the members, and the other with the community at large, who would on his [*sic*] account come to the Institutions, and add to its funds."[35] Dawson was noted as "an earnest and stirring lecturer" who "had a most biting, satirical talent" that attracted "even those who feared the tendency of his pulpit teaching"; Robert Spence Watson, looking back on decades of lectures at the Newcastle Lit.-&-Phil., wrote that he "singled out individuals in the audience and made them the recipients of curiously personal criticisms or observations," although he supplied no examples.[36] Balfour, on the other hand, was universally praised as delivering "beautiful discourses" with "graceful and touching eloquence" and described as "the talented lecturess ... attentively listened to by an admiring audience"; her lectures "met with the most entire and unqualified approbation of a numerous audience."[37] Balfour had 59 separate engagements reported by Union affiliates during this period; Dawson had more than double that number at 124. While many lecturers were reported as speaking at half a dozen or more affiliates, only a few platform speakers were noticeably more prolific.[38]

However, Balfour and Dawson could not carry entire seasons. A survey of half a dozen institution seasons between 1852/3 and 1864/5 shows how individual committees sought to provide programming that attracted and held subscribers and that also took into account an institution's mission, location, demographics, and resources. They include the Leeds Mechanics' Institute; the Birmingham Polytechnic; the Hastings Mechanics' Institute; the Bradford Mechanics' Institute; the Croydon Scientific and Literary Institution; and the Wakefield Mechanics' Institute.

As we saw in Chapter 2, the Leeds Mechanics' Institute (LMI)[39] in 1852 was well-established as a space for popular lecturers—in contrast to the Leeds Phil.-&-Lit., which at this point remained conflicted about opening its program up to the general public—and as a consequence had far and away the most varied program of the six examined here. The twenty-six lectures of the season, delivered by eighteen speakers, spread across most of the categories explored above: ten were in the sciences; nine in literature, art, and music; five in the social sciences; and one in domestic morality. This season is one of the few of the LMI not to include Balfour or Dawson; instead, the most well-known of these speakers were chemist and educator John Henry Pepper, who would become famous for the optical illusion known as "Pepper's Ghost," and Shakespearean Charles Cowden Clarke.[40] Ten of the eighteen speakers were reported in the *Journal* as appearing only locally, either at the LMI or at both the LMI and the Phil.-&-Lit. (Mr. Henwood, Frank Howard, John Ingham Ikin, Gideon Mantell, Thomas John Pearsall, James Rodgers, Adam Sedgwick, William Sinclair, Leeds Town Hall organist William Spark, Theodore West, and Charles Wicksteed). Only four of these ten speakers were also listed in at least one of the lists of lecturers. This suggests that of the eighteen speakers at this prominent and nationally respected institution, one-third were completely local and did not regard themselves as available to speak in other venues. The remaining twelve, however, included Cowden Clarke; Pepper; the nationally known musician and performer Henry Phillips; and German historian Reinhold Solger. Four of the speakers were clergy. Lectures in the sciences and the applied sciences accounted for half of the season; most of the remaining fell into the categories of literature and music. In this way, the LMI season was a continuation of the programs of the late 1840s, where lectures in science and literature were consistently the most numerous and where programming combined the showmanship of a Pepper with the hint of international sophistication emanating from Solger.

The other well-established institution in this cross section was the Birmingham Polytechnic Institute, here represented in 1853. It would soon be overburdened with fatal debt—debt that was in part a function of its commitment to the well-known names appearing on its platform—but it enjoyed a national reputation and the patronage of men such as Charles Dickens, who served as president in 1844.[41] Balfour and Dawson account for five of the lectures in its remarkably full program of thirty offerings, of which only two were in the sciences (astronomer William Radcliffe Birt's general "Objects and Advantages of Science" and naturalist Edmund Wheeler's "Curiosities of Insect Life"). Instead, the institution featured some of the most popular names in literature and music; in addition to Balfour and Dawson, the Polytechnic hosted harpist Frederick Chatterton, poet Georgiana Bennett, and American historian and lecturer John Lord, whose fourteen-volume *Beacon Lights of History* appeared between 1883 and 1896.[42]

Both the LMI and the Birmingham Polytechnic mounted programs pitched to a middle class that could appreciate the sophistication of nationally known musicians, poets, and men of science, and who could enjoy being a part of a national conversation about culture. These were large institutions with robust subscriber bases. The LMI reported a membership of 1,873 in 1849, with annual subscription rates ranging from 5s. and 10s. for ladies and 8s. for "youth" to 12s. and 15s. for adult men; in that year it delivered 54 lectures at a net cost of £96. The Polytechnic reported an 1848 membership of 664, of whom 108 were ladies, with the normal subscription rate set at 6s. per quarter or 24s. per year, and a lecture season that ran for some 36 weeks of the year at an annual cost of £100.[43] Their years of service—the LMI was founded in 1824, the Polytechnic was founded in 1843—suggested that by the early 1850s their growing pains were behind them; their lecture programs suggested that they occupied sturdy and permanent positions in the purveyance of knowledge-based culture in their cities. For the Polytechnic, this was a mirage, as it would close its doors within another year; for the LMI, this position of influence would remain intact for several more decades. Both institutions, however, had prospered when few mechanics' and literary societies existed to compete for subscribers, and their early strengths drew speakers eager to reach appreciative audiences.

Institutions with less wealthy subscribers perforce took a more conservative approach to filling a lecture season. The Hastings Mechanics' Institution, whose 1854–5 season was its twentieth, had grown to 394 subscribers paying annual dues of 12s.[44] Its committee routinely called upon its own membership to fill a season: in

1855, secretary John Banks (who had helped found the institution and would serve as vice president in 1864/5) delivered five of the twenty lectures, while vice president Frederick North, MP, and C. J. Womersley, who would become president in 1863, each delivered one. Other slots were filled by local men, nine of whom (William Caveler, R. Dawson, Mr. Dobell, Thomas Hudson, Mr. Keyworth, Joseph Pitter, the Rev. John Stent, the Rev. G. Stewart, and the Rev. R. N. Young) were reported as speaking only at this institution. Young and Stent were from the neighboring town of St. Leonard's-on-Sea, whose own mechanics' institute would amalgamate with the Hastings Institute in 1865. Eleven of the lectures were on scientific subjects; eight were on the social sciences; and only one—"Oliver Goldsmith"—was on a literary subject. This heavy reliance on local men, as well as the preponderance of science lectures, suggests an institution still working to establish itself; its programming would pivot strongly away from the sciences and into literature, music, and current events beginning in the late 1850s, and during the 1860s its seasons would come to resemble those of many other middlebrow institutions around the kingdom, with regular engagements by Balfour, Dawson, and Grossmith in addition to natural history artist Benjamin Waterhouse Hawkins and musical entertainer George Buckland.

Indeed, that middlebrow programming was well-established by the late 1850s. The Bradford Mechanics' Institute's 1858 season was relatively brief, but among its fourteen lectures were appearances by Grossmith, with three humorous lectures; Balfour and Dawson, with one lecture each; and relatively familiar local names like the Rev. G. W. Conder, who appeared eight times in and around his home in Leeds during the 1850s, and the artist and poet Joseph Woodfall Ebsworth, who would eventually become a clergyman near Bradford and who spent much of his later life as an antiquarian and editor of the ballad literature of the sixteenth and seventeenth centuries. Three gratis lectures were delivered by local clergy (the Rev. Canon Joshua Fawcett, "On some of the Former Inhabitants of Our Old Town and Neighbourhood"; the Rev. S. G. Green, "Old Times: How to Understand Them, and What They Teach"; and the Rev. J. Gregory, "West-Riding Dialect"). Other local speakers included S. H. Kerr, whose lecture on the electric telegraph was delivered gratis. Regional lecturer W. Richardson, "Electricity, Galvanism, and Pneumatics," had delivered series of lectures on electricity and galvanism in Blackburn, Huddersfield, and Hartlepool several years earlier, advertising his work as "Illustrated by a SPLENDID APPARATUS, with which the whole subject of Thunder, Lightning, Tempests, Tornadoes, Whirlpools, Waterspouts, and the whole range of Meteoric Phenomena will be scientifically delineated and demonstrated."[45] Richardson's lecture here in 1858 continued the work of the performative amateur science lecturer, whose showmanship had become an attractive alternative to the more serious science lecture by the 1840s. Overall, Bradford's organizing committee leaned heavily on men from the region, and its low subscription fees—10s. a year, payable quarterly—limited its command of expensive lecturers, especially in the higher-priced sciences.

By 1859, we can see a shift away from programs wholly defined by the spoken lecture. The Croydon Literary and Scientific Institute (founded 1838), just south of London, filled its season with twenty-one offerings, three of which were musical entertainments by George Barker, George Buckland, and D. W. King; another three were literary readings or entertainments by Adolphus Francis, Henry Phillips, and poet and essayist Daniel Puseley, who had recently returned from a lengthy stay in Australia and whose *Rise and Progress of Australia, Tasmania, and New Zealand. By an Englishman* had just been printed for a fourth time.[46] The fifteen formal lectures included five in the arts (literature, music, and fine arts); three on some less-rigorous aspect of the sciences (an inventor, an invention, and a general "Science in a Drop of Water" exploration); one on empire, and half a dozen miscellaneous offerings that ranged from "National Flags" to Grossmith's popular "Wit and Humour." Well-known names anchored the program; in addition to Grossmith, the committee had secured the services of Balfour, art historian Johann Gottfried Kinkel, and historian J. C. Daniel. Croydon had begun to follow the interests of its suburban membership away from the serious content urged by educationists and critics, although as an institution it would become increasingly central to suburban life. This trend away from serious content was not unique to Croydon, but could be seen in institutions across the kingdoms; at the Newport (Wales) Athenaeum and Mechanics' Institute in 1861, for example, the twentieth annual lecture season featured such entertaining speakers as George Dawson, Henry Phillips, J. K. Applebee, George Grossmith, and Walter Rowton, as well as four musical entertainments and a performance by the local rifle corps.[47]

Science as a category of public and popular interest was not eclipsed; when we turn to the Wakefield Mechanics' Institution, where both Balfour and Dawson appeared in 1865, we can see more balanced programming.[48] The 1865 season included twenty-one lectures, ranging from "The Age of the Great Reptiles" and "On the Colouring Principles of Coal Tar" to biographical lectures on Samuel Johnson, John Milton, Lord William Russell, and Henry VIII. Two lectures explored the prehistory of man, and Edmund Wheeler led his listeners through "an inquiry respecting the rational and intellectual powers of animals, and their instinctive faculties as compared with man." All but two of the named lecturers were on the formal "Lists of Lecturers," and one of those two, the Rev. Hugh Stowell Brown, was a well-known reformer and lecturer in Liverpool; all but four—Balfour and Wheeler, from London; Brown, from Liverpool; and Dawson, from Birmingham—were from the region. Wakefield, like the other institutions examined here, was still resolutely local and regional in its programming. For all of these institutions, the reliance upon and preference for regional speakers would begin to modify only after about 1870.

Filling a Single Lecture Season: Five Snapshots of 1863/4

A more revealing picture emerges when we compare a single season—1863/4—across several well-established institutions: the Midland Institute, the Leeds Phil.-&-Lit., the Newcastle Lit.-&-Phil., the Ulverston Mechanics' Institute, and the Hartley Institute. By 1864, the Midland, Leeds, and Newcastle institutions were all experienced hands at the provision of knowledge-based culture, not only locally but also regionally; the Ulverston Mechanics' Institute was five years old and buoyed by a not entirely justified optimism; and the Hartley Institute was a year old and tentatively claiming its space as "an unquestionable, though, perhaps, in many respects, a silent influence on the mental culture of the town and neighbourhood."[49]

We begin with the more established institutions. As we saw in the previous chapter, the Leeds Phil.-&-Lit. had slowly begun its move away from lectures solely by and for members; by 1864, the governing committee had opened up programming to selected "men of stature from a distance" and also increased the society's attractions to suburban families through its holiday "juvenile" lectures. This season, six of the seventeen lectures were "juvenile," all in the sciences; most of the eleven "adult" lectures were also singularly serious in nature, ranging from the emerging fields of anthropology, archaeology, and ethnography to geology and physics, and delivered by men who among them sported a veritable alphabet of credentialing, with six RSAs, four FLS or FSAs, three MAs, and one FRGS. The single biographical lecture was on Roger Bacon; the single historical lecture was by local archaeologist Thomas Wright, "The History of Leeds before the Norman Conquest"; and a general lecture on the institution, by the local Rev. Thomas Hincks, asked listeners to consider "The Relation of the Philosophical and Literary Society, and Kindred Institutions, to the Intellectual Want of a Large Manufacturing and Commercial Town."[50] The Phil.-&-Lit. was still only cautiously entering the world of the popular lecture, still wedded to the idea of producing new knowledge rather than disseminating established knowledge. Wright's history lecture followed that established model, as did naturalist Alfred Russel Wallace's "The Varieties of Man in the Malay Archipelago" and geographer Charles T. Beke's "The Sources of the Nile, and on the Main Requisites for Their Final Determination."[51]

Newcastle, too, chose its own path. Alone of all its peers, it remained wedded to the course of lectures, claiming a space that regarded knowledge-based culture as both a venue for popular content and an opportunity for serious and deep exploration. These courses were regarded as "miscellaneous," in the contemporary use of the word, because they were delivered by "a host of thinkers and workers, … the leading representatives of the principal divisions of discovery and thought." Short series of up to six lectures each formed a string of what might be understood as unconnected minicourses rather than a semester-long course in a single topic. In 1863/4, its offerings included six on chemistry, four on physical geography, four on ornamental art, three on German literature, and half a dozen on the philosophy of mathematics. George Dawson delivered three biographical lectures (on Samuel Johnson, Erasmus, and Martin Luther), while professor Thomas King Greenbank delivered a series of three on oratory and elocution.[52] All told, forty-nine lectures were delivered by fourteen speakers, only one of whom—local man Percy Westmacot, speaking on "Hydraulic Machinery"— gave merely one lecture. The Society had introduced family season tickets in 1861, so successfully that within a few years the governing committee doubled its ticket prices in order to keep the demand under control; even then, as the Society's historian writes, "when in 1866, Mr. J. A. Froude gave three lectures upon 'The Times of Erasmus and Luther,' the room was packed full half-an-hour before the time for the lecture, and the audience overflowed into the hall, and so crowded it and the staircase as to make access to the building from the street all but impossible."[53] This emphasis upon short courses rather than stand-alone lectures was not based on the sense that only "charlatans" offered a program of knowledge within sixty or ninety brief minutes; instead, it reflected the institution's own conviction that what had worked so successfully in the past, attracting "men from a distance" who would otherwise be reluctant to embark on a journey so far from London, had by mid-century become a badge of local and lovable character. Watson would recount in his 1897 history that, since its founding in 1793, 140 series of lectures had been delivered, each offering between 6 and 30 lectures, and linked this local preference to the ongoing efforts to found a college in Newcastle that would "embrace every department of literature, and natural and mental science," efforts that resulted in the establishment of a College of Physical Sciences in 1871 and, six decades later, the University of Newcastle.[54]

The newer societies—the Midland Institute, Ulverston, and Hartley (Southampton)— delivered programs that reflected their own growing pains. The first of these, by now already outgrowing its purpose-built rooms, took seriously its responsibilities as the center of the region rather than the city. In 1864, the Midland was still almost wholly reliant on local talent, much of it delivered without compensation, and its programming included a number of local worthies: J. H. Chamberlain, Samuel Timmins, Sebastian Evans, and George Dawson grounded the season in literature and the arts, while other Birmingham men filled out the programming with offerings in architecture and travel, and two local men of science delivered five lectures on chemistry and physics. The few "lecturers from a distance" included Robert Owen, FRS, who gave a series of four lectures on "The Classification, Geographical Distribution, and Geological Relations of the Class Mammals," and industrial artist and designer Christopher L. Dresser, who delivered a pair of lectures on nature and ornament entitled "The Leaf and the Flower." While the subjects of the season were generally more complex and intellectually framed than those delivered in 1852 at the Birmingham Polytechnic Institute—the amiable reminiscences of a trip to Switzerland had been replaced by "The Aymara Indians of Peru and Bolivia," while "An Hour with the Poets" had given way to "The Three Centenaries of Shakespeare"— this season illustrates how difficult it might be for an institution to leave behind its dependence upon local good will, to move from an aspirational provider of the most up-to-date names and faces to a recognized center of "intellectual power and literary acquirements."[55]

Two other institutions help illuminate these difficulties. The Ulverston Lecture and Scientific Association, grandly staking out an aspirational field of labor, was in its fifth year in 1864. Its season of eighteen lectures included a few well-known names: Dawson and Greenbank, who also appeared at Newcastle in this season, delivered lectures on "Ill-Used Men" (Dawson) and "Readings from Shakespeare" (Greenbank); the Rev. Hugh Stowell Brown spoke on "Common Sense"; and meteorologist and balloonist James Glaisher—whose reliably entertaining lectures had already become a staple of popular science lecturing, and who would appear at the Hartley Institute this season as well— delivered his lecture on "Ballooning." The balance of the season was filled with a raft of local men, all but one of whom donated their services. Of the thirteen gratis lectures, ten were the only lectures listed for the speakers. Their offerings ranged from "A Visit to Antwerp," "Wants: Real and Imaginary," and "Cardinal Wolsey" to "Lord Bacon" and "Macbeth." Despite its formal name as a scientific institution, only four lectures—Glaisher's "Ballooning," phrenologist Spencer T. Hall's "Origin, History, and Destiny of a Drop of Blood," the Rev. W. Till's "Geology, and Its Practical Results," and the Rev. H. Field's rather old-fashioned "Natural History, Illustrated by the Magic Lantern"—addressed topics in or adjacent to the sciences. The report for this season claimed that these lectures, all "of a high class," were not uniformly "successful from a pecuniary view, but intellectually they were so." While the institute could attract and pay for the big names of this season, its tenuous hold on survival was suggested by its low number of subscribers (122, including 5 honorary, 12 ladies, 12 apprentices, and 93 ordinary) and a discussion class that "from some unexplained cause ... gradually dwindled into oblivion."[56] It reported lectures only in the 1864 season, and disappears from view after that year.

Our final example, Hartley, presents a somewhat sober but unequivocally more successful counterpoint to Ulverston. In its first annual report, the honorary secretary reported that "the Hartley Institution is gradually coming to be looked on as the recognised centre of all associations. If the Institution had been of no further service during this the first year of its organization, than to gather all these associations together within its walls, the Council would have, on these grounds alone, reasonable cause for congratulation."[57] The institution, founded through a generous grant with the specific goal of becoming a space for university education, took a cautious approach to programming in order not to outstrip its resources. Its first year was a season of stand-alone lectures, despite the council's view of "isolated lectures on literary and scientific subjects" as providing "so imperfect an idea of their subject as to be of but very limited utility for educational purposes."[58] Yet, this first season was remarkable in its scope and level of sophistication: reflecting the institution's founding goals, its seventeen lectures were largely delivered by well-known names in the sciences, including naturalist Philip Henry Gosse (recovering his reputation after the disastrous 1857 publication of *Omphalos*), James Glaisher, Benjamin Waterhouse Hawkins, Edwin Lankester, Sir John Lubbock, and John Henry Pepper. The Rev. J. M. Bellew delivered literary lectures on Milton and Goldsmith, and the Royal Army's Captain Drayson spoke on "The Weapons of the Modern Artillerist." These latter pieces offered a cursory balance to the sciences. The reserved tone of its first report notwithstanding, the Hartley Institution—to become Hartley University College in 1902, and the University of Southampton fifty years later—appeared free of the widespread dependence on local and gratis lecturers. Founded generously and with a specific path forward to university status, it provided the same center for knowledge-based culture as its peers, but in a more organized, less choppy form that marked it as both significantly more modern—it secured and paid for the services of the most up-to-date science speakers—and more intentional than institutions that had not been fortunate enough to leapfrog over the years of financial worry, audience attrition, demographic change, and competing pressures from critics and supporters alike to be all things to all people.

"Noteworthy Material for Thought": Debate and Discussion at Mid-Century

In 1861, the editor of the *British Controversialist* posed a question that specifically linked the lecture circuit with the world of debate and discussion: "It is often a matter of legitimate curiosity with members of literary societies, and indeed with reflective men in general: What are our lecturers about to do, and what are our literary institutes of various sorts about to present to the audiences that assemble in them during the winter season? There can be little doubt that if we knew the men who are to instruct the public from the platform, and the matters upon which they are to prelect, that we could form a fair idea of the general culture to which they may appeal."[59] These questions signaled the extent to which many young men, members of discussion and debating societies embedded within larger institutions or operating as small independent mutual improvement sites, believed that their own work was an extension and even a deepening of the knowledge-based culture of the lecture society. The mutual bonds between these branches of culture were also increasingly acknowledged and supported by the *Journal*, which occasionally compiled lists of topics for discussion and debate based upon reports submitted by clubs that were supported by Union affiliates. In the analysis that follows, the lists of questions for discussion and debate are drawn from twenty years of the *Controversialist*, the 1862 list compiled and printed by the Society of Arts, the affiliate reports within the *Journal*, the topics listed in Frederic Rowton's 1850 *The Debater*, and the records of one middle-class debating society, the Birmingham and Edgbaston Debating Society, whose members routinely numbered among the elite of the city.[60] Nearly 1,000 items were presented for discussion and debate at these sites or within these publications, and they help us flesh out an important, if much less public, aspect of the ecosystem of knowledge-based culture. This analysis is necessarily male: as we will see in Chapter 5, it was not until about 1870 that women began to create these same spaces for themselves, in some cases forming women-only debating societies and in others, especially in spaces like the emerging provincial colleges, dominating the leadership and membership of student and hobby societies. At mid-century, however, "the ladies," however young and ardent, were largely confined to the audience or the refreshments table.

The undisputed leader within this area of "argument culture" was the *Controversialist*, a national journal that appeared for over two decades (1850–72) and whose editors constantly reiterated that controversy, "far from being a wrangling contentiousness, and an opinionated, self-satisfied anxiety to cavil, … is a reasoning and a reasonable exertion of human thought" and "a justifiable educational agency."[61] Its interest in the work of the lecture season often included informative details that would help its readers appreciate the bona fides of a speaker: for example, in 1864 it noted that in addition to the well-known George Dawson, George Grossmith, and Hugh Stowell Brown, the Faversham Institute's season included a lecture on "Heat" by mineralogist Robert Hunt, professor at the Government School of Mines, whose extensive credentials—probably already familiar to regular lecture-goers—were reprinted for readers less likely to afford season tickets.[62]

Michael Wolff's analysis of the editorial decisions made by proprietor J. A. Cooper and editor Samuel Neil suggests that the overall profile of the young men in their late teens and twenties who formed the readership of this journal was primarily Anglican, urban rather than rural (even when "urban" simply signified a mid-sized town rather than a village), generally engaged in some branch of manufacturing and commerce, fearlessly curious, and convinced that they were as capable as their social and educational betters of debating sensitive topics.[63] Its mostly unsectarian

Christianity was compatible with an "editorial commitment to impartiality," inviting readers and contributors to debate the merits and problems of a broad selection of religious, philosophical, and political questions. As Wolff shows, the confidence of these self-improving readers increased steadily over the two decades of the journal, an increase that can be seen in the growing complexity and contemporaneity of the topics suggested by the editors. The wholly imaginary "Is an Hereditary Monarchy Preferable to an Elective One?" in 1850 gave way to the more concrete and practical question, "Is an Hereditary House of Legislature Desirable?" in 1869, while "Is Crime Insanity?" in 1857 yielded to the more specific "Is the Law of Lunacy Founded on Correct Principles?" in 1862. In this, the editors and readers mutually reinforced the growing emphasis on energetic discussion as a formative part of citizenship. They also reiterated at every turn the need to ensure "mutual friendship and communication" even when "opinion necessarily varies."[64]

The *Controversialist's* assertion that "controversy cultures reflectiveness"[65] was not merely a justification for the journal's existence, it was also a decided rebuttal to contemporary political, social, and educational norms. While institute founders and committee members generally barred not only lectures and library acquisitions but also debate and discussion on topics of religion and politics, younger members in particular found "restriction as to the subjects of discourse" both irritating and patronizing.[66] Some groups, like those in the Manchester Athenaeum, used subterfuge to introduce banned topics: as early as 1850, it was noted with some asperity that the members of the Athenaeum Essay and Discussion Society would dodge the formal prohibition against political discussion by simply notifying members of a debate on an "undefined" subject, a label that was widely recognized as code for topics that were formally proscribed.[67] Older and more socially networked members of these restrictive societies often simultaneously belonged to smaller and more exclusive groups with no such limits, thus both policing the overall community of knowledge-based culture and enjoying freedom of discussion within their vetted subcommunity. In Leeds, for example, members of the Phil.-&-Lit. and other local institutions founded the Leeds Conversation Club specifically as an institution for the debate of local and national issues; membership was limited to twelve, with each hosting the monthly meeting in turn, thus keeping their discussions private and avoiding "debating society dialectics."[68] Others flirted with complete freedom of expression but drew back after "social harmony" appeared to be threatened; the Halifax Mechanics' Institution, for example, repealed its "no politics, no religion" rule after it absorbed the Halifax Mutual Improvement Society in 1849, but then reinstated it after less than two years when controversy shaded into conflict.[69] A decade later, the Middleton Literary Institute found itself embroiled in a minor tempest after Conservative MP Algernon Egerton canceled his appearance "because I was informed, on what I considered good authority, that the society consisted mainly of persons of extreme political opinions, and that no churchmen and few respectable persons belonged to or supported it."[70] In the case of the Blaydon and Stella Mechanics' Institute, the conflict over an "infidel" lecture was so intense that a spin-off institution, "under the patronage of Lord Ravensworth," attempted unsuccessfully to siphon off members.[71]

No matter how discordant, however, politics and religion were consistently important to these young men, and in fact helped define the world of the discussion club. In many ways, this aspect of knowledge-based culture—linked through a kingdom-wide journal and lists of common topics for discussion—was more national than the world of the mid-century lecture, where regional differences and preferences continued to temper programming decisions. Many of the more than 900 questions collected here appear across several sources: Rowton's list of debate topics fed into the editorial decisions of the *Controversialist*, and the young men reading the *Controversialist* pursued these topics in their own clubs; they, in turn, forwarded many of these subjects to the *Journal* when affiliates were asked to provide questions for the Society's published lists. As we will see, below, in several cases these topics were also widely considered by popular lecturers.

Appropriate Topics for Discussion and Debate

As with the earliest attempts by Hudson and others to categorize lecture subjects, these sources often used a limited number of categories as they disaggregated individual discussion topics. The *Controversialist* separated its offerings into nine categories: Religion; Philosophy; History; Politics; Social Economy, &c.; Literature; Education; Science; and "The Topic," a question of current importance. The *Journal* used a similar but not identical set of categories: History; Politics; Political Economy; Social Science and the Amendment of the Law; Ethics; Education, Science, &c; Literature; and Miscellaneous. Other sources, including Rowton's *Debater*, used no categories at all. In this analysis, therefore, these subjects have been coded with the same categories as the lectures, above, with one exception: because the number of discussions on topics in philosophy and religion—subjects rare in lectures during this period—are so much more significant than any other subset of mental science, they have been pulled out into a separate subcategory. Figure 3.9 shows how topics spread out over these categories.

The vast majority of questions—almost half of the 926 total—fell into the social sciences. Within this category, all but three fell within the fields of biography (18), economics (84), education (39), history (114), and national progress (151). Within the 188 topics in current events, all but 9 fell within the two subcategories of politics (117) and foreign affairs (62). Within "Philosophy/Religion," 98 topics fell under the category of religion and 62 under philosophy. Most striking, of course, is the almost complete invisibility of the sciences in these figures. The mid-century compendia of printed lectures had moved away from the sciences because they were increasingly difficult to illustrate or bring to life. For debate and discussion groups, the problem was a different one: science was not a subject for discussion, but rather a fixed presentation of fact, however it might be dressed up as entertainment. Even the most surprising new discoveries in geology and astronomy were guided by established principles of scientific investigation and assimilation. In contrast, topics in history, biography, ethnography, literature, philosophy, and religion, as well as newsworthy events, could be picked apart, parsed, and reassembled. Thus, while these subjects lacked the "mental

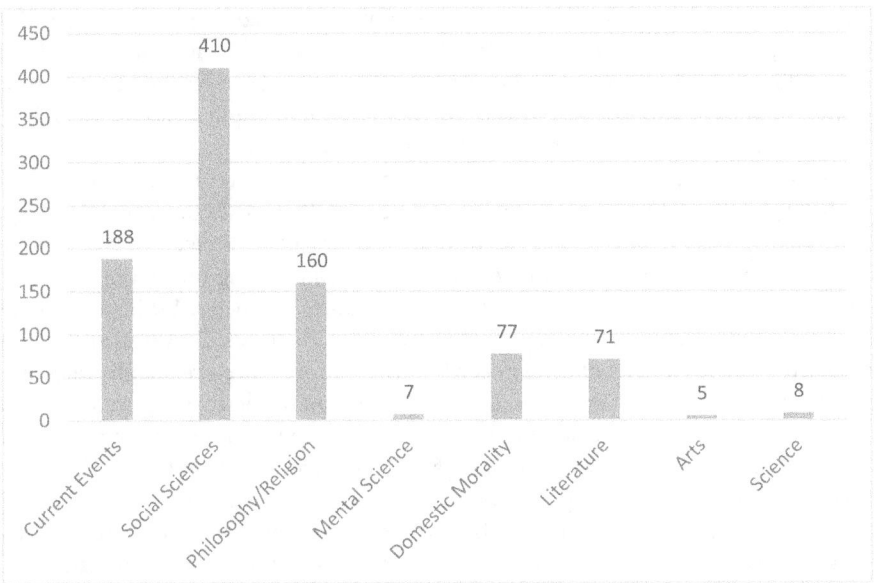

Figure 3.9 Subject categories for discussion and debate.

Sources: *British Controversialist*, 1850–72; Society of Arts, *Subjects for Discussion Classes in Institutions*, 1862; "Proceedings," *J. Soc. Arts*, 1850–1872; Frederic Rowton, *The Debater: A New Theory of the Art of Speaking*, 2nd. edn., 1850; Birmingham and Edgbaston Debating Society, *Annual Reports* 1850–1870; *Birmingham Mirror* (January–December 1866); *Birmingham Mutual* (January–December 1870).

grandeur and dignity" of mathematics and the physical sciences, they provided almost unlimited scope for the disciplined argument that characterized "controversy."[72]

What were the subjects most wrangled over during these decades? While Wolff refers to "that perpetual blister, marriage with a deceased wife's sister," the most popular questions were both more immediate and less risqué.[73] Many were chosen to help provide context for contemporary political and imperial issues. Was war justifiable? Four general debates on this question were recorded at mid-century, while two debates at the Birmingham and Edgbaston Debating Society delved into the specific mismanagement of the Crimea, and one volume of the *Controversialist* was devoted to the publication of members' disquisitions on that war.[74] Should slavery be abolished, and how? Young men considered this question in the context of the American Civil War several times between 1862 and 1864.[75] Debate questions attempted to energize even the most staid of topics: while lecture-goers heard nearly a dozen lectures on the rather snoozy history and principles of banking and commerce, debaters focused instead on the contentious plans to repeal the 1844 Bank Act and the potential benefits and dangers of a £1 bank note.[76] Similarly, while lecture audiences heard about spiritualism only in comic form, debaters earnestly considered more serious questions about the existence of "spiritual manifestations."[77] Even theoretical questions were framed in ways that assumed discussants were widely read and could both marshal knowledge in several fields and also defend their analyses. "Is the Spendthrift more

Injurious to Society than the Miser?" for example, required a speaker to consider issues of political economy and psychology, while "Do we, or did our ancestors of the 'good old time,' enjoy a greater amount of social happiness?" necessitated a rehearsal of history, philosophy, and economics. "Is Public Opinion a sufficient rule of Right?" incorporated issues of law, democracy, rhetoric, and morality, while "Is exclusive monopoly a greater evil than reckless competition?" combined economics and ethics.[78]

Institute secretaries knew from experience that literary lectures and readings were easy to mount and guaranteed to draw a crowd of interested but not terribly critical listeners: of the lectures reported in the *Journal* during this period, 74 were on Shakespeare and another 112 were on other poets or poetry. While a similarly large number of debate questions focused on literary topics, however, they were couched in comparative rather than contemplative form. A lecturer might venture a gentle opinion, as when "The poets, male and female, of the present day, were glanced at; the lecturer leaning to the notion that the female poets have the supremacy in inspiration."[79] In contrast, debaters were asked to vigorously defend the relative value of pairs of writers: Browning and Tennyson, Shakespeare and Milton, Milton and Homer, Dryden and Pope, Byron and Burns, Byron and Scott, Chatterton and Cowper, Chaucer and Spencer, Mrs. Howitt and Mrs. Hemans, Tennyson and Longfellow. In list form, it seemed as though an editor or club secretary simply shook names into a hat and pulled out two at random, but these discussions required a facility with literary and rhetorical analysis, not just personal taste.[80]

Other preferences linking lecture audiences and debaters emerged in the field of history. Just as dozens of lectures took listeners back to the sixteenth and seventeenth centuries, 29 of these 926 reported discussion topics focused on the Tudor-Stuart period. One correspondent in the *Controversialist* gently mocked the tendency among these clubs to go back to the same well: "How many versions have we had of the character of Cromwell?" he asked.[81] The answer, among these sources, was eight. Indeed, so popular was Cromwell that Rowton's *Debater* wrote out a detailed script on this topic, providing points of argument and response for thirteen participants and including a bibliography of nine volumes of Cromwell's speeches and biographies. The speeches provided by Rowton exemplified the earnest gentility that he argued was necessary to the development of boys into men: the penultimate speaker, for example, in disagreeing with his previous discussants, was to avoid insults and instead model "clearness and propriety": "Sir, Neither the indignation, nor the eloquence, of the speaker who has just addressed us shall, if I know it, mislead my judgment on this matter: I am yet unconvinced that Cromwell's is a character to be admired, and I am about to venture a few words upon that side of the question."[82]

Controversy and Competition

This emphasis on gentlemanly disagreement was aspirational, not actual: Rowton's advice was widely ignored, for Cromwell as for other popular topics from this period of history. For example, a multipart debate in the *Controversialist* on the character of Queen Elizabeth included the somewhat prurient suggestion that her reputation as "virgin queen" was as self-evidently undeserved as her ranking among the kingdom's most able rulers.[83] In stark contrast, George Dawson's "Good Queen Bess" lecture, a perennial favorite, poked fun at the royal nose, gently mocked those who preferred the unintelligent prettiness of Mary, Queen of Scots, and then drew his audience along with him in what became a rousing celebration of English spirit and world power: "She knew the whole world hated England. The hatred of the world is our dowry; we have it now, and we ever shall have it. This nation was never loved yet, and never will be; and if this nation be wise, it will trouble its wise head very little about the love of the world."[84] Dawson, in typical fashion, sprinkled his own potentially contentious opinions over his listeners, but he did not ask them to choose among perspectives and then defend their choices. Debate participants, in contrast, engaged in a kind of secular proof-texting that was highly performative. They reveled in the win, even when a club's formal rules urged debaters not to vote on "merely abstract or general questions." Societies of older debaters tended to remain "highly respectable," especially when performing in front of "numerous ladies," as evidenced by an 1853 report of the Birmingham Debating Society.[85] Younger debaters, however, ignored the advice to "leave the discussion to produce its effects on individual minds," and instead incorporated into their performances "grand sarcastic allusions to an inability to supply brains, as well as arguments, scarifyings, and 'cuttings up,' over which dummy members will chuckle, whatever may be the emotions of the victim, and the charge of sinister motives will be craftily insinuated or rudely blurted out."[86] As a result, audiences of friends, sweethearts, and fellow members voted not only on the rhetorical ability of the speakers but also on the extent to which these speakers had "proven" the inherent worth of the side they had represented and had bested their opponents. In such verbal war, one of the most important skills was the extent to which a debater could step just up to the line that separated gentlemanly from ruffianly behavior without delivering an unforgivable insult; such a skill was not required for the lecturer, whose focus instead was on avoiding "forced expression, the want of perfect naturalness, and the use of long words."[87]

This jostling for victory concerned many Union affiliates when the Society of Arts began formally to consider supporting institutional discussion classes and clubs. "Depend on it, the meetings will take their character from a few of the most active members," reported Blake, who warned that while the strong opinions of young men would impart "zest and vivacity" to gatherings, this energy would come at the sacrifice of "some of the amenities of discussion."[88] We can see this sacrifice, as well as the energy with which lecturers and discussants could approach a complex question, when we turn to a single question over "the plurality of worlds" and whether there was intelligent life on planets other than earth.

Exploring the Many Claims to Knowledge-Based Culture: Lectures and Debates on "the plurality of worlds"

In 1853, the Rev. William Whewell published, anonymously, *Of the Plurality of Worlds: An Essay*, following it with *Dialogue on the Plurality of Worlds* under his own name in 1854. He repudiated here the main thesis of his 1833 Bridgewater Treatise,

Astronomy and General Physics, in which he had argued that there was no reason to dismiss the idea of many inhabited worlds as incompatible with Christianity. The treatise was one work in a well-established body of philosophical debate that stretched back centuries, and in his 1854 essay he admitted that his contributions to this body of debate had helped persuade most Christians to accept the idea as a "natural" part of their faith. By the early 1850s, however, he had himself concluded that it was nearly impossible to support, theologically or scientifically, the idea of plural worlds—that is, worlds inhabited by beings that were similar to man. His anonymous book drew immediate criticism. One of his critics, the Rev. David Brewster, not only reviewed Whewell's book at length but also published his own argument supporting the arguments in favor of plural worlds in his 1854 *More Worlds than One: The Creed of the Philosopher and the Hope of the Christian*.[89]

This dispute, complicated and often arcane, riveted the world of knowledge-based culture, asking observers to draw on their reserves of theology and science. While many well-known figures—Adam Sedgwick, Sir John Herschel, T. H. Huxley, and John Henry Newman—took up the cudgels, so too did a number of obscure lecturers and debaters. Here we turn to the lectures and debates on this topic that were reported in the *Journal* and enumerated in the *Controversialist*. The latter devoted four issues to a lengthy debate, "Is the Notion of a Plurality of Worlds Consonant with Science and Revelation?" while the former listed four individual lectures on this topic in 1856 and 1857. One of these lectures, "A Plurality of Worlds" by Unitarian minister Edward Higginson, was based upon a collection of his lectures on the controversy delivered in Wakefield and published in 1855 as *Astro-Theology; or, The Religion of Astronomy*.[90]

Higginson dedicated his published lectures to his congregation in Wakefield, describing them as "earnest and successful votaries of Natural Science," "proficients in Literature and Art," and "Rational Christians." He launched his examination of the controversy by stating that Unitarians had a much easier time harmonizing nature and scripture than did Trinitarians, and much of his lecture focused on the theological stumbling blocks raised by both Whewell and Brewster.[91] Astronomy, properly conceived, he argued, has a "peculiar *religiousness*" stemming from the vastness of the universe, and he began his critique of both Whewell and Brewster by observing that each man was bound by his own orthodoxy—Whewell as an Anglican minister, Brewster as a minister in the Scottish Kirk—to an extent that prevented him from adequately addressing "that most interesting and ennobling question of scientific religion, the Plurality of Worlds."[92] Higginson briefly rehearsed the argument from analogy, that life on earth suggested "similar, but varied, arrangements in other planetary bodies." He also explored the counterargument, that lack of evidence of "similar, but varied" life indicated an absence of divine purpose elsewhere in the universe. His main focus, however, was on the knotty theological problem of salvation through Christ. "Do the intelligent beings who may be supposed to people other words, need a Redeemer, to do for them what Christ did for the inhabitants of this world?" he asked. "Can the Second Person of the Divine Trinity be believed to have made his incarnation and his expiatory sacrifice in each habitable world in succession?"[93] The idea that Christ was crucified on every possible habitable planet in a rapid sequence of suffering was repulsive to "the orthodox believer," who then retreated to an "astro-theology" that must reject any other habitable world. Higginson ignored the established scientific brilliance of both men and instead excoriated first Whewell, for "maintaining for man 'a nature and a place unique and incapable of repetition in the scheme of the universe,'" and then Brewster, for arguing not only that Christ's sacrifice "extended backwards ... and forwards" in time but also literally and figuratively swept across the universe to all planets "formed out of the same material element" as God's created earth. Both refused to consider "intelligent life" in any form except man. Whewell, "lively, dashing, and bold" in his prose, retreated into his safe orthodoxy, Higginson argued, while Brewster's "heavy" and "overstated" argument produced only a "humiliating" dogma worthy of "a child or a submissive servant of church creeds." "The truth is, that the realms of scientific thought and those of the distinctive orthodox theology, so called, have *nothing in common*," Higginson argued. As a Unitarian, free of that orthodox theology, Higginson protested that "we are involuntarily making [God] like ourselves, when we ignore the vast "diversities of condition" and "orders of being" that may have been "endowed with varied life, intelligence, and happiness."[94]

Higginson's language—despite his biographer's contention that "his preaching was not attractive"—was equally poetic and prosaic. Uncowed by the scientific expertise of his targets, he built from point to point in an argument that was primarily theological, but presumed a broad basic knowledge of geology, astronomy, and theology among his readers and listeners. He and they were bound by interest, curiosity, and careful attention to argument, which gave them the right and the responsibility to enter respectfully but not timidly into this intellectually thorny debate. When we turn to the *Controversialist*, we can see assumptions that are perhaps even higher, as the series of young men debating this topic in print strove to reconcile respectful controversy, "the life-blood from the heart of our social greatness," with their need to demonstrate not only cultural competence but also, effectively, cultural competition. They instantiated "the mutual desire for self-improvement" but also scrambled to score a victory over their fellow improvers.

The debate, "Is the Notion of a Plurality of Inhabited Worlds Consonant with Science and Revelation?" opened in 1856 with "Philalethes" leading the charge. While noting that any intelligent life on other planets would be "of no practical utility" due to the vast distances of space, he acknowledged that this debate "opens to us a grand field of the exercise of our reasoning powers."[95] He pivoted almost immediately to a grand field of imagination, urging his readers to dream not only of the "boundless expanse" of the world, from its yellow corn to its "thousand chimneys," but also of the "heaving bosom" of the ocean and "heaven's pale queen," the moon. Subsequent debaters would suggest that Philalethes padded his lecture with description to hide his lack of argument—he "has produced a very *pictorial* but unargumentative paper"[96]— but he introduced the important argument from analogy and provided streams of numbers to establish the mathematical relationships of planetary gravity and temperature. Reminding his readers that geologists had shown the vast age of the earth but also that scripture provided evidence for the world's mere 6,000 years of existence, he turned to the nature of God to introduce his main—albeit late—argument: we cannot imagine God alone and solitary; we cannot imagine the angels without a sphere in the heavens; and we certainly cannot imagine that God would limit his own infinite nature to the creation of a single earth and its people. This brief opening salvo, he argued somewhat defensively, was merely "to lay down the groundwork of an argument upon which others might build, rather than to raise up an elaborate superstructure of our own."

His respondent, "H.D.L.," who would acknowledge in a later number that "we were so hurried" that the premises in his negative position were "not very accurately" articulated, immediately redefined the terms of the debate. "Inhabited," he argued, meant "inhabited by man," and the question he sought to examine was not "Is there a plurality of worlds?" but rather the more specific question, "Is the supposition that there are more worlds than one inhabited by men, consistent with science and revelation?" He argued vigorously that this supposition was, indeed, not consistent.[97] Geology, he argued, "tells us most distinctly that God *has* bestowed particular care and attention upon man," showing us that the vast expanses of time before man have not been wasted but have instead led inexorably to an earth prepared for humans. H.D.L. quoted from both Whewell and Brewster to demonstrate his familiarity with the controversy, and drew as well from Dionysius Lardner, Thomas Dick, and others who had written extensively on this debate. His main weapon in the fight against a plurality of worlds was, like Whewell's, built around the Trinity: any life imbued with reason would necessarily also be "liable to sin," and therefore would inevitably require a redeemer. "Christ must thus have gone to all these different and numerous globes for which our opponents would claim inhabitants, offered to each the same salvation as he did to us, giving them the same revelation, received the same persecution, and endured the same death again and again! How unreasonable!" More reasonable, he argued, was the fact that "the preservation of life" requires "air, moisture, equable temperature, and a certain density of matter," and that no planet but earth could "satisfy these conditions." Deploying exclamation marks with energy, he described the sun—"We hope our opponents will pass a pleasant winter there!"—and Neptune—"900 times colder than our temperature!"—and turned at last to the immense density of Jupiter before moving on to the "fixed stars." Having redefined the question, quoted a variety of authorities in the sciences, and dropped in phrases in Latin and French to demonstrate his cosmopolitan approach to the argument, he retired with one final exclamation point, "in the knowledge and love of our Creator!"

The debate over this controversy would continue for several more months, although the arguments themselves would quickly give way to "remarks of a personal nature," couched in lofty prose. In the next installment, for example, "Threlkeld"—who had suggested that Queen Elizabeth's sexual history was worthy of note—slashed H.D.L. unmercifully for his prose, his logic, and his theology. "H.D.L.'s article is sadly confused," he argued; "We scarcely know what to think of him. ... He makes strange statements, and so misrepresents facts. Has he studied astronomy or geology? Or has he only read over the essay of that 'anonymous author who so electrified us all,' to prepare himself for this debate?"[98] H.D.L., he argued, "runs counter to all the opinions of philosophers and the discoveries of science" and takes "an imaginary tour through the planetary system," providing only an "absurd theory" unsupported by "the facts of science." Threlkeld's own rehearsal of the argument was tame, but it was clear that his goal was to remain just shy of "transgressing the bounds of moderation and decorum" and to avoid by only a hair's breadth the "violent outbursts of temper" and "excess of imprudence and recklessness" condemned by both H.D.L. and the *Controversialist* editors themselves.[99] He refused to engage with either the Trinitarian arguments or the geological arguments, instead dropping in poetry from Tupper, Thomson, and Pope; winning the rhetorical battle was clearly more important to him than engaging in the argument, however weakly articulated by H.D.L., and Threlkeld's deployment of literature as well as the occasional extract from contemporary journalism was, in his own eyes, a mark of polish and power.

Subsequent debaters were both tame and calm by comparison. "S.S." argued that it was possible to believe God had the power to create other inhabitable worlds while also believing that such creation was not necessary to the Divine,[100] while "L'Ouvrier" reminded readers that the debate was rightly over "the reasonableness of assigning to other spheres animated existence" rather than "the comparative truthfulness of arguments" contained in the books of Whewell and Brewster.[101] L'Ouvrier marshaled the "facts" of geology and physics, "so tangible, so real, … court[ing] investigation with a free open-handedness," avoiding rhetorical flourish but dropping in occasional phrases in French and Latin to demonstrate his intellectual breadth. "It is usual, in scientific inquiry, to argue from the known and admitted to the unknown and disputed; and to reverse this principle for the support of an anti-pluralist theory is derogatory to the mental acumen of *British Controversialists*," he scolded. "Vincat Veritum," following L'Ouvrier, dismissed Threlkeld's arguments as "poetic phantasy" while observing that neither side had added any new knowledge to the debate, and—citing Alexander von Humboldt, Robert Chambers, and others—argued that the limited facts of science actually supported the negative side. H.D.L., awarded the final installment of the debate, admitted that "we have been assailed most vehemently" and charged Threlkeld with "compound[ing] a most extravagant dose of nonsense and error."[102] His powers of rational argument exhausted, however, he advised his opponents "to read Edgar Poe's story of Hans P., in which they will find full particulars for making a journey up there. Let them only starve themselves before they go, that their consequent leanness and lightness may counterbalance Jupiter's gravity!"[103]

This debate, classified by the editors under "Philosophy," necessarily also involved a working knowledge of theology and the sciences, garnished with the relishes of poetry and contemporary fiction. Each of these installments, like Higginson's lectures, presumed a broad, if shallow, familiarity with recent intellectual developments. Higginson's lectures were developed within a context of conservative heterodoxy, and his implied relationship to his audiences was one of mutual respect and trust: his purpose was to communicate clearly the messages of the universe refracted through his Unitarianism, to show "how musically those two divine voices sound," rather than to ask his listeners to assess the various iterations of Christianity and declare a victor.[104] The young men in the pages of the *Controversialist*, in contrast, wrote for one another and for others just like themselves; they enjoyed the intellectual combat and the clear emotional pleasure of besting a "fellow-labourer in the field of self-culture."[105] Even when they lacked complete command of their subject matter, their rhetorical manners gave each debater a pleasing feeling of superiority over his fellow discussants and the readers of the journal.

While the worlds of lecture and debate were separate but connected, this *"viva voce"* collection of discussion and lecture had very little overlap with the actual examinations set and administered by the Society of Arts. The breadth of discussion questions and lectures on, for example, the Tudor-Stuart period was infinitely richer than the narrow expectations of examiners on the same historical period: in 1863, these examination questions included "What were the chief causes of the wars of the Roses?" "Give, with dates, a short outline of Queen Elizabeth's Reign," and "What were the grievances for which the Commons demanded redress in the Petition of Right?"[106] In English literature, comparative questions about the "greater poet" were absent, and even the brief section on Shakespeare focused only on close reading of short passages from *Julius Caesar, Macbeth*, and *As You Like It*. Examination questions were, as today, testing content; the discussion and lecture topics were, instead, inviting participants into a broader conversation in which they were expected, in the case of discussions, to develop and defend opinions and preferences supported by evidence, and in the case of lectures, to absorb those opinions as presented in an entertaining form.

However, entertainment—whether through verbal jousting or the well-paced lecture—was not the all-in-all. Many also privileged the lecture and the debate over the examination because audiences and debaters required no credentials to be part of "the discussion of the great questions which affect the interests of every man, woman, and child."[107] Individuals could participate in this kind of citizenship without an MA or an FRS behind their names; indeed, noted one correspondent to *The Mutual* in 1870, "we might even gain more by *viva voce* conversation with a mind of second rate order, than we could from the very highest intellect through the silent conversation of books."[108] This persistent emphasis on orality, previously associated primarily with the illiterate or poorly educated, underscored the conviction that knowledge-based culture was broader than examinations, texts, or classrooms. Chester had sketched a castle-in-the-air picture of the quintessential civic institute; Langford had imagined the hybrid lecture; now discussants and debaters claimed access to "the action of one mind upon another" in a plenitude of forms.[109] The exuberant possibilities invited readers, writers, and speakers into "that system of mutual dependence" wherein they could help one another to exercise "the loftier faculties of the soul."[110]

Moving into the 1870: Shifting Focus, Shifting Content

Despite these popular preferences, and in parallel with the *Journal*'s reporting on affiliate lecture programming, the *British Controversialist* slowly reduced its reports of the mutual improvement and discussion societies that had formed such an important part of its editorial work during its first decade. Wolff speculates that "the *Controversialist*'s plans for creating a momentum of interest in the magazine as a repository of such reports had not succeeded," echoing the same phenomenon recorded in the pages of the *Journal*. In neither case did the editors openly proclaim an end to these reports. The very energy with which knowledge-based culture was pursued across the kingdom suggests strongly that the decline in reporting was an editorial decision based on a changing readership rather than a paucity of material. In the case of the *Journal*, we can see a deliberate shift toward specialized examinations even as it published its lecture lists and lists of discussion questions; in the *Controversialist*, as Wolff notes, the types of questions submitted by readers moved from the elementary ("What is the best German Grammar?") to the specialized ("What were the colour, form, and material of the ancient Roman mourning costume?"), and the focus in "Our Societies" shifted away from what the editor described as "minor 'literary' Institutions more or less public in their character, which it were useless, not to say impossible ... to particularize"[111] and instead began to focus on the web of institutions in Manchester, Birmingham, Leeds, and other large communities. Such overviews of individual cities and towns purported to show the connections between a variety of institutions bound in common pursuit of knowledge-based culture, but in reality they privileged societies that were more complex, less ephemeral, and therefore presumably more important in the common pursuit of participatory citizenship than the smaller and more short-lived institution or club. Thus, "The Literary Societies of Birmingham" focused on the successes of the Midland Institute, outlining its curriculum, its subscription fees and examinations schedules, and its "series of attractive lectures," and noted that "the results of this elaborate machinery it is, of course, impossible thoroughly to estimate."[112] Similarly, "The Literary Societies of Manchester" enumerated that city's complex web of institutions that had facilitated a "revolution" in the spread of "civilization, intelligence, and culture" and had transformed "the obscure into the illustrious, the ignorant into the intelligent and cultivated, the naturally-minded into the spiritually-minded." Smaller societies remained but a tiny piece of this web, which was now, in the 1860s, dominated by "substantial institutions."[113]

This shift in coverage reflected the stabilization of this mid-century model of participatory citizenship and simultaneously presaged an imminent shift in the content and spread of knowledge-based culture. For twenty years, an aspirational model of "*be and do*" drew together hundreds and hundreds of institutions, clubs, and societies, disparate in membership and often defined by regional particularity, but also bound by a belief in the powers of the intelligent and striving individual to fully realize a common human potential. Young men groomed one another to examine, think, and persuade; family audiences supported speakers who addressed them with care and respect; committee members curated programming to incorporate broad fields of knowledge and contemporary events; educationists and institute officers praised these efforts as universal responses to the basic human right to voice and dignity. None of these efforts to privilege an aspirational community of strivers could completely hide the persistent inequalities that characterized Victorian society, however. As we will see in the next chapters, the continued spread of knowledge-based culture would fracture along renewed lines of class and access. The demise of the Union, on the one hand, and the *Controversialist*, on the other, opened up both local and national space for new discussions over education, entertainment, and the raft of institutions which now adopted as their stated mission "the betterment of mankind."

4

Professionalizing the Popular Lecture

A cultured intellect, even though it may be the result of studies that have no bearing upon a man's calling, ennobles him, while it increases his influence and enjoyment.[1]

The past chapters have focused on committees, educators, and critics within the world of knowledge-based culture. In this chapter, we will explore two significant developments: first, the increasingly assertive claims of the platform speaker as "a factor in civilisation that should always command support,"[2] and second, the development of new spaces for those speakers. Both of these developments were responses to the political and social pressures that altered the landscapes of popular education and consumer-driven entertainment after mid-century. Using the *Institute, and Lecturer's Gazette* [*ILG*], a monthly journal edited by Joseph Simpson, we will trace the ways in which the popular lecturer of mid-century, located primarily in "the institutes,"—the small mechanics', literary, and mutual improvement societies rather than the large purpose-built civic spaces—fought to claim new levels of status and power within the civic realm.[3] Their claims to professionalization, however, were ignored or resisted by the growing number of credentialed practitioners, the loosely networked men and women whose platform appearances in the large civic spaces were frequently an adjunct to rather than a substitute for other professional work. Thus, as we will see below, the ranks of the popular lecturer self-segregated into identifiable cliques: the "institute man" (and woman) whose lecture career was painstakingly built upon the demands of the popular platform, on the one hand, and the credentialed men and women who lectured in order to disseminate in easily digestible form the work of their own vocations, on the other. The former group, guided and celebrated by Simpson and his peers, itself fragmented further into "entertainers" and "educators," with entertainers claiming increasingly large pieces of the institute platform pie and educators bemoaning the decline in popular taste. As a result, we can identify at least three separate spheres of popular lecturing in the last decades of the century, each with its own set of aspirations and values: professional popular lecturers who entertained, professional popular lecturers who educated, and credentialed practitioners from other fields who provided lectures as a supplement to their more serious work. The first two were found primarily in the established mechanics' institutes and the newer suburban institutes, while the third populated both the established civic spaces and the new Sunday Lecture Society (SLS) and its many provincial kindred societies.

These emerging categories differed significantly from the three categories defined in 1859 by the Rev. G. W. Kitchin. Kitchin, himself an "amateur sapper and miner," had divided lecturers into "Official Lecturers," who were experts on a topic through education or practice; "Amateur Lecturers," who were motivated solely by personal interest or experience; and "Professional Lecturers, who treat it as their business," and whom Kitchin regarded as "showmen with oxyhydrogen microscopes, or perambulating monsters" whose profit-motive and "humbug" left them "beneath criticism."[4] "Official lecturers" mapped roughly onto the late-Victorian category of credentialed practitioners, while "amateur lecturers" continued to embrace the well-meaning sappers and miners. But "Professional Lecturers" in 1859 were charlatans, motivated only by a desire to part the listener from his money. Simpson, seeking to rescue this last group, reconfigured these categories and erected structures of professionalism emphasizing the centrality of the popular lecturer of every category to both individual and civic culture. Each of these groups was forced to respond to new structures of secondary and higher education, new models of political and social organization, and new modes of leisure. Each of these groups also sought to clearly define their own work in opposition to the wares of the untrained, the fatuous, or the vulgar—Kitchin's "Professional Lecturer," who was not professional at all.

The popular lecture as an artifact of participatory culture competed after mid-century with multiple vehicles for entertainment and improvement, vehicles that rendered the phenomenon of the popular lecture not just commonplace but, in many cases, significantly less attractive than other options. Its survival as a key part of the cultural landscape of the nineteenth century, by the late-Victorian period, appeared increasingly tentative. As we shall see, the popular lecture as an artifact would reemerge as a crucial piece of late-Victorian culture, but the pressures we will explore in this chapter would reshape its meaning, if not its form and content, in important ways.

"A Sort of Beautiful Reproach": The Changing Nature of Institutions

The most significant pressures on popular lecturing came from the changes affecting the mechanics' and literary institutions as a whole. The prototypical mid-century institute linked elementary and advanced classes for working-class men and women with general-interest lecture programming, rhetorically binding these two disparate strands of education and entertainment into a broadly defined ideal of knowledge-based culture built on three important assumptions. First, the working adults compensating for an inadequate childhood education were peculiarly driven not only to attend classes but also to absorb as much "general" programming as possible. Second, they and their economic betters shared a sense that this common intellectual pursuit, even when limited to silent audience participation, conferred a status that was caste-based and should be rigorously defended against those who chose not to join. And finally, such a pursuit would naturally help their city or town cultivate a deeper "appreciation and application of knowledge."[5] For two decades, as institutions added classes and clubs and developed their lecture programming, the link between education and entertainment was perceived as mutually supportive and relatively straightforward, with successful programming responding equally to all three of these foundational assumptions. Even as the Society of Arts reduced its active support of these efforts, substituting its examination system for earlier efforts to provide "eminent lecturers ... on a national scale," institutes continued to curate programming according to local needs and resources.[6]

This relatively brief period of calm was sufficient to ground a caste-based notion of participatory citizenship in the web of institutes that covered the country. By the mid-1860s, with the Education Act of 1870 an inevitability, institute committees, lecturers, and critics began to envision a more mature voluntary network of culture that could be erected on a state-supported foundation of elementary instruction. Institute classes would be more advanced, students more dedicated, lectures more sophisticated, programming more purposeful. Without the burden of providing remedial classes to overworked laborers, and having encouraged unserious subscribers to pursue amusements elsewhere, institutes could focus on the young men and women who would inevitably rise to positions of participatory citizenship in the form of active service to the town and the kingdom.

This dream quickly evaporated after 1870. The transfer of primary education relieved institutes of one burden but made more apparent the equally heavy task of providing secondary instruction to adolescents and young adults.[7] The two decades after the Elementary Education Act witnessed institutes struggling to fill the gaps that persisted long after school-leaving age. Many institutes, assessing available funding, privileged their classes over other programming, committing to "serious and systematic scientific and technical instruction" in evening classes that would funnel students into an expanding program of examinations offered not only by the Society of Arts but also by the YUMI and other unions of institutions.[8] Approximately 40 percent of the examination centers established by the Department of Science and Art in 1864 were located in existing mechanics' institutions, but the sheer numbers of examination candidates far outstripped the spaces available within the web of institutes; by 1899, these institutions comprised only 2 percent of the examination centers across the country.[9]

This statistic did not indicate a declining number of institutes; in fact, the number of named mechanics' institutions increased, especially in villages and small towns, but their functions changed dramatically. As early as the mid-1870s even the larger institutions, substituting examination-based classes for popular lectures and other aspects of what one institution president referred to as "the clubbable element," spoke of their work with "a tone both of cheerfulness and despondency" as they expanded curricula that would permit them to prevail in the competition for enrollment that was "now springing up on all sides."[10] They were, said the Dean of Cowie at one 1873 prize-giving, "follow[ing] the march of mankind" and "adapt[ing] themselves thoroughly to that which was required."[11] At the same time, the move away from mixed programming led the Mayor of Manchester to describe the successes and consequent narrowing of focus of institutes generally as "a sort of beautiful reproach."[12] The inevitable migration of classes to new secondary and technical schools contributed to the erosion of the institutes as a whole: by the late 1880s and early 1890s, many had moved away from both education and entertainment. Instead, taking advantage of the 1866 amendments to the 1850 Public Libraries Act, they operated as local reading rooms and libraries, perhaps occasionally providing the billiards, coffee rooms, and cricket fields now most commonly associated with workingmen's clubs. The rapidly dwindling numbers of smaller institutes that continued to book the occasional lecture relied primarily on speakers known for their pleasant and animated sketch-lectures or "gossips" that were charming rather than intellectually challenging. Such offerings, including the enormously popular "Black Board Lectures" of YUMI secretary Frank Curzon, served as a refreshing balance to the hard work of class study rather than as a conduit for participatory citizenship.[13]

Martyn Walker's assessment of the persistence of mechanics' institutions after the 1850s collapses these late-century reading rooms into the overall tallies of mechanics' institutes even as he examines the "general" institutions within the YUMI that would go on to become important science and art schools, thus presenting a picture of institute success that glosses over the significant contraction of purpose within many post-1880 institutions.[14] Knowledge-based culture shrank in these institutes, first to "knowledge," as the world of the popular lecture appeared both too expensive and too distracting to serve the needs of subscribers, and then to rudimentary programs of "culture" that provided only a faint echo of the complex programming of the institutes at mid-century. Changes in function were often unreflected in the names of these institutions; the 1894 annual report of the Northern Union of Mechanics' Institution, for example, listed among its sixty-seven affiliates not only mechanics' institutes but also reading rooms, libraries, literary societies, mutual improvement societies, and workingmen's clubs, in a jumble of titles evoking the same miscellany collated in 1850 by James Hudson.[15] Their shared purpose enabled even the smallest institutes to adopt the mid-century rhetoric of citizenship, although for most of them "citizen-reader" was both a cumbersome designation and a poorly articulated enterprise, one that would be taken up more successfully within the primary school classroom.[16] Thus, the developing structures of state-sponsored education ultimately forced many institutes to choose: become a formal site of secondary education, or devolve into reading rooms or libraries. Neither path accommodated the popular lecture, as we can see from the declining numbers in Figure 4.1, where the percentage of reporting institutions in the YUMI that offered popular lectures fell from 12 percent in 1878 to a scant 4 percent in 1890.[17]

Popular lectures remained important both to large general institutes like those in Huddersfield and Keighley as well as to the purpose-built civic institutions like the Midland Institute, the Newcastle Lit.-&-Phil., and the Leeds Phil.-&-Lit. When these institutions began to add events billed as "entertainments," such offerings were generally described as including significant serious content. War correspondent John Augustus O'Shea's 1888 "The Humours of Besieged Paris," for example, used comic relief to present the serious history of the Paris Commune: "the first measure of defense these men adopted was to change the names of the streets (laughter)," he joked, before going on to a serious description of the city's occupation. Similarly, Thomas Stevens's 1892 "Across Asia on a Bicycle" was lavishly illustrated with the latest technology but also constructed around the history, politics, and social norms of India, Japan, and

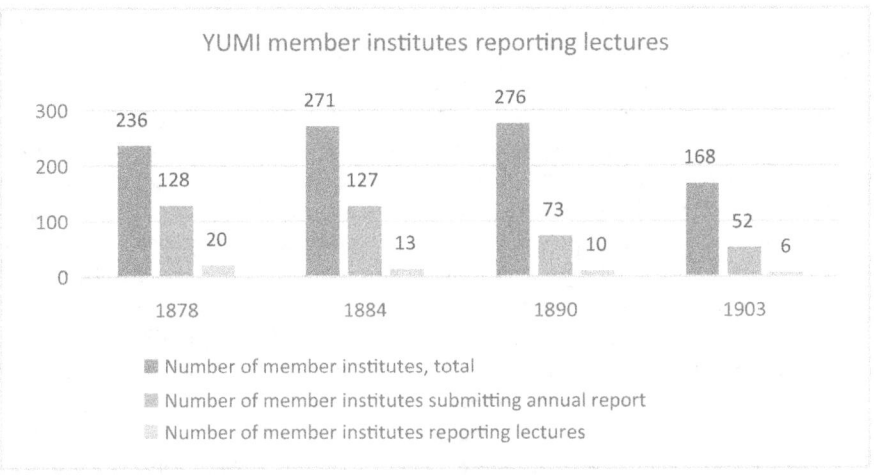

Figure 4.1 Decline in reported lectures, 1878–1903, in YUMI institutions.
Source: Annual Reports of the Yorkshire Union of Mechanics' Institutes, 1878, 1884, 1890, 1903.

China.[18] The new genre of the suburban institute, emerging in the 1870s and examined below, was less committed to this serious mid-century model; their committees courted national speakers but also relied increasingly on orators and musicians, often quite well-regarded, as well as novelty performers such as magicians and hypnotists. The unifying world of mid-century knowledge-based culture was increasingly fractured by the 1890s.

"Recognizing Our Own Real Importance": Professionalization and Boundaries

When Joseph Simpson launched the *ILG* in October 1861, its very title reinforced the relationship of the popular lecture to "the institutes." While the *Journal* focused on reports and correspondence submitted by institute officers, Simpson's periodical, trailing the *Journal* by a decade, focused instead on the voices of the men and women recruited by those committees to fill out a season's programming. Between 20 percent and 40 percent of each monthly issue comprised advertisements placed by lecturers. The balance of each issue contained Simpson's editorials on various aspects of lecturing, alongside correspondence, mediocre poetry by faithful readers, lengthy reprints of lectures (especially on scientific subjects), and "Institute Intelligence" columns that ran reports of lectures and meetings submitted by speakers. Occasionally, such intelligence included reprints of annual reports, as was the practice in the *Journal*, but it more often reproduced accounts of single lectures and brief summaries of upcoming programming; thus, when the *Journal* stopped printing annual reports, the central compendium of lecture programming was replaced by the *ILG*'s patchier approach. Simpson regularly reprinted his own editorial columns over the years, presumably when the press of his work as a printer was especially heavy, so that such items as "Young Institutes," "Old Institutes," "Working Men's Clubs," "Free Lectures," and similar chestnuts all appeared a number of times during his decades of editorship.

When Simpson introduced the *ILG* in 1862 as the organ for his new Lecturers' Association, his purposes were threefold. First, the journal would provide a way for lecturers to advertise both their wares and their schedules, thus "keeping themselves prominently before the notice of the Committees."[19] Second, it would help secretaries and committees run more efficient institutes, not only through easy access to available lecturers but also by printing advice from correspondents on the practical issues of furniture, advertising, and accommodations for lecturers—largely the same topics that had been featured in the first several years of the *Journal*, and that remained chronically problematic. And third, it would provide a space in which to advocate for professionalization. What were the needs of those who earned a living on the platform and whose work, lauded by educators and social critics, still remained meagerly paid and poorly respected? Historian Joe Kember, considering Simpson's work in the context of "the role of impresarios and agencies" in emerging international networks of entertainment, argues that the association was foundational in "creating a trade-based network that might exercise a degree of oversight and quality control over the lectures and the venues in which they were given."[20] The achievements of the association, however, never really came close to these goals. Its work was both aspirational and reactionary, combining lofty ambitions for lecturers and institutions with anxious and skeptical descriptions of modern, market-driven forms of entertainment and audiences.

The first of Simpson's goals was fairly straightforward. In addition to the monthly advertisements, the *ILG* produced an annual list of lecturers and their subjects, sent to the "increasing number of caterers for the instruction and amusement of the public" when the annual work of assembling a program began.[21] Despite Simpson's claims, the number of lecturers listed each year never exceeded seventy, out of the many hundreds of men and women who made their livings upon the platform. Because no official lists survive, it is impossible to accurately estimate how many of the institutes across the kingdom took the periodical every month, although references to "hundreds" of institutes and repeated admonitions to secretaries to rely upon the advertisements as they assembled their seasons suggests that many but certainly not all institutes had paid subscriptions. The monthly editorial leaders, letters, and accounts of lecture seasons made it clear, however, that this group of speakers—self-named "The Lecturers' Association" by 1864—perceived its work as integral to the range of societies and associations across the kingdom.

Simpson's second objective, the advice to institutions, could be observed in every issue of the *ILG*, just as in the correspondence columns of the *Journal*. Secretaries were admonished to provide travel and lodging information, answer correspondence quickly and courteously, adequately heat and light their lecture rooms, repair rickety platforms, provide water for speakers, pay lecturers discreetly but without delay, and coordinate schedules with other secretaries within a region. In addition to these chronic practical complaints, Simpson and his contributors scolded shortsighted committees whose decisions undercut the discipline and sacrifice necessary for the spread of knowledge-based culture. "The Institutes, in many cases, seek only what they call 'prosperity'—that is to have a good balance sheet—they too often ignore their educational and intellectual character, and ... are content to substitute the functions of the Theatre, the Music Hall, and the Ball room, for their own legitimate ones. Unfortunately, too, they cannot do this well," ran an early iteration of this complaint.[22] By early 1880, Simpson could point to "numerous minor Societies and Associations, which, started often under very favorable auspices, in various metropolitan and rural districts, after an ephemeral and frequently trivial existence, speedily collapse," as fatal examples of misdirected energy.[23] "We freely blame a large portion of our Institutes for not recognizing their own real importance," he wrote.[24]

The third of Simpson's goals, that of professionalization, was more ambitious. Lecture agents were almost as rare as a £10 lecture fee until the 1870s, and the rise of the formal lecture agency was still a decade away.[25] "Compared with what is being done in the United States, we, in England are doing nothing," wrote one lecturer in 1865.[26] Lecture engagements continued to be made individually, and thus lecturers and secretaries continued to blame one another for missed opportunities, with secretaries accusing lecturers of neglecting invitations and lecturers responding that "uncourteous secretaries" waited until the last possible moment to fill a programme and then offered the scrambling lecturer a fee well below market price.[27] Simpson and his correspondents insisted that until they agreed upon professional protocols and practices, they would continue to be treated with disrespect by "holier-than-thou" secretaries.[28]

The first proposals for professionalization via an established society or association of lecturers emerged almost immediately in early 1862, with correspondents urging Simpson to lead efforts "to obtain a charter for incorporation, constituting them [lecturers] a legally recognized body, possessing certain privileges, and entitled to certain professional designations." "L. L.," a regular correspondent, suggested the adoption of the title "Professor" by every lecturer, as well as the formation of "The College of Professors" that would include its own board of examiners but that would continue to require individual lecturers to arrange their own schedules of appearances. This combination of self-sufficiency and credentialing would "train a body of well-informed men for a most useful work."[29]

L.L.'s suggestions were too ambitious to be seriously considered. The actual path to the eventual establishment of the Lecturers' Association two years later began with organized sociability. Simpson and his fellow officers—especially barrister and elocutionist Charles John Plumptre,[30] who held the office of president of the association from its inception until his death in 1887—recognized the importance of "clubbability" for the success of their society, uniting as it did speakers and performers whose interests and talents varied but whose shared self-regard as serious professionals bound them together. Annual dinners for "Lecturers who are desirous of uniting" began in London in May 1864 and continued with few exceptions over the following decades.[31] Brief business meetings preceded the dinners, which lasted for several hours and included lengthy toasts and entertainments, usually in the form of orations by members. Attendees at the first dinner—an event referred to as "the Lecturers' Symposium"— were all regular advertisers in the *ILG*, and most specialized in literary or social topics rather than the sciences. The Rev. Henry Christmas occupied the chair, with YUMI secretary Barnett Blake as vice-chair. Toasts and accolades focused on the importance of the profession and the centrality of "Public Lecturing" to education and to public morality: "it was impossible to know, he [Christmas] said, ... to how many thousands they had become guiding stars in the walks of literature, science, and art."[32] Subsequent dinner meetings of interested lecturers, now calling themselves "a Lecturers' College," focused on the need to encourage more *esprit de corps* among the lecturing fraternity and thus to work "for the joint benefit of all." No women were included in this new college, whether by conscious choice or social pressure; the rhetorics of inclusion and exclusion instead focused on ensuring that all lecturers were "men of high Scientific and Literary attainments" since "it is, unfortunately, well-known that they are not always so." Membership in a formal association, it was hoped, would offer sufficient proof of competence and "prevent the more accomplished from suffering by being confounded with the less."[33]

By April 1865, the society had its own officers, including the requisite honorary president (in this case, the Earl of Carnarvon). Simpson was the secretary, a role he would fill for two decades, while Plumptre was president; these two men formed the guiding spirit behind the association, maintaining the tone and tenor of the group until age forced each to retire. Bylaws were adopted in June, and in September Simpson wrote that "by far the majority of the Institutions (including all the principal ones, both in the metropolis and the provinces), are amongst our subscribers," along with lecturers who, "as a body, hav[e] supported us nobly, both by Advertisements and Subscriptions."[34] In October 1866, satisfied that fundamentals of professionalization had been achieved and that the credential of "professor" was both unnecessary and realistically out of reach, the name of the association was changed to the "Society of Lecturers," placing the group's formal title more in line with the Royal Society and other learned societies. It would generally, however, be referred to as the Lecturers' Association after this change, both by members and by outsiders. A brief but unsuccessful campaign to credential lecturers with "MLA"—"Member, Lecturers' Association"—erupted in June 1874.[35] Women were welcomed within the association and to the dinners beginning in 1870, and often provided the semi-domestic labor of entertaining the men after the toasts had ended. Their importance to the profession was urged at regular intervals: for example, "Shakesperian and Musical Lecturer" Clara Sicard chided Simpson in 1874 for consistently referring to lecturers "solely in the *masculine* gender—rather an anomaly, I am inclined to think, in these days of 'Women's Rights' and Lady Lecturers."[36] By 1877, Simpson noted that "as Lecturers, ladies now work worthily with their brothers in the profession."[37] Despite this admission, however, he and many of his correspondents maintained an emphasis on "Institute men" as the primary builders of civilization.

The umbrella of professionalization covered many issues that fell outside the nuts-and-bolts categories of light, heat, and payment. Were year-round lectures "a weekly intellectual feast judiciously served up" or an unwise expansion into "the melting months of June and August?"[38] Should lecturers permit questions and discussions after their talks, or would such opportunities merely encourage bad behavior from an institute's "junior members"?[39] Were *cartes des visites* recommended, and at what price should they be sold?[40] Were dips in attendance and ticket sales due to "want of publicity" or to competition from workingmen's clubs and local chapters of the Rifle Volunteers?

One of the most knotty and persistent questions was the extent to which association members could counteract the reliance of institute secretaries on voluntary amateurs, from enthusiastic but ill-equipped institute members to the local parson. Donated labor had built the mid-century popular lecture model, but the established and paid lecturers associated with the *ILG* now urged institutes to move away from the gratis services that had been indispensable just a dozen years earlier: "Never, under any circumstances, ought any person to be allowed to lecture whose only qualification might be goodness of disposition or extensive learning."[41] Local clergy, who had helped ensure the very survival of many institutes at mid-century, came in for especially harsh criticism: "Gentlemen whose claims to the platform consist in wearing a long coat and waistcoat, buttoned very high, and who prefix the 'Rev.' to their name, and add the magic 'M.A.' at the end, are usually the very worst of failures."[42] Others whose "incompetent endeavours" diluted the field included men who "got up" a puerile lecture or two and whose "painful sense of incompetency" separated them from "men by whom they shrewdly suspect they are greatly looked down upon."[43] Equally problematic were lecturers who submitted their own reviews to the local press, thus engaging in "puffing," "humbug," and "Barnumism." Such reviews, which portrayed lecturers as both naturally brilliant and "highly successful," did great harm to the profession, leading institution secretaries to "expect [association members] to lecture purely for the good of mankind" rather than for a standard fee.

Complaints over inadequate fees resurfaced every summer: "A Lecturer" wrote in mid-1866 that "secretaries make a great mistake if they introduce a huckstering spirit into their financial arrangements with Lecturers. No gentleman of self-respect could condescend to higgle about the price of his literary wares."[44] Those literary wares—already, by the mid-1860s, often rhetorically excluding the work of the popular science lecturer—were the fruits of long hours of research, writing, and rehearsal, and as such deserved as much respect as any other form of investment. "Higgling" was for cheap and nasty consumer goods, not for cultural capital to be shared with a paying, respectful, and self-respecting audience. "The notion of knowledge as a personal, peculiar, selfish possession, is an utterly repulsive one to all right-minded men," wrote Simpson in 1865.[45]

At the same time, such a treasure was not to be scattered carelessly among audiences who could not perceive its value. The intellectual property of the popular platform lecturer was the result of effort and sacrifice, "the mature thought and earnest study" of many months that would be delivered "not half a dozen times, but half a thousand," and deserved to be treated in the same way as the products of older and more well-established professions like medicine and the law.[46] In 1874, the problem of the unappreciative audience led to a "bombshell" letter by art critic and lecturer John Ruskin, responding to a request for services from the Glasgow Athenaeum. Ruskin argued that the "entirely pestilent character" of popular lecture audiences forced lecturers to provide "knowledge it has cost a man half his life to gather, first sweetened up to make it palatable, and then kneaded into the smallest possible pills." Audiences—"the mob"—wanted "your modern fire-working, smooth-downy-curry-and-strawberry-ice-and-milk-punch-altogether lecture," which was an "abominable vanity" on the part of the lecturer as it provided no help to earnest men or women. Ruskin repudiated entirely his practice of popular lecturing, telling the athenaeum committee that he was available only as an extension lecturer for Oxford, and that those lectures could be accessed by the general public through his printed books. "If they don't care for these, I don't care to talk to them," he finished.[47] The letter was widely reprinted, including in the *ILG*. Simpson, whose journal had run intermittent letters and editorials grumbling about underprepared audiences, immediately rose to defend the system. Ruskin's "somewhat hasty but perfectly characteristic utterances" were "egotistical" and "intolerant," missing altogether the civilizing function of the popular lecture. "The ideas of a man of mind are as a rule eminently *suggestive*. Public Lectures are chiefly valuable for the thoughts they suggest to an intelligent or inquiring mind," he argued. The system of popular lecturing "provides a most ennobling source of pleasure, information, and instruction, and an undoubted means of culture to many who, but for such aids and opportunities, might be led to pursuits of a dangerous and baneful tendency." Ruskin, he told his readers, has "entirely misunderstood and … misrepresented a great and noble movement, which does its work in every corner of the land, and is a standing protest against frivolity, and in favor of earnest work."[48]

Simpson's own earnest work, establishing such boundary markers as a recognizable organizational structure, annual meetings, a dedicated journal, and paid advertisements, was intended to place the new and undervalued profession of the popular lecturer on the same footing as other forms of "brain-work." He anticipated, somewhat naively, that the marketplace would continue to stabilize and expand around the popular lecturer as an exemplar of knowledge-based culture, integral to "the intellectual advancement of our race" and organized into an acknowledged professional organization.[49] Ironically, just as this group had laboriously secured a place contiguous to, if not within, the national community of learned societies, its professional bona fides began to lose value.

"A Highly Intellectual Treat": Incorporating Entertainment into the Serious Lecture World

Simpson's work as guide, mentor, publicist, and nanny was tested from the outset, as platform culture ceded significant space to "entertainments" that ranged from musical recitals and evenings with the poets to snappy informal talks on current events and illustrated lectures by adventurous journalists. Simpson's own training and interests ran to traditional mid-century combinations of thoughtful, if unscholarly, sustenance with the occasional relish of amusement, and his editorials continually reiterated the importance of this mode of programming. However, the editorial voice of the *ILG* was consistently at odds with the advertising content of its own pages, as paid promotions for frothy entertainments outnumbered the smaller, more modest ads for staid lectures in the sciences and social sciences. Figure 4.2 illustrates this phenomenon.

In the first issue of the *ILG* (October 1862), the twenty-three paid advertisements by lecturers included seventeen for general "entertainments" by Allan Curr, Arthur Young, Mrs. Holcroft, James Kay Applebee, Basil Young, Walter Rowton, John de Fraine,

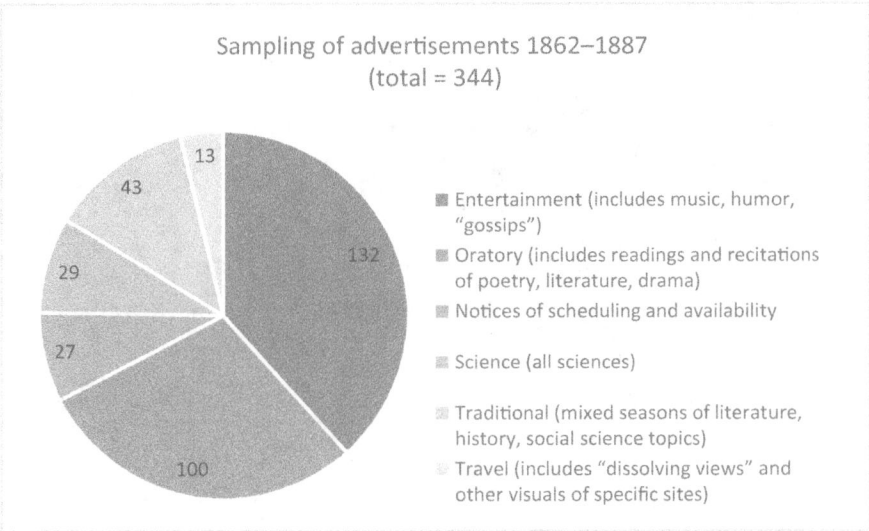

Figure 4.2 Categories of sampled lecture/entertainment advertised in *ILG*, 1862–87 (advertisements of lectures at five-year intervals, two issues per year).

Source: ILG 1862, 1867, 1872, 1877, 1882, 1887.

James Tell Topham, and Nathaniel Bushell, and more specific "musical entertainments" by Professor White, Frederick Chatterton, Fourness Rolfe, Charles Field, C. Fabian, Angus Fairbairn, Frederick Penna, and Mr. Ramsden. Penna, the Royal Harpist to the Prince of Wales, was an admired and seasoned performer, and his decision to advertise his work as "entertainment" after years of appearing on platforms to offer "concerts" reflected a gradual shift within the world of knowledge-based culture to more popular descriptions of established content. A number of experienced lecturers experimented in this way: Basil Young, for example, specifically offered hybrid "musical and mimical entertainments" rather than old-fashioned evenings with the poets, while Walter Rowton emphasized humor, not content, in the fourteenth season of his "Comic Lectures and Entertainments."[50] The half-dozen advertisements for more traditional fare in this issue included two lectures on science, three on literary subjects, and one on "famous men."

"Institute men" were increasingly like Rowton, a fixture since mid-century whose performances were entertaining but decidedly ephemeral, or like John de Fraine, who began lecturing in his teens with such time-tested offerings as "Life in London," "An Evening with the Poets," and "Home, and Household Joys and Trials."[51] These men— and the "Lady Lecturers" of the association—were professional, to be sure, in the sense that they earned often quite substantial livings from their work on the platform. However, their advertisements in the *ILG* and other periodicals, featuring accolades from dozens of satisfied committees around the kingdom, focused on appeals to the senses rather than to the intellect, privileging the "tumblers of amusement" over the "globules of instruction." Smaller institutions found these men and women particularly

Figure 4.3 Sample of advertisements from July 1, 1884 issue of *ILG*.

Source: *ILG*, July 1, 1884.

attractive, as their emphasis on spectacle appeared to guarantee ticket sales and thus profits. In a kind of feedback loop, the success of such entertainments led to ever more eye-catching advertisements. Figure 4.3, showing one page of advertising from the July 1, 1884 issue, illustrates the emerging boldness of such ads, with the visuals used by newer entertainers next to the more traditional descriptive ads of Brearey and Dechman.

Newport Pagnell Literary and Scientific Institute, 1866	
Montem Smith	Our National Melodies: A Musical Entertainment
Rev. J. B. Owen	The Proverbs of Belial
Edmund Wheeler	The Phenomena of Sound and the Sense of Hearing
Moses Coit Tyler	American Wit and Humour
Southport Town Hall Literary Lectures, 1866	
Rev. J. M. Bellew	A Reading
George Dawson	Wellington and Napoleon
Clara Lucas Balfour	Lofty Lessons from Lowly Home
George Grossmith	Pickings from Pickwick
Rev. J. de Kewer Williams	"I"
Moses Coit Tyler	The Orators and Oratory of America
Edmund Wheeler	Ocean Telegraphs
Basil Young	Musical and Mimical Entertainment
Huddersfield Institute, 1883	
George MacDonald and Family	Dramatic Costume Representation of "The Pilgrim's Progress"
R. A. Proctor	The Birth and Death of Worlds (Illustrated)
B. J. Malden	Victoria to Venice, with Sixty Lantern Slides
Rose Seaton	Recitals, Dramatic and Humorous
M. De Jongh	Grand Orchestral Concert
John Lubbock	Savages: Their Mental and Moral Condition
A. Guilmant	Grand Organ Recital
S. Brandon	Dramatic Recital, "Midsummer Night's Dream"
W. F. Barrett	Thought Reading, True and False, with Experiments
R. S. Ball	A Night at Lord Rose's Telescope
Mr. and Madame Edwyn Frith	Vocal and Instrumental Concert Party
F. A. Bridge	A Tour in North Wales, with Lantern Views and Songs
J. William Benn	Sketching Entertainment: Faces from the Streets of London

Figure 4.4 Selected programs in the *ILG*, 1866 and 1883.

Source: *ILG* September 1866: 478–9 (Newport Pagnell and Southport); *ILG* July (1883): 2226 (Huddersfield).

Advertisements were the product of profit-seeking lecturers rather than cash-strapped institutes. As such they necessarily indicate what sellers offered rather than what buyers ultimately purchased, but the persistent placement of large and increasingly creative ads for music, humor, and embellished scientific demonstrations attests to a strong and growing market for these wares. We can see this shift clearly over time, as indicated in Figure 4.4, which illustrates changes in programming within the institute world.

In the September 1866 issue of the *ILG*, the first four engagements at the Newport Pagnell Literary and Scientific Institute comprised a brief but typically mid-Victorian program of respectable eclecticism: three familiar lectures in science, humor, and domestic morality, with one musical offering linked loosely to history. The program of specifically "Literary Lectures" at the Southport Town Hall in the same issue likewise could have been lifted wholly from the previous decade, especially with the enviable triad of Dawson, Balfour, and Grossmith on offer. Cornell University history professor Moses Coit Tyler and naturalist Edmund Wheeler appeared at both of these institutes, offering slightly different lectures at each, and Basil Young's popular "mimical" offering rounded out a Southport season shaped around familiar offerings in music, science, humor, and biography.[52] Seventeen years later, however, these more traditional "mixed programs" had been replaced by newer modes of performative entertainment that included costumes, slides, "lightning sketches," and telepathy. The Huddersfield Institute program for 1883 included nine such entertainments—more than half the season—augmented by illustrated lectures on science and travel.[53] Even well-established traditional science lecturers, like astronomer Richard A. Proctor, archaeologist and ethnographer John Lubbock (Lord Avebury), and Irish Astronomer Royal Robert S. Ball, now made their offerings more entertaining and accessible with slides and demonstrations.

Simpson, as editor of the *ILG*, reaped the financial rewards of expanding advertising revenue, but Simpson as lecturer rued these changes. "The old-fashioned type of Lecture appears to be giving way to the advance of the more modern style of Entertainment," he noted in 1882, reluctantly stating what had been apparent for at least a decade. Lecturers who "[made] amusement the chief feature in their Lectures and Entertainments" would always "secure the greatest number of engagements."[54] Yet, just as he had refused to condemn the audiences so hateful to Ruskin, he also refrained from disparaging the entertainers who had matured as performers alongside himself. Instead, he insisted regularly that this ferment of entertainment performed an important function within the world of knowledge-based culture: "The gossiper, the humorist, the expounder of nature's laws" were there not only "to convulse with laughter the sunny side of humanity," but also, and even more importantly, "to instill into the mind a knowledge of wonders far transcending the skill of the mightiest conjurer to set forth or even to imitate."[55] Thus, while institute lecturers ought to eschew lectures "made out of the odds and ends of old Newspapers," their appropriate subject matter continued to range from "the severe, the literary, the scientific" to "the grave, the gay, the lively."[56]

After all, lecturer-entertainer Walter Rowton and his peers kept the *ILG* afloat through their extensive advertising. So too did the growing number of orators and elocutionists whose efforts were as theatrical as they were intellectual. Simpson's relationship with this field of performance was a difficult one. Carefully curated performances of "good" poetry and literature unquestionably aided in the spread of culture, and as early as the 1850s recitations from Shakespeare, Milton, and others were well-established as part of the work of the institutes. They were, noted Simpson in his editorial debut, "a highly intellectual treat."[57] Plumptre's role as president of the Lecturers' Association also reinforced the claims of the skilled elocutionist that such work was a key element of knowledge-based culture. Plumptre had launched penny readings at mid-century to spread that work further into the working classes, and many institutes originally adopted these to augment rather than replace the work of the popular lecturer. By the debut of the *ILG* a decade later, however, a number of institutes had simply substituted readings for lectures, thus eliminating possible spaces for the popular lecturer. In addition, "good" readings had staled with repetition, to be replaced with the "histrionics" of overly dramatic readings and "coarse songs" that offered only "the lowest depths of dullness or vulgarity."[58] As a result, and in spite of Plumptre's work as president, the columns of the *ILG* were filled with condemnations of "elocutionists" and their "serious damage [to] the Lecture pure and simple." Simpson accused institutes en masse of ignoring the well-crafted lecture and instead choosing the vulgarities of "Ethiopian Serenaders, Performing Dog Troupes, Fat Baby Companies, and other abominations."[59]

Fat babies and performing dogs migrated rather quickly out of the institutes. The penny reading programs did the same, finding more convivial spaces in workingmen's clubs. By the later 1870s, these contagions no longer threatened the dramatic readings and poetic recitations of the serious orator, which now were described as "Entertainments of a higher class, by professional Lecturers."[60] By the early 1880s, Simpson and others had begun to relabel "elocution" as skill rather than content, and to talk about elocution and "oratory" as fundamental tools not only of the modern lecturer but also of the politician and educator.[61]

The Resurgence of the Language of Class

Other, more serious relabeling marked this period of knowledge-based culture as well. The pages of the *ILG* provide a guide to the ways in which the "institute men" grappled with issues of class that had been tamped down at mid-century. Chester and his peers had painted their world in heroic colors, celebrating the men and women participating in institute life as rising above class antagonism; they were self-selected into a caste that valued the model of aspirational citizenship supported by the heady promises of committees and observers. By the mid-1870s, however, "citizen" and "citizenship" were being redirected away from aspiration toward the practicalities of making a living and exercising a limited franchise; that is, away from the third and toward the first of the registers enumerated by Matthew Grant, above. The 1873 YUMI annual report, for example, argued that citizenship—defined here as merely living as a law-abiding, rate-paying subject—entitled men and women to education that would render them "able to do work well, and to get well paid for it." Citizenship "implied having some degree of influence upon the choice of men" who governed, and because boys currently in elementary schools would grow to be "citizens and voters," they should be acquainted with some modicum of geography, history, and other tools for a basic understanding of the empire that these elected officials would rule.[62] In this functionalist redefinition, "citizenship" no longer referred to the path by which a self-selected group of men and women might, in the words of Samuel Smiles, serve as "artisans of civilization" in their own towns and villages.[63] Indeed, the word "citizen" appears in the *ILG* only a handful of times, as when Simpson noted vaguely in the course of an article on formal classes that popular lectures made "better citizens and happier men."[64] By the 1880s, critics and educators sought new language that no longer excluded the indifferent workingman but instead explored ways in which some diluted measure of culture might be poured into the working classes "to purify their moral nature, elevate their intellectual being, and raise them above the mere life of labour to which they have been born."[65]

Importantly, such top-down efforts would require the avid cooperation of the "institute men" (and women). While educationists focused on the role of the institutes as a space for secondary and technical instruction, many institute subscribers and patrons worried that "too great an emphasis on 'specific and technical education'" would prevent "that broad, general development of the mind which enabled a man to grasp any subject which he undertook."[66] Simpson and his peers instead considered how best to enfold the "true working men" in "the cordial bond" of "Literary pursuits"—an adjective that was always capitalized to reinforce its importance.[67] Only "Literary gentlemen" could transform working-class audiences into "men of worth here and heirs of immortality hereafter," and only "Literary institutes" could provide the space for this work.[68] "Whatever encourages among the classes who live by manual labour habits of self-culture, and intelligent recreation, and a rational use of leisure hours, will conduce to the welfare and happiness of the whole community," wrote Simpson in 1872, sounding remarkably like his counterparts from thirty years earlier. This reversion to old tropes of rational recreation and working-class self-culture, now situated almost wholly within the realm of literature and the arts, would elevate and preserve the "Literary gentleman" as a tool of national improvement. "Technical instruction is good," ran an *ILG* editorial the following year, reworking yet another well-worn argument, but "culture is also necessary." Expanded instruction in science and technology, however fundamental to the aims of the state, could not "lift our fellow creatures above the level of mere money-making machines. Literature, with her soft endearing influences, will be brought into request. The Fine Arts will be wanted. Wit and humour, pathos and tenderness, passion and feeling, as exemplified in the page of the historian, the power of the biographer, or the fancy of the poet, must never be ignored, nay *can* never be ignored."[69]

Many popular lecturers thus anticipated a vastly increased demand for their services as a result of the impending changes to elementary, secondary, and technical education. Lecture audiences would inevitably demand more ambitious fare from lecturers who were no longer hobbled by inadequately prepared listeners. Together they would reach for new, dizzying heights of intellectual entertainment. The institutes themselves would be free to fulfill their mission as "the Universities of the working and middle classes,"[70] while the popular lecturer would "*do good* by diffusing noble, pleasing, and useful thoughts, calculated to elevate, purify, and strengthen the minds of our hearers."[71] The world of the professional popular lecturer was poised to become much more interesting, as audiences were educated up and out of their preferences for anodyne amusement.

Even before 1870, however, pessimistic voices warned that working-class adults were deficient "in general intelligence" and were "the dumb brutes of the field."[72] A decade later, as the first generation of young adults produced by the Education Act joined the institutes for a combination of education and entertainment, very little had changed. J. C. Buckmaster, the polymath who had led the Battersea Literary and Scientific Institution for decades and was by now also an active lecturer and examiner at the South Kensington Department of Science, argued in 1878 that the elementary schools thus far had provided only a modicum of basic instruction and no culture whatsoever, while "the platform of Mechanics' Institutes up and down the country had long since been cleared of lecturers and teachers of science to make room for conjurers, mountebanks, low jokers, decayed actors, and comic singers."[73] Buckmaster's colleague, YUMI secretary Frank Curzon, rather weakly protested that the act had effected "the mental enfranchisement of millions of its citizens," but his voice was in the minority.[74]

It became clear by the 1880s that the schools and institutes, whether by themselves or in combination, had not become "a passport to all civilized society." Mental enfranchisement via the schools did nothing to lift boys and girls up to the higher economic or social rungs of the working classes; the institutes' role as a fount of culture in "a land aspiring to a chief position in education and letters" appeared equally unfulfilled.[75] No longer was the "pack of knowledge" to be exuberantly diverse; instead, it should be markedly utilitarian. Educationist and lecturer Henry Crosskey, who surveyed the state of education in an 1885 address to the NAPSS, argued that the "average" student at the elementary school and the higher board school should be satisfied with enough knowledge to "give dignity to their daily toil" and appreciate "the majestic marvels of the world in which they will have to labour."[76] His remarks evoked the language of the local clergy who had dominated the provincial lecture program in its earliest stages, where workingmen and women were urged to understand, but not seek to change, the wonders of the God-created world. Here in 1885 such language, translated into the classroom, operated to erase the more optimistic language of men like Curzon and to eradicate as well any rhetorical traces of mid-century participatory citizenship. Crosskey's "average students" would not actively "*be* and *do*," but might instead be helped to see and to accept the systems within which they lived and labored.

Popular lecturers were still perceived as important to the spread of a general culture, but by the mid-1880s they were advised to participate in this process of acquiescence without inspiring their listeners to reach beyond their grasp. Simpson had argued in the earliest issues of the *ILG* that "institute men" and their audiences were peculiarly linked; lecturers "mix[ed] with their hard-working fellow-students" and thus "know their taste, and … have felt their pulse."[77] By the time of the 1885 NAPSS meeting, this mutuality had been replaced by a more top-down model. Popular lecturer and clergyman William Tuckwell articulated the new class divisions that had replaced the old caste relationships: within the world of the institutes, he said, the subjects most favored by his fellow speakers—art, poetry, and music, but only in such vernacular forms as heliographs, "art-pottery," and tonic sol-fa—were the key to "the great problem of our day—the intellectual and social elevation of [the] irresistible masses" in a broad effort organized and directed by teachers and lecturers in the arts and literature.[78] His argument sought to acknowledge both the realities of late-Victorian urban life and to hold a space for the work of his fellow institute men, a task that increasingly emphasized the work of the literary in "keep[ing] young men in our great cities and country towns from the casino and beershop."[79] Without this influence, these young men would continue to prefer "amusements of the most degrading type," "mere animal gratification," "trashy sensationalism," "vice and ignorance," and "gutter literature."[80] This language, sprinkled throughout the pages of the *ILG* from 1862 to 1889, was a far cry from the mid-century characterizations of working-class institute subscribers as striving, serious learners; instead, it revived the conceit of the willfully ignorant worker, a bundle of sense-experience who chose to ignore the cultural riches available for mere pennies within the walls of the institute and instead drank his wage-packet or spent her pocket money on gaudy bonnets and trashy novels.

The End of an Era?

In 1883, surveying the field around him with some melancholy, Simpson declared that "The Lecture is still a powerful engine for influencing and elevating mankind"[81]—or at least the part of mankind that still attended the institutes. He had spent two decades tending that engine, laboring in a variety of ways to keep the "noble work" of the popular lecturer intact. Arguing from the launch of the *ILG* that eliminating traditional lectures was "the most suicidal act an Institution can commit," he reprinted whole speeches, especially in the sciences, with advice on how lecturers could adapt them to expand their own offerings.[82] He regularly offered column space to proponents of "faddish" intellectual ideas that might pique the interest of committees and audiences; recommended controversial topics that could revive a worn-out repertoire; and even occasionally published exchanges that remained just barely on the side of respectable discourse, as when Walter Rowton attacked the supporters of the Newtonian worldview or when Florence Fenwick Miller printed private correspondence critical of her lecture on "Women Warriors."[83] By the mid-1880s, however, Simpson was aging and so too were the institutes and their programming needs. Larger institutes that had maintained their commitment to knowledge-based culture as a set of practices and beliefs—Huddersfield and others—had survived by tempering, not abandoning, those commitments, as we shall see in our analysis of late-century topics below. But their sturdy support of traditional and even old-fashioned offerings like "Popular Lectures on Literary and Historical Subjects" was increasingly diluted by sensational presentations of sleight-of-hand, music-hall ribaldry, and death-defying feats of physical courage, with which neither the traditional popular lecture nor the culturally curated musical and oratorical entertainment could compete. Simpson mourned the arrival of a new era where "real talent and earnest endeavour" met with "scant success" in the institute world, forcing the professional popular lecturer to beg for engagements in the less worthy spaces associated with "Mutual Improvement Associations connected with our Churches and Chapels, Sunday School Unions, Co-Operative Societies, Working Men's Clubs, Church Institutes, Winter Evening Entertainment Committees, Coffee Taverns, and such-like organizations."[84] When Simpson retired in 1887, it appeared that his decades of work to establish professional boundaries for his peers could not counteract the structural changes to the institutes, with the result that the "institute man" driven to these smaller, noisier, less-refined spaces was now no better than the untalented local curate, "wearing a long coat and waistcoat, buttoned very high."[85]

New Physical Spaces: The Suburban Institutes

All was not high-buttoned coats and fat baby contests, however. Simpson's work was undeniably important in providing structures and advice to one large segment of platform speakers after mid-century, but the Lecturers' Association and the *ILG* were never a full reflection of the world of platform culture. One important locus of innovation was the suburban institute, which emerged late enough in Simpson's career that he never incorporated it into the world of "the institute men," although it shared many features of Simpson's universe. The conception of suburban life as sharply distinct from life in town and village emerged late in the century, with critics suggesting that suburbs needed nurturing if they were to compete with the "superficial attractions" of London.[86] By the 1880s, many observers agreed that "culture has too few centres," rendering thousands in the respectable and hard-working middle classes "outcasts of culture."[87] The challenge of how to establish resources for the "thoughtful, refined, socially disposed people" who would otherwise be "positively ostracized from Society" was the inevitable result of this realization.[88] Within just a few years, a reporter for the *Birmingham Daily Mail* observed that "there is scarcely a suburban neighbourhood of any account which has not been infected by this irresistible desire for scientific and literary cultivation."[89] How to meet that desire became a potent question.

The suburban institutes that were established in response took seriously their charge of "preventing everything from being centred in London."[90] They adopted not only the descriptive language but also many of the programming features of the mid-century institutions: popular lectures and classes; reading rooms and libraries; recreation grounds; and meeting facilities for debating clubs, mutual improvement societies, and other groups. At the same time, however, their founding committees insisted that they were demonstrably different from the world of "the institutes," arguing that to go "strictly on the lines of the old Mechanics Institutes … would have been a complete and disheartening failure."[91] "Suburban centres of population and influence" should aim to serve "the middle and higher as well as … the industrial ranks."[92] Their committees crafted programmes of "an all-round character, not having too many scientific lecturers nor yet overwhelmed with the purely literary element, but at all risks keep[ing] out 'Professor Dry-as-dust.'"[93] The cultural demands of suburban life required "Dramatic and Pianoforte recitals" and "miscellaneous entertainments" rather than purely educational programming, although "faddish" performances in hypnotism, mind reading, and the like were generally kept to a minimum.

This preference for entertainment is easy to trace within season programming. Nearly half of the offerings in many suburban institutes fell under the category of fine arts, and most of these were musical or theatrical performances. Within the category of literature, an increasing number of offerings were also performative in nature; similar trends characterized the categories of current events, where personal travel stories were accompanied by illustrations and examples of derring-do, and of science, as when John Henry Pepper transformed physics into "The Scientific Probabilities of Jules Verne's 'Twenty Thousand Leagues Under the Sea.'" Suburban institutes followed the models of the larger civic institutions to the extent that their committees could afford the expensive lions like Oscar Wilde, humorist Max O'Rell, and Henry Stanley. At the same time, they provided numerous outlets for the members of Simpson's Lecturers' Association, who had adapted their offerings to be as broadly appealing as possible; ventriloquist Colvil Dyke promoted his work as a "Scientific Magician," while photographer B. J. Malden developed "dioramic lectures" with "Unrivalled Dissolving Views." And finally, they offered spaces for local amateur musical, dramatic, and oratorical groups to perform for one another as well as for their friends and families, in a faint echo of the earliest Leeds Phil-&-Lit. programs, where audiences consisted primarily of loving mothers and sisters.

The desire to secure national headliners and well-established entertainers, combined with adequate but not spectacular treasuries, led a number of these suburban institutes to consider amalgamation—something that had been beyond the desires and abilities of the mid-century institutions, despite the constant hectoring of the Society of Arts and the less frequent suggestions in the *ILG*. Suburban institutes acknowledged that suburban leisure was not so very different across the kingdom that a union would crush local character. Birmingham, with the Midland as its flagship, provided the natural hub for this experiment. By 1884, there were seven institutes in the immediate area, encircling the city in a space whose radius was generally no more than 3 miles—an easily traversable distance for lecturers, subscribers, and class instructors. The combined membership of these institutes—Acocks Green, Erdington, Harborne and Edgbaston, King's Heath, Leamington, Moseley, Perry Barr, Sutton Coalfield, and Wednesbury—exceeded 3,000 and their combined annual income was more than £2,000.[94] There were significant differences across institutions, with the Harborne and Edgbaston Institute on the most elite rung of the suburban ladder and the Moseley and Perry Barr institutes near the bottom. Despite social gradations, "the inhabitants of the district are bound together … by intellectual characteristics and by the common pursuit of broad and generous public purposes," noted Crosskey in 1887.[95] Their formal combination into the Birmingham Suburban Institute Union allowed individual institutes to attract the caliber of lecturers at the Midland Institute, with speakers such as William Morris and Thomas Huxley engaged to deliver the same lecture at all member institutes for a set fee.

Yet, the reality of amalgamation was difficult to sustain beyond the first years of the suburban institutes, in part because of the very social gradations that Crosskey and others had dismissed. Records of the 1880s and 1890s show almost no overlap across union programs; only rarely would a regional name like William Tuckwell or a nationally known midrange speaker like the Rev. C. H. Grundy deliver undemanding moral fare like "English Home Life" at such disparate institutes as the well-to-do Harborne and Edgbaston Institute and the significantly less wealthy King's Heath Institute. It was far more common for the former, whose residents included city and business leaders, to share speakers and programming with the Midland Institute, while shedding a nimbus of intellectual respectability on the less ambitious of the suburban institutes. The latter were increasingly dependent upon their own members to volunteer their musical or oratorical talents, inadvertently replicating the efforts of the hobby clubs that had been embedded within the mid-century civic institute.

New Temporal Spaces: The Sunday Lecture Societies

Alongside the world of the "institute men" and the hybrid culture of the suburban institute sat one additional category of platform performance. Still many years away from the bureaucratized American lyceum model, this segment of popular lecture culture would instead mature around the peculiarly English precursor to the centralized speakers' bureau: the society dedicated to the moral transformation of humankind through the spread of a specific type of culture. The most influential of these groups was the London SLS, whose commitment to "the improvement and social well-being of mankind" amplified the interests of a growing body of professional and credentialed men and women in a world that was adjacent to, but distinct from, "the institute men," the suburban institutes, and the regional centers of civic culture housed in Birmingham, Manchester, and Leeds. While some of these practitioner-lecturers circulated among these disparate organizational models, many others chose to limit their appearances to spaces and programs that they deemed most likely to appreciate their expertise. We can see this in the development first of the parent SLS and then of its often unruly offspring.

The London SLS was founded in 1869 by Thomas Huxley and others "to provide for the delivery on Sundays in the Metropolis, and to encourage the delivery elsewhere, of Lectures on Science—physical, intellectual, and moral—History, Philosophy, and Art; especially in their bearing on the improvement and social well-being of mankind."[96] Its early vice presidents included Huxley, Spencer, Darwin, and Tyndall, and its leadership consistently drew from the intellectual elite of the country. The society's ideal members, according to the founders, were the young men and women whose pursuit of wages left only the limited hours of a Sunday for the pursuit of knowledge, and who sought "intellectual food better than can be obtained either in the church or in the public-house" or extracted from nature walks or music-hall performances.[97] According to the experience of one unnamed rural clergyman, 90 percent of "the English working classes" in his parish preferred "Beer and Backy" to sermons, lectures, or even high-toned "entertainments," but SLS secretary W. Henry Domville argued that urban workers were made of sterner stuff and would form "an attentive audience" for the new society's efforts.[98] Such audiences were not, the SLS asserted, being diverted from attendance at church or chapel; they were among the consistently high percentage of nonattenders so worrisome to clergy and social critics, and they sought, in the words of Huxley's *Lay Sermons*, "a knowledge of the phenomena of Nature and of man's relation to Nature."[99] One early editorial noted that the SLS aimed to ameliorate not only the intellectual poverty of the working classes but also "the ignorance of the counting-house, and the drawing-room."[100] Sunday lectures on serious topics, pitched to the level of the aspiring young adult and crafted as well to hold the interest of the businessman and "the cultivated lady of fashion,"[101] would offer another entrée into the world of knowledge-based culture, familiar in form and content but staking out a new temporal space for the work of the professional popular lecturer. This reclamation of the "English Sunday" from the bleak constraints of conservative Christianity would not only lighten the lives of individual seekers after knowledge, it would also inspire cities and towns across the kingdom to embrace a more modern approach to changing modes of labor and leisure. In yet another echo of mid-century discourse, this later generation of reformers argued that any accumulation of knowledge that was good for the individual would by definition be good for the locality.

The SLS mission statement carried a great deal of heavy water, not only in the lofty claim that the society could thus "improve mankind" but also in the assumption that this society would provide a national web of lecture culture where earlier efforts had failed. The Union of the Society of Arts had been unable to persuade member committees to work together; the YUMI and its fellow organizations had also met with resistance in centralizing their programming; the members of Simpson's Lecture Association had likewise experienced a kind of organizational entropy; and the suburban institutes had adopted the platonic ideal of cooperation but generally ignored the realities of shared programming. The London SLS asserted confidently that it would be the fixed point in a new network of knowledge-based culture, linking "elsewhere" to the metropolis through the medium of intellectual food and drink. Many were skeptical: London had proven remarkably infertile ground for such work in the past. It hosted a number of elite learned societies producing new knowledge as well as a multiplicity of ephemeral sites for the consumption of knowledge, but high taxes and cramped spaces made it very difficult for these sites to survive and thrive, let alone combine into regional or national webs of culture. Much of this failure was economic: the chronic debt of the London Mechanics' Institution, noted in year after year of the *Journal*, underscored the peculiar financial difficulties under which the pursuit of knowledge labored in the capital. The depth of outraged mourning sparked by the end of the London Polytechnic in 1880 would reinforce how even the most beloved traditional institutions could not survive these pressures. What, then, made the SLS so confident that its work would not only shape the mental world of the striving young adult of the capital but also anchor a network of kindred societies in the provinces?

The hubris of the SLS's lofty goals invited gentle mockery for attempting to save the world on the backs of "slightly educated, half-educated, or fairly educated" young Londoners, while the preponderance of secularists among its founding members earned it a description as "a genteel Secularist sect."[102] The potential for confrontation with the various Sabbatarian movements in and around London loomed large from the establishment of the society, and the SLS mission statement, strongly implying the failure of traditional moral teaching, invited scrutiny and promised defiance. Unsurprisingly, a variety of Sabbatarian groups quickly linked SLS lecture programming to efforts seeking to open museums and other leisure spaces on Sundays. The SLS founding committee, for its part, continually reminded these critics of the legal loopholes in the century-old Sunday Observance Act, which forbade paid organized amusements on the Sabbath but seemed to promise that lectures for "*bona fide* ... instruction" would be immune from prosecution.[103]

The SLS had to balance its open distaste for Sabbatarianism with a genuine desire to reach men and women repelled by Anglican orthodoxy but seeking some meaningful appreciation of the world around them. Lectures in the sciences seemed the perfect solution. However, by the early 1870s, as we have seen, many popular science lectures were built upon "magical exhibitive effects," and the society was urged to minimize these sensuous pleasures in favor of programming built around history and literature, while ignoring experiments in oratory and performance altogether.[104] The SLS's paradigm of "social well-being" was far more traditional than its critics claimed, echoing and extending the well-established mid-century model of knowledge-based culture: "education, and not amusement," was "the great object of the Society."[105] The structures of each season were, like the programming itself, reassuringly familiar: between twenty-one and twenty-four lectures were offered at St. George's Hall on Sundays between November and April, with tickets at 3d., 6d., and 1s. Season subscribers—about 150 per year—paid £1. Such familiarity guaranteed a consistent Sunday audience of about 400 individuals each week, but even these respectable numbers could not counterbalance the chronic financial stresses that had sunk earlier London societies. The SLS could only afford to pay its lecturers £5 per lecture, a relatively modest fee by 1870 and quite low by the standards of London, where Robert Ball could earn between £25 and £40 for a single exuberantly illustrated science lecture. But even with this moderate outlay for talent, income consistently lagged behind costs; the venue had to be rented for the entire year, even for the summer months when no lectures were given, while fees for advertising, printing, lighting and cleaning, and a salaried secretary were always higher than ticket income. Within the first months of the society's operations, the lecture time was moved from 7:00 p.m. to 3:30 p.m. (up to 4:00 p.m. beginning in the second season), in order to save the extra costs of lighting and heating in the evening, and the lowest tier of admission fees dropped from 3d. to 1d., ensuring a packed balcony most Sundays. Despite these moves, the annual reports often urged members to help find ways to sublet the hall during the off season, to promote the sale of printed volumes of lectures, and to encourage their friends and acquaintances to make donations and to remember the SLS in their wills.

Within the first five years, and ignoring the specter of financial doom, the SLS claimed that its "undefined, but very practical, shape" had led to success where earlier London-based societies had failed: "It has become firmly established and may now be reckoned as one of the permanent institutions of this vast metropolis."[106] There had been no "fanatical outburst" by Sabbatarian groups to mar the society's work. Average attendance was healthy and many in the 6d. and 1d. seats were "recurring attendees," eager to take advantage of "lectures of a class so superior as generally to be only within the reach of the members of our learned and scientific societies and of their personal friends."[107] Indeed, wrote secretary Domville in the 1882 annual report, "artisans and families" looked to these lectures as a source of "desirable knowledge" and often outnumbered the middle-class men and women in the more expensive seats.[108] It cost almost nothing, he noted, to hear such well-known speakers as Karl Pearson, John Addington Symonds, Florence Fenwick Miller, Elizabeth Blackwell, and Edward Aveling, all of whom were by now also regulars at the large civic institutions.

Here we see, however, the question that dogged the SLS throughout its decades of service. Who were the programming committees targeting and who were they reaching, with their catalogue of well-credentialed professionals rather than the wealth of amateur "sappers and miners?" Early observers in the periodical press noted that the lectures were often "too dry to be at all likely to draw those for whom they are chiefly designed, or to form a counter attraction to the public-house," and that "the subjects generally treated [were] ... such that none but the educated and refined can feel pleasure in them."[109] Many were pitched at a level of complexity by now reserved primarily for the secondary or post-secondary classroom, like J. S. Bristowe's technical lecture in 1872, "The Ear, and How to Hear," which required a written guide for listeners.[110] Others were "racy" entertainments rather than serious fare: The *Globe*'s assessment of the first year of programming described it as "lively, though erudite, gossip" and "spiritual pabulum."[111] The first season of effecting "the improvement and social well-being of mankind" was much easier to structure than to fill. By the second year, however, the programming committee began to find its feet, a development reflected in more positive press coverage. For example, speaker Arthur Elley Finch's "The Inductive Philosophy" was labeled "a model lecture" and Finch himself was described as "something more than a popular lecturer, although in that he thoroughly succeeded."[112] However, the gap between ideal and actual audience remained a chronic source of criticism: although "the society spreads its net to catch all classes," the editor of the *South Wales Daily News* noted in 1885, "the company has always been more select than numerous."[113]

What formed the nucleus of this programming? The broad scope of "science, history, philosophy, and art" permitted the SLS to recruit a variety of lecture luminaries. A typical season of lectures—this one from 1874, by which time the SLS had settled on a general model of programming—included three members of the Lecture Association: orator Charles Plumptre on "The Religion and Morality of Shakespeare's Works," art historian G. G. Zerffi on "Egypt from a Religious, Social, and Historical point of view," and social reformer Florence Fenwick Miller on "Funeral Rites and Cremation—Shall we bury or burn our dead?" Other well-known names speaking on particularly topical issues included physician W. B. Carpenter on "Recent Investigations into the Functions of different parts of the Brain," paleontologist and geology professor Harry Seeley on "The Position of the English Universities with regard to National Education and Progress," Icelandic scholar Jon A. Hjaltalin on "Iceland: Its Physical Features and Inhabitants," and war correspondent J. S. Blackie on "War: Its causes, character, and consequences," all alongside James Glaisher's ballooning lectures and Spencer Cobbold's lectures on fossils, which were a coveted part of any institute season.[114] Speakers like Blackie and Glaisher could be vastly entertaining, combining as they did flashy visuals with stories of personal heroism. Their appearances at the Midland Institute and other civic spaces were publicized as desirable combinations of education and entertainment, but the SLS presented their work as fundamentally serious rather than diverting. This approach appeared to work in London, but within a decade the SLS's kindred societies would choose to augment these instructive lectures with an array of popular entertainment, in some ways diluting the mission of the parent society but simultaneously vastly expanding the reach and draw of the Sunday lecture.

Many of these lectures received fairly extensive press coverage in the London papers, coverage that was routinely reprinted in provincial daily and weekly papers. By the 1870s, it was no longer prohibitively expensive to send a writer to cover such events, nor was it difficult to find column space in provincial papers to reprint entire lectures submitted by speakers. Most often, however, editors relied on the work of freelance attendees who provided "fair epitomes of these lectures," which were submitted for

Society approval before being printed. This system was efficient and inexpensive, although the esoteric nature of early SLS lectures could lead to confusion. When homeopathic physician Robert Ellis Dudgeon criticized the press coverage of his 1871 lecture on "The Optical Construction of the Eye," the freelance "lady journalist" who had covered the lecture responded that "Dr. Dudgeon's exposition of his peculiar theory was given so confusedly in his lecture that I found myself unable to give a faithful report of it."[115] The SLS quickly adopted the general practice of distributing lecture syllabi at the door, a system that increased printing costs but decreased audience confusion, especially when the topic was unfamiliar. The society also collected seasons of lectures and printed them for sale. By 1893, annual reports were full of self-congratulation for "making a public-spirited endeavour to afford opportunities for self-improvement and innocent recreation … for the humbler classes," even while much of its lecture programming was more intellectually accessible to the relatively well-educated.[116]

The SLS's success in eluding the ire of Sabbatarian groups encouraged the development and expansion of Sunday programming elsewhere in the city. Some of these associations, including the British Secular Union and the National Sunday League, took the radical step of introducing secular Sunday music, without apparent resistance.[117] By 1890, lecture programming that was secular in nature and pitched generally to working-class and middle-class audiences was offered at St. Andrew's Hall, where the Sunday Evenings for the People carried on under the auspices of the National Sunday League; the Ethical Society at Essex Hall; the South Place Ethical Society, Finsbury; St. Philip's Church; and St. Nicholas Cole Abbey, where the Rev. H. C. Shuttleworth, a Christian Socialist, oversaw lectures on "Education Reform and the London School Board," "Novels and Novelists," "Darwinism," and "Selections of Sacred Music."[118] Non-secular Sunday lectures also multiplied, as Martin Hewitt has shown, in order to examine "great public questions that bore on the life of the Church."[119] Central London was suddenly so teeming with options that the SLS committee began to consider a move to the East End, hoping to stanch the steady loss of subscribers and income.[120]

"Improving Mankind" in the Provinces: The Kindred Societies

While competition within the heart of the metropolis occasioned a mix of approbation and concern, the development of "kindred societies" outside of London appeared to SLS subscribers and patrons to be an unmitigated good. As early as 1874, a small number of Sunday lecture societies were established along the general lines of the SLS, including the Sunday Evening Meetings for the People in Birmingham, the Scottish Secular Union in Edinburgh, and a Sunday Lecture Society in Walsall.[121] The latter two societies echoed the general secular goals of the SLS, while the Birmingham Sunday Evening society was unequivocally both Christian and unsectarian, targeting the unchurched but "preparing them for the reception of more distinctively religious teaching" through "social, moral, and intellectual elevation."[122] The Birmingham society was replaced in 1881 by a Sunday Lecture Society "of a more representative character," pitched at a slightly higher social stratum than its predecessor and drawing members from "some of the chief local, literary, and scientific men, as well as clergymen of the Established Church, and of various Dissenting Denominations."[123] Other kindred societies followed in Newcastle, Tyneside, Manchester (Ancoats), Bradford, Liverpool, and Glasgow. While the SLS could not and did not offer financial support for these offspring, it took the lion's share of credit for "so healthy a growth in our large outside centres,"[124] providing "papers and information" to new chapters and helping arrange for SLS lecturers to appear in these new provincial spaces. As was the case with other provincial cultural institutions, these kindred chapters faced significantly less competition for audiences than the London SLS and as a result enjoyed much higher attendance at each engagement. Societies in Birmingham and Newcastle each averaged 2,000 or more listeners per lecture, while the Glasgow Sunday Society claimed that during one winter "the audience at each lecture was more numerous than at many of the best attended churches in that city."[125]

These kindred societies, like the mid-century institutes and civic associations, were largely guided by local need as they constructed committees and programs. The well-rehearsed commitment to union, for example, characterized the Birmingham SLS, where a central organizing committee could coordinate the rotation of speakers drawn from both "gentlemen conspicuous for their ability in the literary, religious, and scientific world" as well as "fresh and no less eminent local talent," to speak among board schools "in the four quarters of the town."[126] This central committee achieved what many earlier attempts at coordination had not: seasons where each of two dozen speakers would appear at four different locations on a dependable schedule, with fees paid by the committee rather than by the individual site. It ventured within its second year to add musical selections to some lectures, and by 1890 included regular appearances by the Birmingham Amateur Orchestral Society. Other kindred societies also successfully added musical interludes to their Sunday programming. And while the Glasgow Sunday Lecture Society was particularly lauded as a hopeful sign that the notorious Scottish Sabbatarianism was loosening its hold on the city, other local committees rarely alluded to issues of church or faith as they built their programming.[127] Instead, many used the local society to stake out cultural space apart from, but adjacent to and thus more flexible than, the multilayered offerings of the established civic institution, creating lecture programming without the burdens of classes, clubs, and circulating libraries.

In many ways these offshoots of the SLS provided a second outlet for the same lecturers who formed the backbone of civic institution lecture programming in Newcastle, Birmingham, Manchester, and Leeds as well as at the most robust of "the institutes" at Keighley and Huddersfield. While the venerable Newcastle Lit.-&-Phil. was a full-service institution with its own commanding (if aging) physical space, the Tyneside SLS (founded 1883) borrowed a theater, eschewed any formal curricula, and launched its efforts in "a brilliant opening" with a lecture by SLS president W. L. Carpenter to 1,500 men and women. An account of its first two years noted that its lecturers included "gentlemen ... drawn from all classes and ... the most varied opinions," speaking in front of "audiences of a similarly varied character" who were "intelligent and discriminating," and attributed its success to engaging "men already popularly known."¹²⁸ Within five years, it was regarded as "a regular institution in Newcastle," complementing rather than competing with the Lit.-&-Phil. and consistently attracting the same speakers.¹²⁹ The Ancoats SLS, carving out a space contiguous to but significantly different from other Manchester institutions, inaugurated its free Sunday lectures with talks by artist William Morris and chemist Sir Henry Roscoe and also offered "Sunday Evening 'At Homes,'" which were "attended by over 800 working people, besides a good number of their more wealthy fellow citizens."¹³⁰ The Bradford SLS, founded in 1887, offered free lectures "attended almost exclusively by thoughtful, earnest working men," while "a large section of citizens" met in Norwich in the autumn of 1891 to discuss a smaller adjunct to the nine-year-old Tyneside SLS. The first efforts by the Norwich committee were attacked for trying to "exercise its mighty influence on the Municipal Elections," but within a few months a new committee adopted a more typically apolitical and unsectarian approach to programming.¹³¹ Discussions of a society in Sunderland began in autumn 1892, with an initial lecture by the Rev. H. R. Haweis on "Tennyson, the Poet of the Age" in November. Liverpool "at last moved in the right direction" and formed its own SLS in 1886, with its opening session described by the London SLS as "a brilliant success" and its first president claiming it had done much "to break the monotony of the British Sunday." Representatives of this society and the Birmingham SLS met in 1890 to discuss "a bond of union" that would demonstrate a general, undemanding principle of brotherhood.¹³² Leeds, a surprisingly late entrant to the web of Sunday Lecture Societies, finally announced its plans to inaugurate a society "entirely unsectarian" and "free from class prejudice" that same month. The inimitable Robert Ball gave the inaugural lecture, an illustrated "Evening with the Telescope," on November 27, "a triumphant success" to "a huge audience."¹³³

While the programming at these kindred societies generally hewed closely to the mix of subjects that had come to define the civic institutions of mid-century, the relationships between speaker and audience were often less stringently policed. The London SLS, for example, pointed to its "preemptory rule prohibiting even the common and useful practice of asking the lecturer a question, lest the question and answer should lead to debate,"¹³⁴ but many kindred societies permitted audience queries, echoing the assertion decades earlier by the editors of the *British Controversialist* that "controversy does not mean confrontation." While the London SLS aspired to "spread its net to reach all classes," and often reiterated that its audiences were generally "the more solid and steady class of artisans," its ticket-holders tended, as we have seen, to come from "the educated and the refined."¹³⁵ Provincial societies, in contrast, often pointed to packed audiences from all classes, and congratulated themselves when they were able to host annual meetings of such gatherings as the British Association for the Advancement of Science.¹³⁶ Overall, the provincial iterations of the SLS enjoyed more varied speakers, more mixed audiences, and more engaged local newspaper coverage than the London parent society. Indeed, adapting their founding ideals, many kindred societies moved deliberately away from the London SLS's pledge "to regenerate society" and instead focused on "brightening and cheering the lives of many persons whose existence needed very much brightening and cheering."¹³⁷ On the whole, the provincial chapters were more popular and more robust than their metropolitan parent.

"He Had Not Merely Picked Out the Jokes": The 1894 LDOS Lawsuit and the Nexus of Education and Amusement, Revisited

The widespread public appreciation of these Sunday societies was jolted by the 1894 prosecution of the infant Leeds SLS by the Lords' Day Observance Society (LDOS), under the auspices of the apparently moribund Sunday Observance Act.[138] The LDOS lawsuit argued that the Leeds SLS was operating as a "disorderly house" by charging entrance fees for lectures that were humorous and lively. The law had rarely been invoked in the nineteenth century, but the LDOS persuaded a Mr. Henry Reid to bring the suit as a "common informer" under the law. The suit targeted two lectures in January 1894, one on "The Chicago Exhibition of 1893" by George Villiers and another on "The Distinctive Character of the English, Scotch, and Irish People; or, John Bull, Sandy, and Pat" by Max O'Rell, both highly sought-after popular lecturers.[139] These lectures, the prosecutors claimed, were a commercial enterprise operating illegally on the Sabbath; they were also both entertaining and amusing, and as such violated the 1781 Act on two counts. Members of the hastily formed Federation of Sunday Societies responded that the long reach of the Sabbatarians represented a "wanton and intolerant interference with the liberty of British subjects," while the use of the "common informer" was "a relic of a barbarous age."[140] The prosecution was mocked for its witnesses, including one who "said he had given a fair account of the lecture to the best of his recollection. He had not merely picked out the jokes. He did not remember that the lecturer gave a history of Chicago, and accompanied it with statistics."[141] Many critics focused primarily on the absurdity of the suit—if a lecture produced laughter in the audience, it was illegal; if it put the audience to sleep, it remained within the letter of the law and the sponsoring society was not liable—but the court case clearly had implications for the work of many groups seeking to expand leisure options on Sundays.[142] To the surprise of many observers, Reid won the case in July, but the verdict was quickly appealed and overturned on the grounds that his suit had actually named the wrong persons as keeper and manager—had in fact sued the wrong persons. Post-appeal analyses continued to attack the LDOS, describing the suit as a "determination to make everybody gloomy and stupid on Sunday."[143] LDOS secretary Frederic Peake pointed out, however, that despite the results of the appeal, "the lectures complained of have been pronounced illegal and the Coliseum a 'disorderly house' in the eyes of the law."[144] A series of attempts to repeal the law came to nothing.

Within the world of the popular lecture, the lawsuit targeted anew the connection between education and entertainment. Laughter and music were now embedded into lecture culture, even for "serious" speakers like James Blackie, whose lecture on "Christianity and Social Organization" was infused with "well-turned joke[s] or gesture[s] ... full of meaning," or the Rev. William Tuckwell, whose press reviews routinely noted "loud laughter," "much laughter," "renewed laughter," and "enthusiastic applause."[145] The Leeds defense team implied that any separation between education and amusement was by now completely artificial. Sir Arthur Hobhouse, the longtime director of the London SLS, argued that a law that criminalized enjoyment was itself laughable: "Now, according to the law recently expounded, he could not help thinking that if he had not brought himself within the provisions of the Act it was only due to the most melancholy of all causes—that nobody could be found to aver that his lecture was either entertaining or amusing."[146]

The failure to repeal the Sunday Act, however, cast a temporary pall over the SLS and a number of its provincial progeny. Venues demanded indemnities or refused to allow Sunday lectures to take place at all; lecturers canceled engagements; "persons of position" resigned their directorships.[147] The societies in Norwich and Bristol temporarily shut down.[148] The Leeds SLS continued for a brief period without charging admission fees, while noting that "the audience … were at liberty to give as much as they pleased," but eventually suspended operations.[149] The Liverpool Sunday Society had not been set up to charge at the door and thus, its supporters noted, "has been more regardful of legal requirements, and for that reason has gone on without interruption."[150] The LDOS itself was quiescent, having made its point, although it was characterized in the *Westminster Review* as "continu[ing] the system of intimidation by means of threatening letters."[151] Newspapers and weekly reviews kept the issues of the suit before the public as fruitless attempts were made to amend or appeal the act. It would be several more years before several of the kindred societies could confidently offer the diverse programming of the early 1890s.

Revisiting the Ecosystem of Knowledge-Based Culture

Recuperating the late-Victorian ecosystem of knowledge-based culture presents challenges that were not at issue at mid-century. First, of course, is the end of the *Journal* as a compendium of institute programming. No single periodical appeared after 1870 to fill that niche. As a result, especially for smaller institutes, records of lectures and entertainments became increasingly ephemeral, perhaps reported in highly truncated form in local newspapers but often simply disappearing. Many of these smaller institutes failed after 1870, as we have seen. No sources specifically trace the decline of these institutes, although the *Journal*'s own appendices indicate a steep drop in the number of union members, from 116 in 1867 to 29 in 1898 (see Figure 4.5). Thus, the data for any analysis of the late-Victorian state of popular lecturing depend primarily upon the well-preserved records of the SLS and the larger civic institutions, most of which published annual reports and also enjoyed regular coverage by local journalists.

Despite these gaps, we can see patterns that help illustrate the ways in which popular lecturing and lecturers fared after 1870. Figure 4.6 shows the distribution of lectures by category after 1870, while Figure 4.7 shows a comparison of lecture categories as a percentage of total lecture for the mid-century period and this late-century period.

As these figures show, "Sciences" retained its position as the most popular topic in institutes and societies, accounting for 26 percent of lectures at mid-century and 23 percent at late century. However, the nature of these offerings had already changed significantly by 1870, with spectacle and coziness increasingly working together to attract family audiences to the institutes. During the 1860s, "spectacle" led to the

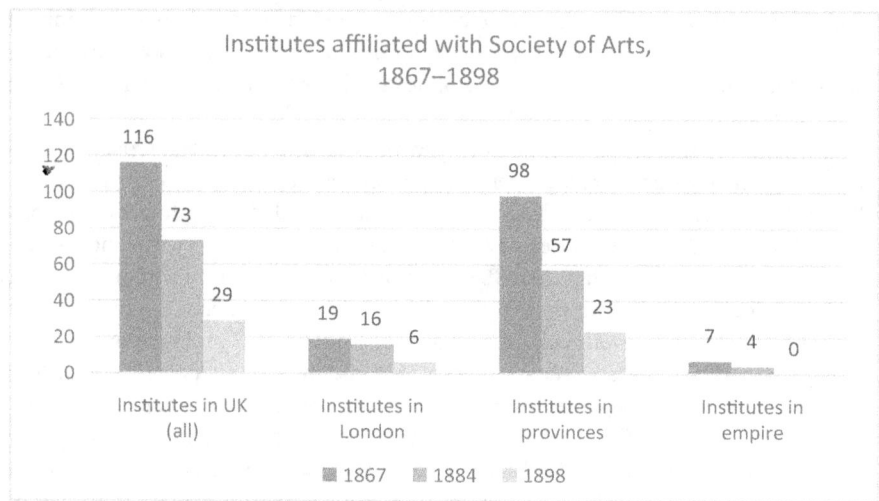

Figure 4.5 Decline in institutions affiliated with the Society of Arts, 1867–98.
Source: *J. Soc. Arts* 1867, 1884, 1898.

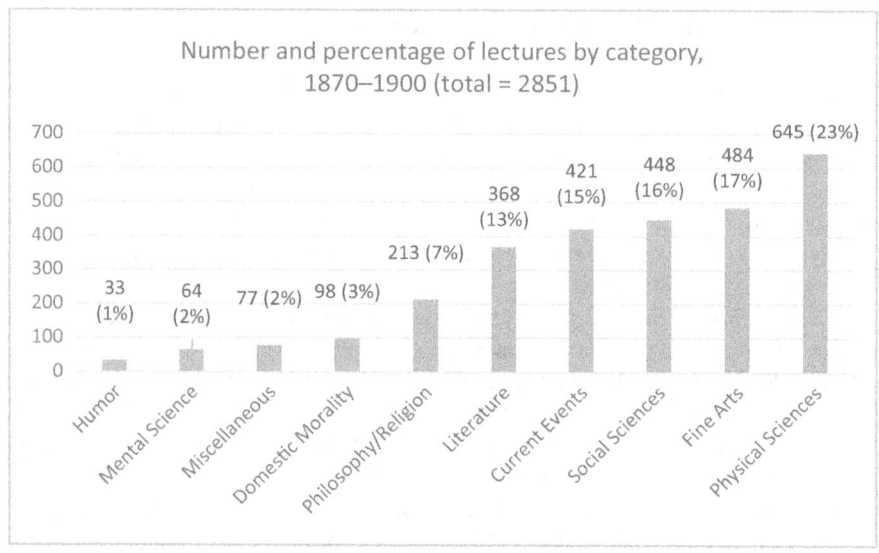

Figure 4.6 Lectures delivered by category, 1870–1900.

Source: *J. Soc. Arts*, 1870–90; *ILG* 1861–89; Birmingham and Midland Institute, *Annual Reports* 1870–1900; Leeds Phil.-&-Lit. *Annual Reports*, 1870–1900; Robert Spence Watson, *History of the Newcastle Literary and Philosophical Institute*; Sunday Lecture Society, *Annual Reports* 1870–1900.

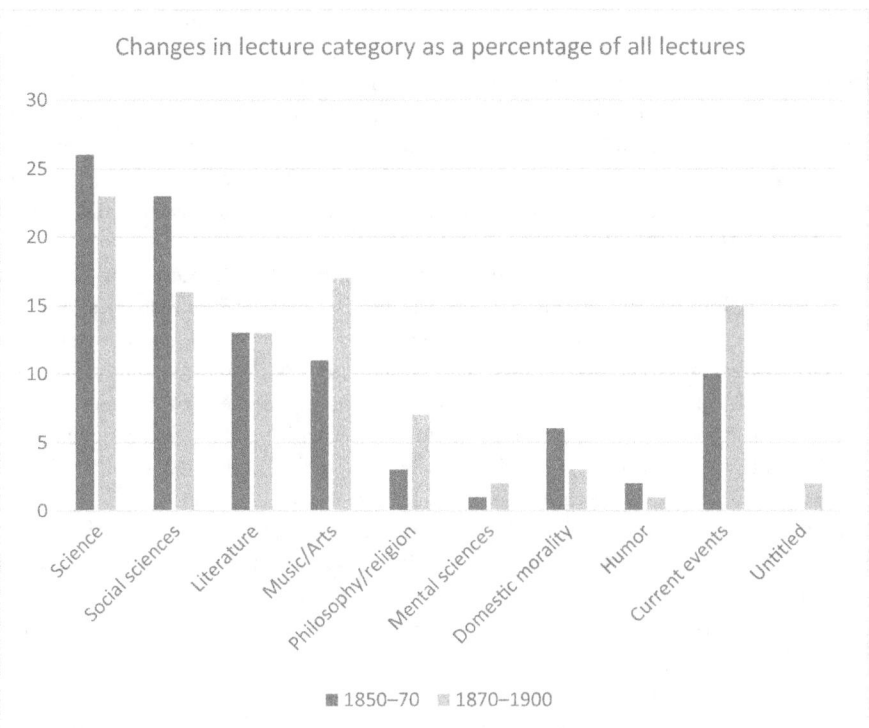

Figure 4.7 Changes in lecture categories as a percentage of all lectures.

Source: *J. Soc. Arts*, 1852–90; *ILG* 1861–89; Birmingham and Midland Institute, *Annual Reports* 1870–1900; Leeds Phil.-&-Lit. *Annual Reports*, 1870–1900; Robert Spence Watson, *History of the Newcastle Literary and Philosophical Institute*; Sunday Lecture Society, *Annual Reports* 1870–1900.

continuous engagements of speakers like geologist and astronomer William R. Birt, who appeared on hundreds of platforms to deliver such lectures as "The Lunar Tourist" and "A Night among the Stars," all accompanied by lantern slides and other illustrations (including, famously, a working model of a volcano). His performative work made him a solid draw for a mixed audience, but the printed versions of these same lectures—which appeared regularly in the *ILG* as part of Simpson's efforts to encourage association members generally to adopt new content—were challengingly ponderous when unrelieved by visuals.[152] "Coziness," on the other hand, came in the frothier work of naturalist William Kidd, whose serious labor on birds and insects was transmuted into a series of enormously popular "gossips" that rejected "fine-spun theories, clothed in the scientific formula of the day" in favor of "a budget of delightful anecdotes" in botany, meteorology, and other natural sciences.[153] Not every listener found his presentations appealing, of course; the official notice of Kidd's 1862 lecture at the Chichester Mechanics' Institution, "Popular and Laughable Gossip about Birds, Beasts, and Fishes," described it as "an intellectual treat," while the report of the lecture in the *West Sussex Gazette* described it as "vapid and puerile."[154] But Kidd's "racy" pace and homely vernacular delighted family audiences, and his ability to use that tone and style across subject matter—there were "familiar anecdotal gossips" and "popular gossips," as well as "gossips" on famous people and contemporary events—made him a top choice for many institutions up to his retirement due to ill health. Together, Kidd and Birt marked a transition point for the science lecture, as the speaker with only his notes and a carafe of water by his side gave way in the 1870s to the costumed performer with such offerings as "The Fairyland of Science" that were designed to amuse rather than to enlighten.[155]

The other major change over time lies in the nature of the "entertainer" who was so vexing to Simpson and so welcoming to secretaries of suburban institutes. At mid-century, "literature" and "fine arts" together accounted for about one-quarter of all platform offerings, and most of these were serious presentations of writers and artists or their cultural output. By the 1880s, these totaled 30 percent of offerings, but at least half of these were performative in some way. The driver for this change was the wealthy suburban institute. At the Harborne and Edgbaston Institute, for example, the ratio of performances to lectures was 3:1 in response to local demand, while that ratio remained 1:3 at both the Midland Institute and the Newcastle Lit.-&-Phil. Thus, mid-century lectures on the world of the Romantic poets gave way to recitations and songs from the period, while analyses on Shakespeare's villains were replaced by costumed or dramatic performances of Iago and Macbeth. Pedagogical programs of the music of Dibden were replaced by "Humorous Pianoforte Recitals," performed by family groups. The "entertainments" most troubling to Simpson—the hypnotists, magicians, and "thought-readers"—formed the bulk of offerings in "mental science," "humor," and "miscellaneous," accounting for about 5 percent of recorded lectures in these sources; this was a small percentage but it was nearly double the number of these performances recorded at mid-century. Even "current events" had become more entertaining, with the heroics of war journalism or imperial travel replacing the careful analyses of foreign policy. Frederick Villiers and H. H. Pearse were especially popular "war artists" and insisted that their goals were "simply to entertain," with one *Newcastle Courant* editor noting acerbically that "people don't go to hear bloodthirsty tales, any more than they would stand in front of a stationer's shop to gloat over the Police News. They go just out of patriotism, of course."[156]

This broad picture does not show us how different types of institutes made their choices and secured their programs. What follows is an analysis of individual institutes, chosen as generally representative of the variety of spaces associated with some form of knowledge-based culture. These include the three major civic institutions in Birmingham, Leeds, and Newcastle: the wealthy suburban institution serving Harborne and Edgbaston; a smaller local institute in Chichester; the London-based SLS; and its "kindred society," the Birmingham SLS, which was still referred to during much of this period as the Sunday Evening Meetings for the People (SEMP). This selection of sources allows us to assess subject matter and speakers across several matrices. First, the three large civic institutions all identified themselves and were perceived as cultural leaders for the entire region, not just the city, and that regional responsibility drove choices in programming. Second, the London SLS battled for audience share with a variety of other culture resources, and its programming decisions were driven by complicated issues of economy and attractiveness. Third, the choice of the Harborne and Edgbaston Institute, as a well-to-do suburban society, and the Birmingham SEMP, designed specifically to attract the working classes, provides an interesting set of data about the similarities and differences within a single city, a city that already shouldered the burdens of a regional culture provider. Further, the comparison of programming between the parent SLS and its Birmingham offshoot demonstrates very different perceptions of programming "for the improvement and social well-being of mankind." Every institute continued to try to balance a season's programming. However, as we take these institutions in turn by category, we can make several general observations.

First, the large civic institutions. We have seen how the Leeds Phil.-&-Lit., the Midland Institute, and the Newcastle Lit.-&-Phil., as represented by Figures 4.8, 4.9, and 4.10, each evolved specific programming to represent both city and region. The Midland, for example, established a music program that became nationally renowned, while the Leeds Phil.-&-Lit. always relied heavily on programming that incorporated the knowledge-producing work of its elite members. The Newcastle Lit.-&-Phil. had its own eccentricities, many of which were rooted in its relative isolation at mid-century but that persisted even as modern transportation made it easier to get to and from the city, and those eccentricities were referenced with indulgence by local reporters: "In Newcastle it does not matter much who the lecturer is; the call is for matter, not men," wrote one journalist, previewing the 1888 season.[157] Such a cheerful preference was not the case at the Midland or the Leeds Phil.-&-Lit., where "men" mattered very much.

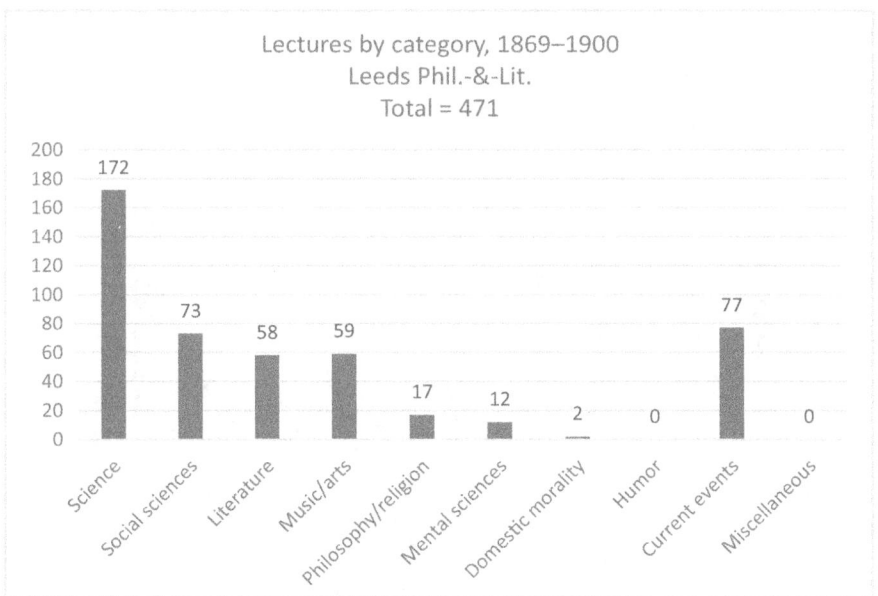

Figure 4.8 Leeds Phil.-&-Lit., 1869–1900.

Source: Leeds Philosophical and Literary Society, *Annual Reports*, 1869–1900.

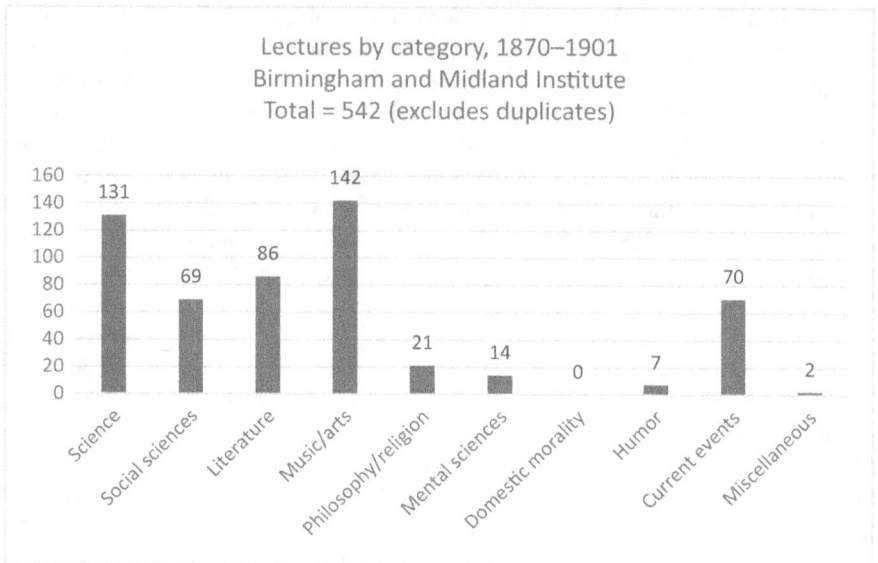

Figure 4.9 Birmingham and Midland Institute, 1870–1901.
Source: Birmingham and Midland Institute, *Annual Report*, 1870–1901.

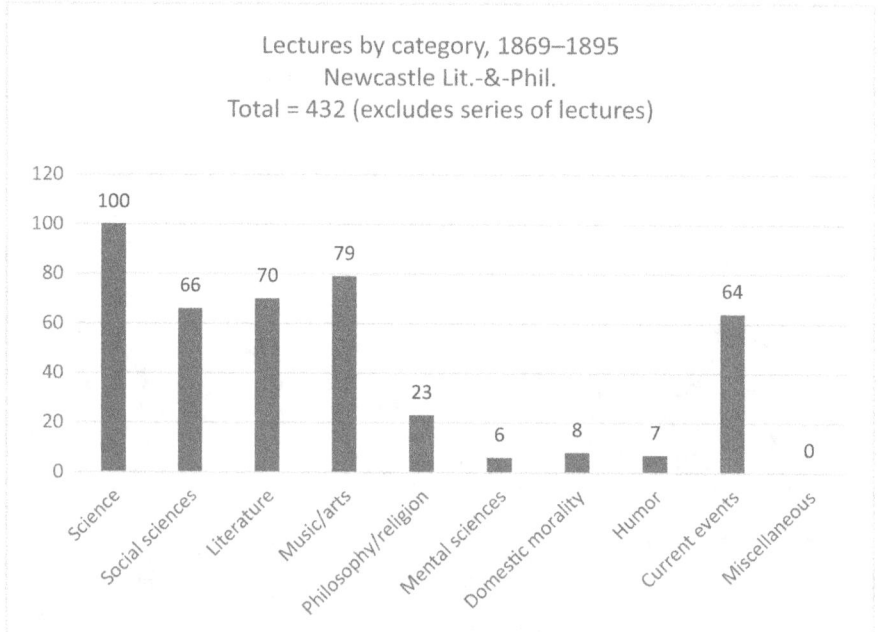

Figure 4.10 Newcastle Lit.-&-Phil., 1869–95.
Source: Robert Spence Watson, *History of the Newcastle Literary and Philosophical Society*.

At the Leeds Phil.-&-Lit., continuing decades of preferences, lectures in the sciences far outstripped those in other fields. Of the ten most popular lecturers during these decades, seven were well-known men of science (Sir Robert Ball, W. F. Barrett, Henry Crowther, Dr. John Edwin Eddison, Sydney Lupton, Louis Compton Miall, and Professor T. E. Thorpe), and only Ball and Barrett were not local members of the Society. The other three most popular lecturers were all local men, two of whom lectured on history and one on literary figures. Humor, performative recitations, and oratory were absent from most Leeds seasons, and "entertainments" were entirely relegated to Christmas programming for children.

At the Midland, Ball and Barrett also made the list of most popular lecturers, as did other national science figures including Sir James Crichton Browne, the Rev. W. H. Dallinger, R. A. Proctor (whose astronomy lectures were extravagantly advertised in the *ILG*, putting him in the tiny minority of speakers in these civic institutions who were associated with the Lecturers' Association), entomologist Edward Bagnall Poulton, paleontologist H. G. Seeley, and zoologist Andrew Wilson. Austrian pianist Ernst Pauer, historian John Robert Seeley, and Birmingham Art Gallery director Whitworth Wallis rounded out the list alongside George Dawson, who had been the most sought-after speaker in the early years of the Midland and continued to appear until his death in 1876. Only Dawson and Wallis were local, although in the first ten years of the Midland (1854–64) nearly three quarters of the speakers had been local men who donated their services. The Midland's offerings in the arts remained traditionally lecture-based; only 30 percent of fine arts in this post-1870 period were "performances," and these relied primarily upon the institute's Madrigal Choir and its Amateur Orchestral Association, which offered traditional classical works rather than more modern or vernacular programs.

At the Newcastle Lit.-&-Phil., Dawson, Seeley, and Proctor were among the most sought-after speakers, linking the institute to other regional centers. Equally popular was local alderman T. P. Barkas, whose offerings ranged from "Festus, the Epic Poem of the Nineteenth Century," to "The Opinions of Ancient Philosophers, Historians, and Poets respecting Comets," placing him squarely in the mode of knowledge-based culture favored by Simpson and other mid-century men. Other local favorites were historian and nonconformist minister John Collingswood Bruce, chemist Joseph Wilson Swan, historian and philosopher John Theodore Merz (who also founded the region's electrical company), and institute secretary Robert Spence Watson, while favorite "lecturers from a distance" included microscopist William Henry Dallinger, physiologist Ernest Albert Parkyn, musician W. Rea, and Shakespeare scholar Richard Green Moulton.[158] As with the Midland, Newcastle's offerings in the fine arts were much more likely to be traditionally lecture-based than performative.

Of all these speakers at the three institutions, only Dawson and Barkas lectured in the increasingly old-fashioned eclectic model of mid-century. By this later period, large civic bodies wanted well-established expertise from practitioners rather than the more generalized or "dilettantish" offerings of the lecturer who had defined mid-century platform talk. This expertise was most often scientific, but history, philosophy, law, and music were equally respected fields of professionalized knowledge. One result of this preference was a dearth of women speakers among the top ten at each site; women were often invited as musical or dramatic performers, and increasingly presented important topical issues in the social sciences, but even in this later period few could break into the male-dominated spheres of physical science or history that produced the more serious speakers. It was only at the end of the century, as we will see in the following chapter, that women lecturers could translate their increasingly professionalized experience into the popular lecture world.

Thus far, we have looked at the world of the dedicated physical institute, where lecture programming was linked spatially to a web of other leisure offerings. What of the phenomenon of the Sunday lecture, which stood apart from a curriculum of classes and clubs and had no permanent physical home? The SLS and its kindred societies offer a different perspective on the culture of the late-Victorian lecture. These societies were not institutes; they lacked the loyal students, the devoted teachers, the small and large tempests over rules, clubbability, and youthful misbehavior. Founded with a single goal that appears today to be naively optimistic—to uplift humanity through the two-hour lecture—the SLS offers a distillation of the Victorian belief in the inspiring nature of those "noble, pleasing, and useful thoughts" lauded by Simpson. What can we make of its programming and that of its provincial offshoots?

The most frequent speakers for the London society were generally well-known men of science, moderately well-known women in the social sciences, and a number of speakers addressing topics in literature and religion. Almost none had any apparent relation to the Lecturers' Association. Acknowledged experts in various sciences lent their names to the SLS: W. B. Carpenter in zoology, W. K. Clifford in physics, and T. Spencer Cobbold in physiology and anatomy were all frequent speakers. Millicent Garrett Fawcett and Elizabeth Ormbe both appeared regularly to speak on issues of women and family, while Anna Kingsford spoke about the gendered work of the anti-vivisectionists. A number of lectures on ancient and non-Western religious and philosophical practices threaded through each season, so that London audiences became quite familiar with specialists G. G. Zerffi, T. W. Rhys Davids, and George Wotherspoon. A few generalists appeared regularly as well, with repertoires that evoked the mid-century "pack of knowledge" now fast giving way to specialization: for example, American Moncure D. Conway offered frequent lectures on topics including "Shakespear's [sic] Merchant of Venice: an Atonement," "Studies of War made at Prussian Headquarters," and "The condition and out-look of the British Stage," while Arthur Nichols delivered popular lectures on folklore and anthropology and Benjamin Richardson delivered a selection of biographies of famous men, evoking the content if not the style of the late George Dawson. As Figure 4.11 shows, almost entirely absent from the first two decades of the London SLS were lectures on the fine arts, literature, or most current events; even the contemporary wars of imperial rivals were unimportant, although a deeper understanding of the religious or philosophical history leading to war was considered an important programming item.

The kindred societies were less rigid about programming. Some committees followed the general lead of the London SLS, so that Newcastle and Leeds, for example, frequently featured R. S. Ball, Andrew Wilson, and many of the other prominent names of the parent organization, securing for themselves a reputation equal to the local Lit.-&-Phils. The Newcastle *Courant* argued that both the local SLS and the Lit.-&-Phil.

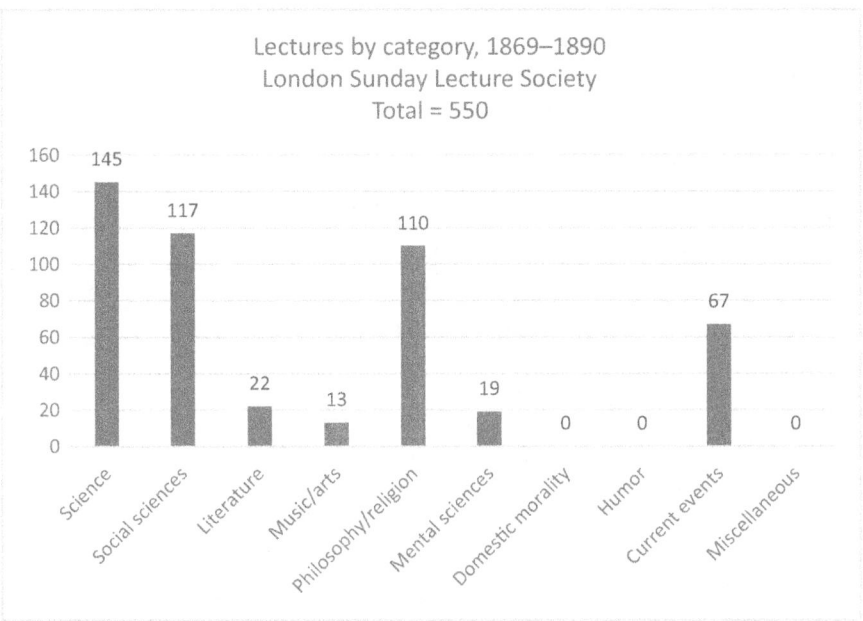

Figure 4.11 London Sunday Lecture Society, 1869–90.

Source: Sunday Lecture Society, *Annual Reports*, 1869–90.

were equally "great lecturing organisations" who consistently secured a variety of well-known names including actress Sarah Siddons and statesman Sir George Trevelyan.[159] In contrast, the Birmingham SLS deliberately retained its founding focus as the Sunday Evening Meetings for the People by relying heavily on well-known local men like Samuel Timmins, Thomas Hewins, John Alfred Langford, and alderman R. F. Martineau, augmented only rarely by national figures like R. S. Ball and W. J. Lancaster. Familiarity rather than cost drove these programming choices, along with a desire not to replicate the work of the Midland Institute, which was tacitly acknowledged to be the appropriate space for national headliners.

The SLS and its kindred societies generally honored their founding pledges to focus on science, history, and literature, eschewing the innovations in entertainment that so troubled Joseph Simpson. We see those innovations instead in the wealthier suburban institutes whose goals were to secure the caliber of speakers that had characterized the American lyceum's "star system" at mid-century. This might occasionally translate to transatlantic celebrities but more often built upon national names like Wilde, Ball, O'Rell, and Stanley, augmented with familiar "institute men" like Walter Rowton and Frank Curzon and the more exotic works of light opera performer C. H. Snazelle and "prestidigitateur" Charles Bertram. The well-funded Harborne and Edgbaston Institute devoted some 50 percent of its programming to entertainment in the fine arts, but also regularly secured beloved regional speakers like William Tuckwell and local art gallery director Whitworth Wallis. Its fellow suburban union members often

Plymouth Mechanics' Institute

J. D. Cogan	Pottery and porcelain
Harry Furniss, Esq.	Art and artists
Wilmott Dixon, Esq.	Historical oration
F. Austin, Esq.	Musical sketch
Edward Ash, Esq.	Dioramic lecture-entertainment

Leeds Mechanics' Institute

J. Carrodus and family	Concert
B. J. Malden	My holiday in Norway, a dioramic entertainment
E. S. Bruce	Light, optics, and optical illusions
William Lant Carpenter	The sun
J. N. Ellaby	Readings
Professor Archibald	Eddison's [sic] loud speaking phonograph
William Dawson and family	Concert
Rev. Arthur Mursell	Breathing books and living libraries
C. C. Maxwell	The humour of our own time
Adelaide Detchon	Recital

Wakefield Mechanics' Institute

Westgate Chapel Choir	Concert
Joseph Thompson, Esq	Civilization and progress
Rev. Andrew Chalmers	An unknown chapter in Wakefield history
Rev. J. J. Christie	Letters and letter writers
R. Marchant, Esq.	Quaint old York, with lime light views
Rev. William Heaton	The Rev. Sydney Smith: his life and writings
Rev. L. S. Calvert	Common applications of chemistry, with experiments
Rev. G. Grantham Collins	Life amongst the gold diggers and sheep farmers in New Zealand
Prof. Rogers	Chopin and his works
W. Miles, Esq.	Miscellaneous recitals
Frank Curzon	Hogarth the painter, historian, and moralist, illustrated on the black board

Leeds Phil.-&-Lit.

Earl of Carnarvon	Liberty of speech
Rt. Hon. Lord Houghton	Thomas Wentworth, Earl of Strafford
C. V. Boys	Quartz fibres
Henry Blackburn	Algeria and Morocco
L. J. Rogers	History of dance music
Edward Bagnall Poulton	The use of colour in the animal kingdom, illustrated in insects
Archibald Barr	Some scientific questions concerning pictures
Dr. Tempest Anderson	The Sicilian volcanoes
Arthur Sidgwick	Robert Browning

Prof. Marshall Ward	Timber, and some of its diseases
Harborne and Edgbaston Institute	
Rev. Dr. Dallinger	Contrasts in nature: the infinitely great and the infinitely small
Dunbar Steen	Dramatic recitals
Whitworth Wallis	In search of Pharaoh
Harriet Kendall	Dramatic recitals
Rev. William Tuckwell	The Great Ice Age. Illustrated.
J. Deykin and J. Redfern	Amateur dramatic performance
A. B. Chamberlain	The application of natural foliage to decorative art
Amateur Opera Company	A grand vocal and instrumental concert
Midland Institute	
Wyke Bayliss	The legend of beauty; or Art as representing the passion of our lives
Edmund Gosse	Leigh Hunt
James Crichton-Browne	Brain Growth and Brain Stress
Carl Armbruster	Modern composers of classical song
Rev. A. R. Vardy	A day in the streets of ancient Athens
C. H. Bothamley	The photography of to-day
T. Matesdorf, Esq.	Old illuminated manuscripts
The Institute Madrigal Choir	Concert

Figure 4.12 Selected programming at institutions, January–May 1889.

Source: *ILG* 1889; Birmingham and Midland Institute, *Annual Report*, 1889; Leeds Phil.-&-Lit. *Annual Report*, 1889; Robert Spence Watson, *History of the Newcastle Literary and Philosophical Institute*; Harborne and Edgbaston Institute, *Annual Report*, 1889; Yorkshire Union of Mechanics' Institutes, *Annual Report*, 1889.

could not afford the stars, despite union pledges to share costs, but they could augment appearances by Tuckwell and Wallis with amateur dramatics and homegrown musical programming. Such member-driven performances had earned the gentle sarcasm of Blake and other mid-century institute men, who believed "amateur theatricals" would only dilute the importance of institute offerings, but by the 1880s and 1890s the enthusiastic performances of younger subscribers appeared increasingly necessary to long-term survival.

If we place programming from a selection of these societies side by side, we can trace some important connections and discern the continuing efforts to maintain autonomy while participating in a national web of culture. Figure 4.12 shows a brief portion of one season across several societies.

Two major points emerge from these data. First, nearly all of these performers were well-established rather than unknown amateurs. Only Wakefield relied heavily on local talent that did not appear outside the region; even the Plymouth Mechanics' Institution could boast of Furniss and Dixon, busy lecturers of many years' experience. The warnings of American critics, that a new lecturer had about a year to prove himself, appears not to be the case in the English system, where familiarity generally bred affection rather than contempt. Many of these lecturers had been active for decades and appeared in the mid-century lecture lists of the Society of Arts as well as in the *Journal*. Further, none of these performers appeared in more than one of these institutions during this season, suggesting again that the oft-repeated desire for regional and unified programming remained largely performative, and that the pool of available lecturers was deep enough to satisfy the needs of quite disparate programming committees and audiences.

Second, taken as a group, these programs generally follow the overall choices outlined above: a healthy percentage of lectures that dealt with some aspect of scientific thought, whether that was the manufacture of porcelain, the geologic formations of the Ice Age, or the emerging science of psychology. Some fifteen of these fifty-three offerings—nearly 30 percent—were identifiably "entertainment" of some kind, from the musical recitals of Kendall and Detchon—both heavily advertised in and reviewed by the *ILG*, now under the direction of Alfred Simpson—to the famous blackboard sketches of Frank Curzon. Within these lists, we can see that the Leeds Phil.-&-Lit. continued to ignore "entertainment" in favor of science, while the Harborne and Edgbaston Institute devoted half its program to musical and dramatic performance. Harborne shared none of its seasons with the Midland, underscoring the very different purposes of these geographically and socially similar institutions. The Leeds Mechanics' Institution hewed most closely to the mid-century model of lecture programming.

"The Perfecter of Knowledge and a Recreation after Labour": The Future of the Popular Lecture

What, then, do we make of the late-Victorian world of the popular lecture? Simpson, in one of his final columns for the *ILG*, reviewed for his readers the ways in which entertainment that was "fitted for the amusement-loving side of human nature" had rendered the "scientific or literary Lecture ... something of a failure." Simpson mourned the vanishing world of the institutes, where the intellectual altruism of the popular lecturer had helped fit two generations of individuals with the "packs of knowledge" necessary for a good life. Changes to elementary and secondary education had robbed the popular lecture of its foundational place within active knowledge and participatory citizenship, as forces well beyond the control of the platform speaker transformed the listener into a consumer and diminished the robust spaces of knowledge-based culture into attenuated sites for classes and examinations. Yet, all was not lost: "Art and science, history and poetry, can only be followed into their remote recesses, and their hidden beauties brought to light, through the platform Lecture—alike the perfecter of knowledge, and a recreation after labour."[160]

We have seen in this chapter how the world of the popular lecturer split into three distinct but still related categories. Generalist lecturers like Simpson, who built their work on the mid-century pairing of education and entertainment, came to describe their work as "Literary," even when these offerings spilled over into the social sciences, religion, and philosophy. Their efforts, retaining the strong moral flavor associated with mid-Victorian self-improvement, were juxtaposed to the performance and spectacle increasingly associated with both the fine arts and the sciences, as oratory, costume, and experiment captured the imagination of a public generally indifferent to or unable to appreciate the intellectual innovations of modernist art or late-century physics. Thus, "Entertaining" lectures formed a second segment of late-century knowledge-based culture, and, like the "Literary" lectures, enabled the hard-working and enterprising speaker to make a living on the platform. Simpson's tireless work to professionalize these efforts touched hundreds of these speakers, many of whom never joined the Lecturers' Association but who reaped the benefits of standards, boundaries, and practices that transformed the amateur world of mid-century. Finally, intellectuals and practitioners willing to share their interests with educated but unspecialized audiences emerged as a new and important segment of this same world. Many popular speakers could move easily across these porous boundaries. In the following chapter, we will see one more wave of fragmentation, as the popular lecture was adapted to serve two very different functions: first, it anchored the decades of the University Extension movement, finally pushed out of the realm of adult education after 1903 and the establishment of the Workers' Education Association, and second, it became an undisputed consumer good, marketed by new and expanding commercial lecture agencies.

5

The Late-Victorian Popular Lecture

I have not been one of those fortunate persons who are able to regard a popular lecture as a mere hors d'oeuvre, *unworthy of being ranked among the serious efforts of a philosopher.*[1]

The popular lecture as an artifact changed very little in late-Victorian England: its form and content were generally stable, its functions within civic culture remained broadly understood and appreciated, and its practitioners continued to discern, reflect, and shape the tastes and preferences of listeners. Subscribers at mid-century had come to expect lecture programs that ranged across subject matter and increasingly included contemporary and even controversial topics, presented in tightly constructed and liberally illustrated one- to two-hour segments; subscribers some forty years later could count on the same basic guarantees of well-crafted topicality and variety. By the mid-1890s, the popular lecture needed no crusaders like Harry Chester and Barnett Blake, no defenders like Joseph Simpson and Frank Curzon. The LDOS lawsuit had targeted the Sunday societies for their timing, not their content. The popular lecture was perceived as, and treated as, a fact as well as an artifact: fundamental to Victorian culture, immovable in its centrality to middle-class performances of status, and indispensable as a tool in working-class self-improvement. It was uniquely able to "awaken an interest in scientific and literary subjects among persons whose attention might otherwise have never been directed to such matters," educationist Sir Phillip Magnus told an 1893 audience. Popular lectures continued to serve as "a source of refreshment" as well as a means of "enlarg[ing] our mental wealth and add[ing] to our enjoyment of life."[2]

Indeed, late-Victorian popular lecture culture had changed significantly only in two related respects. First, the middle range of dedicated sappers and miners had nearly vanished, to be replaced on the platforms of most civic institutions by the credentialed practitioners whose lectures reflected an established and recognized career. The professional popular lecturer who entertained had generally relocated into suburban institutes and other venues that sought music and magic, while the professional popular lecturer who gently educated had become outmoded and had steadily disappeared from the platform. This evolution was uneven, more rapid in large centers than in small towns and more complete in younger societies than in old. Several of these latter spaces, especially the older and smaller mechanics' institutes and lit.-&-phils., retained their hold on local sentiment and support through the use of homegrown talent. At the small Keswick Lecture Society, for example, local vicar Hardwicke D. Rawnsley appeared regularly on the platform to deliver gratis lectures pulled from his own tourist memories, such as the descriptively named "Some Royal Mummies" and "Some More Royal Mummies," rather than more sophisticated presentations of his work in land conservation and local politics.[3] In general, however, and outside the shrinking number of such spaces in villages and small towns, the credentialed practitioner became increasingly central to late-Victorian knowledge-based culture.

The second major development, which fed and was fed by the first, was the normalization of the SLS as the primary vehicle through which these popular lectures were delivered. As we saw in the previous chapter, kindred branches of the SLS were established in many large and midsized towns in the 1880s and 1890s, all of them independent from but loosely modeled after the London society. While these provincial offshoots adopted various strategies to attract and retain local audiences—Birmingham's use of board schools to guarantee access to audiences across the city or Halifax's policy of free admissions just before the lectures began—their participation in the overall project of "the improvement and social well-being of mankind" helped attract the credentialed practitioners who had formed the backbone of the London SLS programming from its inception. Provincial societies often interspersed these practitioners with familiar local faces, but the overall dependence on established speakers created increasingly homogenous audiences across the kingdom. SLS programming on Sunday nights did not preclude other weekly programming; the Midland Institute, the Newcastle Lit.-&-Phil., and a number of other civic institutions used Monday evenings for their own lecture programs, while smaller mutual improvement, debating, and literary societies spread their meetings across the week. "Those fond of hearing lectures have had plenty of opportunity for gratifying their wishes during the week," noted one Newcastle reporter with satisfaction.[4] However, the kingdom-wide association of Sunday afternoons or evenings with a variety of offerings that were reliably entertaining, moderately serious, topical, and generally inexpensive preserved and expanded the importance of the popular lecture in provincial culture. Even small and limited societies, such as the tiny Barkerend Sunday Lecture Society and the Belle Vue Hotel Sunday Evening Lectures, took advantage of the normalization of Sunday as a space for secular offerings. Not all of these efforts were successful, of course; the Morpeth *Herald* warned that the local SLS was so poorly regarded by city residents that "it will kill the movement so far as Morpeth is concerned," despite the fact that "the lecturers are men of marked ability, and specially skilled as popular entertainers."[5] By the 1890s, however, the popular lecture as a vehicle for knowledge-based culture had become both more general and more generally accessible, no longer implicitly limited to a privileged caste of participatory citizens.

Thus, even as Simpson and others had rued the decline of "the institutes" as the primary space for popular lectures, and lamented the choices of many popular lecturers to embrace entertaining appeals to the senses rather than more sober appeals to the generally educated intellect, the popular lecture as an artifact became more, not less, robust through the 1880s and 1890s. Simpson's work ironically obscured the ways in which the popular lecture adapted and survived. His position as the acknowledged champion of the "institute men" like himself and the ways in which he mourned their narrowing opportunities implied an overall collapse in the phenomenon of the popular lecture. In reality, however, that perceived collapse was a reconfiguration of the late-century cultural landscape. By about 1890, the very abundance and ephemerality of the popular lecture made it an ideal tool for those individuals and institutions ushering in modernization and change. It was flexible enough to initiate and accommodate intense debates over privilege and responsibility, national fitness and individual capacity, duty to self and commitment to empire. As we will see below, it continued to be closely associated with new models of adult education. At the same time, it was increasing one consumer good among many, purchasable and disposable, and thus in competition with other forms of leisure culture.

From Participation to Sympathy: Changing Models of Citizenship

While the basic structures of the popular lecture remained relatively stable over time, the broader field within which it operated had changed significantly. At mid-century, a caste of unenfranchised but participatory citizens was expected to enthusiastically pursue culture through voluntary institutions that provided crucial practice in civic duty alongside instruction and amusement. Within the institutes, the popular lecture and its accompanying structures of sociability would both nurture this understanding of citizenship and provide the local spaces for its performance. According to this paradigm, the liberal subject would be inexorably shaped by the artifacts of knowledge-based culture, and his children would unfailingly seek those opportunities even if he himself could not: "The next generation will be much like the last in all essentials, but will be more intelligent, more patient, more careful, more successful in all the arts and in all the graces of life," argued one institution president.[6] In the relatively peaceable decades of mid-century, this vaguely articulated future, peopled by productive but not disruptive citizens, seemed inevitable.

As we have seen, however, the realities of the 1867 Reform Act and the 1870 Education Act illuminated just how limited that caste of participatory citizens was and might be. The facts of elementary education and suffrage created new citizens, but the mid-century ideal of participatory citizenship, now exposed as narrow and exclusive, could no longer be confidently invoked as the certain outcome of these changes. As an ideal, it was largely replaced by a pair of discourses aimed at both children and adults. For children, as Stephen Heathorn has shown, a relatively straightforward patriotism was embedded in new curricula developed by and within the primary schools, emphasizing empire and Englishness as two halves of a modern whole.[7] For adults, this discourse focused on working-class men, newly enfranchised and often unevenly educated, who needed to be guided into their proper roles. Simpson and his institute men had argued that "literature, with her soft endearing influences," was a crucial conduit to civic duty for the working classes, but this view gained little traction outside the narrow world of the Lecturers' Association. Instead, as Beaven and Griffiths have shown, civic leaders undertook a broad variety of efforts to engage these new voters in a carefully regulated "civic spirit" that replaced the ideal of active participation with models of carefully regulated public and private behaviors. Persistent worries that the workingman in particular remained "imperfectly civilized"[8] reinforced the shift away from autonomous self-culture toward a more prescriptive late-Victorian citizenship, where the good citizen was defined as a law-abiding wage earner whose knowledge of larger local, national, and imperial issues was limited in breadth and framed within emotive patriotism rather than rational self-improvement.[9] The civic, cross-classing functions of knowledge-based culture had flourished in the capacious mid-century institutes, but as these spaces were inexorably folded into new models of secondary and technical education, little room was left for what Samuel Barnett would call "the widely spread eagerness to get knowledge" defined by shared social interests and a common "public conscience."[10]

Many who had cut their teeth on the mid-century model fought hard to preserve the link between participatory citizenship and knowledge-based culture, as we can see in the old-fashioned language of one Yorkshire clergyman who in 1888 condemned the local branch of the Primrose Society for wooing new voters with "amusement rather than instruction, … catering for men and women's weaknesses instead of offering opportunities for self-improvement and the acquisition of knowledge."[11] In the changing world of the institutes, there were two responses, neither sufficient to preserve the mid-century model. One common reaction, as we saw in the previous chapter, was to try to rehabilitate the notion of the citizen-reader—the village reading room and library, where literacy became a rough surrogate for civic duty. In 1890, for example, one YUMI speaker told his listeners that reading rooms and libraries, "well-stocked with good books" from the Union, "enabled those who are now citizens to discharge their [unenumerated] duties more fitly and intelligently than they would otherwise have done."[12] Village libraries "made people better citizens" who would be able to encourage "local assemblies" to "get things right." This model of nonspecific local engagement differed significantly from the spiritual, intellectual, and physical capacities lauded by Chester and his colleagues, however; citizen-readers were tasked only with "one patriotic purpose, the trying to make the world better than they had found it."[13] This discourse was generally a failure, presenting the world of the book not as intoxicating space for imagination and self-realization but rather enfolding it into the functionalist work of the franchise.

At the other end of the spectrum ran a more affective thread of citizenship, where men and women were urged to discern and pursue "a common good" built on individual growth and self-expression.[14] This language was most common in the suburban institute, where members and patrons easily accessed suffrage, organized charity, and other recognized pathways to civic engagement. Presidents and members together spoke regularly of "the personal duty of each and the common interest of all," "general sympathy," "working for the good of [our] fellow-citizens," and "promot[ing] the welfare and happiness of all our citizens."[15] This familiar and generalized language of sympathy and support, which had also figured largely in mid-century rhetoric, supplied an emotive link between individual and community. "Sympathy" had, of course, been used for at least a century in ways well beyond the simple expression of emotional affinity and "the imagination of other people's thoughts and feelings."[16] Its malleability had made it particularly useful within discourses of religion, politics, and the sciences, and it was also a well-established tool for novelists, poets, and essayists as they sought over the century to generate social change. Now, a model of "sympathetic citizenship" emerged to provide a temporary bridge from caste-based and localized participation to a set of emotional attachments that would form the basis of late-century patriotism, attachments that were simultaneously more broadly English and less activist than the mid-century vigor that had promised so much.

This model of sympathetic citizenship was particularly evident in the rhetoric of institute committees and students, where the well-established trope of "sympathy of mind with mind," had long been one way of bridging differences within the classroom, the lecture theater, and the library. Langford had used the phrase in prescribing the hybrid lecture model at the Midland; three decades later, "the collision of mind with mind" had become a common description of the relationship not only between student and teacher but also, more broadly, between self and other.[17] Because "mind with mind" suggested no immutable class hierarchy but rather a mutual and disciplined curiosity, it preserved a loose sense of corporate belonging that required no specific social action beyond the recognition of a shared appreciation for the pursuit of knowledge. "English literature binds the race in fetters of sympathy," noted one speaker at the YUMI annual meeting in 1897.[18] This sense of sympathy had been embedded in the mid-century world of knowledge-based culture, and it would be threaded through new late-Victorian spaces for the popular lecture as well.

Building University Extension around the Popular Lecture

This language of sympathetic citizenship was peculiarly embedded within the University Extension movement, an enterprise built upon the popular lecture and described by one student as "guiding thought into better ways, ... larger views, wider sympathies, deeper insight."[19] Founded in 1873 by James Stuart, it was "the outcome of two great modern institutions, universal Elementary Education and free public Libraries ... [and] the recent development of our railway system" to provide "extramural" education, that is, education outside of Oxbridge but linked to the universities through teachers, curricula, and access to examinations.[20] Embedded within the web of knowledge-based culture that produced and nurtured the civic institutions, its programming was similarly attractive to skilled artisans and young, mostly middle-class women, two groups who leaned strongly away from vocational subjects and were already eager consumers of novels, periodicals, and popular lectures in literature, history, and the arts. Early extension directors, sketching out the parameters of the movement, deployed familiar language about the dangers of undisciplined access to these instruments of culture: "The dangers are chiefly two," they wrote. "The power of reading gives new opportunities for indulging directly in evil; it presents also a new temptation to dissipate mental energy. ... Higher education obviates them by introducing new benefits. It gives intellectual interest to life; it conduces to sobriety of political judgment; the study of national literature and national history inspires patriotism. In short, by giving contact with the greatest thoughts of the world, such training imparts higher ideals of life, of citizenship, and of religion."[21] These sweeping claims were updated versions of the arguments that had marked debates over mid-century reading rooms, access to periodical literature, and other innovations within the institutes. Now they focused on the "liberal education" accessed through the Extension movement and "primarily directed to something quite other than the material needs of life," designed to combat "narrowness, whether of home or of school, of class or profession, of nation or locality."[22] Critics were quick to begin parsing the movement's complex amalgamation of political conservatism, social activism, philosophical idealism, Oxbridge self-preservation, and educational utility, but for Extension students, the claim was simple: "There are moral influences at work through University that tend to ennoble and beautify life."[23]

Extension courses began with a popular lecture and generally consisted of six to twelve public lectures over three to six months, supplemented by classes, tutorials, and exams for the 20 percent of audience members who then chose to enroll as Extension students.[24] Initial lectures for every course needed to be popular in nature, for several reasons. A good popular lecture, open to an audience of habitual lecture-goers who would pay fees already associated with a choice platform speaker, would both defray the administrative costs of the Extension course and attract the small number of listeners who were willing to pursue the academic portion of the course itself. Extension lecturers and many local secretaries commented at length on how and how easily a well-crafted popular lecture could lead to the acquisition of "systematized knowledge," and for many years it was accepted as a norm that the lecturer who "serves the cause of true education by giving a lecture on Monday in Oxford" would "repeat the same lecture on Tuesday at Birmingham."[25] "The popular side of higher education should be kept steadily in view as the essential feature of the scheme," wrote one secretary about a proposed set of courses, explaining that "the popular lectures would feed the smaller classes."[26]

The first dozen years of Extension programming, as it moved from a highly localized and limited enterprise to a kingdom-wide phenomenon, mapped the popular lecture clearly onto this specific threshold space, where students and general audience members could share a well-crafted platform performance by a sophisticated speaker—"a living cultured teacher"—whose bona fides included, by definition, university-level knowledge and experience.[27] Thus, a science lecture by Cambridge professor Henry Roscoe—already a desirable addition to a civic lecture program—would inevitably coax new learners out of old subscriber bases. A number of established institutions incorporated Extension programming into their existing lecture offerings. The Newcastle Lit.-&-Phil. was an enthusiastic early adopter of Extension lectures into its seasonal programming, so that its offerings might include some two dozen individual lectures one year and one or two courses the next. The SLS in Ancoats (formally known as the Ancoats Recreation Committee), ushered in its twelfth year not only with lecturers by William Morris, writer and poet Richard LeGalliene, Russian political exile Prince Pyotr Kropotkin, and other coveted speakers but also with a pair of Extension courses, including Oxford lecturer Hudson Shaw's popular course on "English History for Workmen," and a series of Gilchrist Lectures featuring Sir Robert Ball and others.[28] The Darlington Lecture Association was founded in 1881 specifically "to get an extension scheme in place," although it took another decade to secure the programming.[29] The Midland Institute pointed to its own early efforts "to bring the blessings of University learning into the midst of work-a-day life."[30] Introductory popular lectures of Extension courses fit relatively seamlessly into the existing civic programs, while the subsequent classes and examinations could be placed adjacent to the work in the older mechanics' institutes and cooperative societies as well as the courses of programming at the redbrick universities and the established "industrial departments" at the Midland and similar sites.

This hybrid experiment spread rapidly from Oxford, Cambridge, and the University of London, driven by a combination of local demand, available funding, and persistent reminders that "Oxford and Cambridge will be false to their trust if they allow general culture to perish."[31] By 1891, as SLS branches spread across midsized towns, extension centers were also operative in these and hundreds of smaller sites, with nearly 1,000 discrete courses serving over 50,000 enrollees.[32] The establishment of an extension center in these early years was remarkably similar to the establishment of an SLS. The process for each type of organization required a local worthy to "get the subject up" and assemble a committee, which would in turn hire a secretary, coordinate with the university for a lecturer, secure adequate newspaper coverage, and guarantee "a local chorus" of supporters.[33] Like early institute committees who called for cooperative programming to fill a region's roster of popular lecturers and then ignored practical suggestions for unified planning, local extension committees could be equally stubborn, "refus[ing] to work amicably with their railway neighbours" and therefore unable to be "placed in a circuit round which a lecturer travels weekly or fortnightly."[34] The similarities between filling an extension program and filling an institute lecturing season led to fears that "the University might slide into the position of a popular lecturing-bureau," and as late as 1891, Extension speakers were reassuring their audiences that "the university extension scheme ... was not, by any means, a mere lecture agency."[35] It was, instead, particularly attuned to local need, just as the mid-century institutes had been: "The university informs the town what lecturers it has at its disposal and what courses they are able to give, and the town determines what kind of lectures it desires to receive. The subjects vary very much," explained Extension lecturer Oscar Browning. "The northern miners are keen for instruction in science; suburban ladies prefer the literature and art of medieval Italy or Germany."[36] Centers consistently chose courses in literature, history, the social sciences, and the arts over those in the sciences, following patterns of preference evident since 1850 in the institutes and the civic institutions. The spring 1893 list of courses offered through Oxford, for example, showed that courses in nonscience subjects outnumbered science courses by about two to one.[37] Extension directors, echoing language from the heyday of the institutes, noted that the course content itself was less important than the discipline of the experience. Extension courses were key to "mental training" rather than simply mastery of facts: "in the hands of a capable lecturer, a course on literature can be made to inculcate much [sic] of the same principles of accuracy, method, and research (which after all are the most important things) as a course on science."[38]

The self-reflective musings of the early Extension movement also strongly echoed the discourse that had surrounded the earliest discussions of the popular lecture. Might University Extension "teach people to think for themselves?" Would "lighter courses on novels, on art, on architecture, on lime-lit Italian towns" distract from the serious work of the movement? How could the movement prevent the profusion of cheap novels and the penny press from "emasculat[ing] the national mind?" Were the popular lectures so crucial to the Extension program merely "dessert before dinner, all plums and no pudding?" Could extension students elevate their own lives through "the principle of real dignity in Knowledge?" Would such a movement add to "the national interests?"[39] Students and secretaries responded as their earlier counterparts had done, arguing that "the revived popularity of the lecture" was crucial to new, broader access to higher education: "it is the business of the lecturer to give a push to the mind, not to provide it with peptonized pabulum."[40]

A New Caste of "Brain Workers"

These early Extension centers similarly emphasized the place of "social intercourse, the play of mind on mind, the stimulating effect of a corporate life" within this new iteration of knowledge-based culture.[41] Popular lectures were a starting point not only for the academic framing of an Extension course but also for the shared social and intellectual delights of pursuing knowledge, whether or not that knowledge was deepened through tutorials and examinations. Much early content in the Oxbridge Extension periodicals explored the intellectual growth spurred by the good popular lecture. "The superiority of lectures over books, as teaching instruments, depends on the contact between the personality of the lecturer and that of the student," argued one Extension secretary in a lengthy column in the *Oxford University Extension Gazette [OUEG]*, and thus students were strongly advised to listen without taking notes in order to take full advantage of "those subtle currents of sympathy" expressed through "voice, gesture, [and] changing expression of feature."[42] Another correspondent, revisiting John Ruskin's notorious public scolding of the popular lecture audience, noted that "Mr. Ruskin would himself be the first to allow that the impressive power of all good teaching lies in the personality of the teacher."[43] Extension work, synthesizing the language of mid-century institute men with the rhetoric emanating from Oxbridge, provided a purposeful "sympathy with and desire for knowledge, because it broadens life, heightens pleasure, and puts us in communication with the best that has been said and thought and known."[44]

Students also consistently emphasized the social benefits of their shared corporate experiences in language that revived the idea of caste, a concept that had been dismissed by Simpson in the mid-1860s as "a *fiction*" that would inevitably dissolve as education in general became more broadly available.[45] Extension cofounder Richard Moulton argued that "we know nothing of social classes in University Extension. We wish our audiences to include all kinds of people, all ages, all degrees of previous education ... . It is for all classes alike."[46] In reality, of course, hierarchies and divisions were rife within the Extension movement, both within the centers and within the various student groups that coalesced around the classes.[47] Instead of using the language of class, however, students claimed a shared devotion to "brain-work," a phrase made endlessly flexible through the popular lectures of practitioners like Sir James Crichton and Dr. Andrew Wilson. Descriptions of the brain as a physical organ provided "proof" that the students of the institutes and the extension classrooms, no matter how they earned their wage, were all "brain workers" and thus were as crucial to civic improvement as the brick-workers and bankers whose contributions might be more physically tangible.[48] As the world of local participation was slowly homogenized and diluted, "brain work" became increasingly important as a way to differentiate those who pursued knowledge from those who did not: "the very democracy of intellect is parted from outer barbarians by a gulf far deeper than that which parts the aristocracy of wealth or rank from social inferiors."[49] By 1890, one popular lecturer noted that English society in its entirety was "divided into two classes—the brain worker and the manual worker," a division more quaintly described by an Extension student as "brain-spinners or hand-workers."[50]

Importantly, within the extension world, this division did not reflect simple class boundaries but rather the caste-based division between "real students ... and dilettante amateurs."[51] "Brain-work" carried important emotional value even as many students discovered it actually did little to improve the economic or social position of the possessor. As Thomas Wright, "the journeyman engineer," had argued a generation earlier, "enjoying the literature of your country" was entirely separate from rising socially or economically.[52] Predictably, this struggle made the unspoken promises of extension-based liberal education that much more irresistible, and the Extension lecture became increasingly differentiated from the "merely-popular." By the mid-1890s, Extension administrators, lecturers, and students began to draw carefully back from the popular lecture as such: "University Lectures are not 'popular' in the sense of descending to the people's taste," emphasized one student in 1894; "Their purpose is rather to cultivate the popular taste and raise it to the University standard."[53] A few years later, the boundary between "popular" and "extension" lectures was made even more explicit: Captain J. H. Cooke, scheduled to appear in January 1902 at the Halifax SLS, requested a change in his advertised lecture, "England in the Mediterranean," as he had "come to the conclusion that it is of a type that is more suited to a "University Extension" audience. ... It does not therefore lend itself to the relation of those personal narratives and experiences which go so far to render travel lectures amusing *and interesting.*" Cooke offered to the SLS instead his tried-and-true "Etna," with "thrilling limelight views," which was less focused on "the political element" and had fewer maps, and thus would more easily "commend itself to the average audience."[54]

This resurgence of both class and caste was articulated as well in new language about citizenship. Extension students consistently referred to themselves not only as "brain-workers" but also as "citizens of the world," and argued that Extension education "aim[ed] at training the citizen rather than the scholar."[55] Robert Halstead, an ardent Extension student and missionary for the cause, reminded his fellow students that "we are not only members of a great nation and of a complex society, but we may become citizens in a no less important realm of knowledge and thought that knows no nationality and no social distinction."[56] University Extension would help students perceive both "higher ideals of life and ... their duties as citizens."[57] Unsurprisingly, then, courses on citizenship were especially popular.[58] "The aim, we are far from saying the achievement, but certainly the aim, of University Extension is to bear witness to the double need of the education of scholars and the education of citizens."[59]

Erasing the Popular Lecture from Adult Education

The Extension movement, built as it was upon a reluctance to force significant structural or ideological change at Oxbridge, was important to the culture of the popular lecture for reasons of both timing and ideology. Unlike their successors in the Workers' Education Association (WEA) or the Labour College movement, Extension organizers in the mid-1870s understood that success was, for a number of practical reasons, dependent upon the web of institutes and societies already in existence. The movement could not survive financially without linking itself to the culture of the popular lecture as it existed in civic institutions across the kingdom. Like those institutions, University Extension provided a crucial space to explore the connections between instruction and education, on the one hand, and citizenship and its duties and responsibilities, on the other. Extension students and secretaries, most of whom had been born after the mid-century period of seemingly unshakeable social, political, and economic expansion, faced the resurgence of class antagonisms as they sought to reestablish the boundaries of an updated caste of those who might "*be and do*." The movement's "whole eager, vigorous, impressionable body of mostly young people"[60] wrestled with limited social mobility and a lack of seriousness on the part of educators and critics as the extension movement continued to grow.

However, given the limits of the old established universities, it was inevitable that students and educationists would seek a more radical system of opportunity and access. As many scholars have shown, the WEA (founded 1903) ran alongside the Extension movement for a number of years, slowly pushing aside the older organization as founder Albert Mansbridge and others constructed a "highway" to university education that was built not only on existing popular lecture programming but increasingly on the offerings of formal education associations and the newer universities.[61] Five years after its founding, the WEA published a lengthy assessment of the field of play, which functioned as a manifesto of a new iteration of adult education. According to the report, University Extension as a system was insufficient for several reasons, all of which had been analyzed and debated almost since the first Extension course some thirty years earlier. First, because Extension centers had to be completely self-funded, "both the lectures and the subject to be studied must be chosen not solely or chiefly on account of their educative value, but with a view to the probability of their drawing such large numbers that the lectures will 'pay.'" Second, its "unsystematic" nature made "its courses too little of a continuous education." Finally, neither Extension lecturers nor their audiences had any real close connection with the university. "It is desirable," noted the *Report*, "that both lecturers and students should feel that they share in the dignity which comes from belonging to an ancient academic body." The existing system should not be destroyed outright but rather should be "recognized as merely subsidiary to the tutorial classes."[62]

The *Report* set an ambitious agenda that had as one of its effects the slow but irrevocable separation of the popular lecture from post-secondary education. Local universities and colleges might still gesture toward the work of the civic institutions as providing ancillary or purely recreative lectures, but the popular lecture as a conduit for higher education was finally declared a failure. "Valuable though lectures to audiences of more than one hundred persons may be in stimulating interest and attracting genuine students, they are necessarily, when taken by themselves, of very little real educational value. They make the lecturer into an orator, and the audience into a public meeting."63 Such lectures might continue until the WEA was able to establish a complete network of centers, but it was clear that knowledge-based culture was fracturing permanently along that same boundary between education and entertainment that had persistently challenged educators, committees, social critics, and subscribers. The report reassured readers that both were needed; university education, not merely through Oxbridge but now also organized by the redbrick universities, would provide "liberal" study that "gives access to the thoughts and ideals of the ages," while popular lectures would be associated with "civic qualities" necessary for satisfactory corporate life. The former "stands for culture in its highest and truest sense," while the latter might help shape the individual as "a member of a self-governing nation."64

Establishing this ambitious program necessitated some dependence upon frameworks already in place, provided both by the Extension programs and the surviving mechanics' institutes and other sites of mid-century culture, and the transition could be bumpy. For example, in 1910 the Handsworth WEA *Annual Report* noted upcoming "lectures on miscellaneous subjects," that would be "of a very interesting and instructive character," including "Venice," "The Life of the People in Switzerland," "The Romance of the Solar System," "The Old Stone Crosses of the British Isles," "The Nile, Its History and Mystery," and "Four Hundred Years of Piano Music."65 This program replicated many mid-century programs of mechanics' institutes, and the Handsworth WEA, building on the Handsworth Working Men's Association, found it easiest in its early years to continue this pattern of general popular lectures by local or regional men rather than secure university lecturers for courses and tutorials. By 1912, however, its lecture program was firmly oriented around WEA-approved courses of lectures: the fall 1912 course was on "Germany and the Germans," delivered by Mr. Herbert Heaton, MA, of the University of Birmingham, while the spring 1913 course was "Selected Plays of Shakespeare" by Mr. Gordon Hilsop, MA, also of the University of Birmingham.66

The language of the WEA journal, *The Highway*, continued to deploy much of the rhetoric of both university extension and mid-century knowledge-based culture. The WEA was "a Missionary Association, not for the purpose of making all men and women scholars, but to awaken their interest in education, and to give them such pure and true things as they demand. Pure recreation, even, for such is a harbinger of progress: reasoned, physical culture, the necessary concomitant of mental development, glorious and inspiring simple books, for by thought awakened in such a manner a nation can live."67 Local supplements regularly spoke of a focus on "sympathy of mind with mind," the importance of "education for life" rather than for making a living, and the rejection of a life of "soul-deadening toil, made palatable by intervals of sensational amusement—which is not recreation."[68] The language of mid-century knowledge-based culture had been appropriated and remade for the purposes of access to liberal education, even as the cornerstone of that culture—the popular lecture itself—no longer provided the foundation for this education. Instead, the popular lecture was firmly relocated into the civic institutions and societies where it had begun.

Managing the Popular Lecture: The Halifax Sunday Lecture Society

What did the collision of mind with mind look like in the context of late-Victorian popular lecturing? By the 1890s, the process of curating this programming followed a stable and predictable general pattern, as we can see if we turn to one of the younger kindred societies. The Halifax SLS (HSLS) was founded in November 1895, after the Leeds lawsuit, in order to extend the work of the Sunday societies more fully into West Yorkshire. Founder Henry Greenwood had helped establish the Leeds society and would go on to help launch chapters in Hull, Sheffield, and other northern cities and towns. Halifax had its own decades-old mechanics' institute, which by the 1890s had "only a meagre account to give of itself"; it had a reputation among some former members as elitist and unresponsive, "monopolized as a privilege for the few."[69] With only negligible programs of classes and lectures, by late in the century it was primarily used as a space for annual meetings of local societies, including the HSLS.

The organizing committee, led by Greenwood, followed the by now well-established path to the establishment of a kindred society, just as committees in Sunderland, Norwich, Sheffield, Stockton, and other areas were doing at this time: enrolling sufficiently well-connected committee members, engaging an honorary president, contemplating the costs of a secretary, and polling neighborhoods for supporters who were willing to pay anywhere from a shilling to a guinea to help establish the society. Halifax mayor and alderman G. H. Smith served as president for the first several years of the society, underscoring the connections of the HSLS to the city as a whole. The boilerplate language of the parent SLS was adopted, with two alterations. First, the Halifax committee pledged to deliver not only "Lectures on Science—Physical, Intellectual, and Moral—History, Philosophy, and Art," but also lectures on literature and sociology, which by the mid-1890s were regarded as importantly modern. Second, the lofty goal of the new society was now "the mental and moral well-being of mankind," rather than the London SLS's 1859 "improvement and social well-being of mankind."[70] "Mental and moral" improvement implied individual self-care; "social well-being" had embraced a much larger world, now no longer necessarily responsive to individual effort. The Halifax committee was not staking out new ground in these changes. Other new societies, like the one in Sheffield, made these same updates as well.[71]

The minute-books of the HSLS reflect a simultaneous commitment to financial prudence and to contemporary trends in platform performance. Reflecting these commitments within a season's program required a specific sequence of work on the part of the committee. Members would compile an extensive wish list of names and topics to be forwarded to a subcommittee and the secretary. They in turn would negotiate dates, fees, and even titles. Such negotiations, especially the frequent requests that speakers lower their fees, often came up short, so that new speakers had to be proposed, vetted, contacted, and cajoled within a matter of a few weeks in order to finalize and print the season's programs and to place notices in the local press. The 1896–7 program, for example, began with a list of sixty-three men and women, including national stars like Henry Irving, William Morris, and Max O'Rell; well-regarded specialists in the sciences like Andrew Wilson and Boyd Dawkins; regional favorites like Birmingham Art Museum director Whitworth Wallis; and such literary figures as adventure writer Arthur Montefiore (the chronicler of Henry Stanley's African adventures), war journalist Frederick Villiers, and novelist Mrs. Humphrey Ward. Several names on this initial slate were represented by Gerald Christy's Lecture Agency, Ltd., now in its twentieth year of operation, although negotiations over fees and titles were made directly with potential speakers.[72] A few backup choices were invited when members of the original wish list did not respond quickly enough, reinforcing the chronic complaints made in Simpson's journal that committees often operated on timelines too tight for many speakers. Within three weeks from the first suggestions for the season, the entire committee was able to vote on a final program list, shown in Table 5.1.

The two most expensive lecturers were the best-known; Max O'Rell, of course, was cheerfully notorious for being named in the Leeds lawsuit for his humorous lectures on contemporary society, while Canon William Stubbs was a well-regarded historian and cleric who would eventually become bishop of Oxford. The least expensive, S. L. Mosley, was a local ornithologist; the Rev. Thomas Hicks, also inexpensive, was a regional favorite whose subject matter focused on a by now old-fashioned look at nature as God's book. Speakers in the middle range of fees were familiar faces on the mid-1890s lecture circuit, including Villiers; Wilson; Thomas Cradock Hepworth, whose inventions included a modernized magic lantern; and Arthur Diosy, founder of the Japan Society of London. Just three years before, the *Lichfield Mercury* had heralded the opening of the winter lecture season by noting that "three guineas a lecture is the customary honorarium for lecturers," but, as the HSLS records show, this figure was significantly lower than the actual fees charged by the most sought-after speakers.[73] The outlay by the HSLS to the Lecture Agency, Ltd., for its limited brokerage services in 1896 was not recorded, although a decade later the charge to the society by Christy's agency was £14 for a season.[74]

This system of assembling a season's programming, starting with a long list of "possibles" and winnowing it down to twenty or so names that would include some of the lecture world's most sought-after speakers, remained the norm at least until the Great War. As we can see, lecture fees varied widely by individual—a significant departure from the mid-century model, where national lecturers generally all expected fees of about 5 guineas and local lecturers often donated their services. By 1890, payments for service could be notably low, as with Mosley and Hicks, or shockingly high. In the 1903–4 season, for example, the Halifax society contracted to pay 15 guineas to Sarah Grand for a lecture on "Things we Forget to Remember" and a whopping 36 guineas to Mrs. Harriet Kendall for her single evening of readings from "As You Like It," but only 1 guinea to local Captain H. L. P. Benson for "Jamaica, the Isle of Springs."[75] One of the highest paid of the day was explorer Henry Stanley, whom the Darlington Lecture Association considered in 1894 but rejected because his £50 fee was out of reach.[76]

Table 5.1 Program of Lectures, Titles, and Fees for Halifax SLS, 1896–7 Season

Date	Lecturer	Title	Fee	On original list?
October 18	S. L. Mosley	Local Birds	1 guinea	yes
October 25	J. W. Robertson	Past and Present of Women	5 guineas	yes
November 1	Frederick Villiers	War on a White Sheet	7 guineas	yes
November 8	Rev. Canon William Stubbs	James Russell Lowell: Poet and Prophet	10 guineas	yes
November 15	Arthur Montefiore	Arctic Exploration	7 guineas	yes
November 22	Dr. Robert Wallace	The Philosophy of Can	8 guineas	no
November 29	Max O'Rell	Americans at Home	10 guineas	yes
December 6	T. C. Hepworth	Photography Up To Date	7 guineas	yes
December 13	D. W. Allport	Famous Scenes in the British Parliament	4 guineas	yes
January 10	Dr. Drinkwater	Home	5 guineas	no
January 17	Rev. Haskett Smith	Camping Tours through the Holy Lands	5 guineas	no
January 24	W. Herbert-Jones	New Zealand	5 guineas	no
January 31	Dr. Andrew Wilson	Curiosities of Brain Action	6 guineas	yes
February 7	Arthur Diosy	Japan and the Recent War	7 guineas	no
February 14	A. W. Fletcher	Nineteenth-Century Ideals	5 guineas	yes
February 21	Thomas Hicks	Botanicals	3 guineas	yes
February 28	J. Pendleton	The Humorous Side of Newspaper Toil	5 guineas	no
March 7	Harry How	Interviews and Interviewing	6 guineas	yes
March 14	Rev. Hutchinson	Cochineal Monsters	5 guineas	no
March 21		Musical Evening		

Source: Halifax Sunday Lecture Society *Minute Book*, June–July 1897.

Membership fees and ticket pricing were structured to support these expenses: by 1896, basic annual subscription fees for the HSLS (granting membership in the society but not covering any ticket costs) had been raised to 2s., while the more common subscription-plus-ticket fee structure had five levels: 1 guinea for membership plus 2 season tickets; 10s. 6d. for membership plus 1 season ticket; 7s. for membership plus 1 "second reserve" season ticket; 6d. for a single "front seat" at the door; and 1d. for admission to the gallery. These fee structures followed the pattern set by institutes across the country.

The presence of the Lecture Agency appeared to signal the development—finally—of a national speakers' bureau along the lines of the lyceum network in the United States. Working through the Lecture Agency promised to guarantee a high caliber of speaker, but at this point, after the initial contact brokered by the Agency, negotiations over dates, topics, and fees were always carried out between the society secretary and the individual speaker. Societies felt free to reject speakers who would not reduce a rate or accommodate a locality's schedule, and the Lecture Agency, still stabilizing under Christy's reorganization, tended not to get involved in these granular negotiations nor even to take any significant action when its sponsored speaker failed to satisfy. In one highly emotional episode in 1899, for example, the HSLS committee reported that Morley Roberts, "an unknown man" secured through the Agency, delivered a lecture that was "a perfect fiasco." The local paper described it as "A Sunday Lecture Farce."[77] "We have sustained incalculable damage," the committee wrote to Christy. Roberts had been secured to give a travel lecture but failed to bring any slides, and most of the audience walked out; as a result, "our Vice-President requested his name removing [sic] from our list, and many subscribers demanded their money back."[78] Christy sent back "a wandering letter" and the HSLS, with no practical alternative available, continued to use his services.

The HSLS, like most of the SLS's kindred societies, bore little resemblance to its parent in terms of focus or structure. By the 1890s, it and other Sunday societies had established themselves securely as important partners in civic culture, providing sophisticated and varied programming well beyond the London SLS's emphasis on serious secular topics, often at significant cost in lecture fees. Weekly attendance, mostly from the upper working and middle classes, averaged about 500 at most of these kindred societies, and newspaper coverage referred to ticket-holders as "*au fait*" both with contemporary issues and, to a modest degree, with a wide range of specialist knowledge. Committee members in Halifax observed that only art-historical lectures failed to keep audience interest.[79] (Halifax was not alone in this observation; half a dozen years earlier, lecturer J. Ernest Phythian had observed that "art is unfortunately supposed to have an interest for the few only, not for the many," with the result that many localities ignored lecturers and courses built around "visible beauty."[80]) There were no gratis lectures necessary to fill a season: ticket prices covered costs and often provided a cushion of profit that could be donated to a local charity, reinforcing the importance of the society to overall civic life. Similarly, there were almost no generically moral lectures illustrating the wonders of God's world through the workings of insects or sea life. Instead, lectures on the most modern developments in the sciences were balanced by presentations on empire, history, and literature by "eminent people," seasoned by an organ program here or a recital of folk songs there. The 1899–1900 season, for example, included such "tried favourites" as Arnold Dolmetsch, Madame Annie Grey, H. R. Haweis, Alfred H. Fison, Whitworth Wallis, J. Foster Fraser, and chemistry professor Arthur Smithells, with "new visitors" including "distinguished names" like Mary Kingsley and Israel Zangwill.[81] Local amateurs became less and less important to these societies over time. Simpson's goal, to professionalize the popular lecture, had been achieved; lecturers were remunerated and generally respected, even as committees often waited until the last minute to finalize programs and nearly always pushed to reduce the costs of the lecture season.

The HSLS enjoyed broad coverage in the local paper, as was the case with most other provincial chapters, and this coverage often served to replicate the lecture itself as closely as possible, with cues to readers' appropriate emotional reactions. J. M. Bacon's lecture "Voyages of Cloudland," for example, occupied some 1,500 words in the *Courier*, with detailed descriptions of Bacon's well-known photographs of scenery and apparatus, laid out by the editor with such set-off subheads as "All the World Went Mad" and "Ascent by

Night" that likened the story to a magazine feature. The report, most likely submitted by Bacon or his representative, included the reported speech typical of newspaper reporting at this time, alongside Bacon's own words and several interpolations of "(laughter and applause)" to support the editorial claim that this lecture was "one of the finest ... ever given under the auspices of the Halifax Sunday Lecture Society."[82] Other lecturers, presenting material that was significantly less hair-raising, also attracted editorial judgment; H. R. Haweis, for example, who appeared regularly in Halifax and exemplified a moderate and even traditional approach to his material, spoke in November 1899 on "Garibaldi" with "some personal reminiscences." "Mr. Haweis is a firm believer in the use of the platform for lectures and similar work as a means of reaching many different classes of people," noted the reporter, who gave a short *precis* of Haweis's lecture career and reprinted rather dated remarks by the lecturer on the superiority of "this personal method ... of imparting knowledge and enthusiasm for knowledge."[83]

Editorial interventions were typical of the coverage of these late-Victorian lectures. Scissors-and-paste reprinting remained quite common, especially for well-known speakers who had submitted long summaries of their work ahead of time, but frequently individuals or their topics merited specific commentary. In some cases this was highly critical; Wilfrid Scawen Blunt's anti-imperialist lecture on "Egypt" at the Newcastle Lit.-&-Phil. in October 1885 drew scathing coverage in the *Shields Daily Gazette*, whose editor warned that "The Sunday Lecture Society is doing itself a very positive injury by extending its invitations to lecturers with Mr. Blunt's [political] proclivities." In contrast, the *Newcastle Courant* eschewed editorial comment and merely replicated the substance of Blunt's lecture in some 1,000 words of reported speech, including "(Loud applause") and "(Laughter and applause)."[84] Similarly, Arnold Lupton's 1902 string of appearances to lecture on "The South African War" led to a flurry of correspondence from readers condemning his "pro-Boer stance" as well as strong editorial condemnation of "his fling at the Government."[85] When there was little subject matter of substance to critique, editors might happily offer commentary on the skills "usually devoted to amusing [rather than] instructing audiences."[86] Newspaper accounts regularly noted the "graphic word pictures of an extremely interesting character" of one lecture, the "piquant explanations" of another, the "rich, modulated tones" of a third.[87] Disappointing performances were openly disparaged: Sarah Grand's 1900 lecture on "The Art of Happiness," delivered on a series of SLS platforms, was criticized as a "vigorous championship of the obvious" and a "flimsy, superficial, and inadequate" lecture "by a person of shallow attainments" who had "an irresistible tendency to pose as public mentor on any or every subject under the sun."[88]

Lecture Programming at the Turn of the Century: A Comparison

Late-Victorian popular platform speakers were more skilled, more disciplined, and generally more devoted to contemporary issues than their mid-century predecessors, and both institutes and audiences expected well-crafted seasons that placed significant responsibilities on secretaries and program committees. These expectations, like the elaborations of "sympathy" by suburban institute organizers or the strictures against unregulated reading by Mackinder and Sadler, continued to be couched in familiar language. We can see a digest of fifty years of this advice in the words of an anonymous organizer in "a northern society." He reminded committees "always to aim at obtaining lecturers of the highest class" who could help "large masses of men" appreciate "the noblest ideas." Such speakers, imbued with sympathy, would "deliberately appeal to the best instincts and the highest intelligence" of the audience. The strongest guarantee of a good slate of lecturers, argued this organizer, was a committee drawn from "almost every rank of persons in the city, from the wealthy, the learned, the professional, the tradesmen, the workmen" who would keep the programs "out of narrow grooves" and prevent a few from "weary[ing] the public with [their] individual hobbies."[89]

In Tables 5.2–5.5 that follow, we can see what a late-century interpretation of that advice looked like. Choosing the 1899–1900 seasons of the Leeds Phil.-&-Lit., the Midland Institute, and the Halifax SLS allows us to compare societies that grew out of very different contexts but which, by the turn of the century, had become part of an increasingly homogenous field of knowledge-based culture. As we have seen, the HSLS catered for working-class as well as middle-class listeners, but neither the Leeds Phil.-&-Lit. nor the Monday Evening Lectures at the Midland offered the tier of very inexpensive or even free seating that we see at the HSLS. Despite this, the three institutes shared similar preferences and instincts in building their programs, largely relying on the lists of speakers represented by the Lecture Agency (see Figure 5.1).

Comparing these programs to that of the Bradford Mechanics' Institute—by the turn of the century, one of the few old-established institutes that still offered a robust program of popular lectures—we can see how the choices of civic institutions

Table 5.2 Leeds Phil.-&-Lit. Lecture Program, 1899–1900

W. M. Flinders Petrie, DCL, LLD, PhD	Egypt, from Abraham to Athanasius
Walter Crane, ARWS	The Language of Line
Karl Pearson, MA, FRS	Some Recent Contributions to Our Knowledge of Heredity
Francis Gotch, MA, FRS	The Electrical Fish of the Nile
Thomas Marshall, MA	Homeric Topography; Troy, Mykenae, Delphi
H. J. Palmer	Sydney Smith as a Yorkshire Country Parson
H. E. Berthon, MA	Balzac; ses oeuvres et Son Influence
Albert Forbes Sieveking, FSA	The History of Gardens
Sir Oliver J. Lodge, LLD, FRS	Wireless Telegraphy
Rev. Charles Hargrove, MA	The City of Rome; Its Rise, Its Grandeur, and Its Ruin
Edmund Gosse, LLD	Robert Louis Stevenson
Israel Zangwill, BA	Fiction the Highest Form of Truth
William Hancock, FRS, FLGS	Travels in Guatemala, Salvador, and Nicaragua
Henry Crowther, FRMS	Lanuvium, a Buried Roman City; The Clerk of the Weather; Some Marvels of Bird Life (Three Lectures)

Source: Leeds Philosophical and Literary Society, *Annual Report*, 1900.

Table 5.3 Midland Institute Monday Evening Lectures, 1899–1900 Season

A. C. Haddon, DSc, FRS	Our Papuan Fellow-Subjects
W. Hall Griffin	Robert Browning—the Spirit of His Work
Albert Forbes Sieveking, FSA	The History of Gardens
Sir Martin Conway, MA, FSA, FRGS	Climbs in the Bolivian Andes
C. H. Bothamley, FLC, FCS	The Colour of the Sky and the Sunset
C. H. Bothamley	Sunlight and Its Effects
Sebastian Evans, LLD, and F. Bennett-Goldney	Caesar's Invasions of Britain
Alfred Sidgwick, MA	Milton's Minor Poems
The Birmingham Amateur Orchestral Society	Concert
W. H. Hadow, MA	Expression and Description in Music
Whitworth Wallis, FSA	The Pictorial Art of Burne-Jones
Rev. J. M. Bacon, MA, FRAS	Voyages in Cloudland
Alexander Hill, MA, MD	The Brain as the Apparatus of Thought
Rev. John Watson, DD ("Ian Maclaren")	Books and Bookmen
Sir James Crichton-Browne, MD, LLD, RFS	The Fight with Tubercle (Two Lectures)
Hugh Robert Mill, DSc, LLD	The Story of a Map Sheet
Louis C. Miall, FRS	The History of a Fly
The Birmingham Amateur Orchestral Society	Concert

Source: Midland Institute, *Annual Report*, 1900.

Table 5.4 Halifax Sunday Lecture Society, 1899–1900 Lecture Program

Morley Roberts	Round the World in a Hurry
Rev. J. M. Bacon, MA, FRS	Voyages in Cloudland
Arnold Dolmetsch and Family	Music of Shakespeare
Arthur Smithells, CMG, FRS	Liquid Air
Rev. H. R. Haweis, BA	Garibaldi, with Personal Reminiscences
Richard Kerr	Beauties of Nature
Dr. A. H. Fison, DSc	Life of a Star
Mr. Charles Fry	Lecture-Recital: Gems of Poetry
Miss Mary Kingsley	West Africa
John Foster Fraser	Among the Picturesque Burmese
Whitworth Wallis	The Art of Lord Leighton
Rev. Haskett Smith	Athens and the Isles of Greece
Frank T. Bullen	Whales and Whale Fishing
Madame Annie Grey	The Gathering of the Clans
Arthur Diosy	The End of the Century
Israel Zangwill	The Ghetto
J. W. Gregory, DSc	Africa in the 19th Century

Source: Halifax Sunday Lecture Society, *Minute Book*, August 1899.

Table 5.5 Bradford Mechanics' Institute Lecture Program, 1903–4

Rev. W. H. Dallinger, LLD	May Our Neighbouring Planets Be Habitable?
Rev. C. H. Grundy, MA	Lodgings, Boarding Houses and Hotels
Dr. Vaughan Bateson, FRGS	The Forbidden Frontier
Mr. Harry Rice	Musical and Humorous Entertainment
Mr. W. F. Wray ("Kuklos")	The Art of the Hoardings
Mr. Henry Hibbert, FRGS	The Isle of the Shamrock
Mr. John Foster Fraser	America Up-To-Date
Mr. William Miles	Dramatic and Humorous Recitals
Mr. Graham Moffatt and Miss Kate Moffatt	Dramatic and Humorous Entertainment
Mr. Percy French	Humorous and Artistic Entertainment
Mr. Frederick Lambert	The Mammoth Cave of Kentucky
Mr. George Grossmith	Humorous Musical Entertainment
Mr. H. Morgan-Browne	Travel and Sport in Abyssinia
Mr. Henry Hibbert, FRGS	Across Sweden
Mr. Alex Watson	Dramatic and Humorous Recitals
Rev. Haskett Smith, MA	The Marvels of the Nile
Mr. Samuel Wells, FRGS	A City of Silence: La Grande Chartreuse
Rev. Arthur C. Hill	The Morals of Modern Fiction
Miss Grace Jean Crocker	An Evening with American Authors
Mr. John Wilson, FRGS	In the Heart of Peru
Sarath Kumar Ghosh	The Romance and Mystery of India
Rev. J. Gleeson	Rambles in Ireland
Rev. Theodore Wood	Wonders of Bee Life
Mr. D'Arcy Clayton's Musical Entertainers	The Gipsies and Their Jester
The Elocution Class	Recitals

Source: Yorkshire Union of Mechanics' Institutions, *Annual Report*, 1903.

overlapped with or parted from the selections made by the programming committee of an institute now firmly built upon secondary and technical education for the working classes.

In Leeds, we see a heavily credentialed roster of speakers,[90] including three of the most noted names in the sciences: Egyptologist W. M. Flinders Petrie, eugenicist Karl Pearson, and physicist Oliver Lodge. Gosse and Zangwill were equally well-known in literature, while Walter Crane was already famous as an illustrator. Four of these speakers—Marshall, Hargrove, Hancock, and Palmer—were members of the society (Hargrove and Marshall served as presidents) and delivered their lectures gratis. Crowther was the curator of the society's museum and served as president or vice president of several institutes, including the Bristol Lecture Society and the Huddersfield Microscopical Society. Total fees paid to lecturers for this season amounted to £24 12s. 4d., or less than £3 per speaker, indicating strong personal ties between many of these speakers and the Society; these bonds encouraged voluntary lectures and reduced the Society's reliance on the work of the Lecture Agency. Crowther, for

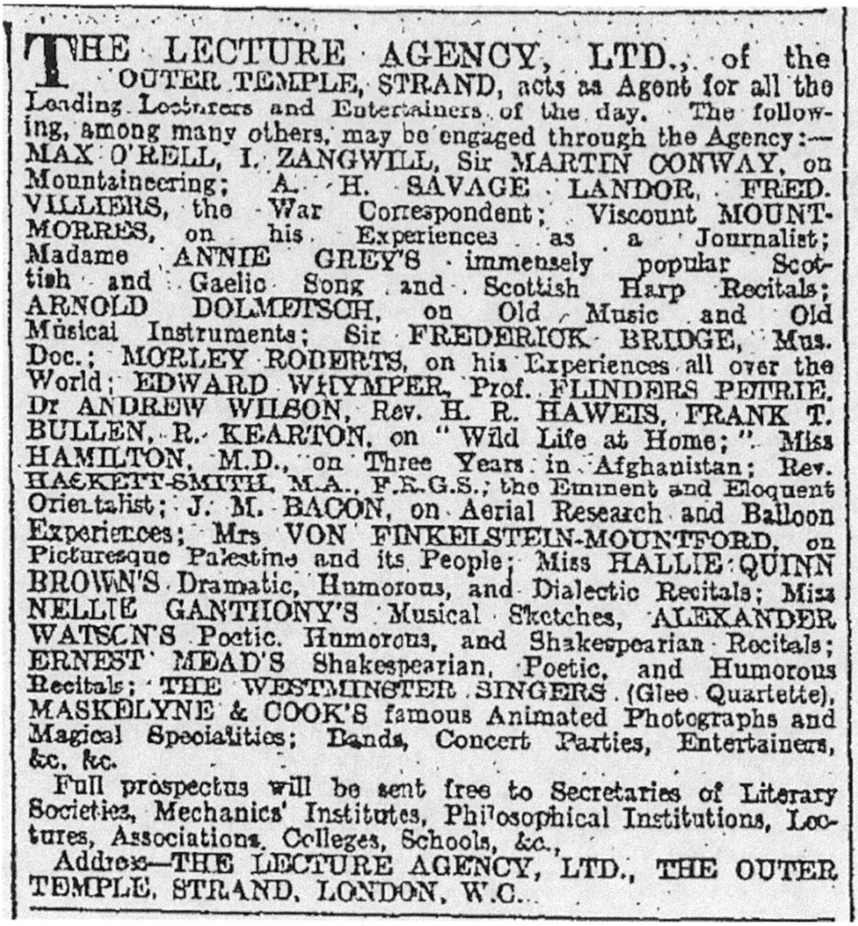

> THE LECTURE AGENCY, LTD., of the OUTER TEMPLE, STRAND, acts as Agent for all the Leading Lecturers and Entertainers of the day. The following, among many others, may be engaged through the Agency:— MAX O'RELL, I. ZANGWILL, Sir MARTIN CONWAY, on Mountaineering; A. H. SAVAGE LANDOR, FRED. VILLIERS, the War Correspondent; Viscount MOUNTMORRES, on his Experiences as a Journalist; Madame ANNIE GREY'S immensely popular Scottish and Gaelic Song and Scottish Harp Recitals; ARNOLD DOLMETSCH, on Old Music and Old Musical Instruments; Sir FREDERICK BRIDGE, Mus. Doc.; MORLEY ROBERTS, on his Experiences all over the World; EDWARD WHYMPER, Prof. FLINDERS PETRIE. Dr ANDREW WILSON, Rev. H. R. HAWEIS, FRANK T. BULLEN, R. KEARTON, on "Wild Life at Home;" Miss HAMILTON, M.D., on Three Years in Afghanistan; Rev. HACKETT-SMITH, M.A., F.R.G.S.; the Eminent and Eloquent Orientalist; J. M. BACON, on Aerial Research and Balloon Experiences; Mrs VON FINKELSTEIN-MOUNTFORD, on Picturesque Palestine and its People; Miss HALLIE QUINN BROWN'S Dramatic, Humorous, and Dialectic Recitals; Miss NELLIE GANTHONY'S Musical Sketches, ALEXANDER WATSON'S Poetic, Humorous, and Shakespearian Recitals; ERNEST MEAD'S Shakespearian, Poetic, and Humorous Recitals; THE WESTMINSTER SINGERS (Glee Quartette), MASKELYNE & COOK'S famous Animated Photographs and Magical Specialities; Bands, Concert Parties, Entertainers, &c., &c.
>
> Full prospectus will be sent free to Secretaries of Literary Societies, Mechanics' Institutes, Philosophical Institutions, Lectures, Associations, Colleges, Schools, &c.,
>
> Address—THE LECTURE AGENCY, LTD., THE OUTER TEMPLE, STRAND, LONDON, W.C.

Figure 5.1 Advertisement by the Lecture Agency, Ltd., 1899.

Source: *Sheffield Daily Telegraph*, July 17, 1899. This ad ran in a number of papers in July 1899, including *The Scotsman*, July 17, 1899, and *Daily News* [London], July 12, 1899.

example, handled all of his own bookings, here and elsewhere, for "Lectures on Personal Travel and Science," "delivered without recourse to Notes of any kind" and "illustrated by an excellent series of original Lantern Slides ... described by the Press as the finest ever shewn."[91] The ability to secure the talents of Flinders Petrie and Lodge signaled the Society's continued self-identification as a space of and for the sciences, broadly conceived, even as "science" as a part of knowledge-based culture was increasingly difficult to parse. The rejection of anything musical also signaled a continuation of its founders' emphases away from the fine arts, while the inclusion of Gosse and Zangwill acknowledged the continued general conviction that, in the words of John Morley, "literature is one of the instruments, and one of the most powerful instruments, for forming character, for giving us men and women armed with reason, braced by knowledge, clothed with steadfastness and courage, and inspired by that public spirit and public virtue of which it has been well said that they are the brightest ornaments of the mind of man."[92] Thus, this program managed to secure several of the season's stars, reinforce a commitment to the production of knowledge, and "inspire public virtue."

The program at the Midland Institute was a broader representation of late-century culture than we see in Leeds.[93] The Midland shared only one lecturer with the Leeds Phil.-&-Lit.: Albert Sieveking, who had just published *Gardens Ancient and Modern: An Epitome of the Literature of the Garden-Art* and was speaking about his work across the country.[94] And while Leeds only reluctantly brought the arts into its programming, the Midland continued its well-established emphasis on literature, the arts, and music, with lectures on Browning, Milton, Burne-Jones, and "bookmen" generally, as well as two concerts by the local Amateur Orchestral Society, which occupied a well-respected place in the city's rich musical world and was nationally recognized for "the performance of orchestral music at a high standard."[95] Topicality drove this programming: "brain-science" was represented by Alexander Hill and James Crichton-Browne, aeronautics and meteorology by John Bacon and Alexander Mills, mountaineering by Martin Conway, and photography by C. H. Bothamley. Only two of these speakers were local men: Sebastian Evans, one of the earliest supporters of the Midland, and Whitworth Wallis, the curator of the Birmingham Art Gallery. The season was contemporary and balanced, reflecting the Midland's many decades of designing seasons that would attract subscribers from across the region.

In Halifax, the HSLS also focused on topicality and balance.[96] Its program featured three speakers who appeared as well at Leeds or Birmingham: Wallis, Bacon, and Zangwill, all highly popular and all reflective of the Society's commitment to choose only lecturers who had been vetted by the public through prior appearances at other Societies. Science was represented here by chemistry professor Arthur Smithells, astronomer Alfred Henry Fison, and microscopist Richard Kerr; lectures on Africa, India, and Greece, with limelight views, included the "round the world cyclist" John Foster Fraser and focused on the excitements of exploration. Music and oratory accounted for three lectures. The program had been assembled through the multistep process noted above, with several last-minute substitutions: John Foster Fraser replaced W. B. Bottomley, who would have lectured on "Microbes, Friendly and Otherwise," Whitworth Wallis replaced E. Page Gaston, "The Lost Races of America," and J. W. Gregory replaced R. W. Roberts, "Buildings of the British Isles." On the whole, the end result achieved the committee's desire for well-known speakers and performers and even, despite the reputation of the Halifax audiences, included a well-received art-history lecture. This season was not without its problems, including as it did the "disastrous" appearance of Morley Roberts, but overall it represented a solid, popular, and safe collation of knowledge-based culture.

In contrast to this nearly wholesale rejection of the local lecturer, the Bradford Mechanics' Institute continued to occupy the space that had once spread across the kingdom.[97] Bradford's program differed significantly from the previous three examples, and indeed continued to look much more like a mid-century mixture of "sappers and miners" alongside an occasional nationally known speaker. Dallinger's talk on habitable planets recalled, dimly, the mid-1860s fascination with the same subject, examined in Chapter 3; "The Wonders of Bee Life" by the Rev. Wood evoked the mid-century approach to the natural world as part of divine creation; and both "Lodgings, Boarding Houses and Hotels" and "The Morals of Modern Fiction" similarly pointed backwards to a type of lecture that was no longer part of the programming at civic institutions and kindred societies. George Grossmith, son of the George Grossmith so beloved at mid-century, delivered a comfortable "humorous musical entertainment." "Kuklos," the "bicycling journalist" from the *Daily News* whose pieces recounted his adventures, was well-chosen as an exciting and up-to-date speaker, reinforcing the contemporary fascination with bicycling that also made Fraser's lectures so popular. Only these two, as well as Haskett Smith and Grossmith, would have been part of the Lecture Agency list, and the large proportion of general "entertainments," on the one hand, and travelogues, on the other, marked the Bradford program as an unrepentantly old-fashioned approach to the popular lecture: it was undemanding, entertaining, and inexpensive to mount.

Importantly, all of these programs were almost wholly male. Many of the women who appeared at established institutes were not lecturers but performers in music, drama, and the arts. "Lady Lecturers" continued to form only a tiny fraction of serious speakers in these public civic spaces. In smaller societies, however, they were increasingly present as powerful voices for a variety of causes, speaking as Poor Law Guardians, health reformers, crusaders for legal change, and other agents of civic and national improvement.[98] Two attempts to organize included the London-based Women Lecturers' Association, founded in 1893 to provide lectures on subjects "from Dante to domestic sanitation" to audiences ranging from members of workingmen's associations to "the idle women of the suburbs," and the Association of Women Pioneer Lecturers, founded the same year to supplement the often slow spread of Extension centers into both suburbs and villages.[99] In 1895, Edith Bradley, the managing director of the Women Lecturers' Association, led a failed attempt to establish a Women Lecturers' Institute that would replicate many of the functions of Simpson's Lecture Association, credentialing women lecturers and elevating their work as "a distinct profession."[100] The proposed basis for credentialing would include not only subject knowledge but also "power of dramatic expression in Literary, and of vivid demonstration on Scientific, subjects" and, importantly, "sympathy and interest." The proposal itself indicated two important developments: first, the growing demarcation of lecturing from classroom teaching, and second, a significant growth in the number of serious, educated, non-"entertaining" women lecturers—a phrase with much more gravitas than "Lady Lecturers." Neither was sufficient, however, to ground an institute in 1895.

"You Want the Man Who Has Been There!"

The severing of ties between adult education and popular lecture culture was slow and difficult, leaving many secretaries and organizations once again wondering how best to draw and keep a subscriber base. The multiplication of both sites and speakers led to a certain amount of cynicism. Many participants in this world of culture had expected the popular lecture to lift all men and women into the state of grace predicted by Joseph Simpson. Instead, as the Lord Mayor of Leeds argued in 1903, it uniformly failed to reach "the same objectless, vacant crowd perambulating up and down, back and back again."[101] Yet as a consumer good, it was unshakably popular.

By the turn of the century, the appetite for popular lectures seemed inexhaustible. This was especially true when joined to the growing demands for speakers at the broad range of interest- and hobby-based societies excluded from this study, from spiritualists, secularists, and socialists, on the one hand, to conservation societies and charity organizations, on the other. While these smaller societies continued to depend on limited numbers of men and women who could craft specialized offerings, and Extension centers drew from the universities, civic institutions turned more and more frequently to the services of the lecture agency in order to build programming. Turning to Gerald Christy's Lecture Agency, Ltd., we can see how the popular lecture was marketed as indispensable to "the healthy throb of intellectual life." The agency's 1911 publication, *Concerning Popular Lectures*, promoted "the leading lecturers and entertainers of the day," including such stars as Henry Stanley, Winston Churchill, Arthur Conan Doyle, Ernest Shackleton, Hilaire Belloc, and Charles Dickens the Younger, and also provided a blueprint for those "enlightened citizens" who wished to found a new institution or resuscitate a moribund one.[102]

Now "a far bigger factor in the life of the people than ... twenty years ago," popular lecturing served a somewhat jumbled set of purposes. According to the anonymous author, a good program of lectures would raise "the general standard of thought," encourage "a fuller national life," inspire a love of books, bring individuals back to the church, break down international prejudice, provide mental refreshment after a long day of labor, build "civic spirit," inspire laughter, and entertain children: "there is no end to the high causes that will be admirably served by the popular lecture." Good lecturers would present "oratory rigorously cleansed from the flamboyant and the meretricious," "amusement ... couched in plain language, terse and vigorous, ... [and] admirably illustrated," and "plenty of racy, nervous, idiomatic English readily understood by the people." They would avoid "ornament" and "high-sounding words to cover poverty of thought," and should never merely "talk to their slides," although good illustrations and competent lantern operators were imperative.[103] Instead, "the alchemy of the human voice"—that twentieth-century iteration of "the collision of mind with mind"—would provide mental recreation unavailable at music halls, skating rinks, and "kinematograph theatres." "The theatre and the music-hall cannot suffice for the whole intellectual side of man," argued the writer. Lecturers should have "achieved ... something of genuine merit and importance in the arts, literature, or science" or "travelled to almost unknown lands and brought back vivid recollections." Audiences wanted "life as it comes to the mass of the people ... the romance, the pathos, and the tragedy of everyday existence" rather than the "avowedly educational." "You want the man who has been there!" advised the author.

All of these benefits were couched in "civic spirit," the motivating force that would transform popular lecturing for the modern world. This new vision retained, in indiscriminate form, the broad outlines of mid-century institutions. A combination of (very) limited instruction and curated amusement would bind together eager individuals across lines of class and gender; these listeners would, through their participation, enhance public spirit, support artistic and intellectual creativity, and reap the benefits of sympathy and the action of mind on mind. Gone from this vision, however, was the individual man or women who might attempt to tie such work to the duties of participatory citizenship, the structures of adult education, or the long-term personal enrichment that might come from a well-curated "pack of knowledge." Gone, too, were those on whose labor the early popular lectures had depended; the curates, the sappers and miners, the earnest women painting vivid word pictures of enviable domestic peace. The world of knowledge-based culture had broadened to include "the man on the street," but it had also narrowed in scope; it provided less room for that same man to participate in a world defined by shared curiosity and determination to make change.

Importantly, while the popular lecture reflected evolving paradigms of education and entertainment, it did not exhaust the variety of offerings that characterized the end of our period. The ecosystem of knowledge-based culture continued to embrace the debating and discussion societies, learned societies, and mutual improvement societies that had spread since mid-century. Many of these sites continued to promote the engaged citizenship developed at mid-century. Literary societies were "an association of enlightened citizens in their collective capacity" whose "sense of obligation should be full and keen."[104] Debaters continued to rehearse both the familiar questions of Shakespeare's genius, the compatibility of commerce and Christianity, the influence of the press, and the importance of trial by jury, on the one hand, and topicalities like compulsory vaccination, the necessity of an Egypt protectorate, and proposed changes to licensing laws, on the other. As they had done at mid-century, these questions absorbed the interests of both the small "mutual" and the elite suburban institute.[105] The veritable explosion of such societies for women was similarly marked by the appropriation of the language of mid-century knowledge-based culture. Members argued that "the cultivation of the mind by the acquisition of knowledge and a familiarity with the writings of great authors" helped develop and guide "a deep interest in the events which are agitating the nations around us, and the desire to know something of the concerns affecting the country and the town in which she lives."[106] Women debaters attacked many of the same topics on the lists of male-only societies: the occupation of Egypt, the benefits and drawbacks of compulsory education, the theater as a means of culture, and the relative benefits of town and country life.[107] All of these societies, claimed one report, were "preparing [members] for the higher duties of citizenship."[108] But these claims to citizenship, now so important to the small private society, had been stripped out of the culture of the popular lecture by the eve of the Great War. No longer embedded into the scaffolding of civic improvement, no longer expected to reflect local and regional needs or changing standards of modernity, the popular lecture was now expected to be "distinctly pleasant and commendable" rather than a necessary tool in "cultivating intellect as we cultivate corn." Platform speech was increasingly one type of commodity, competing with an overwhelming set of other consumer choices.

Conclusion

The Great War did not destroy the popular lecture, but the relationship between knowledge-based culture and participatory citizenship did not survive the war. After 1918, the large civic institutes remained and continued to provide rich programs of music, lectures, and special-interest classes. Sunday lectures continued to provide a homogenized program of culture to middle-class and upper-working-class audiences. Specialized societies thrived as they constructed programs around focused interests. The Selborne Society, for instance, which had been founded in the late 1880s, became the premier interwar supplier of lectures and educational materials on conservation, ornithology, and botany.[1] Other educational bodies, like the Gilchrist Trust, continued their efforts as well. But popular lectures no longer formed a de facto vehicle for a kingdom-wide spread of culture. Nor did they figure in adult education, whether inside or outside of the colleges and universities. Citizenship, for its part, underwent a series of remarkable transformations in response to the stresses and opportunities of the 1920s and 1930s. Where once the Victorian model of knowledge-based culture promised to enable the individual "to obtain a clearer and juster idea of the religious, moral, social, and political circumstances amid which his lot is cast,"[2] postwar society no longer defined itself around this aspiration. The deliberate shedding of old forms of entertainment and education radically minimized (but did not eliminate) the importance of popular lectures after 1918. They seemed increasingly a relic enjoyed by one's elders, a kind of tedious performance to be superseded by modern forms of leisure.

This book has been one attempt to examine how and why this artifact became so embedded in Victorian culture, and to explore the ways in which the popular lecture anchored a shared project of social and intellectual growth for many men and women. The ecosystem of knowledge-based culture provided space across lines of class and gender where groups could explore troubling questions, enjoy new models of entertainment, and participate in the performance of invigorating inquiry. Those efforts were welcomed by provincial towns and cities wrestling with the physical and social challenges of civic expansion. Interpreting the work of institutes and societies as a key part of modernization allowed city leaders to help shape the boundaries of citizen participation, while the men and women enfolded by these spaces accepted as a given their right to listen, judge, and advise. The moral and social power of this acquisition of knowledge more than balanced any lack of political and economic power.

As we have seen, the stability of this type of shared social enterprise was strongest in the period of 1850 to the 1880s, and began to erode as the first generation of students shaped by the Education Act of 1870 reached adulthood. During this first, heroic period, the crusaders for inclusion and professionalization opened up the world of knowledge-based culture to anyone who chose to participate, ignoring hidden or inconvenient barriers to access. Those barriers were increasingly apparent after about 1880, as educationists and reformers began to shift focus to purposeful educational efforts. Lecture culture, for both providers and listeners, broadened to accommodate new forms of entertainment and narrowed to exclude specialized fields of knowledge. By the early twentieth century, as we saw in Chapter 5, the popular lecture was severed from education as such, ending a partnership that had been troubled but persistent since 1850.

Within these six decades of knowledge-based culture, the Victorians experienced a range of lecture options that ran from the feeble efforts of the untrained junior institute member and the well-meaning but equally raw curate to the robust, engaging work of men and women who took their platform responsibilities as a charge to share history, drama, current events, literature, and the sciences as enticingly as possible. "Give them something popular, attractive, and high-sounding, and depend upon it they'll come in their thousands," advised one columnist in 1888.[3] While many of the lectures mentioned in this book have not survived—and were so ephemeral as to leave almost no trace—very many of them helped Victorian men and women to shape the "pack of knowledge" that they carried with them throughout their lives. Exploring this kingdom-wide web of institutions and individuals places the popular lecture squarely back into Victorian culture.

This recuperation seems especially timely today. The lecture as an essential core of higher education has been challenged, tested, and often abandoned (and then reclaimed) over the past decade. The classroom lecturer has similarly been devalued and often derided as "the sage on the stage," performing but not teaching. And the connections between lecturer and student have been buffeted by trends ranging from the MOOCS (massive open online courses) of the 2010s to the rapid and often difficult transition to online teaching necessitated by Covid-19. The current crises of higher education echo many of the same concerns over access, regulation, and purpose that occupied Victorian educationists and learners, intensified by the more potent ideological clashes of the present.

At the same time, of course, "thank you for coming to my TED talk" has come to signal the ways in which the general-interest lecture engages, inspires, provokes, and entertains. These contemporary audiences are bound not by time and space but by programming accessed through the same online tools that have helped to diminish the importance of the curricular lecture. Similar to the radio broadcasts of the early twentieth century, these offerings reach across more rigid lines of identity to forge new webs of belonging. They show no sign of diminishing as an important aspect of shared culture: Technology, Entertainment, Design [TED] LLC estimates that nearly 50,000 discrete talks have been delivered between 2009 and 2023. Brief—each less than twenty minutes long—and accessible on demand, they have become embedded within our modern "pack of knowledge." And, like the Victorian popular lecture, they speak to a voracious curiosity on the part of listeners. What is markedly different today is the extent to which popular lectures no longer signal a monolithic knowledge-based culture. Such a culture fractured and disappeared more than a century ago, even as the popular lecture has proven more robust than the culture which nurtured it. However, it survives today as a personal choice rather than as a commercial transaction: as the centerpiece of the monthly club meeting, the content of an online hour or two, the basis for a vigorous discussion with a few close friends.

This book has explored the structures of the Victorian popular lecture through both institution and culture. Many aspects of the Victorian lecture deserve further study. The ways in which individual lecturers perceived the cultural world they helped create and nurture remain largely unexamined, especially in ways that might further illuminate the divisions between the old-fashioned educators, the entertainers, and the credentialed professionals. The degree of ease with which individual lecturers crossed these category boundaries, as well as the boundaries delineating the religious and the political, remains to be examined. Personal memoirs might also help us flesh out the multiple ways in which the lecture season fed the social as well as the intellectual needs of the provincial man and woman. How did the season ticket compare to other markers of local status? Can we discern generational conflict beyond that outlined in these chapters, by investigating the worries of parents and families? Was the lecture hall also a site for courtship, or horseplay? How did these social concerns affect the ways in which listeners experienced insights into worlds beyond their immediate reach? These worlds were intellectual, but they were also political, social, and economic. Thus, how did the spread of lecture institutions—not just individual lecturers—across the colonies do the work of empire, reinforcing hierarchies and behaviors in spaces that might seem frighteningly devoid of familiar structures for leisure or learning?

While this book has deliberately set aside the platform speech associated with church and politics, two additional lecture spaces have also been omitted from this study, and each merits further exploration. First is the social world of small clubs and gatherings outside the civic institutions, where lectures were selected by and delivered to audiences sharing specific and often quite narrow common interests such as hobby groups and mothers' clubs. Second is the geographic world of London, birthplace of both the science lecture and the Sunday lecture, where the sheer volume and diversity of platform offerings posed challenges of time, money, and audience that provincial committees did not have to negotiate. A deep dive into the fortunes of the London Polytechnic Institute, for example, might provide a textured counterpart to the aspirations and accomplishments of the provincial lecture society. Finally, a comparative assessment of the two major lecture agencies operating in Victorian and Edwardian England, Gerald Christy's Lecture Agency and the Lecture League, would yield new insights into how and how much the platform world in England continued to deviate from the well-established American model, and how the commodified lecture was marketed to audiences beyond the civic institutions studied here. As with any starting point, this book raises almost as many questions as it seeks to answer. I hope it serves as a valuable foundation for future explorations of the question, "What did the Victorians talk about?"

Notes

Introduction

1. Arthur Hervey, *A Suggestion for Supplying the Literary, Scientific, and Mechanics' Institutes of Great Britain and Ireland with Lecturers from the Universities* (Cambridge: Macmillan, 1855), 19.
2. See "Introduction," in Paul Barlow and Colin Trodd, eds., *Governing Cultures: Art Institutions in Victorian London* (Aldershot: Ashgate, 2000), 3.
3. Martin Hewitt, "Beyond Scientific Spectacle: Image and Word in Nineteenth-Century Popular Lecturing," in *Popular Exhibitions, Science and Showmanship, 1840–1910*, ed. Joe Kember, John Plunkett, and Jill A. Sullivan (London: Pickering and Chatto, 2012), 81.
4. Ibid.
5. Martin Hewitt, "Aspects of Platform Culture in Nineteenth-Century Britain," *Nineteenth-Century Prose* 29, no.1 (2002): 12. For the decline of the political lecture in workingmen's clubs, see John Davis, "Radical Clubs and London Politics, 1870–1900," in *Metropolis London: Histories and Representations Since 1800*, ed. David Feldman and Gareth Stedman Jones (London: Routledge, 1989), 103–28; see also T. G. Ashplant, "London Working Men's Clubs, 1875–1914," in *Popular Culture and Class Conflict 1590–1914: Explorations in the History of Labour and Leisure*, ed. Eileen Yeo and Stephen Yeo (Sussex: Harvester Press, 1981), 241–70. Political and temperance lecturing before 1860 are explored in Janette Lisa Martin, "Popular Political Oratory and Itinerant Lecturing in Yorkshire and the North East in the Age of Chartism, 1837–1860" (PhD dissertation, University of York Department of History, 2010), while Aled Jones shows how lecturing could be one part of a larger campaign for specific political or civic goals, in Aled Jones, "The *Dart* and the Damning of the Sylvan Stream: Journalism and Political Culture in the Late-Victorian City," in *Encounters in the Victorian Press: Editors, Authors, Readers*, ed. Laurel Brake and Julie F. Codell (New York: Palgrave Macmillan, 2005), 177–94. The need to employ women lecturers as part of a larger program of philanthropy and outreach can be found in *Women Workers. Papers Read at a Conference, Convened by the Birmingham Ladies' Union of Workers among Women and Girls, In November, 1890* (Birmingham: Lawrence, 1891).
6. See Catherine Clare Feely, "Scissors-and-Paste Journalism," *Dictionary of Nineteenth-Century Journalism in Great Britain and Ireland*, ed. Laurel Brake and Marysa Demoor (London: Academia Press, 2009), 561.
7. Robert Vaughan, *The Age of Great Cities; Or, Modern Society Viewed in Its Relation to Intelligence, Morals, and Religion* (London: Jackson and Walford, 1843), 141. See also Robert Lawton, "An Age of Great Cities," *The Town Planning Review* 43, no. 3 (1972): 199–224; Andrew Lees, *Cities Perceived: Urban Society in European and American Thought, 1820–1940* (New York: Columbia University Press, 1985).

8. *Report of the Proceedings Connected with the Grand Soirée of the Manchester Athenaeum, Held on Thursday, October 3rd, 1844: From the Manchester Guardian of Saturday, October 5th, 1844* (Manchester: Cave and Sever, 1844), 28.
9. Lees, *Cities Perceived*, 50, quoting William Fordyce ("moral, social, and political progress") and Robert Lamb ("go-ahead sort"), and 51, quoting Thomas Baines, *History of the Commerce and Town of Liverpool, and of the Rise of Manufacturing Industry in the Adjoining Counties* (London: Longman, 1852), 676–7.
10. Samuel Timmins, *Address, Delivered at the Annual Meeting of Members, 12th January 1874 (at the Birmingham and Midland Institute)* (Birmingham: Offices of the Journal, 1874), 10.
11. Lees, *Cities Perceived*, 50–4; see also Arline Wilson, "'The Florence of the North'? The Civic Culture of Liverpool in the Early 19th Century," in *Gender, Civic Culture and Consumerism: Middle-Class Identity in Britain, 1800–1940*, ed. Alan Kidd and David Nicholls (Manchester: Manchester University Press, 1999), 34–46 .
12. Hewitt refers to these built spaces as "elements of modernization" in Martin Hewitt, "Confronting the Modern City: The Manchester Free Public Library, 1850–80" *Urban History* 27, no. 1 (2000): 68.
13. Deborah Tannen famously introduced this lens into a critique of modern American culture, where it has been taken up and refined by a number of scholars. See Deborah Tannen, *The Argument Culture: Moving from Debate to Dialogue* (New York: Random House, 1998) and David Zarefsky, "What Does an Argument Culture Look Like?" *Informal Logic* 29, no. 3 (2009): 296–308. Carly S. Wood, examining debating societies built around institutions of women's higher education in the United States and the UK, defines debate as "a structured activity that brings individuals together to collectively engage in the ritual practice of argumentation," in Carly S. Wood, *Debating Women: Gender, Education, and Spaces for Argument, 1835–1945* (East Lansing, MI: Michigan State University Press, 2018), 2. For an excellent overview of the historiography of debate and argument, see her introduction, 1–18.
14. For "rational recreation," see Peter Bailey, "'Will the Real Bill Bailey Please Stand Up?' Towards a Role Analysis of Mid-Victorian Working Class Respectability," *Journal of Social History* 2 (Spring 1979): 336–53; Hugh Cunningham, *Leisure in the Industrial Revolution* (London: Croom Helm, 1980); and Gary Cross, *A Social History of Leisure since 1600* (State College, PA: Venture Publishing, 1990.) The divide between leisure and idleness was a fruitful one for early scholarly work on nineteenth-century adult education, especially in studies of the founding and first decades of the mechanics' institutes and similar spaces. Many historians, building on the two key contemporary accounts by James Hudson and James Hole in the early 1850s, have generally accepted their conclusions that these institutes "failed to reach those for whom they were intended" and thus were institutional and educational failures: James William Hudson, *History of Adult Education, in Which Is Comprised a Full and Complete History of the Mechanics' and Literary Institutions, Athenaeums, etc.*
(London: Longmans, 1851) and James Hole, *An Essay on the History and Management of Literary, Scientific, and Mechanics' Institutions: And Especially How Far They May Be Developed and Combined so as to Promote the Moral Well-Being and Industry of the Country* (London: Longman, Brown, 1853). Mabel Tylecote, Edward Royle, and Roger Fieldhouse, for example, examine the shift in membership away from "mechanics" to a higher social stratum and conclude, in the words of Tylecote, that by mid-century these institutions "had nearly everywhere ceased to be regarded as a medium for the instruction of the masses and had become select rather than popular institutions."

Mabel Tylecote, *The Mechanics' Institutes of Lancashire and Yorkshire before 1851* (Manchester: Manchester University Press, 1957), 259; see also Edward Royle, "Mechanics' Institutes and the Working Classes, 1840–1860," *Historical Journal* 14, no. 2 (1971): 305–21, and Roger Fieldhouse, *The Workers' Educational Association: Aims and Achievements 1903–1977* (New York: Syracuse University, 1977). John P. Hemming picks up the story of these institutes in "The Mechanics' Institutes in the Lancashire and Yorkshire Textile Districts from 1850," *Journal of Educational Administration and History* 9, no. 1 (1977): 18–33. Writing within the history of science, Steven Shapin and Barry Barnes have argued that the type of education provided in these institutes transformed mechanics' institutions into conduits for practical, job-based skills rather than for any true disciplinary exposure to chemistry, botany, engineering, or the like; Steven Shapin and Barry Barnes, "Science, Nature and Control: Interpreting Mechanics' Institutes," *Social Studies of Science* 7, no. 1 (1977): 31–74. C. M. Turner argues that these institutes' main function was to reinforce early-nineteenth-century social and economic stability; C. M. Turner, "Sociological Approaches to the History of Education," *British Journal of Educational Studies* 17, no. 2 (1969): 146–65; see also his "Political, Religious, and Occupational Support in the Early Mechanics' Institutes," *Vocational Aspect of Secondary and Further Education* 20, no. 45 (1968): 65–70. Even those scholars who reject this dualistic paradigm accept as a given that "the failure of most mechanics' institutes was already patent" by 1848, as Marcella Pellegrino Sutcliffe has argued in her exploration of the development of workingmen's colleges after mid-century. Marcella Pellegrino Sutcliffe, "The Origins of the 'Two Cultures' Debate in the Adult Education Movement: The Case of the Working Men's College *c*. 1854–1914," *History of Education* 43, no. 2 (2014): 144. An extreme version of the good-versus-evil model characterizes J. Jeffrey Robinson, *Social Control and the Education of Adults in the Nineteenth and Early Twentieth Centuries: The Role of Religion, Natural Law, Science and Useful Knowledge in Curbing Licentiousness, Promoting Moral Rescue and Averting Working-Class Dissent* (Boca Raton, FL: BrownWalker Press, 2013). In contrast, Ian Inkster uses what he calls a "functionalist" frame to explore how and why these institutions changed over generations: Ian Inkster, "The Social Context of an Educational Movement: A Revisionist Approach to the English Mechanics' Institutes, 1820–1850," *Oxford Review of Education* 2 (1976): 277–307; see also Ian Inkster, "Science and the Mechanics' Institutes, 1820–1850: The Case of Sheffield," *Annals of Science* 32 (1975): 451–74. Martyn Walker's recent work substitutes a paradigm of change for the model of failure in his exploration of the transformation of mechanics' institutes into workingmen's colleges, arguing that mechanics' institutions in particular experienced a temporary drop in membership in the late 1840s, and that it was this brief decline that prompted Hudson and Hole to conclude that such institutes had failed. After 1850, however, Walker argues that such institutions grew apace as interest in formal adult education pressured civic leaders and educators alike to support what eventually became an established web of workingmen's colleges. In Walker's model, which generally minimizes the importance of popular lectures and other forms of leisure culture, the mechanics' institutions largely continued their class-based educative work after 1850, albeit attracting significantly less scrutiny than that during the previous decades of radical political agitation. Martyn Walker, *The Development of the Mechanics' Institute Movement in Britain and beyond* (London: Routledge, 2017). More recently, Douglas Watson has shown how these institutions added other essential services, including an array of financial instruments, which helped propel many working-class men and families into an economic stability that was not intrinsically linked to secondary education or even to "culture," broadly considered, while Susan Barton has shown how some institutes during this period committed significant resources to travel and other leisure activities. Douglas Robert Watson, "The Road to Learning": Re-evaluating the Mechanics' Institute Movement" (PhD dissertation, University of Plymouth, 2018); see especially chapter 2, "Social and Economic Aspects of the Mechanics' Institute Movement (1820–1869)"; Susan Barton, "The Mechanics Institutes: Pioneers of Leisure and Excursion Travel," *Transactions of the Leicestershire Archaeological and Historical Society* LXVII (1993): 47–58. Michael Ian Watson's work a decade later applied this functionalist frame to a collection of institutions in and around Preston, Blackburn, and Darwen, ranging from small church-based mutual improvement societies to mechanics' institutions and libraries, arguing that "the mechanics' institutes of North Lancashire were not primarily agencies of social control or social legitimization but even if they had been either or both of these in the eighteen-twenties, external pressures would have forced them to make major compromises by the eighteen-fifties," and cautioning that "the development and changing social roles of these institutes cannot be adequately analysed in isolation from their local communities and the economic and social structure of North Lancashire." Michael Ian Watson, "Adult Education in North Lancashire in the Second Quarter of the Nineteenth Century" (PhD dissertation, University of London Institute of Education, 1988), 163, 208. See also Martin Hewitt, *The Emergence of Stability in the Industrial City: Manchester, 1832–67* (Aldershot: Scholar Press, 1996), where he argues that early mechanics' institutions in Manchester were part of a temporary but widespread campaign of "middle-class moral imperialism" that faded after mid-century; Hewitt draws upon and expands the work of R. J. Morris, *Class, Sect and Party: The Making of the British Middle Class: Leeds, 1820–1850* (Manchester: Manchester University Press, 1990) in his discussion of middle-class moral imperialism. Elizabeth Neswald's exploration of two iterations of the Galway Mechanics' Institute demonstrates how the first failed because of perceived political activism while the second, more successful, institution was closely tied to the local temperance movement; Elizabeth Neswald, "Science, Sociability and the Improvement of Ireland: The Galway Mechanics' Institute, 1826–51," *British Journal for the History of Science* 39, no. 4 (2006): 503–34. In the same vein, Séamus Duffy has shown how the successes and failures of the Belfast Mechanics' Institution and other similar societies were strongly linked to the state of trade rather than to overt class antagonism or controversial programming, while Jana Sims has explored the thread of paternalism that inevitably wound its way through the governing bodies of these institutions, especially the smaller societies that were the least protected against the effects of industrial or agricultural contraction. Séamus S. Duffy, " 'Treasures Open to the Wise': A Survey of Early Mechanics' Institutes and Similar Organisations," *Saothar* 15 (1990): 39–47; Jana Hilda Sims, "Mechanics' Institutes in Sussex and Hampshire, 1825–1875" (PhD dissertation, University of London, 2010). See also R. A. Thomas, "The Mechanics' Institutes of the Home Counties, *c.* 1825–70," *Vocational Aspect of Education* 31, no. 79 (1979): 67–72 (Part 1) and 31, no. 80 (1979): 103–8 (Part 2). More recent work has focused on the intensely local, adding essential context to the changing understandings of these institutions; see Janet Flexner, "The London Mechanics' Institution: Social and Cultural Foundations 1823–1830" (PhD dissertation, University College London, 2014); C. Stockdale, "Mechanics'

Institutes in Northumberland and Durham" (PhD dissertation, University of Durham, 1993).

15. Harry Chester, *Schools for Children and Institutes for Adults. An Address on National Education* (London: Longman, Green, 1860), 19–20. Henry "Harry" Chester became chair of the Council of the Society of Arts in 1853 and was the moving force behind the founding of the Union of Institutions and one of the main voices pushing for the system of examinations eventually established in 1855. Son of Sir Robert Chester and educated at Charterhouse and Cambridge, Chester entered the civil service in 1826 via the Privy Council Office and in 1840 became Assistant Secretary to the Committee of the Privy Council on Education under Sir James Kay (later Kay-Shuttleworth). He was an early and tireless advocate of examinations within the civil service, which he regarded as a counterpart to the Society of Arts examinations. He helped found the Highgate Literary and Scientific Society in 1839 and was one of its early presidents. He lectured occasionally at institutions within the Union, usually on the subject of mechanics' and other institutes; his other areas of interest within the overall scope of the Society included the work to establish universal musical pitch and a committee to examine food supplies, especially for the working classes, in the 1860s. He was a vice president of the Society at the time of his death in October 1868 at age sixty-two. See "Obituary: Harry Chester," *Journal of the Society of Arts [J. Soc. Arts]* 16 (1867/68): 800; *The Register, and Magazine of Biography, Vol. 1* (London: Nichols and Sons, 1869); J. S. Hurt, "General Notes: Studies in the Societies Archives. Harry Chester: The Early Years," *Journal of the Royal Society of the Arts [J. R. Soc. Arts]* 116, no. 5138 (1968): 156–9; J. S. Hurt, "General Notes. Harry Chester: The Middle Years," *J. R. Soc. Arts* 116, no. 5139 (February 1968): 262–4; J. S. Hurt, "General Notes. Harry Chester: The Later Years," *J. R. Soc. Arts* 116, no. 5140 (1968): 321–3. See also "Proceedings of the Society. Chairman's Address," *J. Soc. Arts* 17 (1868/69): 2–3, where Chester was eulogized as "our lamented and beloved colleague" (3).

16. This relationship is explored in T. H. Marshall, *Citizenship and Social Class and Other Essays* (Cambridge: Cambridge University Press, 1950). For a provocative set of essays that interrogate the ways in which Jose Harris and subsequent scholars have used Marshall's work, see Lawrence Goldman, ed., *Welfare and Social Policy in Britain since 1870: Essays in Honour of Jose Harris* (Oxford: Oxford University Press, 2019).

17. Matthew Grant, "Historicizing Citizenship in Post-War Britain," *Historical Journal* 59, no. 4 (2016): 1189.

18. H. S. Jones, "The Civic Moment in British Social Thought: Civil Society and the Ethics of Citizenship, *c.* 1880–1914," in *Welfare and Social Policy in Britain*, ed. Goldman, 29–43.

19. For helpful overviews of the development of concepts of citizenship in the nineteenth and twentieth centuries, see the following: Michael Freeden, "Civil Society and the Good Citizen: Competing Conceptions of Citizenship in Twentieth-Century Britain," in *Civil Society in British History: Ideas, Identities, Institutions*, ed. Jose Harris (Oxford: Oxford University Press, 2003), 276–81; Derek Heater, *Citizenship in Britain: A History* (Edinburgh: Edinburgh University Press, 2006); Eugenia Lowe, "The Concept of Citizenship in Twentieth-Century Britain: Analysing Contexts of Development," in *Reforming the Constitution: Debates in Twentieth-Century Britain*, ed. Peter Catterall, Wolfram Kaiser, and Ulrike Walton-Jordan (London: Frank Cass, 2000), 179–99; Julia Parker, *Citizenship, Work and Welfare: Searching for the Good Society* (New York: St. Martin's Press, 1998); Charles Pattie, Patrick Seyd, and Paul Whiteley, *Citizenship in Britain: Values, Participation and Democracy*

(Cambridge: Cambridge University Press, 2004). For examinations of citizenship and the working classes, see Brad Beaven, *Leisure, Citizenship and Working-Class Men in Britain, 1850–1945* (Manchester: Manchester University Press, 2005); Brad Beaven and John Griffiths, "Creating the Exemplary Citizen: The Changing Notion of Citizenship 1870–1939," *Contemporary British History* 22, no. 2 (2008): 203–25. Works focusing on how urban leaders interpreted "citizenship" include John R. Griffiths, "Civic Communication in Britain: A Study of the *Municipal Journal c.* 1893–1910," *Journal of Urban History* 34, no.5 (2008): 775–94 and Helen Meller, "Urban Renewal and Citizenship: The Quality of Life in British Cities, 1890–1990," *Urban History* 22, no.1 (1995): 63–84. Meller has also interrogated the intersections of citizenship and gender: see Helen Meller, "Women and Citizenship: Gender and the Built Environment in British Cities 1870–1939," in *Cities of Ideas: Civil Society and Urban Governance in Britain, 1800–2000. Essays in Honour of David Reeder*, ed. Robert Colls and Richard Rodger (Aldershot: Ashgate Publishing, 2004), 231–57; see also Catherine Hall, Keith McClelland, and Jane Rendall, *Defining the Victorian Nation: Class, Race, Gender and the Reform Act of 1867* (Cambridge: Cambridge University Press, 2000). Women fighting for the franchise were especially prone to emphasize the ideas of duty and responsibility inherent in definitions of citizenship; see Simon Morgan, *A Victorian Woman's Place: Public Culture in the Nineteenth Century* (London: Tauris Academic Studies, 2007); Kathryn Gleadle, *Borderline Citizens: Women, Gender, and Political Culture in Britain 1815–1867* (Oxford: Oxford University Press, 2009); Rosemary O'Day, "Women and Education in Nineteenth-Century England," in *Women, Scholarship and Criticism: Gender and Knowledge c. 1780–1900*, ed. Joan Bellamy, Ann Laurence, and Gill Perry (Manchester and New York: Manchester University Press, 2000), 91–109; Geoff Eley, "Culture, Nation and Gender," in *Gendered Nations: Nationalisms and Gender Order in the Long Nineteenth Century*, ed. Ida Blom, Karen Hagemann, and Catherine Hall (Oxford: Berg, 2000), 27–40; Ulrike Walton-Jordan and Jutta Schwarzkopf, "Transforming Relations of Gender: The Feminist Project of Societal Reform in Turn-of-the-Century Britain," in *Reforming the Constitution*, ed. Catterall, Kaiser, and Walton-Jordan, 158–78. For the ways in which elementary school teaching grappled with the challenges of "teaching" citizenship, see Heather Ellis, "Elite Education and the Development of Mass Elementary Schooling in England, 1870–1930," in *Mass Education and the Limits of State Building, c. 1870–1930*, ed. Laurence Brockliss and Nicola Sheldon (New York: Palgrave Macmillan, 2012), 46–70; Stephen Heathorn, "'Let Us Remember that We, Too, Are English': Constructions of Citizenship and National Identity in English Elementary School Reading Books, 1880–1914," *Victorian Studies* 38 (1995): 395–428; Brian Simon, "Education and Citizenship in England," in *The State and Educational Change: Essays in the History of Education and Pedagogy*, ed. Brian Simon (London: Lawrence & Wishart, 1994), 75–83; Susannah Wright, "Citizenship, Moral Education and the English Elementary School," in *Mass Education*, ed. Brockliss and Sheldon, 21–43; Peter Yeandle, *Citizenship, Nation, Empire: The Politics of History Teaching in England, 1870–1930* (Manchester: Manchester University Press, 2015), 395–427; see also Roger Fieldhouse, *A History of Modern British Adult Education* (Leicester, England: National Institute of Adult Continuing Education, 1996). For the exploration of civic participation as citizenship, see Brian Harrison, "Civil Society by Accident? Paradoxes of Voluntarism and Pluralism in the Nineteenth and Twentieth Centuries," in *Civil Society in British History: Ideas, Identities, Institutions*, ed. Jose

Harris (Oxford: Oxford University Press, 2003), 79–96; Anthony Everitt, "Culture and Citizenship," in *Citizens: Towards a Citizenship Culture*, ed. Bernard Crick (London: Blackwell, 2001), 64–73.
20. Heater, *Citizenship in Britain*, 116; quoting John Stuart Mill, *Considerations of Representative Government* (1861).
21. A. Vincent and R. Plant, *Philosophy, Politics and Citizenship: The Life and Thought of the British Idealists* (Oxford: Blackwell, 1984), 1. See also Brian Harrison, "Planning in Modern Britain: Its History and Dimensions," in *Welfare and Social Policy*, ed. Goldman, 79–102; and Julia Moses, "The Reluctant Planner: T. H. Marshall and Political Thought in British Social Policy," in *Welfare and Social Policy*, ed. Goldman, 127–6.
22. Oscar Browning, *The Citizen: His Rights and Responsibilities* (London: Blackie and Son, 1893), 10–11; quoted in Heathorn, "'Let Us Remember that We, Too, Are English,'" 37.
23. Percy E. Matheson, "Citizenship," *International Journal of Ethics* 8, no. 1 (1897): 22–40, 28, 34, 39.
24. Samuel Smiles, *Self-Help: With Illustrations of Character and Conduct* (London: John Murray, 1859; revised and enlarged edition, New York, n.d.), 331.
25. I examine the development of caste in detail in Anne B. Rodrick, *Self-Help and Civic Culture: Citizenship in Victorian Birmingham* (Surrey: Ashgate, 2004); see especially pp. 49–132.
26. Frances Power Cobbe, *Why Women Desire the Franchise* (London: National Society for Women's Suffrage, 1877), 4.
27. Meller, "Women and Citizenship," 234.
28. Lectures on this topic, which became particularly timely with the 1874 publication of an essay by London Cremation Society founder Sir Henry Thompson, were delivered under the auspices of various lecture societies, including the offshoots of the London-based SLS, while the question was also included in lists of debates and discussions produced by the Society of Arts and other groups. Henry Thompson, *Cremation: The Treatment of the Body after Death* (London: Henry S. King, 1874).
29. This charge was reprinted in all publications of the SLS, including the published lectures as well as advertisements and annual reports.
30. George H. Snazelle (1848–1912) was a popular baritone better known for his comic opera and musical theater than the traditional Italian opera performances with which he launched his career. His "considerable reputation as singer, raconteur, and entertainer" was described in his 1898 autobiography, *Snazaparilla*; see http://www.operascotland.org/person/3375/George-Snazelle (accessed June 23, 2020).

Chapter 1

1. "Report of Council: General Meeting," *Journal of the Society of Arts* [hereafter *J. Soc. Arts*] 1 (1852/3): 347 (remarks by Mr. Buckmaster). Published in London by George Bell (later Bell and Daldy), the *Journal* appeared every Friday beginning November 26, 1852. It was supplied free of charge to individual members and to institutions within the Union; for others, it was 3p. (4p., stamped). Each issue ran twelve pages of text and four pages of front and back matter, which included advertisements and a list of Union affiliates. The online *Journal* (accessed for this project via the Hathi Trust) is

digitized by entire volumes with pagination for each volume starting with page one. Each new volume begins in November and runs for twelve months. The reference style used here indicates volume number, year (e.g., 1852/3), and page number within the entire volume.

2. An excellent overview of American lecture culture in the nineteenth century can be found in Donald M. Scott, "The Popular Lecture and the Creation of a Public in Mid-nineteenth-Century America," *Journal of American History* 66, no. 4 (March 1980): 781–809; Donald M. Scott, "The Profession that Vanished: Public Lecturing in Mid-nineteenth-Century America," in *Professions and Professional Ideologies in America*, ed. Gerald L. Geison (Chapel Hill, NC: University of North Carolina Press, 1983), 12–28; and Angela G. Ray, *The Lyceum and Public Culture in the Nineteenth-Century United States* (East Lansing, MI: Michigan State University Press, 2005). See also Carl Bode, *The American Lyceum: Town Meeting of the Mind* (Carbondale, IL: Southern Illinois University Press, 1956). A recent collection of essays has examined the American lecture circuit as one way in which Americans gained a greater understanding of global history and culture: Tom F. Wright, ed., *The Cosmopolitan Lyceum: Lecture Culture and the Globe in Nineteenth-Century America* (Amherst, MA: University of Massachusetts Press, 2013); see especially the essay by Angela G. Ray, "How Cosmopolitan Was the Lyceum, Anyway?" 23–41. Wright also explores the ways in which prominent American lecturers carried "civic speech" across the pond in *Lecturing the Atlantic: Speech, Print, and an Anglo-American Commons 1830–1870* (Oxford: Oxford University Press, 2017). Richard D. Brown discusses lecture culture in the context of the American emphasis on citizenship in *The Strength of a People: The Idea of an Informed Citizenry in America 1650–1870* (Chapel Hill, NC: University of North Carolina Press, 1996). For a discussion of literary lecturers in the United States after about 1870, see Philip Waller, *Writers, Readers, and Reputations: Literary Life in Britain 1870–1918* (Oxford: Oxford University Press, 2006), chapter 16: "Lecture Tours," 575–614.

3. "How They Manage Their Lectures in England," *Putnam's Magazine* 13, no. 13 (1869): 98–106.

4. "How They Manage Their Lectures In England," 105–6.

5. Tom F. Wright, "The Results of Locomotion: Bayard Taylor and the Travel Lecture in the Mid-nineteenth-Century United States," *Studies in Travel Writing* 14, no. 2 (June 2010): 113.

6. Scott, "The Popular Lecture." Scott identifies four key characteristics that made this public lecture circuit so successful: a coherent season, running from November to April; a consistent schedule, so that an individual lyceum's lectures were predictably held on, say, Monday evenings at 6 pm; good advance publicity; and "the avid reporting of lectures [which] surrounded them with an aura that stamped them as important events and identified and spread the reputation of a corps of regional and national lecturers." Scott, "The Profession that Vanished," 19. For the star system, see Peter Cherches, "Star Course: Popular Lectures and the Marketing of Celebrity in 19th Century America" (PhD dissertation, New York University, 1997) and Waller, *Writers, Readers, and Reputations* (chapter 9, "The Star Turn"), 364–97. For the ways in which post-1875 lyceum practices began to change, see Sara Lampert, "Bringing Music to the Lyceumites: The Bureaus and the Transformation of Lyceum Entertainment," in Wright, *The Cosmopolitan Lyceum,* 67–89; and Evan Roberts, "The Peripatetic Career of Wherahiko Rawei: Maori Culture on the Global Chautauqua Circuit, 1893–1927," in Wright, *The Cosmopolitan Lyceum,* 203–20. For a discussion of the role of the

press in creating an audience for certain kinds of lectures, see Wright, "The Results of Locomotion"; Amanda Adams, *Performing Authorship in the Nineteenth-Century Transatlantic Lecture Tour* (Aldershot: Ashgate, 2014); Ronald J. Zboray and Mary Saracino Zboray, *Literary Dollars and Social Sense: A People's History of the Mass Market Book* (New York: Routledge, 2005).

7. "Lectures and Lecturing," *Meliora* 2 (1860): 198–9; quoted in Phillip Collins, "'Agglomerating Dollars with Prodigious Rapidity': British Pioneers on the American Lecture Circuit," in *Victorian Literature and Society: Essays Presented to Richard D. Altick*, ed. James R. Kinkaid and Albert J. Kuhn (Columbus, OH: Ohio State University Press, 1984), 3.

8. "Correspondence. Lectures," *J. Soc. Arts* 1 (1852/53): 385 (letter from E.W.).

9. The two general histories of the Society of the Arts are Henry Trueman Wood, *A History of The Royal Society of Arts* (London: John Murray, 1913) and Derek Hudson and Kenneth W. Luckhurst, *The Royal Society of Arts 1754–1954* (London: John Murray, 1954). The word "Royal" was added to the Society's title in 1908. See also Anton Howes, *Arts and Minds: How the Royal Society of Arts Changed a Nation* (Princeton: Princeton University Press, 2021); Susannah Gibson, *The Spirit of Inquiry: How One Extraordinary Society Shaped Modern Science* (Oxford: Oxford University Press, 2019); Adrian Tinniswood, *The Royal Society and the Invention of Modern Science* (New York: Basic Books, 2019); and D. G. C. Allan, "The Society of Arts and Government, 1754–1800: Public Encouragement of Arts, Manufactures, and Commerce in Eighteenth-Century England," *Eighteenth-Century Studies* 7, no. 4 (1974): 434–52.

10. Wood, *History of the Royal Society of Arts*, 370; quoting a letter from member Harry Chester to the Council of the Society in 1851.

11. For discussions of the local and imperial nature of club culture during the eighteenth and nineteenth centuries, see Mrinalini Sinha, "Britishness, Clubbability, and the Colonial Public Sphere: The Genealogy of an Imperial Institution in Colonial India," *Journal of British Studies* 40, no. 4 (2001): 489–521. For discussions of the learned societies of the period, which by 1850 ranged from the venerable Royal Academy of Arts (established 1768) and the Linnaean Society (1788) to the newer Geological Society of London (1807), the British Association for the Advancement of Science (1831), and the Philological Society (1842), see Peter Clark, *British Clubs and Societies 1580–1800: The Origins of an Associational World* (Oxford: Oxford University Press, 2000) and William C. Lubenow, *"Only Connect": Learned Societies in Nineteenth-Century Britain* (Woodbridge: Boydell Press, 2015).

12. Historians of science have examined the culture of the science lecture from many angles. See, as a start, the following: J. N. Hays, "The London Lecturing Empire, 1800–1850," in *Metropolis and Province: Science in British Culture 1780–1850*, ed. Ian Inkster and Jack Morrell (London: Hutchinson, 1983), 91–119; Ian Inkster, "Culture, Institutions and Urbanity: The Itinerant Science Lecturer in Sheffield 1790–1850" in *Essays in the Social and Economic History of South Yorkshire*, ed. S. Pollard and C. Holmes (Sheffield: South Yorkshire County Council, 1976), 218–32; Ian Inkster, "Science and Society in the Metropolis: Preliminary Examination of the Social and Institutional Context of the Askesian Society of London, 1796–1807," *Annals of Science* 34, no. 1 (1977): 1–32; Aileen Fyfe and Bernard Lightman, "Science in the Marketplace: An Introduction," in *Science in the Marketplace: Nineteenth Century Sites and Experiences*, ed. Fyfe and Lightman (Chicago: University of Chicago Press, 2007), 1–19; Bernard Lightman, "Lecturing in the Spatial Economy of Science," in

Science in the Marketplace, 97–132; Ian Inkster, "The Public Lecture as an Instrument of Science Education for Adults: The Case of Great Britain, c. 1750–1850," *Paedagogica Historica* 20, no.1 (1980): 80–107; Ian Inkster, "Popularised Culture and Steam Intellect: A Case Study of Liverpool and Its Region, Circa 1820–1850s," in *The Steam Intellect Societies: Essays on Culture, Education, and Industry Circa 1820–1914*, ed. Ian Inkster (Nottingham: Department of Adult Education, University of Nottingham Press, 1985), 44–59. For a discussion of the functions of the conversazione within the community of the science society, see Samuel J. M. M. Alberti, "Conversaziones and the Experience of Science in Victorian England," *Journal of Victorian Culture* 8, no. 2 (2003): 208–30.

13. This development would eventually extend to the most prominent of science groups, the British Association for the Advancement of Science, where the lay public was present in the form of "ladies," wives, and daughters of BAAS members who helped turn the annual meeting into the "Philosophers' Picnic"; Rebekah Higgitt and Charles W. J. Withers, "Science and Sociability: Women as Audience at the British Association for the Advancement of Science, 1831–1901," *Isis* 99, no. 1 (2008): 1–27. See also Louise Miskell, "Meeting Places: The Scientific Congress and the Host Town in the South-West of England, 1836–1877," *Urban History* 39, no. 2 (2012): 246–62.
14. Bernard Lightman, "*Knowledge* Confronts *Nature*: Richard Proctor and Popular Science Periodicals," in *Culture and Science in the Nineteenth-Century Media*, ed. Louise Henson, Geoffrey Cantor, Gowan Dawson, Richard Noakes, Sally Shuttleworth, and Jonathan R. Topham (Aldershot: Ashgate Publishing, 2004), 205.
15. Howard M Wach, "Culture and the Middle Classes: Popular Knowledge in Industrial Manchester," *Journal of British Studies* 27, no. 4 (1988): 377.
16. R. J. Morris, "Middle-Class Culture, 1700–1914," in *A History of Modern Leeds*, ed. Derek Fraser (Manchester, UK: Manchester University Press, 1980), 201.
17. Edward Schunk used this phrase in a speech to the lit.-&-phil. reviewing its fortunes over the previous century, reported in Manchester Literary and Philosophical Society, *Proceedings* 41 (1897), xlvii; quoted in Robert H. Kargon, *Science in Victorian Manchester: Enterprise and Expertise* (Baltimore: Johns Hopkins University Press, 1977; 2nd. edn., New Brunswick NJ: Transaction Publishers, 2010), 148. For an exploration of the slow professionalization of "science" in the nineteenth century, see Heather Ellis, "Knowledge, Character and Professionalisation in Nineteenth-Century British Science," *History of Education* 43, no. 6 (2014): 777–92.
18. Institutional rules generally cordoned off religion and theology as inappropriate for general discussion; Martin Hewitt, "Ralph Waldo Emerson, George Dawson, and the Control of the Lecture Platform in Mid-nineteenth Century Manchester," *Nineteenth-Century Prose* 25, no.2 (1998): 1–25. See also Edward Kitson Clark, *A History of 100 Years of the Life of the Leeds Philosophical and Literary Society* (Leeds: Jowett and Sowry, 1924) and Edward Kitson Clark, *Leeds Conversation Club, 1849–1939* (Leeds: Conversation Club, 1939); Simon Gunn and Rachel Bell, *Middle Classes: Their Rise and Sprawl* (London: Weidenfeld and Nicolson, 2011).
19. See, for example, Job Legh in Gaskell's *Mary Barton* (1848) and Mr. Venus in Dickens's *Our Mutual Friend* (1865).
20. A number of recent works have examined the use of spectacle in the second half of the century. Samuel Alberti lists "phantasmagoria, zoetropes (or 'wheels of life'), stroboscopes (or iconoscopes), stereoscopes and ... that simple classic, the magic lantern" as typical of the professional lecturer's equipment by mid-century; Alberti, "Conversaziones and the Experience of Science," 218.

21. Hays, "The London Lecturing Empire," 94.
22. Ibid., 109.
23. Ibid., 99.
24. Simon Naylor, "The Field, the Museum and the Lecture Hall: The Spaces of Natural History in Victorian Cornwall," *Transactions of the Institute of British Geographers (NS)* 27 (2002): 497.
25. Diarmud A. Finnegan, *Natural History Societies and Civic Culture in Victorian Scotland* (London: Pickering and Chatto, 2009).
26. Ibid., 3.
27. Enda Leaney, "'Evanescent Impressions': Public Lectures and the Popularization of Science in Ireland, 1770–1860," *Eire-Ireland* 43, nos. 3–4 (Fall/Winter 2008): 157–82, 179.
28. Robert Spence Watson, *The History of the Literary and Philosophical Society of Newcastle-upon-Tyne (1793–1896)* (London: Walter Scott, Limited, 1897), 202–4; Manchester Athenaeum, *Addresses, 1835–1885, also, Report of Proceedings of the Meeting of the Members in Celebration of the 50th Anniversary of the Institution, October 28th, 1885* (Manchester: printed for the directors, 1885), 217. The Athenaeum lectures were delivered in 1835 by John Phillips, FRS, who was, at the time of these lectures, the secretary of the Yorkshire Philosophical Association as well as a professor of geology at King's College, London.
29. Leaney, "'Evanescent Impressions,'" 178. See also Hewitt, "Aspects of Platform Culture" and Lightman, "Lecturing in the Spatial Economy of Science." This liminality continued into the second half of the nineteenth century, frequently combining political economy with a generally Christian theology; see Martin Hewitt, "Popular Platform Religion: Arthur Mursell at the Free Trade Hall, 1856–65," *Manchester Region History Review* 10 (1996): 29–39. Waller argues that the "preacher-lecturer" was more an American than an English phenomenon, and that by the 1870s "it was as if there were two separate worlds in Britain, secular and religious"; Waller, *Writers, Readers, and Reputations*, 578–9. However, as we shall see in the chapters that follow, these two worlds remained interconnected until at least the mid-1880s, especially in the provinces.
30. Hays points specifically to the Crystal Palace and the University of London as agents of this change in London and the surrounding areas; "The London Lecturing Empire," pp. 111–12. See also Juliana Adelman, *Communities of Science in Nineteenth-Century Ireland* (London: Pickering and Chatto, 2009) for a discussion of the growth of government-controlled institutions first augmenting and then replacing the local private societies discussed by Leaney. Leaney notes that this change was not universally appreciated; lecturer William Kirby Sullivan referred to government-sponsored lecture series as "a system of intellectual outdoor relief." Leaney, "'Evanescent Impressions,'" 181, quoting *Report from the Select Committee Appointed to Inquire into the Condition of the Scientific Institutions of Dublin Which Are Assisted by Government Aid, with the Proceedings, Minutes of Evidence, Appendix, and Index* HC 1864 (495) xiii, I, p. 194. For one example of the ways in which "science" became both specialized and often simply odd, see Lara Karpenko and Shalyn Claggett, eds., *Strange Science: Investigating the Limits of Knowledge in the Victorian Age* (Ann Arbor, MI: University of Michigan Press, 2017). Scientific references and descriptions of experimentation showed up in a variety of unexpected spaces; see Anne Rodrick, "Melodrama and Natural Science: Reading the 'Greenwich Murder' in the Mid-century Periodical Press," *Victorian Periodicals Review* 50, no.1 (2017): 66–99.

31. See generally Thomas Kelly, "The Origin of Mechanics' Institutes," *British Journal of Educational Studies* 1, no.1 (1952): 17–27, and Thomas Kelly, *George Birkbeck: Pioneer of Adult Education* (Liverpool: Liverpool University Press, 1957).
32. Manchester Mechanics' Institution, *Preamble* (Manchester, 1824); quoted in Mabel Tylecote, "The Manchester Mechanics' Institution, 1824–50," in *Artisan to Graduate: Essays to Commemorate the Foundation in 1824 of the Manchester Mechanics' Institution, Now in 1974 the University of Manchester Institute of Science and Technology*, ed. D. S. L. Cardwell (Manchester: Manchester University Press, 1974), 55.
33. Kelly, "Origin of Mechanics' Institutes," 20–1.
34. Hudson, *History of Adult Education*, vi. There has been little written on Hudson (1812–1884), despite his involvement in so many institutions and projects for the education of working men. The brief biography by B. R. Villy provides a good basic overview: He worked as a bookseller until 1843, when he began his career as an educator and officer of a series of educational societies in Manchester, London, Glasgow, Liverpool, and Leeds. Hudson founded or helped found the Scottish Union of Popular Literary and Scientific Institutes in Glasgow, the Northern Union of Literary and Mechanics' Institutes, and the Association of Lancashire and Cheshire Mechanics' Institutes, and also served variously as secretary, librarian, lecture agent, or committee member at the Greenwich Society for the Acquisition and Diffusion of Useful Knowledge, the Leeds Mechanics' Institute, the Yorkshire Union of Mechanics' Institutes, the Glasgow Athenaeum, the Manchester Athenaeum, and the Manchester Free Library. See B. R. Villy, "James William Hudson, Ph.D.," *Manchester Review* 1 (1862/3): 352–61. By 1860, he had cut most of his institutional ties and poured his efforts into the founding of Trafford College in Manchester. In 1867, he was elected a fellow of the Chemical Society, London: "Proceedings of Societies. Chemical Society," *The Chemical News and Journal of Physical Science* 15 (1867): 77. Robert Bud and Gerrylynn K. Roberts refer to him as "professional chemist" and "organiser and chronicler of the mechanics' institutes," in *Science versus Practice: Chemistry in Victorian Britain* (Manchester: Manchester University Press, 1984), 102.
35. *Census of Great Britain, 1851. Education. England and Wales. Report and Tables. Presented to Both Houses of Parliament by Command of Her Majesty* (London: E. Eyre and W. Spottiswoode, 1854), lxx.
36. John Laurent, "Science, Society and Politics in Late Nineteenth-Century England: A Further Look at Mechanics' Institutes," *Social Studies of Science* 14, no. 4 (1984): 589. Laurent notes the YUMI's consistent growth: numbers of affiliates rose to 122 in 1868 and 276 by 1890, with membership numbers at 18,500 in 1850, 23,000 in 1868, 46,000 in 1879, and "upwards of 60,000" in 1890; 589. The YUMI was officially founded in 1838, replacing the West Riding Union of Mechanics' Institutes, which had been founded the previous year. See Walker, *The Development of the Mechanics' Institute Movement*, 7. The Union of Lancashire and Cheshire Institutes grew out of the Manchester District Association of Literary and Scientific Institutions, founded in 1839, and reorganized in 1847 into the Lancashire and Cheshire Union of Mechanics' Institutions; its more informal name, the Union of Lancashire and Cheshire Institutes, immediately became the default reference in periodicals and speeches during the period. A. P. Dent, "The Union of Lancashire and Cheshire Institutes. An Outline of Its Functions and Work," *Journal of the Textile Institute Proceedings* 29, no. 7 (1938): 365–73.

37. By 1865, the number of "unions in union with the Society" had reached 10: The Aldershot and Farnham District Association (4 member institutions); the Bucks and Berks Adult Education Society (no members listed); the East Lancashire Union (10 member institutions); the Kent Association of Institutes (9 member institutions); the Manchester Association of Mechanics' Institutions of Lancaster and Cheshire (86 member institutions); the Metropolitan Association for the Promotion of the Education of Adults (49 member institutions); the Southern Counties Adult Education Society (186 member institutions); the South Staffordshire Union (25 member institutions); the Yorkshire Union of Mechanics' Institutions (132 member institutions): and the Worcestershire Union of Educational Institutes (26 member institutions). "Programme of Examinations for 1865," *J. Soc. Arts* 13 (1865/66), appendix.
38. Hudson, *History of Adult Education*, viii–ix.
39. See appendix, "Mechanics' Institutions, Literary and Scientific Institutions and Similar Bodies Recorded in Great Britain up to and Including the Year 1851" in Kelly, *George Birkbeck*, 302–28. In 1852, the initial issue of the *Journal* listed 231 affiliates in the following categories: Mechanics' Institute (72), Athenaeum (11), Literary Institute or Society (17), Reading Room or Library (5), Literary and Science Institute or Society (36), Literary, Scientific, and Mechanics' Institute or Society (9), Mechanics' Institute and Literary Society (10), Mechanics' Institute and Scientific Society (1), Mutual Improvement Society (9), Literary and Philosophical Institute or Society (4), Useful Knowledge Institute or Society (8). There were also 16 with some other combination of these categories (e.g., the Dawlish Literary and General Knowledge Society), 13 with no descriptor (e.g., the Bilston Institute), and 20 with descriptors that fell into none of these categories (e.g., the Camberwell Institute for the Industrial Classes, the Bootle Educational Society, and the Folkestone Harveian Institution). "List of Institutions in Union with the Society of Arts, November 23rd, 1852," *J. Soc. Arts* 1 (1852/3): i–ii.
40. Flexner, "The London Mechanics' Institution," 430–2.
41. E. Renals, Esq., "On Mechanics' Institutions and the Elementary Education Bill. Read before Section F, British Association for the Advancement of Science, at Liverpool, September, 1870," *Journal of the Statistical Society of London* 33, no. 4 (1870): 452.
42. Hole, *Essay*. Hole (1820–1895) was the honorary secretary of the YUMI (a position he held from 1848 to 1867) when he wrote this essay for a competition sponsored by the Society of Arts; a similar essay, "Light, More Light!: On the Present State of Education amongst the Working Classes of Leeds," followed in 1860. Such competitions were relatively common during this period; see Chapter 3 in this volume for information on John Alfred Langford of Birmingham, whose literary career was launched through two similar essay competitions. Hole also served on the committees of the Leeds Mechanics' Institution and the Leeds School of Art, as well as a number of cooperative and preservation societies in London, and worked with many of the important figures in the adult education movement, including Harry Chester, James Hudson, and James Booth. See J. F. C. Harrison, *Social Reform in Victorian Leeds: The Work of James Hole, 1820–1895* (Leeds: Thoresby Society, 1954); Martin Hewitt, "James Hole," *Oxford Dictionary of National Biography* (online edn.), Oxford University Press (accessed September 23, 2004).
43. Hudson, *History*, vii; Hole, *Essay*, 17.
44. Hudson, *History*, vii–viii.
45. Ibid., 167.

46. Ibid., 96 (Liverpool), 146 (Nottingham), 155 (Preston), xii ("social necessities").
47. Hole, *Essay*, 25.
48. Ibid.; Hudson refers to these rivals as "casinos," *History*, 140.
49. "Proceedings of Societies. Yorkshire Union of Mechanics' Institutions," *J. Soc. Arts* 1 (1852/3): 320.
50. "Proceedings of Institutions. Swindon," *J. Soc. Arts* 1 (1852/3): 130; "Correspondence. Causes of the Failure of Institutions," *J. Soc. Arts* 2 (1853/4): 665 (letter from Joseph Simpson, Islington Literary and Scientific Society, July 26, 1854).
51. "Proceedings of Institutions. Yorkshire Union of Mechanics' Institutions," *J. Soc. Arts* 2 (1853/4): 529 (remarks by Edward Baines). Edward Baines, Jr. (1800–1890), like his father, was integrally involved in a number of Leeds political and social institutions, including the Leeds Lit.-&-Phil., the Leeds Mechanics' Institution, and the YUMI; he took over the proprietorship of the *Leeds Mercury* upon his father's death in 1848 and served as MP for Leeds from 1859 to 1874. Like Hudson, he was a committed voluntaryist, only reluctantly conceding that state involvement in education was necessary for reform. J. R. Lowerson, "Baines, Sir Edward," *Oxford DNB* (online edn.) (accessed September 23, 2004).
52. W. H. J. Traice, "Home Correspondence. Lectures," *J. Soc. Arts* 1 (1852/3): 431–2. Traice (1813–1885), an engineer, taught miners and foremen for some two decades in the colliery night schools of the Bridgewater Collieries and delivered a number of lectures on equipment and ventilation to various learned societies; see, for example, W. H. J. Traice, "Coal-Cutting Machinery," *Transactions of the Manchester Geological Society*, 13 (1876): 83–99. He served for many years as the secretary of the Leeds Mechanics' Institute and Literary Society, agent to the Union of Lancashire and Cheshire Institutes, and secretary of the Institutes in Union, in which capacity he dispensed advice and delivered lectures on educational as well as entertaining subjects to member institutions. He served as a trustee of the Manchester School of Art and was a member of the Manchester Literary Club. See Carole A. O'Reilly, "Professional Identity and Social Capital: The Personal Networks of Victorian Popular Journalists" (2019). Available online: http://usir.salford.ac.uk/id/eprint/48332/ (accessed September 23, 2019).
53. See, for example, "Correspondence. Popular Lecturers," *J. Soc. Arts* 1 (1852/3): 444 (letter of July 18, 1853).
54. "One Hundred and Second Anniversary Dinner," *J. Soc. Arts* 4 (1855/6): 559–60 (remarks by the Right Hon. Lord Ashburton, FRS, in the chair).
55. "The Birmingham and Midland Institute. Address by Sir John Pakington," *Birmingham Daily Gazette*, September 30, 1862: 3.
56. Leeds Mechanics' Institute, *Annual Report of the Committee of the Leeds Mechanics' Institute and Literary Society [for 1855-1856], Presented to the Annual Meeting on the 30th of January, 1856* (Leeds: The Institute, 1856), 10–11.
57. "Report, First Ordinary Meeting, Wednesday, November 24, 1852," *J. Soc. Arts* 1 (1852/3): 1 (remarks of Mr. Cole, Chairman of Council).
58. Leeds Mechanics' Institute, *Annual Report [1856]*, 3.
59. "Proceedings of Institutions. Kelvedon," *J. Soc. Arts* 2 (1853/4): 345.
60. "Proceedings of Institutions. Basingstoke," *J. Soc. Arts* 2 (1853/4): 472.
61. Eneas Mackenzie, "Literary Institutions: Literary and Philosophical Society," *Historical Account of Newcastle-upon-Tyne Including the Borough of Gateshead* (Newcastle-upon-Tyne, 1827), 461–86. Available online: *British History Online* http://www.british-hist

ory.ac.uk/no-series/newcastle-historical-account/pp461–486 (accessed January 24, 2019).
62. Watson, *Newcastle Lit.-&-Phil.*, 202–7. The Newcastle Lit.-&-Phil.'s success as a general institution of culture stands in marked contrast to the town's Literary, Scientific, and Mechanical Institution (est. 1824), which could not compete on the grounds of "lectures and concerts" and amalgamated with the Tyne Polytechnic Institution in 1847; see Hudson, *History*, 141–2.
63. W. H. J. Traice, *Hand-Book of Mechanics' Institutions, With Priced Catalogue of Books Suitable for Libraries. 2d edition* (London: Longman Green, 1863), 20.
64. Roger Boswell [Hugo Reid], *The Art of Conversation, Giving Hints, Suggestions, and Rules for Cultivating and Promoting Social Intercourse* (London, 1867; 1st edn., 1862); quoted in Andrew St. George, *The Descent of Manners: Etiquette, Rules and the Victorians* (London: Chatto and Windus, 1993), 55. Reid was a Scottish writer and educationist who served as the president of the Hunterian Society of Edinburgh, the principal of the People's College, Nottingham, and the headmaster of Dalhousie College, Nova Scotia, where he spent the years 1855–9 before returning to Britain. He was also a member of the Glasgow and Liverpool Mechanics' Institutions. A member of the Society of Arts, he produced two series of textbooks in the sciences as well as a number of lectures, articles, and volumes on education and self-education. Within the pages of the *Journal*, Reid was a regular correspondent on the need to establish workingmen's colleges throughout the kingdom. See Anita McConnell, "Reid, Hugo," *Oxford DNB* (online edn.), https://doi.org/10.1093/ref:odnb/23329 (accessed September 23, 2004).
65. An earlier list had proposed an even more highly aspirational and exhaustive program of culture: "astronomy, botany, geology, ethnology, mythology, psychology, biography, history, sculpture, mathematics, mechanics, manufactures, microscopic research, malaria, sanitary arrangements, sleep and suspended animation, instinct and reason, the laws of colour, the causes of rain and wind, commerce, currency, political economy, nerve force, vision, the habits of animals, and many other topics which cannot be so succinctly described." "Reporter for the Press," *Monthly Literary and Scientific Lecturer, Vol. 4* (London: T. W. Grattan, 1853), iii–iv.
66. "Reports of Institutes. Macclesfield Useful Knowledge Society," *J. Soc. Arts* 1 (1852/3): 20–1; "Home Correspondence. Lectures," *J. Soc. Arts* 1 (1852/3): 22–3 (letter from William Hughes). The category of "Reports of Institutes" was short-lived and within a few weeks had been replaced by "Proceedings of Institutions."
67. See, for example, one correspondent from Wellingsborough going so far as to say of Henry Vincent, whose early political radicalism gradually shaded into a well-organized lecturing career, "As an orator, he almost stands unequalled amongst perambulating lecturers." "Proceedings of Institutions. Wellingsborough," *J. Soc. Arts* 3 (1854/5): 107.
68. "Correspondence. Lectures," *J. Soc. Arts* 1 (1852/3): 385 (letter from E.W.); G. H., "Lectures," *J. Soc. Arts* 1 (1852/3): 128.
69. "Proceedings of Institutions. Poole Mechanics' Institute," *J. Soc. Arts* 3 (1854/5): 232.
70. "First Ordinary Meeting. Wed, Nov 21, 1855. Address by Rev. Dr. Booth, Chairman of Council," *J. Soc. Arts* 3 (1854/5): 4–5.
71. Anonymous, "Union Correspondence. Journal and Lectures," *J. Soc. Arts* 1 (1852/3): 9.
72. Michael Faraday, *A Course of Six Lectures on the Chemical History of a Candle*, ed. W. Crookes (London: Griffin, Bohn & Co., 1861). Faraday delivered this course of lectures in 1848 as part of the "Christmas lectures for young people," an annual series at the Royal Institution of Great Britain in London.

73. Traice, "Home Correspondence. Lectures," 431–2.
74. For Sunday schools, see Thomas Laqueur, *Religion and Respectability: Sunday Schools and Working Class Culture, 1780–1850* (New Haven: Yale University Press, 1976); K. D. M. Snell, "The Sunday-School Movement in England and Wales: Child Labour, Denominational Control and Working-Class Culture," *Past and Present* 164 (1969): 122–68.
75. Hugo Reid, "Suggestions for the Conversion of Mechanics' Institutions into Colleges for the People," *J. Soc. Arts* 1 (1852/3): 535. Reid had his article reprinted and distributed as a pamphlet to Union affiliates.
76. "General Meeting, June 8, 1853," *J. Soc. Arts* 1 (1852/3): 348 (remarks by Lyon Playfair, chair of the 1853 general meeting); see also "First Ordinary Meeting. Wed, Nov 21, 1855: Address by Rev. Dr. Booth, Chairman of Council," *J. Soc. Arts* 5 (1855/6): 5, where Booth described in tragic terms the "silent, patient study" of the uninstructed adult.
77. Alexander John Scott, "*Self-Education: An Opening Lecture Delivered to the Members of the Salford Mechanics' Institution, on Wednesday Evening, January 11th, 1854*" (Manchester: A. Ireland and Company, 1854), 4. Scott was the principal of Owens College, Manchester, when he delivered this lecture.
78. "Almondbury Mechanics' Institution Soiree," *Huddersfield Chronicle*, February 25, 1860, 6 (remarks of R. Houghton).
79. Scott, *Self-Education*, 4. Lowe made his comment after the passage of the 1870 Education Act.
80. F. W. Naylor, *Popular Libraries in Rural Districts* (London: Simkin, Marshall, & Co., 1855), 17.
81. J. P. Dodd, *Ten Letters on Self-Education, with Introduction and Notes* (Newcastle: Hamilton & Adams, 1856), "Letter I," p. 7; see also his *Lecture on the Best Means of Promoting the Intellectual Improvement of Youth. Delivered in the Lecture Room of the Literary and Philosophical Society of Newcastle, on September 26th, 1846* (London: Longman, Brown, Green, and Longmans, 1847). Dodd would campaign tirelessly, albeit unsuccessfully, for the formation of a university in Northumbria; see Joan Allen, *Rutherford's Ladder: The Making of Northumbria University 1871–1996* (Chicago, IL: Northumbria University Press, 2005).
82. Scott, *Self-Education*, 6.
83. "Almondbury … Soiree," 6 (remarks of R. Houghton).
84. Reid, "Suggestions for the Conversion of Mechanics' Institutions," 535.
85. "Huddersfield Mechanics' Institution. Annual Meeting," *Huddersfield Chronicle*, February 3, 1855, 6 (remarks of Joseph Batley, president).
86. "Proceedings of Institutions. Leeds Church Institute," *J. Soc. Arts* 12(1863/4): 88 (remarks of Lord R. Cecil, MP). Cecil noted, however, that education was not a cure-all: "they had expected that education … would eradicate the tendencies to crime from the human heart," but were forced to admit that "education" had generally failed in this respect.
87. Ibid.
88. "Longwood Mechanics' Institution. Annual Soiree," *Huddersfield Chronicle*, April 14, 1860, 6 (remarks of John Haigh, president of the Linwood Mechanics' Institution).
89. "Almondbury … Soiree," 6 (remarks of R. Houghton).
90. Dodd, *Ten Letters*, 7.

91. *Report of the Proceedings at the Eleventh Annual Soiree of the Blaydon and Stella Mechanics' Institution, Held in the Lecture Hall, Blaydon, on Monday, 31st August, 1857* (Blaydon: Thomas Francis Moseley, 1857), 8 (speech of Rev. Ralph Fenwick).
92. "Leeds Philosophical and Literary Society. Address by the President, the Vicar of Leeds," *Leeds Intelligencer*, October 30, 1858: 9.
93. Chester, *Schools for Children*, 3.
94. "The Fifth Annual Conference between Representatives from the Institutions in Union, and the Council of the Society, Held July 23, 1856," *J. Soc. Arts* 4 (1855/6): 560 (remarks of Lord Ashburton delivered at the anniversary dinner).
95. "Reports of Institutions. Macclesfield Useful Knowledge Society," *J. Soc. Arts* 1 (1852/3): 20.
96. "Report of Council, 'General Meeting,' June 8, 1853," *J. Soc. Arts* 1 (1852/3): 347; remarks of Rev. Edward Bull.
97. "Home Correspondence. On the Examination of Members of Literary and Mechanics' Institutes," *J. Soc. Arts* 2 (1853/4): 451-2 (letter from J. C. Buckmaster). John Charles Buckmaster (1819-1908) served for many years as the honorary secretary of the Battersea Literary and Scientific Institution, receiving an engraved silver tea service valued at £40 for his work in 1853; "Proceedings of Institutions. Battersea," *J. Soc. Arts* 2(1853/4): 241; he was also a chemistry instructor, writer, and eventually an examiner for the Department of Education.
98. "Letters. List of Lecturers," *J. Soc. Arts* 2 (1853/4): 721 (letter from Frederick Parker).
99. "Proceedings of Institutions. Sydney, New South Wales," *J. Soc. Arts* 5 (1856/7): 621 (remarks of Dr. Woolley). Martyn Walker briefly addresses the spread of the mechanics' institute movement throughout the empire; see *The Development of the Mechanics' Institute Movement*, chapter 10; see also John Ramsay McCulloch, *A Descriptive and Statistical Account of the British Empire: Exhibiting Its Extent, Physical Capacities, Population, Industry, and Civil and Religious Institutions, Volume 2* (London: Longmans, 1854); Bronwyn Lowden, *Mechanics' Institutes, Schools of Arts, Athenaeums, etc.: An Australian Checklist - 3rd Edition* (Donvale, Australia: Lowden Publishing Co., 2010); Pam Baragwanath and Ken James, *These Walls Speak Volumes: A History of Mechanics' Institutes in Australia* (Victoria: Ken James, 2015); Adele Perry, *On the Edge of Empire: Gender, Race, and the Making of British Columbia, 1849-1871* (Toronto: University of Toronto Press, 2001).
100. "First Ordinary Meeting. Wednesday, November 21, 1855. Address by Rev Dr. Booth, Chairman of Council," *J. Soc. Arts* 4 (1854/5): 5.
101. Benjamin Scott, *Practical Hints to Unpractised Lecturers to the Working Classes: Fourth Edition* (London: Q. P. Baron, 1858): 13-21, 32-40.
102. "Proceedings of Institutions. Darlington Mechanics' Institution," *J. Soc. Arts* 1 (1852/3): 22 (iron); "Proceedings of Institutions. Liverpool Collegiate Institution," *J. Soc. Arts* 4 (1855/6): 541(extinction); "Proceedings of Institutions. Wakefield Mechanics' Institution," *J. Soc. Arts* 5(1856/7): 15 (jet).
103. "The Conference," *J. Soc. Arts* 1 (1852/3): 347 (remarks of the Rev. A. Bull).
104. "Report of Council, 'General Meeting,' June 8, 1853," *J. Soc. Arts* 1 (1852/3): 348 (remarks of W. J. Fox, MP).
105. "Proceedings of Institutions. Carlisle. The Sixth Annual General Meeting of the Members of the Church of England Religious and General Literary Association," *J. Soc. Arts* 5 (1857/8): 592 (remarks of Chancellor Burton).
106. "Correspondence. Mechanics' Institutions," *J. Soc. Arts* 8 (1860/1): 852 (letter from Thomas Marshall).

107. Hugo Reid, "Suggestions for the Conversion of Mechanics' Institutions into Colleges," *J. Soc. Arts* 1 (1852/53): 536.
108. "Fourth Annual Conference, July 2, 1855," *J. Soc. Arts* 3 (1854/5): 574–5 (remarks of Mr. Cameron, of the Institutions in Union in the Midland Counties and Yorkshire).
109. "Mechanics' Institutions," *Chambers' Papers for the People* 3:23 (Edinburgh: William and Robert Chambers, 1850), 12, 16.
110. Traice, *Hand-book*, 23.
111. Ibid., 89.
112. "Report of Council, General Meeting, June 8," *J. Soc. Arts* 1 (1852/3): 350 (remarks of J. W. Hudson).
113. "Home Correspondence. Lecturers, Lectures, Apparatus," *J. Soc. Arts* 1 (1852/3): 420 (unsigned letter).
114. "Correspondence. Mechanics' Institutions," *J. Soc. Arts* 6 (1857/8): 610 (letter from Barnett Blake). Blake (1812–1866) served as secretary of the YUMI from 1856 until his death from typhus. He edited the *Exeter Gazette* (1843–52) and the *Liverpool Standard* (1852–6) and was a member of a number of culture institutions, including the Southwark Literary and Scientific Institution, the Exeter Literary and Scientific Institution, and the Western Literary and Scientific Union. His obituary in the *Journal of the Society of Arts* noted that he was "a clear, fluent, and interesting speaker and lecturer," while the *Leeds Intelligencer* noted that while he was "somewhat too impatient in his nature to make a good teacher of individuals, he often succeeded admirably in laying before his audiences that knowledge which to the great majority was complicated and unfamiliar." "Obituary. Mr. Barnett Blake," *J. Soc. Arts* 14 (1865/6): 350; R. V. Taylor, "Barnett Blake," in *Supplement to the Biographia Leodiensis; or, Biographical Sketches of the Worthies of Leeds and Neighbourhood* (London: Simpkin, Marshall, 1867): 611–14, which included the *Leeds Intelligencer* obituary. Blake was succeeded as secretary of the YUMI by Henry H. Sales, who had been secretary to the Metropolitan Association for Promoting the Education of Adults ("Proceedings of Institutions," *J. Soc. Arts* 14 (1865/6): 458.
115. "Proceedings of Institutions. Poole," *J. Soc. Arts* 3 (1854/5): 232–3; "Proceedings of Institutions. Derby," *J. Soc. Arts* 3 (1854/5): 232.
116. Watson, *Newcastle Lit.-&-Phil.*, 202–7.
117. A. D. Garner, "The Society of Arts and the Mechanics' Institutes: The Co-ordination of Endeavour towards Scientific and Technical Education, 1851–54," *History of Education* 14, no. 4 (1985): 258–9.
118. Ibid., 259 (quoting letter from R. G. Latham).
119. Hervey, *A Suggestion for Supplying Lecturers*, 15.
120. "Correspondence. Lectures," *J. Soc. Arts* 1 (1852/3): 385 (letter from E.W.).
121. "The New List of Lecturers," *J. Soc. Arts* 4 (1855/6): 579 (letter from Walter Rowton).
122. "List of Lecturers and Their Subjects," *J. Soc. Arts* 1 (1852/3): 491 (letter from "A Working Man").
123. "Report of Council, 'General Meeting,' June 8, 1853," *J. Soc. Arts* 1 (1852/3): 350 (remarks of Dr. Prior Purvis, Greenwich Useful Knowledge Society).
124. "Report, Sixth Annual Conference between Representatives from the Institutions in Union and the Council of the Society of Arts (June 24, 1857)," *J. Soc. Arts* 5 (1856/7): 465 (remarks of S. L. Rymer, Croydon Literary and Scientific Institution).
125. "List of Lecturers," *J. Soc. Arts* 2 (1853/4): 664 (letter from Robert Dalgliesh).
126. "The Society's List of Lecturers," *J. Soc. Arts* 3 (1854/5): 785–6 (letter from "X. Z.," quoting *The Pembrokeshire Herald*, October 26, 1855).

127. "Society's List of Lecturers," *J. Soc. Arts* 3 (1854/5): 804 (letter from "A. B."). A similar complaint concerned a spurious lecturer, Frederick Young, who was not on the Society's list; instead, using the London Mechanics' Institution as a reference, he demanded a down payment for his services and then absconded without lecturing. "Notice to Institutions," *J. Soc. Arts* 3 (1854/5): 628 (notice from E. W. Martin, Hon. Sec. to the Guilford Institution).
128. "Fifth Annual Conference between Representatives from the Institutions in Union and the Council of the Society," *J. Soc. Arts* 4 (1855/6): 545.
129. "First Ordinary Meeting, Wednesday, November 21, 1855," *J. Soc. Arts* 4 (1855/6): 4–5 (remarks by Rev. Dr. Booth, Chairman of Council).
130. "Fifth Annual Conference between Representatives from the Institutions in Union and the Council of the Society," *J. Soc. Arts* 4 (1855/6): 555 (remarks by Rev. Dr. Booth).
131. "Correspondence. The New List of Lecturers," *J. Soc. Arts* 4 (1855/6): 560 (letter from Walter Rowton).
132. Ibid.
133. "Popular Lecturers," *J. Soc. Arts* 1(1852/3): 444–5 (letter from "One of the Lecturers of the Western Literary and Scientific Union").
134. "Gratuitous Lecturers," *J. Soc. Arts* 1(1852/3): 613 (letter from "Mercator").
135. "Home Correspondence. Lecturers, Lectures, Apparatus," *J. Soc. Arts* 1 (1852/3): 420 (unsigned letter).
136. "List of Lecturers," *J. Soc. Arts* 2 (1853/4): 664 (letter from Robert Dalgliesh).
137. "Home Correspondence. Lectures," *J. Soc. Arts* 1 (1852/3): 22–3 (letter from William Hughes).
138. Hole, *Essay*, 148.
139. "Home Correspondence. Lectures," *J. Soc. Arts* 1 (1852/3): 431 (letter from W. H. J. Traice).
140. Hole, *Essay*, 63; italics in original.
141. "Home Correspondence. Gratuitous Lecturers," *J. Soc. Arts* 1 (1852/3): 457 (letter from Harry Chester).
142. "List of Lecturers," *J. Soc. Arts* 2 (1853/4), 721 (letter from Frederick Parker).
143. Hole, *Essay*, 148.
144. Janet Cunliffe-Jones, "A Rare Phenomenon: A Woman's Contribution to 19th-Century Adult Education," *Journal of Educational Administration and History* 24, no. 1 (1992): 1–17. Balfour (1808–1878) married James Balfour at sixteen and, when he joined the local temperance movement and took the pledge in 1837, she also embraced the temperance cause. She converted from Anglicanism to the Baptist faith in 1840. Cunliffe-Jones's reconstruction of Balfour's lecturing schedule is drawn from private family papers, including her letters to her son John, one of four surviving children, and her travel diaries from the mid-1850s. See also Kristen G. Doern, "Balfour, Clara Lucas," *Oxford DNB* (online edn.) (accessed September 23, 2004).
145. Society for the Encouragement of Arts, Manufactures, and Commerce, Union of Institutions, *List of Lecturers and Their Subjects, Together with a List of the Institutions in Union. Revised Edition, 14 August 1854* (London: W. Trounce, 1854) and *List of Lecturers and Their Subjects, Together with a List of the Institutions in Union* (London: W. Trounce, 1862).
146. George Grossmith (1820–1880) was chief reporter for the London *Times* and covered court proceedings for other newspapers as well. His two sons, George and Weedon,

were successful and prolific writers and published the comic bestseller, *Diary of a Nobody*, in 1892.
147. Union of Institutions, *List of Lecturers 1854* and *1862*.
148. Wright Wilson, *The Life of George Dawson, MA, Glasgow, Being an Account of His Parentage and His Career as a Preacher, Lecturer, Municipal and Social Reformer, Politician and Journalist* (Birmingham: Percival Jones, 1905), 18. See also Hewitt, "Emerson and Dawson."
149. W. E. [William Edwin] Adams, *Memoirs of a Social Atom* (New York: Augustus M. Kelley Publishers, 1968; originally published in 2 vols., 1903): 114–15. Adams was born in 1832 and would have been a young adult when he heard Dawson and Balfour lecture.
150. "Correspondence. Lectures," *J. Soc. Arts* 1 (1852/3): 385 (letter from E.W.).
151. "Proceedings of Institutions. Bolton Mechanics' Institute," *J. Soc. Arts* 6 (1857/8): 99–101.
152. "Proceedings of Institutions. Birkbeck Literary and Scientific Institution," *J. Soc. Arts* 18 (1869/70): 875.
153. Wood, *History of the Royal Society of Arts*, 372–3.
154. Traice, *Hand-Book*, 5.

Chapter 2

1. Holyoake, *Literary Institutions*, 5.
2. "One Hundred and Second Anniversary Dinner," *J. Soc. Arts* 4 (1855/6): 559–60 (remarks by Right Hon. Lord Ashburton, FRS, in the chair).
3. "Manchester Athenaeum Conversazione," *Manchester Times*, December 10, 1859: 5 (remarks of John Pender).
4. "Manchester Athenaeum. Social Soiree," *Manchester Courier*, March 29, 1856: 10 (remarks of John Ashton Nicholls, FRAS).
5. "Proceedings of Institutions. Birmingham and Midland Institute," *J. Soc. Arts* 11 (1861/2): 705.
6. *An Act to Exempt from County, Borough, Parochial, and Other Local Rates, Land and Buildings Occupied by Scientific or Literary Societies* [1843] (6 & 7 Vict. c. 36).
7. *An Act to Explain and Amend the Act for Exempting from Local Rates Land and Buildings Occupied by Scientific and Literary Societies* [1857] (8 Vict. c. 35).
8. For the Athenaeum, see "Court of Queen's Bench, Westminster, Nov. 12," *Manchester Courier*, November 15, 1851: 5. For the Society of Arts, see "Annual Conference," *J. Soc. Arts* 21 (1872/3): 635–45. The 1843 Act stipulated that any institution or society that provided living space for porters or housekeepers could lose its exemption.
9. *Literary and Scientific Institutions Act, 1854* (17 & 18 Vict. c. 112) was passed in August 1854 "to afford greater facilities for the establishment of institutions … and to provide for their better regulation."
10. "Proceedings of Institutions. Yorkshire Union of Mechanics' Institutions," *J. Soc. Arts* 13 (1864/55): 656 (secretary); "Surbiensis," "Lecturers," *J. Soc. Arts* 1 (1852/3): 373 (hospitality); Barnett Blake, "Management of Mechanics' Institutions," *J. Soc. Arts* 8 (1859/60): 676 (advertising); "Proceedings of Institutions. Yorkshire Union of Mechanics' Institutions," *J. Soc. Arts* 13 (1854/5): 656 (scheduling); "Proceedings of

Institutions. Saffron Walden," *J. Soc. Arts* 2 (1853/4): 186 (ticket fees). The Saffron Walden Institute charged nonmembers the following rates for season lecture tickets: 15s. for reserved seats, 8s. for unreserved seats in the front, and 2s. 6d. for unreserved seats in the back, with "a proportionate reduction" for members. Other institutes charged lower fees; the Falkirk School of Arts, for example, priced season tickets at 3s. 6d. for adults and 2s. 6d. for youth; "Proceedings of Institutions. Falkirk School of Arts," *J. Soc. Arts* 6 (1857/8): 254 (remarks of George Hamilton, MD, secretary). Thomas Newbigging of the Bacup Mechanics' Institution recommended surcharges for every lecture, of 2p. for subscribers and 6p. for nonmembers: "Home Correspondence. Lectures and Entertainments at Mechanics' Institutions," *J. Soc. Arts* 10 (1861/2): 560–1. Barnett Blake suggested that institutional subscription fees be set at 21s. per year for honorary members and 2s. 6d. quarterly for regular members, with surcharges of 3d. weekly for classes and some small surcharges for lecture tickets: "Mechanics' Institutes," *J. Soc. Arts* 8 (1859/60): 676. In 1867, "Amicus" suggested that a secretary be paid £250 annually, a sum significantly out of reach for most institutions: "The Manchester Mechanics' Institution. To the Editor of the *Manchester Guardian*," *Manchester Guardian*, December 18, 1867: 4. For a typically heated exchange over how to manage penny lectures, see "Report, Sixth Annual Conference between Representatives from the Institutions in Union and the Council of the Society of Arts (June 24, 1857)," *J. Soc. Arts* 5 (1856/7): 466.
11. "Proceedings of Institutions. Ipswich Mechanics' Institution," *J. Soc. Arts* 11 (1862/3): 48; "Proceedings of Institutions. Redditch Mechanics' Institution," *J. Soc. Arts* 1 (1852/3): 22.
12. "Proceedings of Institutions. York Institute," *J. Soc. Arts* 1 (1852/3): 11–12; "Proceedings of Institutions. Chatham, Rochester, Strood, and Brompton Mechanics' Institution," *J. Soc. Arts* 6 (1857/8): 524; "Proceedings of Institutions. Windsor and Eton Literary, Scientific, and Mechanics' Institution," *J. Soc. Arts* 6 (1857/8): 611.
13. "Proceedings of Institutions. Darlington Mechanics' Institution," *J. Soc. Arts* 1 (1852/3): 33, 160.
14. "Proceedings of Institutions. Boston Athenaeum," *J. Soc. Arts* 1 (1852/3): 165.
15. "Proceedings of Institutions. Cheltenham Literary and Philosophical Institution and Athenaeum," *J. Soc. Arts* 5 (1856/7): 306.
16. "Proceedings of Institutions. Newport [Wales] Athenaeum and Mechanics' Institution," *J. Soc. Arts* 6 (1857/8): 601. The society had launched an unsuccessful fundraising campaign in 1854, hoping to build before its lease expired: "Proceedings of Institutions. Newport Athenaeum and Mechanics' Institution," *J. Soc. Arts* 4 (1855/6): 444.
17. "The Societies Section. Hartlepool Mechanics' Institution," *British Controversialist and Literary Magazine* 1 (1859): 187–8. This institution was founded as the Hartlepool Literary, Scientific and Mechanical Institute in 1833; according to the anonymous history of the town published in 1844, "It rapidly increased in prosperity for the first year, after which time it declined, and had it not been for the efforts of one or two individuals, it would long ago have been dissolved." Anon., *The History of Hartlepool* (Hartlepool: Alfred Moore, 1844): 47.
18. "Proceedings of Institutions. Lockwood Mechanics' Institution," *J. Soc. Arts* 9 (1860/1): 183; "Proceedings of Institutions. Avenham Institution for the Diffusion of Knowledge (Preston)," *J. Soc. Arts* 10 (1861/2): 93–4.

19. Much of this rescue work was carried out by Samuel Ogden, who served as secretary from 1849 to 1853 and president from 1870 to 1885. He recounted the success of his efforts at the anniversary dinner in 1885; see "Address by Samuel Ogden, Esq., J.P., President of the Athenaeum, in Celebration of the 50th Anniversary of the Foundation of the Institution," *Manchester Athenaeum. Addresses 1835–1885"* (Manchester, 1888), 195–6. For an account of the fiscal crisis, see also Hudson, *History,* 112–15.
20. "Proceedings of Institutions. Liverpool Institute and School of Art," *J. Soc. Arts* 7 (1858/9): 157.
21. "Proceedings of Institutions. Crosby Hall Evening Classes," *J. Soc. Arts* 7 (1858/9): 771. The debt faced by the London Mechanics' Institution, founded in 1823, had exceeded £1,500 by 1857 and appeals to both the government and other institutions peppered the "Proceedings" of the late 1850s; see, for example, "Proceedings of Institutions. Crosby Hall Evening Classes," *J. Soc. Arts* 4 (1855/6): 727. Crosby Hall, located in London, would be forced to find new accommodations "on account of the expense of rent," becoming the Sussex Hall Evening Classes in 1859 and the City of London College in 1861–2; *J. Soc. Arts* 10 (1861/2): 714.
22. "Proceedings of Societies. Beechin Mechanics' Institute," *J. Soc. Arts* 4 (1855/6): 369–70; other institutes reporting such "extras" included societies in Barnet, Poole, Portsea, and Salisbury.
23. "Proceedings of Societies. Blackburn Literary, Scientific, and Mechanics' Institution," *J. Soc. Arts* 5 (1856/7): 473; "Proceedings of Societies. Bacup Mechanics' Institution," *J. Soc. Arts* 11 (1862/3): 174–5.
24. "Correspondence. Mechanics' Institutions," *J. Soc. Arts* 6 (1857/8): 610 (letter from Barnett Blake).
25. Holyoake, *Literary Institutions,* 7.
26. "Accommodation and Expenditure in Mechanics' and Similar Institutions," *J. Soc. Arts* 10 (1861/2): 737–8 (remarks of John Jones, Secretary, South Staffordshire Educational Association).
27. "Proceedings of Institutions. Radcliffe and Pilkington Lyceum and Mutual Improvement Society," *J. Soc. Arts* 1 (1852/3): 129–30.
28. "Proceedings of Institutions. Chester Mechanics' Institution," *J. Soc. Arts* 5 (1856/7): 581.
29. "Proceedings of Institutions. Royston," *J. Soc. Arts* 3 (1854/5): 233; "Proceedings of Institutions. Much Wenlock," ibid., 787. Focusing specifically on the need for stand-alone libraries in the countryside where even small societies were absent, F. W. Naylor recommended an annual member subscription of 2s., or the charge to nonmembers of ½d. per volume, and the elimination of late fees for members and nonmembers alike. Naylor, *Popular Libraries in Rural Areas,* 44.
30. "Proceedings of Institutions. Macclesfield Society for Acquiring Useful Knowledge," *J. Soc. Arts* 7 (1858/9): 127 (annual presidential address by Lord Stanley of Alderley). For an overview of reading rooms and the growth of public libraries, see Thomas Kelly, *A History of Public Libraries in Great Britain 1845–1975* (London: The Library Association, 1973); Alistair Black, "Lost Worlds of Culture: Victorian Libraries, Library History and Prospects for a History of Information," *Journal of Victorian Culture* 2, no. 1 (1997): 95–112; Martin Hewitt, "Confronting the Modern City: The Manchester Free Public Library, 1850–80," *Urban History* 27, no. 1 (2000): 62–88. The concerns over the "problem" of fiction were as old as fiction itself; see, for instance, Ana Vogrinčič, "The Novel-Reading Panic in 18th Century England: An Outline of

an Early Moral Media Panic," *Medijska istraživanja* 14, no.2 (2008): 103–24; see also Richard Altick, *The English Common Reader: A Social History of the Mass Reading Public, 1800–1900* (Chicago: University of Chicago Press, 1957; 2nd. edn., Ohio State University Press, 1998); Kate Flint, *The Woman Reader 1837–1914* (Oxford: Oxford University Press, 1993); Helen Small, "Dickens and a Pathology of the Mid-Victorian Reading Public," in *The Practice and Representation of Reading in England*, ed. James Raven, Helen Small, and Naomi Tadmor (Cambridge: Cambridge University Press, 1996), 263–90; Pamela K. Gilbert, *Disease, Desire, and the Body in Victorian Women's Popular Novels* (Cambridge MA: Cambridge University Press, 1997); Matthew Bradley and Juliet John, eds., *Reading and the Victorians* (Farnham: Ashgate, 2015); Paul Raphael Rooney and Anna Gasperini, eds., *Media and Print Culture Consumption in Nineteenth-Century Britain: The Victorian Reading Experience* (London: Palgrave Macmillan, 2016).

31. "Proceedings of Institutions. Carlisle Church of England Religious and General Literary Association," *J. Soc. Arts* 7 (1858/9): 141 (remarks of Chancellor Barton); Naylor, *Popular Libraries in Rural Districts*, 3 ("pernicious," "immoral," and "evil" reading).
32. B. F. Duppa, *A Manual for Mechanics Institutions. Published under the Superintendence of the Society for the Diffusion of Useful Knowledge* (London: Longman, 1839), 49–50.
33. Traice, *Hand-book*: 42, 53–5.
34. George Campbell, 8th Duke of Argyll, "Address Delivered to the Members of the Glasgow Athenaeum, on the 21st January, 1851," *The Importance of Literature to Men of Business: A Series of Addresses Delivered at Various Popular Institutions* (London: John J. Griffin and Company, 1852), 262.
35. "Mechanics' Institutions," *J. Soc. Arts* 9 (1860/1): 115.
36. John F. Godwin, "The Bradford Mechanics' Institute," *Transactions of the National Association for the Promotion of Social Science [Trans. NAPSS] 1859* (London: John W. Parker & Son, 1860): 341–2.
37. "Proceedings of Institutions. Bingley Mechanics' Institute," *J. Soc. Arts* 13 (1864/5): 106–7.
38. "Proceedings of Institutions. Carlyle Mechanics' Institution," *J. Soc. Arts* 4 (1855/6): 110.
39. "Mechanics' Institutions," *J. Soc. Arts* 8 (1859/60): 852–3 (correspondence from Barnett Blake, who was referring to books by Sarah Stickney Ellis and similar authors). Blake, Duppa, Traice, and dozens of secretaries and library directors acknowledged that collections, especially in small towns and villages, were often built primarily by donations of books rather than funds to purchase books, which limited the extent to which institutions could wholly control their volumes.
40. Edward Edwards, *Memoirs of Libraries, Including a Handbook of Library Economy*, Vol. 1 (London: Trubnor & Co., 1859), 776. Edwards argued that the free library "must contain, in fair proportions, the books that are attractive to the uneducated and the half-educated, as well as those which subserve the studies and assist the pursuits of the clergyman, the merchant, the politician, and the professional scholar," 775–6.
41. "Proceedings of Institutions. Nottingham Mechanics' Institution," *J. Soc. Arts* 6 (1857/8): 590.
42. *Annual Report of the Committee of the Leeds Mechanics' Institute and Literary Society, Presented to the Annual Meeting on the 30th of January, 1856* [hereafter LMI, *Annual Report*] (Leeds, 1856), 10 ("Literature"). The LMILS library in 1856 reported that

nearly 15,000 of the total of 47,500 volumes issued that year were "Fiction," with only some 3,700 in "Fine Arts, Literature, &c."

43. "Proceedings of Institutions. Dorking Literary and Scientific Institute," *J. Soc. Arts* 7 (1858/9): 12 ("contributions to general literature"); "Proceedings of Institutions. Manchester Mechanics' Institution," *J. Soc. Arts* 9 (1860/1): 306 (convenience). See Lewis Roberts, "Trafficking in Literary Authority: Mudie's Select Library and the Commodification of the Victorian Novel," *Victorian Literature and Culture* 34, no. 1 (March 2006): 1–25; Guinevere L. Griest, "A Victorian Leviathan: Mudie's Select Library," *Nineteenth-Century Fiction* 20, no. 2 (1965): 103–26; David E. Gerard, "Subscription Libraries," in *Encyclopedia of Library and Information Science, Volume 29*, ed. Allen Kent, Harold Lancour, and Jay Elwood Daily (New York: Marcel Dekker, 1980).

44. "Proceedings of Institutions. Halifax Mechanics' Institution," *J. Soc. Arts* 1(1852/3): 179 and 7(1858/9): 204 (remarks of Sir Charles Wood, MP); "Proceedings of Institutions. Macclesfield Society for Acquiring Useful Knowledge," *J. Soc. Arts* 3 (1854/5): 63.

45. "Proceedings of Institutions. Bacup Mechanics' Institution," *J. Soc. Arts* 11 (1862/3): 115 (expansion of hours to 8 a.m.–10:30 p.m. six days a week); "Proceedings of Institutions. Newington Working Men's Association," *J. Soc. Arts* 9 (1860/1): 573 (discrete visits).

46. "Proceedings of Institutions. Macclesfield Society for Acquiring Useful Knowledge," *J. Soc. Arts* 3 (1854/5): 63 (three times a day); "Proceedings of Institutions. Bury Athenaeum for the Diffusion of Useful Knowledge," *J. Soc. Arts* 10 (1861/2): 535 (expense).

47. "Manchester Athenaeum. Annual Meeting," *Manchester Courier*, February 3, 1855: 9 (remarks of Mr. Robinson, responding to the annual report).

48. This common phrase was the title of a mid-century collection of essays to athenaeums and literary societies in commercial cities: *The Importance of Literature to Men of Business: A Series of Addresses Delivered at Various Popular Institutions* (London: John J. Griffin and Company, 1852).

49. "Manchester Athenaeum," *Manchester Times*, February 3, 1855: 10 (annual report for 1854; remarks of Mr. Currie).

50. Ibid.

51. "Manchester Athenaeum. Annual Meeting," *Manchester Courier*, February 3, 1855: 9 (remarks of James Hudson, secretary).

52. J. F. W. Herschel, "Address Delivered to the Subscribers to the Windsor and Eton Public Library, on the 29th January 1833," *The Importance of Literature to Men of Business*, 35 ("floating literature"); "Proceedings of Institutions. Carlisle Church of England Religious and General Literary Association," *J. Soc. Arts* 7 (1858/9): 141 (remarks of meeting chair, Chancellor Barton).

53. Campbell [Duke of Argyll], "Address ... Glasgow Athenaeum," 262.

54. "Proceedings of Institutions. Carlisle Church of England Religious and General Literary Association," *J. Soc. Arts* 7 (1858/9): 141 (remarks of Chancellor Barton).

55. Chester, *Schools for Children and Institutes for Adults*, 20.

56. Ibid., 19–20.

57. "Proceedings of Institutions. Manchester Athenaeum. Soiree," *J. Soc. Arts* 6 (1857/8): 704.

58. "Proceedings of Institutions. Yorkshire Union of Mechanics' Institutions," *J. Soc. Arts* 12 (1863/4): 459 (remarks of "several delegates" at the annual conference of the union, May 18, 1864).
59. "Warminster Conference on Adult Education. Athenaeums," *J. Soc. Arts* 8 (1859/60): 834.
60. "Correspondence. Recreation at Mechanics' Institutions," *J. Soc. Arts* 10 (1861/2): 444–5 (letter from Barnett Blake).
61. "South Staffordshire Association for Promoting Adult Education," *J. Soc. Arts* 12 (1863/4): 737.
62. "Proceedings of the Society. Thirteenth Annual Conference of the Institutions in Union," *J. Soc. Arts* 13 (1864/5): 534 (remarks of Sir Thomas Phillips, chair).
63. "Proceedings of Institutions. Cheltenham Literary and Philosophical Society," *J. Soc. Arts* 1 (1852/3): 105 (relaxing rules against political and theological debate); "Proceedings of Institutions. Coupar Angus Nautical Improvement Society," *J. Soc. Arts* 5 (1856/7): 254 (extending "usefulness" by adding smaller clubs).
64. "Proceedings of Institutions. Greville House Working Men's Library and Reading Room, Paddington," *J. Soc. Arts* 12 (1863/4), 320.
65. "Proceedings of Institutions. Much Wenlock Agricultural Reading Society," *J. Soc. Arts* 3 (1853/4): 743–4; *J. Soc. Arts* 8 (1859/60): 642–3.
66. "Thirteenth Annual Conference of the Representatives of the Institutions in Union, and the Local Educational Boards, with the Council of the Society," *J. Soc. Arts* 12 (1863/4): 536.
67. "Proceedings of Institutions. Haley-Hill Working Men's College," *J. Soc. Arts* 10 (1861/2): 410.
68. "Proceedings of Institutions. Hull Young People's Christian and Literary Institute," *J. Soc. Arts* 11 (1862/3): 762.
69. "Lancashire and Cheshire Institutional Association," *Manchester Examiner and Times*, March 28, 1855: 4 (annual report read by James Hudson, secretary).
70. Hudson, *History*, xii.
71. Ibid., 118–19; *Report of the Proceedings Connected with the Grand Soiree of the Manchester Athenaeum, from the Manchester Guardian of Saturday, October 5th, 1844* (Manchester: Cave and Sever, 1844), 4 (remarks of George Greaves, director of the Athenaeum).
72. Hudson, *History*, 120.
73. "Proceedings of Institutions. Croydon Literary and Scientific Institute, Annual meeting," *J. Soc. Arts* 10 (1861/2):156 (Edward Westall, MD, in the chair).
74. "Proceedings of Institutions. Macclesfield Society for Acquiring Useful Knowledge," *J. Soc. Arts* 3 (1854/5): 63.
75. Leeds Mechanics' Institute, *Annual Report, 1856*, 10–11.
76. "Proceedings of Institutions. Reading," *J. Soc. Arts* 5 (1856/7): 492.
77. "Proceedings of Institutions. Manchester Mechanics' Institution," *J. Soc. Arts* 6 (1857/8): 695.
78. "Proceedings of Institutions. Bingley Mechanics' Institute," *J. Soc. Arts* 12 (1864/5): 105–6 (Alfred Harris in the chair).
79. Ibid.
80. "Proceedings of Institutions. Sudbury Literary Institute," *J. Soc. Arts* 1 (1852/3):143 (describing Mr. Rouse lecturing on astronomy); italics added.
81. *Monthly Literary and Scientific Lecturer, Vol. 1*, iii.

82. "Proceedings of Institutions. Tunbridge Literary and Scientific Institute," *J. Soc. Arts* 4 (1855/6): 408; "Proceedings of Institutions. Brighton Mechanics' Institute," *J. Soc. Arts* 3 (1854/5): 45; "Proceedings of Institutions. Wirksworth Mechanics' Institute," *J. Soc. Arts* 4 (1855/6): 411 (describing lecture of Rev. J. Edwards); Leaney, "Evanescent Impressions," 178.
83. "Manchester Mechanics' Institution," *Manchester Guardian*, November 4, 1868: 6 (remarks of Oliver Heywood); "Yorkshire Union of Mechanics' Institutes. The Evening Meeting," *Manchester Guardian*, May 19, 1864: 1 (remarks of the Duke of Argyll).
84. "Institutes for Working Men," *London Quarterly Review* 113 (1863): 20.
85. "Eleventh Annual Conference of the Institutions in Union," *J. Soc. Arts* 10 (1861/2): 531 (remarks of Benjamin Shaw, Greville House Working Men's Library and Reading Room).
86. Alan White, "Class, Culture, and Control: The Sheffield Athenaeum Movement and the Middle Class 1847–64," in *The Culture of Capital: Art, Power, and the Nineteenth-Century Middle Class*, ed. Janet Wolff and John Seed (Manchester: Manchester University Press, 1988), 83–115. For a brief period, there were two competing athenaeums as well as the mechanics' institute vying for membership and financial support.
87. "Eleventh Annual Conference of Institutes in Union, 23 June 1862," *J. Soc. Arts* 10 (1861/2): 532 (remarks of Harry Chester, cofounder of the institute).
88. "Proceedings of Institutions. Leeds," *J. Soc. Arts* 1 (1852/3): 590–1.
89. "Proceedings of Institutions. Saddleworth Mechanics' and Literary Institution," *J. Soc. Arts* 5 (1856/7): 184.
90. "Proceedings of Institutions. Derby Railway Literary Institution," *J. Soc. Arts* 3 (1854/5): 165.
91. James Wall, "Essay on Mechanics' Institutions," in *Prize Essays of the Northern Association of Literary, Mechanics,' and Educational Institutions, 1857* (Newcastle-on-Tyne: John Bell, 1858), 11.
92. "Yorkshire Union of Mechanics' Institutes," *The Watchman*, June 18, 1851; reprinted in *New Zealander* 7, no. 586 (November 26, 1851): accessed at https://paperspast.nat lib.govt.nz/newspapers/NZ18511126.2.9. The *New Zealander*, filling its pages via the scissors-and-paste practices so widespread at mid-century, reprinted for its colonial readers an 1851 article that described a mechanic's institute as "the club, the newsroom, the lecture-room, … the Athenaeum, museum, and sometimes the concert-room" for young middle-class men.
93. "Proceedings of Institutions. Carlisle Church of England Religious and General Literary Association," *J. Soc. Arts* 4 (1855/6): 689.
94. "Yorkshire Union of Mechanics' Institutes," *The Watchman*, June 18, 1851 ("young members of middle-class families"); "Mechanics' Institutions," *J. Soc. Arts* 9 (1860/1): 115 (letter from Frederick Monk, "foppish display").
95. "Mechanics' Institutions," *J. Soc. Arts* 9 (1860/1): 120, 123.
96. *Report … Grand Soiree*, 20. This speech was printed with minor alterations in *Manchester Athenaeum. Addresses, 1835–1885*, 9–28.
97. "Proceedings of Institutions. Denton and Haughton Mechanics' and Literary Institution," and "Basingstoke Mechanics' Institution," *J. Soc. Arts* 1 (1852/3): 19, 285. Several institutes introduced junior membership levels payable quarterly rather than annually; the Manchester Athenaeum charged junior members 5s. quarterly, in contrast to the 6s. 6d. quarterly fee charged to regular members.

98. "Manchester Athenaeum," *Manchester Times*, February 3, 1855: 10. The Athenaeum was governed by a board of directors elected from among the city's elite, who generally held their directorships for decades and thus provided continuity alongside a 24-member executive committee made up of any members of at least three years' standing, elected by their peers to a 12-month term. Samuel Ogden, rehearsing the history of the Athenaeum in 1885, described the 32-member founding board of directors as "the most prominent and best-known men of Manchester of the day;" *Manchester Athenaeum. Addresses 1835–1885*, 189.
99. "Manchester Athenaeum," *Manchester Courier*, January 31, 1857: 10 ("fickle," remarks of Samuel Ogden, president); "Manchester Athenaeum. Annual Meeting," *Manchester Courier*, February 3, 1855: 9 ("coldness," remarks of S. Pope, president).
100. "The Manchester Athenaeum. Annual Meeting," *Manchester Courier*, February 1, 1851: 10 (remarks of Mr. Ginty, Mr. Capes, and Mr. Lowry).
101. *Report ... Grand Soiree*, 22.
102. "The Manchester Athenaeum. Opening of the New Library Hall," *Manchester Courier and Lancashire General Advertiser*, July 6, 1850: 9–10 (remarks of Sir Elkanah Armitage).
103. "In canvassing amongst the merchants and tradesmen of Manchester for the mortgage debt," noted Samuel Ogden in 1852, whose patience was clearly tried on numerous occasions by the youngsters, "he had frequently heard the remark made, with how much greater pleasure they would support this institution, if they could see the members themselves and the young men of Manchester partaking more largely of its privileges." "Manchester Athenaeum. Annual Meeting," *Manchester Courier*, January 31, 1852: 10. The loss of young members during the summer was widespread: The Barnard Castle Mechanics' Institute suspended its classes for the summer but found that there was not enough interest to renew them in the fall; "Proceedings of Institutions. Barnard Castle Mechanics' Institute," *J. Soc. Arts* 8 (1859/60): 99.
104. "Manchester Athenaeum. Annual Meeting," *Manchester Courier*, January 29, 1853: 10; "Manchester Athenaeum," *Manchester Times*, January 28, 1854: 10.
105. "Manchester Mechanics' Institution," *Manchester Guardian*, May 23, 1867: 3. Earlier critiques of Angell and the Board were rehearsed in "Manchester Mechanics' Institution," *Manchester Guardian*, March 1, 1866: 3, and Joseph Wood, "The Manchester Mechanics' Institution. To the Editor of the *Manchester Guardian*," *Manchester Guardian*, March 3, 1866: 6.
106. Watson notes that "the Darwen Mechanics' Institute's fourth annual soiree was disturbed when stones were thrown through the windows by 'a few disorderly blackguards' outside," quoting the *Blackburn Standard*, January 26, 1848; Watson, *The Road to Learning*, 202. See also *Leeds Intelligencer*, January 29, 1853: 7 (expulsion of subscriber for destroying property).
107. Alan Woods, "The Mechanics' Institutes of North-East Lancashire 1851–89: A Comparative Study," *The Vocational Aspect of Education* 29, no. 72 (1977): 43; citing Darwen Mechanics' Institute, *Annual Report*, 1840.
108. Barnett Blake, "The Mechanics' Institutes of Yorkshire," *Trans. NAPSS 1859*, 335–40. Martyn Walker calculates that 310 YUMI members had entered into membership with the Union of the Society of Arts by 1856; Martyn Walker, "'Solid and Practical Education within Reach of the Humblest Means': The Growth and Development of the Yorkshire Union of Mechanics' Institutes, 1838–1891" (PhD dissertation, University of Huddersfield, 2010), 304–7.

109. "Huddersfield Mechanics' Institution. Annual Meeting," *Huddersfield Chronicle*, February 3, 1855: 6 (remarks of Frank Curzon, secretary, and Joseph Batley, president).
110. "Proceedings of Institutions. Worcestershire Union of Educational Institutes," *J. Soc. Arts* 11 (1862/3): 139.
111. "Yorkshire Union of Mechanics' Institutions. Twenty-Third Annual Meeting," *Bradford Observer*, May 31, 1860: 5.
112. "Whitby Mechanics' Institute. Fifteenth Annual Soiree," *Yorkshire Gazette*, November 3, 1860: 4 (remarks of Rev. J. Hughes).
113. "Yorkshire Union of Mechanics' Institutes (From Our Reporter)," *Leeds Intelligencer*, June 2, 1860: 6.
114. In 1859, Barnett Blake noted that most of the classes in YUMI affiliates tended to be elementary in nature, with classes in grammar, mathematics, and French attracting the most students; see "The Mechanics' Institutes of Yorkshire," *Trans. NAPSS 1859*, 337–8. This shifted rapidly after 1870.
115. Renals, "On Mechanics' Institutions," 452–5.
116. Swire Smith, *The Work of Mechanics' Institutes in Our Towns. A Paper Read at the Conference of the Delegates and Members of the Yorkshire Union of Mechanics' Institutes, 1877* (Leeds: Charles Goodall, 1877), 4–6.
117. Laurent, "Science, Society and Politics in Late Nineteenth-Century England," 593. See also Sutcliffe, "The Origins of the 'Two Cultures' Debate in the Adult Education Movement."
118. James Booth, "How to Learn," *J. Soc. Arts* 6 (1856/57): 454.
119. Renals, "On Mechanics' Institutions," 454.
120. "Proceedings of Institutions. Hastings Mechanics' Institution," *J. Soc. Arts* 14 (1866/7): 407.
121. Clark, *History of 100 Years of Life*, 5–11, 26. Original shareholders paid £100 each, to be used to purchase land and erect a building, which opened in 1822. Ordinary members paid an entrance fee of three guineas and an annual subscription of two guineas. Beginning in 1833, a new category of annual subscribers, with no entrance fee, paid one guinea a year. In 1858, family members of subscribers—wives, daughters, and sons under twenty-one—could gain their own privileges for 5s. annually.
122. Museum tickets were generally 6d. for a day or 5s. for a season; the penny admissions were initially limited to Sundays.
123. Hudson, *History*, 93 ("sound commercial English education").
124. "Soiree of the Leeds Mechanics' Institution and Literary Society," *Leeds Intelligencer*, December 21, 1850: 5 (remarks of Rev. George W. Conder). The LMI absorbed the Leeds Literary Institution in 1842 and became the Leeds Mechanics' Institution and Literary Society (LMILS), but dropped "literary society" from its name in late 1868.
125. "Leeds Philosophical and Literary Society," *Leeds Intelligencer*, May 8, 1858: 9 (remarks of John Hope Shaw).
126. "Leeds Mechanics' Institution Soiree," *Bradford Observer*, October 24, 1861: 7 (remarks of Lord Stanley, in the chair).
127. Leeds Mechanics' Institute, *Annual Report, 1856*, 4–7. The report was also printed in the *Journal*.
128. "Proceedings of Institutions. Leeds Mechanics' Institute and Literary Society," *J. Soc. Arts* 3 (1855/6): 209 (remarks of James Hole).
129. Ibid. (remarks of H. Gore).

130. "The Leeds Mechanics' Institute," *Yorkshire Post and Leeds Intelligencer*, January 30, 1869: 5.
131. This "Important Rule Respecting the Property of the Society" was printed on page 2 of each report beginning in 1860, above a form that individuals could use to bequeath property or effects to the Society.
132. *Forty-First Annual Report of the Council of the Leeds Philosophical and Literary Society, at the Close of the Session, 1860-61* (Leeds, 1861), 4.
133. *Forty-Second Annual Report of the Council of the Leeds Philosophical and Literary Society*, 6, 19.
134. Holyoake, *Literary Institutions*, 16.
135. *Forty-Sixth Annual Report of the Council of the Leeds Philosophical and Literary Society*, 3–4.
136. *Forty-Third Annual Report of the Council of the Leeds Philosophical and Literary Society*.
137. O'Callaghan's subjects tended to be general history or literature; for example, "Autographs—Their Collection, and Connection with History" (1856), "The Conditions of the Primeval Inhabitants of the British Isles" (1865), and "Incidents in the Life of Our First Prince of Wales (Edward II) Unrecorded in the Histories of England" (1867); see Clark, *Leeds Philosophical and Literary Society*, 175–82; see also "Proceedings of Institutions. Wakefield Mechanics' Institution," *J. Soc. Arts* 13 (1864/5): 561, and *Forty-Seventh Annual Report of the Council of the Leeds Philosophical and Literary Society*, 3. The number of 5s. subscribers—the wives, daughters, and young sons of members—had increased to 114 by 1863, multiplying almost tenfold since 1860, underscoring the attractions of the institution to the middle-class family.
138. *Fiftieth Annual Report of the Council of the Leeds Philosophical and Literary Society*, 5–7. The work with local schools was notable as a program of cooperation with existing institutions rather than the establishment of a separate school within the Phil.-&-Lit.
139. *Fiftieth Annual Report of the Council of the Leeds Philosophical and Literary Society*, 18–19 (remarks of Edward Baines at the 50th anniversary dinner).
140. Ibid., 24 (remarks of Canon Woodford at the 50th anniversary dinner).
141. For a helpful discussion of how many nineteenth-century urban areas came to embrace their status as not-the-capitol, see Jerome I. Hodos, *Second Cities: Globalization and Local Politics in Manchester and Philadelphia* (Philadelphia, PA: Temple University Press, 2011).
142. Quoted in Rachel E. Waterhouse, *The Birmingham and Midland Institute, 1854–1954* (Birmingham: Council of the Birmingham and Midland Institute, 1954), 5. Within a few years, the institute informally dropped "Birmingham" from its name in all but its official reports.
143. "Birmingham and Midland Institute," *Ward and Lock's Pictorial Guide to Warwickshire* (London: Ward and Lock, 1883), 223.
144. Rodrick, *Self-Help and Civic Culture*, 101.
145. John C. Miller, "Adult Evening Schools," *Trans. NAPSS 1857* (London: John W. Parker & Son, 1858), 197.
146. Waterhouse, *Birmingham and Midland Institute*, 52–3. The Monday evening lectures attracted so many "strangers" paying at the door—1,340 in 1862, up to 1,743 in 1864, with no increase in numbers of lectures given—that many annual subscribers could

not get in. The admission of ladies at the door on Mondays ended in 1873 due to overcrowding and complaints by season ticket-holders that they were turned away.
147. Midland Institute, *Annual Report for 1860*, 4 (leasing of rooms) and *Annual Report for 1861*, 4 ("the centre around which all institutions might cluster").
148. Midland Institute, *Annual Report for 1869*, 5; Midland Institute, *Annual Report for 1865*, 4.
149. Langford was a self-made man whose education at his mother's knee, supplemented by classes at the Birmingham Mechanics' Institution, sparked a love of literature and poetry. The deaths of his wife and three of his young children in 1846, when Langford was twenty-three, led him to George Dawson's Church of the Saviour, and within two years he had moved from chair-making to bookselling and thence to his own printing business. He taught evening classes at the Church of the Saviour Sunday school, wrote abundantly, and in 1847 and 1850 won prizes in two of the omnipresent mid-century contests held for "Essays by Working Men": "On the Temporal Advantages of the Sabbath" and "Essay on the Tendency of Mental Culture." Volumes of poetry and local history, and innumerable essays and reviews for *The Truth-Seeker, Cooper's Journal, The Poor Man's Guardian, Howitt's Journal*, and other mid-century journals of self-culture, established his role as a model self-educated man. "N. L.," "Toiling Upward: John Alfred Langford, LL.D., &c.: Journalist, Poet, Historian, Essayist, and Politician," in *British Controversialist* 3rd ser., 27 (1871): 54–62, 221–30, 303–12, 383–93, 306. See also "The Midland Institute and the 'Gazette,'" *Birmingham Daily Gazette* 19 November 1863, 4.
150. "Iris," "Midland Institute to Let," *Birmingham Daily Gazette*, March 3, 1864: 7 (windows); "W. R.," "Caveat. Midland Institute," *Birmingham Daily Gazette*, September 12, 1854: 6 (mud); "Midland Institute," *Birmingham Daily Gazette*, March 27, 1865: 5 (ventilation and teachers); "Midland Institute," *Birmingham Daily Gazette*, March 28, 1865: 3 (lecture admission); "Local News," *Birmingham Daily Gazette*, January 9, 1865: 5 (wooden panels).
151. "Midland Institute," *Birmingham Daily Gazette*, January 24, 1865: 3.
152. "Ego," "Midland Institute," and "J. C.," "To the Editor of the Daily Gazette," *Birmingham Daily Gazette*, March 28, 1865: 3; "F. D.," "Midland Institute," and "A Member from the First," "The Midland Institute and the Working Class," *Birmingham Daily Gazette*, March 30, 1865: 7–8.
153. "The Birmingham and Midland Institute," *Birmingham Daily Gazette*, January 3, 1865: 4.
154. Untitled editorial, *Birmingham Daily Gazette*, May 15, 1865: 4–5.
155. "M. E." [Foster Barham Zincke], *How Much Longer Are We to Continue Teaching Nothing More than Was Taught Two or Three Centuries Ago?* (London: J. Hatchard & Son, 1850), 5. For an overview of debates on university reform, see Michael G. Brock and Mark C. Curthoys, eds., *The History of the University of Oxford. Volumes 6 and 7: Nineteenth-Century* (Oxford: Oxford University Press, 2000); Paul R. Deslandes, *Oxbridge Men: British Masculinity & the Undergraduate Experience, 1850–1920* (Bloomington, IN: Indiana University Press, 2005); Peter Scott, "The Reform of English Higher Education: Universities in Global, National and Regional Contexts," *Cambridge Journal of Regions, Economy and Society* 7 (2014): 217–31; George Weisz, "The Anatomy of University Reform 1863–1914," *Historical Reflections/Réflexions Historiques* 7, nos. 2–3 (1980): 363–79.
156. Untitled editorial, *Birmingham Daily Gazette*, May 15, 1865: 4–5 ("collision"); August 23, 1865: 4–5 ("average intelligence").

157. Untitled editorial, *Birmingham Daily Gazette*, August 23, 1865: 3; "Proceedings. Birmingham and Midland Institute," *J. Soc. Arts* 11 (1861/2): 705 (remarks of Pakington).
158. Untitled editorial, *Birmingham Daily Gazette*, May 15, 1865: 4–5 ("in looking down the list"); August 23, 1865: 2–3 ("English Feelings," "intermediate in character").
159. Untitled editorial, *Birmingham Daily Gazette*, January 1, 1866: 4–5.
160. Ibid.
161. Ibid.
162. "Manchester Athenaeum Meeting," *The City Jackdaw (Manchester)* 2, no. 65 (February 9, 1877): 5.
163. "Proceedings of Institutions. Manchester Mechanics' Institution: Competitive Examinations," *J. Soc. Arts* 5 (1856/7): 651 (remarks of Dr. Booth).

Chapter 3

1. Leeds Mechanics' Institute, *Annual Report*, 1857, 7.
2. "Proceedings of Institutions. Yorkshire Union of Mechanics' Institutions Annual Meeting," *J. Soc. Arts* 2 (1853/4): 528–9 (remarks of Edward Baines, Esq., in the chair).
3. Naylor, *Popular Libraries*, 39.
4. "Attilus," "Literary Institutions of Manchester," *British Controversialist and Literary Magazine* 2 (1861): 423. The *Controversialist* appeared under slightly different titles. Series 1, volumes 1–6 (1850–5) was entitled *The British Controversialist and Impartial Inquirer* (1850–3) and *The British Controversialist and Magazine of Self-Culture* (1854–5). The new series, volumes 1–6 (1856–1858) was entitled *The British Controversialist and Self-Educator*. The third series, volumes 1–28 (1859–72) was entitled *The British Controversialist and Literary Magazine*. References to this journal will be styled *"British Controversialist* (date)."
5. At the Liverpool Mechanics' Institution for the period 1840–6, the breakdown was as follows: science, one-third of lectures; literature, one-third; music and drama, one-sixth; mental science, one-twelfth; fine arts, one-twelfth; Hudson, *History of Adult Education*, 101.
6. Hole, *Essay*, 30–1 (Manchester); "Proceedings of Institutions. Yorkshire Union of Mechanics' Institutions," *J. Soc. Arts* 1 (1852/3), 5 (1856/7), 11 (1864/5) (YUMI).
7. *Monthly Literary and Scientific Lecturer*, vols. 1–4.
8. Henry Pitman, ed., *Pitman's Popular Lecturer and Reader*. n. s. 9 (London: Pitman, 1864).
9. "Annual Soiree of the Leeds Mechanics' Institution" *Leeds Times*, January 28, 1854: 3 (remarks of Lord Lytton). See Richard Yeo, "Reading Encyclopedias: Science and the Organization of Knowledge in British Dictionaries of Arts and Sciences, 1730–1850," *Isis* 82, no. 1 (1991): 24–49; T. W. Heyck, *The Transformation of Intellectual Life in Victorian England* (London: St. Martin's Press, 1982); and the essays in Martin Daunton, ed., *The Organisation of Knowledge in Victorian Britain* (Oxford: Oxford University Press, 2005), especially Daunton's introduction, 1–28.

10. George Higinbotham, *Self-Education: A Lecture Delivered at the Brighton [Australia] Mechanics' Institute on Friday, August 8, 1862, Published by Request of the Committee* (Melbourne: Blundell and Ford, 1862), 13; "S. N.," "Controversy," *British Controversialist* (1860): 362 ("outgush" and "self-hood").
11. Albert James Bernays, "Chemistry of the Breakfast-Table," *Household Chemistry; Or, Rudiments of the Science Applied to Every-Day Life* (London: Samson Low, 1852), xiii, 4–5.
12. John Ryan, "Essays on Natural and Applied Chemistry: The Chemistry of the Breakfast Table," *Illustrated London Magazine* 1 (1853): 186.
13. Philip Joseph Hartog, "Albert James Bernays," *Dictionary of National Biography, 1901 Supplement*. Available online: https://en.wikisource.org/wiki/Bernays,_Albert_James_[DNB01], (accessed July 19, 2020); Watson, *Newcastle Lit.-&-Phil.*, 172 ("much-lectured people").
14. Ryan, "Essays," 187.
15. Charles Cowden Clarke (1787–1877) wrote and lectured extensively on Shakespeare, Chaucer, and Moliere, and in his later life also produced a literary history of the game of cricket. Fellow Shakespearean Samuel Timmins, also a prolific lecturer, wrote that Clarke "stimulated the public interest in the study of Shakespeare" in part through his "charming humour of expression." Samuel Timmins, "Charles Cowden Clarke," *Oxford Dictionary of National Biography, 1885–1900, Volume 10*. Available online: https://en.wikisource.org/wiki/Dictionary_of_National_Biography,_1885-1900/Clarke,_Charles_Cowden (accessed November 4, 2023).
16. John Joseph Knight, "Isabella Glyn," *Oxford Dictionary of National Biography, 1885–1900, Volume 22*. Available online: https://en.wikisource.org/wiki/Glyn,_Isabella_Dallas[DNB00] (accessed July 18, 2020).
17. Fanny Kemble (1809–1893), the daughter of famed actor Charles Kemble, made her stage debut as Juliet at Covent Garden in 1829 and quickly became one of the stars of the English theater. She retired in 1834 to marry a wealthy plantation owner, Pierce Butler, and moved to the United States. The marriage ended in divorce in 1849. Kemble returned to the English stage and became famous for her Shakespeare readings, appearing on platforms across the country until her retirement in 1868. She published plays, poetry, and a memoir of her time on the plantation, *Journal of a Residence on a Georgian Plantation*, which became an important piece of abolitionist literature. Robert Bernard Martin, "Kemble, Frances Anne [Fanny]," *Oxford Dictionary of National Biography [online]* (2004). Available online: https://doi.org/10.1093/ref:odnb/15318 (accessed November 4, 2023).
18. George Dawson, "The Origin, Character, and Doings of the Anglo-Saxons," *The Working-Man's Friend, and Family Instructor*, n.s. 1, no. 1 (1851): 106–8.
19. Harris's work on the Anglo-Saxons was ultimately published two decades later as part of a series of scholarly essays for the Royal Historical Society. George Harris, "Domestic Everyday Life, and Manners and Customs in This Country, from the Earliest Period to the End of the Eighteenth Century. Part II: From the Coming of the Anglo-Saxons to the Norman Conquest," *Transactions of the Royal Historical Society* 6 (1877): 86–130.
20. "Proceedings of Institutions. Battle," *J. Soc. Arts* 1 (1852/3): 285.
21. The fall of Nineveh was the subject of an epic poem by Romantic poet Edwin Atherstone, published between 1828 and 1868, priming popular interest in the archaeological excavations of the ancient biblical city that began in the 1840s. The remarkable extent of recovered artifacts and ruins, many of which were displayed

in the British Museum, kept the archaeological and historical work at the site in the public imagination well into the twentieth century.
22. "Eleventh Annual Conference of the Institutions in Union, held 23 June 1862," *J. Soc. Arts* 10 (1861/2): 531 (remarks of Benjamin Shaw, Greville House Working Men's Library and Reading Room).
23. "Proceedings of Institutions. Hastings Mechanics' Institution," *J. Soc. Arts* 2 (1853/4): 440 (report read by Mr. J. Banks, secretary).
24. "Proceedings of Institutions. Wareham," *J. Soc. Arts* 1 (1852/3): 58.
25. "Proceedings of Institutions. Chichester," *J. Soc. Arts* 2 (1853/4), 842.
26. "Proceedings of Institutions. Newbury," *J. Soc. Arts* 2 (1853/4): 13–14.
27. John S. Reid, "Faraday's 'Advice to a Lecturer,' " University of Aberdeen Natural Philosophy Collection (2017). Available online: https://homepages.abdn.ac.uk/npmuseum/article/Faraday'sAdvice.pdf (accessed July 2, 2020).
28. "Abstracts of Papers, Lectures, and Discussions. On Classes For Scientific Observations in Mechanics' Institutions," *J. Soc. Arts* 2 (1853/4): 684 (lecture by Robert Hunt, FRS). There were a number of extremely popular exceptions to Hunt's rule, including Robert Ball, John Henry Pepper, and George Buckland; see Lightman, "Lecturing in the Spatial Economy of Science."
29. "The Spectroscope," *Manchester Guardian*, April 22, 1868: 6.
30. "Randolph," "Education. Are Public Lectures Profitable for Instruction?" *British Controversialist* (1866): 26.
31. Watson, *Newcastle Lit.-&-Phil.*, 256.
32. "Proceedings of Institutions. Wellingsborough," *J. Soc. Arts* 3 (1854/5): 107.
33. Watson, *Newcastle Lit.-&-Phil.*, 256.
34. "Proceedings of Institutions. Avesham," *J. Soc. Arts* 10 (1861/2): 93.
35. "Home Correspondence. Lectures," *J. Soc. Arts* 1 (1852/3): 431 (letter from W. H. J. Traice);"Report of Council, June 8, 1853," *J. Soc. Arts* 1 (1852/3): 350 (remarks of James Boorne).
36. George St. Clair, ed., *Biographical Lectures by George Dawson, M.A.* (London: Kegan Paul, Trench & Co., 1886), v; Watson, *Newcastle Lit.-&-Phil.*, 257. See also Wach, "Culture and the Middle Classes," 401, where Wach describes the appearances of Dawson on the lecture platform of the Manchester Athenaeum in the 1840s, describing him as a "deliberate diffuser of knowledge."
37. "Proceedings of Institutions. Cheltenham," *J. Soc. Arts* 1(1852/3): 153 ("beautiful discourses); "Proceedings of Institutions. Derby," *J. Soc. Arts* 3(1854/5): 231 ("talented lecturess"); "Proceedings of Institutions. Whitchurch (Salop)," *J. Soc. Arts* 3 (1853/4): 233 ("unqualified approbation").
38. The top lecturers reported in the *Journal*, in addition to Balfour and Dawson, were as follows: David Thomas Ansted, 15 on geology and geography; James Kay Applebee, 14 on Douglas Jerrold, Thomas Hood, and other literary subjects; George Barker, 17 on musical subjects; Joseph A. Baynes, 10 primarily on ancient Greece and Rome; John Bennett, 10 on watches and watchmaking; Albert James Bernays, 7 multi-lecture series on chemistry; Charles Cowden Clarke, 41 on the works of Shakespeare, Moliere, Chaucer, and others; J. C. Daniel, 38 on Napoleon, Richelieu, Queen Elizabeth, and other historical biographies; George Grossmith, 46 humorous lectures, primarily on Dickens's characters; Benjamin Waterhouse Hawkins, 44 on paleontological subjects such as "The Gorilla" and "Extinct Animals"; William Ballantyne Hodgson, 31 on empire, economics, and sanitary reform; Robert Hunt, 23 on physics and geology, including a popular series entitled "Sermons in Stones

and Books in the Running Brooks"; Fanny Kemble, 9 dramatic performances from Shakespeare; Johann Gottfried Kinkel, 14 on ancient art; Edwin Lankester, 29 on physiology of humans and animals; Henry Nicholls, 21 literary readings; J. H. Pepper, 10 on chemistry and physics, including his famous "Ghost Lecture"; Walter Rowton, 17 readings on literary figures; James Snape, 12 on mathematics and Greek; Henry Vincent, 26 on history; Edmund Wheeler, 56 on subjects in physics, including the steam engine and its application; and Basil Young, 11 humorous lectures on contemporary society.

39. Although the LMI was technically the Leeds Mechanics' Institute and Literary Society (LMILS) for part of this period, it will continue to be labeled here as "LMI."
40. "Pepper's Ghost" appeared to project an ethereal image onstage through the use of lighting and mirrors. The effect was brought to the English stage in the mid-1840s and used to make it seem as though an actor was a ghost or spirit; Pepper expanded on the technique and popularized it as a spectacle in its own right beginning in the 1860s.
41. Dickens's well-known support of these types of institutions is explored in P. A. W. Collins, "Dickens and Adult Education," *British Journal of Educational Studies* 3, no. 2 (1955): 115–27.
42. Georgiana Bennett (sometimes "Bennet") was noted in the 1862 "List of Lecturers" as "author of 'The Studio,' 'Songs of Home,' 'Woman and her Duties,' &c." Her poetry was reprinted in provincial papers and in volumes of contemporary poetry; see, for example, *Guy's Learner's Poetic Task-Book* (London: R. Clay, 1849). See also Andrew Hobbs, "Five Million Poems, or the Local Press as Poetry Publisher, 1800–1900," *Victorian Periodicals Review* 45 no. 4 (Winter 2012): 488–92.
43. Hudson, *History*, 92 (LMI), 64 (Polytechnic).
44. Hudson, *History*, 291.
45. For Huddersfield, see "Meltham Mills Mechanics' Institute." Available online: https://huddersfield.exposed/wiki/Meltham_Mills_Mechanics%27_Institute (accessed July 21, 2020); for Hartlepool, see broadside available online: https://www.bidsquare.com/online-auctions/potter-potter/broadside-for-lectures-on-electricity-galvanism-elec tro-magnetism-pneumatics-979079 (accessed July 21, 2020).
46. George Clement Boase, "Daniel Puseley," *Dictionary of National Biography, 1885–1900, Volume 47*. Available online: https://en.wikisource.org/wiki/Puseley,_Dani el_[DNB00] (accessed July 21, 2020). Puseley also wrote fiction under the name of Frank Foster.
47. "Newport Athenaeum and Mechanics' Institute," *Monmouthshire Merlin and South Wales Advertiser*, April 27, 1861: 3.
48. Founded in 1841, the institution had 576 members by 1848 and charged subscription fees of 10s. and 5s., making it one of the least expensive in the country; Hudson, *History*, 234. Membership rose to a high of 812 in 1856/7, and by 1864/5 it was 710: "Proceedings of Institutions. Wakefield," *J. Soc. Arts* 5 (1856/7): 14–15 and 13 (1864/5): 561.
49. "Proceedings of Institutions. Hartley Institute," *J. Soc. Arts* 11 (1863/4): 771–2.
50. Hincks, a local clergyman, was a consistently popular lecturer and was adept at interpreting various branches of science for a variety of audiences. His biology lectures ranged from "On the Stone Lily and the Star Fish" (LMI, 1858/9 season) and "A Day by the Sea-Side, Illustrated by Specimens and Drawings" (Wakefield Mechanics' Institution, 1856/7 season) to "The Paper Nautilus and Its Story" (Leeds Phil.-&-Lit., 1856/7 season) and "Shells and Their Inhabitants" (a pair delivered at the Newcastle Lit.-&-Phil., 1866/7 season); he also delivered occasional juvenile lectures,

such as "Corals, Illustrated by an Extensive Series of Specimens from the Society's Museum" (Leeds Phil.-&-Lit., 1866/7 season). His entry in the 1854 List of Lecturers also promoted lectures on the life of St. Bernard and "The Philosophy of History."
51. Charles Tilstone Beke, FRS, FSA, helped determine the course of the Blue Nile River in the 1840s.
52. Greenbank was a professor of oratory and the author of *The British Orator: Comprising Observations on Vocal Gymnastics, Articulation, Melody, Modulation, Force, Time, and Gesture* (London: Simkin and Marshall, 1849).
53. Watson, *Newcastle Lit.-&-Phil.*, 208–9. James Anthony Froude was a historian, novelist, and editor. Part of the Oxford movement, he left Anglicanism after publishing the controversial *Nemesis of Faith* in 1849. His most well-known historical works included *History of England from the Fall of Wolsey to the Defeat of the Spanish Armada* and *Life of Carlyle*.
54. Ibid., 261–6.
55. "Our Societies' Section. The Literary Societies of Birmingham," *British Controversialist* (1861): 356.
56. "Proceedings of Institutions. Ulverston," *J. Soc. Arts* 12 (1863/4): 748.
57. "Proceedings of Institutions. Hartley," *J. Soc. Arts* 12 (1863/4): 771–2.
58. Ibid., 772.
59. "The Lecture Season," *British Controversialist* (1861): 356.
60. In addition to the *British Controversialist*, the sources used in this analysis include Society of Arts, *Subjects for Discussion Classes in Institutions* (London: W. Trounce, 1862) (hereafter *Subjects, 1862*); reports and proceedings submitted to the *J. Soc. Arts*, 1850–70; Frederic Rowton, *The Debater: A New Theory of the Art of Speaking*, 2d. ed. (London: Longmans, Green, 1850); the annual reports of the Birmingham and Edgbaston Debating Society; and two brief local journals modeled on the *Controversialist*: the *Birmingham Mirror* (January–December 1866) and the *Birmingham Mutual* (January–December 1870). The Birmingham and Edgbaston Debating Society (hereafter the B&E), was founded in 1846 as the result of the merger of the Birmingham Debating Society and the Edgbaston Debating Society; their early histories may be found in John Alfred Langford, *Modern Birmingham and Its Institutions, Vol. 2: A Chronicle of Local Events, from 1841 to 1871* (Birmingham: E. C. Osbourne, 1873); see also Charles Wade, *The Lucid Expression of Thought: The Birmingham and Edgbaston Debating Society, 1846-2006* (Redditch, England: Brewin Books, 2007).
61. "S. N.," "Controversy," *British Controversialist* (1861): 366. Each volume's preface included some similar reminder for its readers, although the wording differed slightly from volume to volume.
62. "The Societies' Section. The Lecture Season," *British Controversialist* (1864): 237.
63. Michael Wolff, "The British Controversialist and Impartial Inquirer, 1850–1872: A Pearl from the Golden Stream," in *The Victorian Periodical Press: Samplings and Soundings*, ed. Joanne Shattock and Michael Wolff (Toronto: University of Toronto Press, 1982), 367–92. See also Wolff, "The British Controversialist and Literary Magazine: Devoted to the Impartial and Deliberate Discussion of Important Questions in Religion, Philosophy, History, Politics, Social Economy, Etc., and to the Promotion of Self-Culture and General Education," *Victorian Periodicals Newsletter* 1, no. 2 (June 1968): 27–45, where he transcribes the debates and discussion topics for the entire run of the journal.

64. George Dawson, *An Address to the Eclectic Society of Birmingham, at Their First Public Meeting* (Birmingham: E.C. Osbourne, 1846).
65. "S. N.," "Controversy," 366.
66. Thomas Cooper, *Eight Letters to the Young Men of the Working Classes* (London: F. Farrah, 1868).
67. Hudson, *History*, 119.
68. Thomas Wemyss Reid, *A Memoir of John Deakon Heaton, M.D., of Leeds* (London: Longman, Greens, 1883), 107.
69. Toshihiko Iwama, "Voluntary Societies and the Urban Local Community: A Case Study of the Halifax Mechanics' Institution," *Family & Community History* 11, no. 1 (2008): 17–25.
70. "The Middleton Literary Institute," *Manchester Guardian*, January 30, 1860: 4 (letter from Algernon Egerton).
71. "Secular Progress. Blaydon," *The London Investigator: A Monthly Journal of Secularism* 3, no. 33 (December 1856): 329; *Report of the Proceedings at the Eleventh Annual Soiree of the Blaydon and Stella Mechanics' Institution, Held in the Lecture Hall, Blaydon, on Monday, 31st August, 1857* (Blaydon: Thomas Francis Moseley, 1857).
72. "B.S.," "Aids to Self-Culture," *British Controversialist* (1856): 242–3.
73. Wolff, "A Pearl from the Golden Stream." This question actually appears only twice in the sources used in this study: in the *Controversialist* in 1862 and in the debating rooms of the Birmingham and Edgbaston Debating Society in 1856.
74. "Is War in Any Case Justifiable?" (*The Debater*, 1850); "How Far Is War Justifiable?" (*Subjects*, 1862); "Is War under Every Circumstance, Opposed to Christianity?" (*British Controversialist*, 1850); "Is Defensive War in Accordance with Christianity?" (*Birmingham Mutual*, 1870). The Birmingham and Edgbaston Debating Society asked a series of questions: "Whether a diplomatic compromise of the differences between Turkey and Russia would be preferable to war?" (November 1853; no vote recorded), "Ought England to have taken up arms in the present war in defence of Turkey against Russia?" (May 1854; no vote recorded). The *Controversialist* ran a multipart debate in 1855, "Was the British Government justified in entering upon the present war with Russia?" and, in keeping with its policy, presented arguments from both sides without choosing one over the other.
75. "How to Most Efficiently and Morally Abolish Slavery" was included in the 1862 *J. Soc. Arts* list and was debated by the Shrewsbury Discussion Society in 1863 and the Midland Railway Discussion Society in 1864, and featured in the *British Controversialist* over the course of 1864.
76. The evergreen nature of these specific issues can be seen in the questions on money and banking: "Ought the Bank Act of 1844 to be repealed?" (*Controversialist*, 1865); "That the Bank Charter of 1844 is most vicious in principle, and ought not to be renewed" (Birmingham and Edgbaston Debating Society, 1855); "Is an Unlimited Bank Issue beneficial to commerce?" (*Controversialist*,1858); "What are the objections to a circulation of One Pound notes, issued by the Bank of England and by the Provincial Bankers?" and "Is there any adequate foundation for the doctrine that the issue of bank notes is an exclusive function or prerogative of the sovereign or state?" (both listed in *Subjects*, 1862).
77. "Have we sufficient Evidence to prove that Communications are now made to Man from a Spiritual World?" asked the *Controversialist* in 1854; similarly, it posed

the question "Is Spiritualism True?" in 1860, and "Are the Modern Phenomena Designated 'Spiritual Manifestations' genuine? And have we in them Satisfactory Evidence of Intercourse with the Inhabitants of the Spiritual World?" in 1861. The Birmingham and Edgbaston Debating Society considered, in 1856, "Is there reasonable ground for believing in the Existence of Spiritual Manifestations?" but recorded no answer.

78. The "spendthrift" question was listed in the *Debater* (1850) and the *Subjects* (1862) and was discussed in the *Controversialist* (1856); the question on public opinion was debated in the *Controversialist* in 1866; the questions on "the good old times" and "monopoly" were listed in the *Subjects* (1862).
79. "Proceedings of Institutions. Newbury," *J. Soc. Arts* 2 (1853/4): 13–14 (J. T. Topham, "On the History and Utility of Poetry").
80. As examples, the *Debater* asked the following: "Which was the greater Poet, Shakespeare or Milton?"; "Which was the greater Poet, Milton or Homer?"; "Which was the greater Poet, Dryden or Pope?"; "Which was the greater Poet, Byron or Burns?"; "Which was the greater Poet, Chatterton or Cowper?"; "Which was the greater Poet, Chaucer or Spenser?"; "Which is the greater Poet, Mrs. Howitt or Mrs. Hemans?"; and "Which is the greater Poet, Wordsworth or Byron?" The *Subjects* listed the following, sent in from affiliate members: "Which was the greater poet—Byron or Burns?"; "Was Sir Walter Scott, as a Poet, superior to Lord Byron?"; "The English poets from Chaucer to Milton are superior to the modern"; "The merits of Shakespeare and Milton as poets"; and "Are the moderns or the ancients the truer poets?" Contributors to the *Controversialist* considered "Was Byron or Scott the Greater Poet?" (1857) and "Is the Poetry of Tennyson as Healthy in its Tendencies as that of Longfellow?" (1860). The men of the Birmingham and Edgbaston Debating Society considered "Was Byron or Scott the Greater Poet?" (1857); "That the works of the English novelists since the days of Scott are superior to those of their predecessors" (1861); and "That Robert Browning was a greater poet than Alfred Tennyson" (1864). These titles reinforce the general trend of literature recommended for purchase by institution libraries: see Traice, *Handbook*, 53–4, where his recommended works of "miscellaneous literature" included Burns, Byron, Eliot, and Scott.
81. B. S., "Aids to Self-Culture," *British Controversialist* 6 (1855): 242.
82. Frederic Rowton, *The Debater: A New Theory of the Art of Speaking*, 2nd. edn. (London: Longmans, Green, & Co., 1850), 160; see also "Introduction," xiv ("clearness and propriety").
83. Is the character of Queen Elizabeth worthy of admiration?" for example, was listed in *The Debater* and *Subjects 1862*, and formed a lengthy debate in the *British Controversialist* (1856), where "Threlkeld" was the audacious debater who questioned Elizabeth's morals: 27.
84. "Good Queen Bess" in St. Clair, *Biographical Lectures of George Dawson*, 14. Affiliates of the Union reported Dawson's lecture four times during these two decades, and it remained on his list of available lectures well into the 1870s; see Wilson, *The Life of George Dawson*.
85. "Reports of Mutual Improvement Societies. Birmingham Debating Society," *British Controversialist* (1853): 152–3 (reporting a debate over "Whether it is probable that the other European States will suffer from Russian Aggression," in which the affirmative was carried).

86. *Subjects (1862):* 7 (voting); "Home Correspondence. Mechanics' Institutions and Discussion Classes," *J. Soc. Arts* 8 (1860/1): 532 ("scarifyings"). The Society advised that speakers should be limited to 10 to 15 minutes each; other societies, such as the Shrewsbury Discussion Society, allotted 20 minutes for the opening speaker and 15 minutes for each respondent. Most agreed that no member might speak more than once on any question. "Shrewsbury Discussion Society," *J. Soc. Arts* 10 (1863/64): 30.
87. "R.R.R," "Matter and Manner," *The Mutual* 1, no. 8 (1870): 64.
88. "Home Correspondence. Mechanics' Institutions and Discussion Classes," *J. Soc. Arts* 8 (1859/60): 532 (letter of W. H. J. Traice, May 18, 1860).
89. See M. J. Crowe, *The Extraterrestrial Life Debate, 1750–1900: The Idea of a Plurality of Worlds from Kant to Lowell* (Cambridge: Cambridge Univ Press, 1986; 2nd. edn., Dover Publications, 1999); David Clifford, Elisabeth Wadge, Martin Willis, and Alex Warwick, *Repositioning Victorian Sciences: Shifting Centres in Nineteenth-Century Scientific Thinking* (New York: Anthem Press, 2006). William Whewell (1794–1866) was both scientist and clergyman, publishing in areas ranging from geology and astrology to theology and poetry; his work in geology was deeply influential for Charles Darwin. He was a mathematical genius and an inspired wordsmith, most famously coining the word "scientist" in 1833, and served as master of Trinity College, Cambridge, for some two decades. David Brewster (1781–1868), like Whewell both scientist and clergyman, was especially prolific in optics and photography, and was one of the founders of the Free Church of Scotland; he also served as the principal of both the University of St. Andrews and of Edinburgh. See Richard Yeo, "Whewell, William," *Oxford Dictionary of National Biography (online edn.).* (Oxford University Press, 2004). Available online: https://doi.org/10.1093/ref:odnb/29200 (accessed November 4, 2023); A. D. Morrison-Low, "Brewster, Sir David (1781–1868)," *Oxford Dictionary of National Biography (online edn.).* (Oxford University Press, 2004). Available online: https://doi:10.1093/ref:odnb/3371 (accessed November 4, 2023).
90. Edward Higginson, *Astro-Theology; or, The Religion of Astronomy: Four Lectures in Reference to the Controversy on the "Plurality of Worlds," as Lately Sustained Between Sir David Brewster and an Essayist* (London: E. T. Whitfield, 1855). He delivered his lecture to the Wakefield Mechanics' Institution, Normanton Branch; "Proceedings of Institutions. Wakefield," *J. Soc. Arts* 5 (1856/7): 655. The remaining lectures on this subject—C. J. Womersley's "Literary History of the Bible, and the Plurality of Worlds" (Hastings Mechanics' Institute) and Alfred Barry, "The State of the Controversy as to the Plurality of the Worlds" (Leeds Phil.-&-Lit.), both from 1856, and the Rev. H. A. Plow, "The Plurality of Worlds (Plymouth and Portsea Literary and Philosophical Association), 1857—do not survive. An earlier lecture in 1854 by the Rev. E. H. Bickersteth, "Astronomy and Christianity" (Mechanics' Institute, Poole), has also disappeared.
91. Higginson, *Astro-Theology*, "Preface," vii–viii.
92. Ibid., 47.
93. Ibid., 49.
94. Ibid., 77.
95. "Philalethes," "Affirmative Article I.," *British Controversialist* (1856), 16–20.
96. "S. S.," "Negative Article II," ibid., 91.
97. "H. D. L.," "Negative Article I," ibid., 20–5.
98. "Threlkeld," "Affirmative Article II," ibid., 50–4.
99. "H. D. L.," "Negative Article I," ibid., 20.
100. "S. S.," "Negative Article II," ibid., 91–4.

101. "L'Ouvrier," "Affirmative Article III," ibid., 141–5.
102. "Vincat Veritum," "Negative Reply," ibid., 249–52.
103. H.D.L. was referring to Edgar Allen Poe's short story, "The Unparalleled Adventure of One Hans Pfaall," which first appeared as "Hans Phaall—a Tale" in *Southern Literary Messenger* 1, no. 10 (June 1835)" 565–80.
104. Higginson, "Preface," *Astro-Theology*, ix.
105. "Preface," *British Controversialist*, (1856), iii.
106. "Examination Papers, 1863," *J. Soc. Arts* 11 (1862/3): 670–1.
107. Langford, *The Uses of Knowledge*, 17.
108. Charles Hibbs, "The Debating Class," *The Mutual* 1, no. 6 (June 1870): 37.
109. Ibid.
110. R. W. Dale, "*A Sermon on the Tercentenary of the Birth of William Shakespeare, Preached at Stratford-on-Avon, on Sunday, April 24, 1864* (London: Hamilton, Adams, & Co., 1864), 11, 16.
111. Wolff, "'A Pearl from the Golden Stream,'" 387, quoting from the October 1861 number.
112. "Our Societies Section. The Literary Societies of Birmingham," *British Controversialist* (1861): 354.
113. "Our Societies Section. The Literary Societies of Manchester," ibid., 421–2.

Chapter 4

1. Smith, *Work of Mechanics' Institutes*, 12–13.
2. "Is the Lecture Declining?" *Institute, and Lecturer's Gazette* [*ILG*] (December 1885): 2497.
3. Joseph Simpson (1820–1886) was a printer, bookseller, and newspaper editor in London and then, after 1865, in Newport Pagnell, where he published the *Newport Pagnell Gazette* and maintained a busy lecturing schedule, also serving as secretary or other officer to several institutions. The *Institute, and Lecturers' Gazette*—hereinafter the *ILG*—was launched in October 1861 as a monthly publication. It ran eight pages per issue at a cost of 2s. 6d. annually, and was purchased by institutions as well as by individual lecturers. It was supported solely by advertisement, not only by lecturers themselves but also by booksellers, purveyors of patent medicines, shirt and trouser manufacturers, and other miscellaneous businesses. The *ILG* was a quintessentially ephemeral periodical and exists only at the British Library, where the run ends in 1889. The journal's pages are numbered sequentially from the first issue; thus, for example, an article in the October 1, 1889, issue begins on page 2943. This pagination system has been followed here. Although the *ILG* continued for another decade or two, its contents after January 1, 1890, can only be inferred from the few mentions of the periodical or its publisher in other sources. For Simpson's obituary, see "Funeral," *Buckingham Advertiser and Free Press*, January 1, 1887: 6.
4. The Rev. G. W. Kitchin, MA, *A Lecture on Lectures. Delivered before the Members of the Bradford Church of England Literary Institute* (London: Bell and Daldy, 1859), 18–19.
5. "Manchester Athenaeum," *Manchester Guardian*, January 31, 1872: 6.
6. Garner, "Society of Arts and the Mechanics' Institutes," 262.

7. For an overview of the historiography of primary and secondary education in the nineteenth century, see Andy Green, "Technical Education and State Formation in Nineteenth-Century England and France," *History of Education* 24, no. 2 (1995): 123–39; see also Gunn and Bell, *Middle Classes*, especially chapter 4.
8. G. W. Roderick and M. D. Stephens, *Education and Industry in the Nineteenth Century: The English Disease?* (London: Longman, 1978), 58.
9. Ibid., 64.
10. "Manchester Mechanics' Institution," *Manchester Guardian*, February 24, 1872: 8 ("clubbable," remarks of Oliver Heywood in the chair); "Manchester Mechanics' Institution," *Manchester Guardian*, October 31, 1874: 7 ("despondency," remarks of Oliver Heywood in the chair). The institute's fiftieth annual report noted that the rapid increase in night schools all over the city was cutting into institute class attendance; "Manchester Mechanics' Institution," *Manchester Guardian*, February 27, 1874: 6; it also specifically named Owens College, founded in 1851, as drawing many of its potential students away.
11. "Manchester Mechanics' Institution," *Manchester Guardian*, October 30, 1873: 5 (remarks of R. M. Cowie, the Dean of Manchester).
12. "Manchester Mechanics' Institution," *Manchester Guardian*, November 7, 1871: 5 (remarks of Mayor J. Grave, Esq., presiding).
13. Frank Curzon (1819–1907), the son of an Exeter bookseller, helped found the Exeter Literary Society in 1841 and held positions as secretary of institutions in Warrington and Huddersfield before his appointment as organizing secretary at the YUMI in 1871. He published several volumes of poetry and had some early success as a portraitist, a talent that led to his lectures "Illustrated on the Black Board" on subjects "Institutional, Biographical, Artistic, Educational, and General," which he delivered to the several hundred institutes in the Union. His biographer noted that "In this way he has been the means of imparting a love of Art to the masses of the people, and it is pleasant to know that very many have been induced to decorate their homes with works of art suggested by his lectures." W. H. K. Wright, *West-Country Poets: Their Lives and Works* (London: E. Stock, 1896), 130–2. For an expansive list of his lectures, see Yorkshire Union of Mechanics' Institutes, *Annual Report for 1883* (Leeds: Goodall & Suddick, 1883), appendix. These reports will be referenced hereafter as YUMI, *Annual Report for [year]*.
14. Martyn Walker, "'The Yorkshire Union Has Grown to the Most Extensive Educational Confederation in the Kingdom': The Growth and Distribution of the Yorkshire Union of Mechanics' Institutes, 1838–1890," *The Australian Library Journal* 62, no. 2 (2013): 134–9.
15. *The Forty-Sixth Annual Report of the Northern Union of Mechanics' Institutions, Held at Newcastle-upon-Tyne, September 13th, 1894* (Morpeth: George Flint, 1894), 4.
16. H. O. Arnold-Forster, *The Citizen Reader. For the Use of Schools* (London: Cassell, 1885).
17. YUMI, *Annual Reports for 1878, 1884, 1890, 1903*. Figure 4.1 excludes any institution offering only one or two lectures a year, usually by the traveling YUMI secretary.
18. "The Humours of Besieged Paris," *Shields Daily News*, January 17, 1888: 4 (O'Shea's lecture to the Newcastle Sunday Lecture Society). Stevens's lecture formed the basis for a memoir of the same name with his co-traveler; see Thomas Stevens and William Lewis Schactleben, *Across Asia on a Bicycle* (New York: Century Books, 1894).
19. "Our Opening Address," *ILG* (October 1861): 3.

20. Joe Kember, "The Lecture-Brokers: The Role of Impresarios and Agencies in the Global Anglophone Circuit for Lantern Lecturing, 1850–1920," *Early Popular Visual Culture* 17, nos. 3–4 (2019): 287.
21. "The Handbook for the Institutions," *ILG* (July 1883): 2225.
22. "College of Lecturers," *ILG* (December 1864): 307.
23. "Stagnation," *ILG* (February 1880): 1853.
24. "College of Lecturers," *ILG* (December 1864): 307.
25. Only two agents advertised in the first decade of the *ILG*: E. Bartlett, representing Charles J. Plumptre, and Professor Biver, representing Nathaniel Bushell, Esq., both prolific lecturers.
26. "Multum in Parvo. To the Editor of the 'Institute,'" *ILG* (July 1865): 365 (letter from W. Hickman Smith).
27. "The Lecturer," "Co-operation. To the Editor of 'The Institute,'" *ILG* (September 1862): 93. Attempts to push secretaries to engage in "local combination," to meet annually in order to share schedules, continued to be unsuccessful; see, for example, W. Hickman Smith, "Lecturers' Fees. To the Editor of 'The Institute,'" *ILG* (April 1864): 246.
28. Omicron, "A Contrast. To the Editor of 'The Institute,'" *ILG* (November 1862): 110–11 ("holier").
29. Arphad, "Co-operation. To the Editor of "The Institute," *ILG* (February 1862): 38 ("incorporation"); "L. L.," "College of Professors. To the Editor of 'The Institute,'" *ILG* (July 1862): 77 ("College").
30. Plumptre was born in 1818 and practiced law for over a decade. He introduced the first Penny Readings for the public and eventually gave up his law practice to focus on teaching and public speaking. He was appointed lecturer on elocution at Oxford and at King's College and produced several volumes on the physiology and culture of voice and speech. See Richard Garnett, "Charles John Plumptre," *Dictionary of National Biography 1885–1900*, vol. 45; available online at https://en.wikisource.org/wiki/Dictionary_of_National_Biography,_1885-1900/Plumptre,_Charles_John (accessed August 9, 2022).
31. "Lecturers' Dinner and Conference," *ILG* (May 1864): 250.
32. "Lecturers' Dinner and Conference," *ILG* (July 1864): 267–8.
33. "The College of Lecturers," *ILG* (October 1864): 291 ("unfortunately"); "L. L.," "College of Professors. To the Editor of 'The Institute,'" *ILG* (July 1862): 77 ("prevent the more accomplished"). A benevolent fund would be established in 1874.
34. "To Our Readers," *ILG* (September 1865): 379.
35. M. L. A., "Lecturers' Association. To the Editor of 'The Institute,'" *ILG* (June 1874): 1221.
36. "Lady Lecturers. To the Editor of the 'Institute,'" *ILG* (May 1874): 1214. Sicard's letter was one of the first to be printed under the cautionary banner, "We Do Not Hold Ourselves Responsible for the Opinions Expressed by Our Correspondents," which accompanied occasional carefully articulated aspersions from lecturers who felt ignored, misunderstood, or insulted by their fellows.
37. "The Coming Campaign," *ILG* (June 1877): 1565.
38. L. L., "Lectures All the Year Round. To the Editor of 'The Institute,'" *ILG* (March 1862): 46; Basil Young, "Lectures All the Year Round. To the Editor of 'The Institute,'" *ILG* (June 1862): 68.
39. A Subscriber, "Discussions after Lectures," *ILG* (December 1862): 119 ("query"); Henry A. Williams, ""Discussions after Lectures," *ILG* (January 1863): 125–6 ("junior

members"). "The Secretary of a Cornish Institution" noted that his society had permitted structured discussion since its founding fifteen years earlier, with "loss of temper" minimized by regulating how often and for how long audience members could speak (ibid., 126).

40. Simpson was the first to advertise these in the *Gazette*, for a price of 1s. plus postage: *ILG* (May 1864): 256.
41. "A Physician," "Plan to Make Education Popular," *Birmingham Daily Gazette*, May 24, 1869: 7.
42. Young, "Lectures All the Year Round," 68.
43. "The Lecture Session 1872–1873," *ILG* (October 1872): 1059 ("incompetent endeavours"); "The College of Lecturers," *ILG* (February 1865): 323 ("painful sense").
44. A Lecturer, "Lecturers' Fees. To the Editor of 'The Institute,'" *ILG* (July 1866): 461.
45. "The Educational Value of Classes," *ILG* (November 1865): 395.
46. "The Modern Lecture," *The Technologist, or Industrial Monthly: A Practical Journal for Manufacturers, Mechanics, and Builders* (November 1, 1871): 2.
47. "Mr. Ruskin on Public Lectures," *ILG* (July 1874): 1232.
48. "Mr. Ruskin's Bombshell," *ILG* (July 1874): 1228.
49. "A Word for Ourselves," *ILG* (September 1862): 91.
50. For a brief overview of the ways in which lecturers experimented with performance that emphasized manner over matter, see Anne B. Rodrick, "Chatting Up the Sciences: The Mid-Victorian 'Lecture-Gossip,'" *Victorian Review* 49, no. 2 (forthcoming).
51. John de Fraine, *Autobiography* (London: Bowers Brothers, 1900), 39. De Fraine was an extremely sought-after lecturer "On Literary, Social, and Moral Subjects," not because of innovative content but because of his widely acclaimed oratorical abilities. His offerings in 1889 ranged from "Lord Beaconsfield" and "President Garfield" to "My Scrap Book" and "The Age: Its Weakness, its Wants, and its Worth"—all types of lectures that fit neatly into the mid-century model lauded by Simpson. Like Balfour, de Fraine began his career as a temperance speaker.
52. "Institute Intelligence. Newport Pagnell and Southport," *ILG* (September 1866): 478–9.
53. "Institute Intelligence. Huddersfield," *ILG* (July 1883): 2226.
54. "Retrospect and Prospect," *ILG* (December 1882): 2169.
55. "Lectures and Their Mission. Lecturers and Their Capabilities," *ILG* (August 1862): 83.
56. "College of Lecturers," *ILG* (December 1864): 307 ("odds and ends"); "Lectures and Their Mission. Lecturers and Their Capabilities," *ILG* (August 1862): 83 ("grave, gay, lively").
57. "Lectures and Their Mission. Lecturers and Their Capabilities," *ILG* (August 1862): 83.
58. "A New Year's Greeting," *ILG* (January 1874): 1179 ("vulgarity").
59. "A New Year's Greeting," *ILG* (January 1874): 1179 ("dullness"); "A Word for Half-Formed Institutes," *ILG* (April 1878): 1655 ("abominations"); "The Past, the Present, and the Future," *ILG* (May 1883): 2209 ("pure and simple"). The popularity of minstrelsy shows, often referred to as "n*gger troupes," was especially criticized. Other critics shared Simpson's sentiments: In 1871, a review in the *Literary World* noted that the second generation of penny readings have "run riot and become farcical, and have lost almost every philanthropic or praiseworthy element they at first possessed," *Literary World* (August 25, 1871): 117. "Damage" to lectures was everywhere long after the fat babies had migrated: even apparently instructive diversions like the spelling and geographical bees introduced by *ILG* coeditor William Stokes of the Royal Polytechnic, as offshoots of his very popular courses on memory,

were deplored as detracting from the noble work of lecturers; recitation and music bees were introduced in the late 1880s in the context of programming for younger members of institutes. "Chit Chat. A New Geographical 'Bee,'" *ILG* (September 1880): 1914; "Recitation Bees," *ILG* (March 1886): 2521.
60. "A New Year's Greeting," *ILG* (January 1874): 1179; "Entertainment" and "Lecturer," like "Literary," were consistently capitalized throughout the journal.
61. "Jottings," *ILG* (February 1889): 2858. For discussions of oratory specifically, see Janice Schroeder, "Speaking Volumes: Victorian Feminism and the Appeal of Public Discussion," *Nineteenth-Century Contexts* 25, no. 2 (2003) 97–117; Josephine Hoegaerts, "Speaking Like Intelligent Men: Vocal Articulations of Authority and Identity in the House of Commons in the Nineteenth Century," *Radical History Review* 121 (January 2015): 123–44.
62. YUMI, *Annual Report for 1884*, 88, 92 (remarks by W. E. Forster, MP).
63. Smiles, *Self-Help*, 10.
64. "Classes," *ILG* (November 1865): 395.
65. "Middle Class Education," *ILG* (November 1864): 299.
66. "Manchester Mechanics' Institution," *Manchester Guardian*, February 27, 1871: 3 (remarks of the Bishop of Manchester at the annual meeting).
67. "Middle Class Education," *ILG* (November 1864): 299.
68. "Literary Contributions to the Pages of 'the Institute.' To the Editor of 'The Institute,'" *ILG* (December 1864): 304 (letter of S. R. Redman). Within a decade, even the member institutes of the YUMI were being referred to by Simpson as "Literary institutes," leaving the "scientific" modifier out altogether; see, for example, Unions of Institutes," *ILG* (July 1873): 1131.
69. "Unions of Institutes," *ILG* (July 1873): 1132.
70. "Institutions in General, and the Birkbeck Literary and Scientific Institution in Particular," *ILG* (March 1870): 1811 (reporting speech of Earl de Grey and Ripon, president of the council at the annual meeting of the Birkbeck Literary and Scientific Institution).
71. "Young Lecturers," *ILG* (February 1868): 707; italics in original.
72. Green, "Technical education and state formation," 126 (quoting the 1868 Schools Inquiry Commission).
73. YUMI, *Annual Report for 1878*, 89–91 (remarks of J. C. Buckmaster).
74. YUMI, *Annual Report for 1884*, 41 (report submitted by Frank Curzon, secretary).
75. "Unions of Institutes," *ILG* (July 1873):1132.
76. Henry W. Crosskey, "The Peripatetic Method of Instruction in Science and Its Development," *Trans. NAPSS* (1885), 390–1. Crosskey (1826–1893), a Unitarian minister who succeeded George Dawson at the Birmingham Church of the Savior and served from 1869 until his death, was also a writer and lecturer on glacial geography.
77. "Popular Entertainments," *ILG* (January 1877): 1525 ("friends of literature"); "Philosophical Societies and Mechanics' Institutions," *ILG* (May 1862): 58 ("pulse").
78. William Tuckwell, "Art for the People," *Trans. NAPSS (1885)*, 743. Tuckwell, an Anglican minister, was a popular lecturer primarily in the areas around Yorkshire and the Midlands whose work increasingly reflected the principles of Christian socialism.
79. *ILG* (January 1874):1179.
80. See *ILG* (September 1874):1249 ("degrading"); *ILG* (July 1878): 1862 ("animal"); *ILG* (May 1881): 1987 ("trashy"); *ILG* (April 1888): 2750 ("vice"); *ILG* (February 1889): 2858 ("gutter").
81. "The Past, The Present, and the Future," *ILG* (May 1883): 2209.

82. "Lectures—Their Relative Position and True Estimate," *ILG* (November 1862): 107.
83. As one example of faddishness, see the work on "symbolical Comprehensionism" by F. J. Wilson in the March 1885 issue. Rowton, who published "Science's Quarrel with the Bible" in 1876, initiated a months-long quarrel that year with astronomer Richard Dart; he would similarly attack astronomer R. A. Proctor in 1883. Fenwick Miller's letters were printed with Simpson's by now regular prefatory remarks that "we do not hold ourselves responsible for the opinions expressed by our Correspondents." "Correspondence," *ILG* (July 1878): 1684.
84. "The Past, The Present, and the Future," *ILG* (May 1883): 2209.
85. Simpson and Plumptre both retired in 1887 and each died shortly thereafter. The Association fell to the leadership of Simpson's son Alfred Simpson, whose tenure would be reflected in significant shifts within the editorial content of the *ILG*, including a move to theater reviews, biographies of performers, and regular guest columns on acting and elocution.
86. John Morley, *On Popular Culture. An Inaugural Address Delivered [to the Birmingham and Midland Institute] in the Town Hall, Birmingham, on the 5th of October, 1876* (London: Virtue, 1876), 4. For the growth of suburban life, see Sarah Bilston, "'Your Vile Suburbs Can Offer Nothing but the Deadness of the Grave': The Stereotyping of Early Victorian Suburbia," *Victorian Literature and Culture* 41, no. 4 (2013): 621–42; Nicola Bishop, *Lower-Middle-Class Nation: The White-Collar Worker in British Popular Culture* (Bloomsbury Academic Press, 2021); Dion Georgiou, "Leisure in London's Suburbs, 1880–1939," *London Journal*, 39, no. 3 (2014): 175–86; R. Dennis, *Cities in Modernity: Representations and Productions of Metropolitan Space, 1840–1930* (Cambridge: Cambridge University Press, 2008); see also the essays in F. M. L. Thompson, ed., *The Rise of Suburbia* (Leicester University Press, 1982).
87. J. R. Seeley, *A Midland University: An Address Delivered [to the Midland Institute] in the Town Hall, Birmingham, on the 10th October, 1887* (Birmingham: Offices of the *Journal*, 1887), 6.
88. S. Wall Richards, "Suburban Literary Institutes," in *Trans. NAPSS* (1884), 5–9 ("agencies").
89. William J. Clarke, *The Growth of the Suburban Institutes* (Birmingham: For the [Birmingham Suburban and District Institutes] Union, 1883 [reprinted from the *Birmingham Daily Mail*, November 17, 1883]), 3.
90. Birmingham Suburban and District Institutes Union, *An Address Delivered by the Most Honourable the Marquis of Lorne, KT, President, ... on October 5, 1886* (Birmingham, 1886), 8 ("centred in London").
91. S.W.R. [S. Wall Richards], "Suburban Literary Institutes," *Graphic*, November 11, 1882: 7.
92. "Cheadle Literary Institution," *The Manchester Magazine. An Illustrated Northern Serial of Literature, Science, Art, and Social Progress*, II (1879/80), 241.
93. Richards, "Suburban Literary Institutes," 16.
94. Birmingham Suburban and District Institutes Union, *Address ... Marquis of Lorne*, 6.
95. Henry W. Crosskey, "Presidential Address: A Plea for a Midland University," in *Proceedings of the Birmingham Philosophical Society* V, no. ii (1886/7): 245.
96. This charge was reprinted in all publications of the Sunday Lecture Society, including the published lectures as well as advertisements and annual reports.
97. "The Sunday Lecture Society," *Examiner*, January 6, 1872: 15.

98. Sunday Lecture Society, *Mr. W. Henry Domville's Report to the Preliminary Meeting Held at Freemasons' Tavern, on the 25th of November, 1869* (London: Kenny & Co., 1869), 1.
99. Thomas Huxley, *Lay Sermons, Addresses, and Reviews* (London: Macmillan and Co., 1870), 78–9. The passage from which this phrase was taken would be printed in the annual reports in 1876, 1877, and 1878.
100. "The Sunday Lecture Society," *Examiner*, December 31, 1870: 9.
101. Ibid.
102. *The Globe*, November 20, 1869: 5 ("genteel"); "The Sunday Lecture Society," *The Graphic*, January 15, 1870: 2–3 ("half-educated"). Ruth Barton, "Sunday Lecture Societies: Naturalistic Scientists, Unitarians, and Secularists Unite against Sabbatarian Legislation," in *Victorian Scientific Naturalism: Community, Identity, Continuity*, ed. Gowan Dawson and Bernard Lightman (Chicago: University of Chicago Press, 2014), 189–219, examines the leadership of the parent SLS in the context of secularization, focusing extensively on the members of the so-called X Club.
103. The Sunday Observance Act 1781 (21 Geo. 3. c. 49) forbade houses, societies, or clubs from offering paid "publick entertainment or amusement" on Sundays, in order to curtail "the corruption of good morals" and "the encouragement of irreligion and profaneness." Under the law, heavy penalties were levied on the keepers of the house (£200 each), the manager of the entertainment (£100), and ticket-takers, printers of advertisements, and various others associated with the event (£50 each). All fines were to go to the individual suing under the law, the so-called Common Informer. Under the 1623 Common Informers Act, an individual who informed on a party breaking the law was entitled to fines, penalties, and even the private property of the defendant; the act was not abolished until 1951 (*Common Informers Act*, 14 & 15 Geo. 6, c. 39). Despite its confidence, the SLS prohibited all musical entertainments, preferring to "err on the safe side"; Sunday Lecture Society, *Preliminary Meeting*, 2.
104. Sunday Lecture Society, *Preliminary Meeting*, 2–3 (unsigned letter to Domville).
105. Sunday Lecture Society, *Third Annual Report*, October 15, 1872 (London: Kenny & Co., 1872), 6.
106. Sunday Lecture Society, *Fifth Annual Report*, October 1874 (London: Kenny & Co., 1875), 6.
107. Ibid., 7. This phrase was repeated in subsequent annual reports.
108. Sunday Lecture Society, *Thirteenth Annual Report*, October 1882 (London: Kenny & Co., 1882), 6.
109. "The Sunday Lecture Society," *Morning Post*, March 12, 1870: 1 ("refined").
110. "Sunday at St. George's Hall," *Examiner*, November 2, 1872: 6–7.
111. "Our London Correspondent," *Swindon Advertiser and North Wilts Chronicle*, March 8, 1880: 3; *Globe*, April 1, 1870: 1 ("gossip" and "pabulum").
112. "Sunday at St. George's Hall," *Examiner*, 6–7.
113. *South Wales Daily News*, October 19, 1885: 3.
114. Sunday Lecture Society, *Fifteenth Annual Report*, October 1874 (London: Kenny & Co., 1875), 4–5.
115. "Sunday Lecture Society," *Examiner*, December 23, 1871: 10 ("fair epitomes"); ibid., January 6, 1872: 15 ("his peculiar theory").
116. Arthur F. V. Wild, *A Criticism of the Second Report of the Select Committee of the House of Lords on the Lord's Day Act, 1781 (21 Geo. III c. 49), Appointed on Motion*

for the Second Reading of the Sunday Bill, 1895 (London: Sunday Lecture Society, 1897), 24.
117. Sunday Lecture Society, *Eleventh Annual Report, October 1880* (London: Kenny & Co., 1880), 6.
118. Sunday Lecture Society, *Twenty-First Annual Report, September 1890* (London: Kenny & Co., 1890), 8–10; "Clubs, Reading Rooms, and Lecture Halls (From the *Athenaeum*)," *Morning Post*, March 30, 1872: 7.
119. Hewitt, "Preaching from the Platform," 91.
120. Between 1872 and 1878, the number of subscribing members dropped from 201 to 152, while annual subscription income dropped from about £200 to about £136 and total income dropped from £224 to £164. Sunday Lecture Society, *Nineteenth Annual Report, September 1888* (London: Kenny & Co., 1888), 6–7.
121. For Walsall, see Sunday Lecture Society, *Fifth Annual Report*, 6; the other societies were enumerated in Sunday Lecture Society, *Tenth Annual Report, October 1879* (London: Kenny & Co., 1879), 7.
122. Sunday Lecture Society, *Eleventh Annual Report, October 1880* (London: Kenny & Co., 1880), 6–7.
123. *Handbook of Birmingham. Prepared for the Members of the British Association, 1886* (Birmingham: Hall and English, 1886), 359 ("more representative"); see also James Morgan, *A Short History of the Birmingham Sunday Lecture Society* (Birmingham: Allday, 1917).
124. Sunday Lecture Society, *Thirteenth Annual Report, October 1882* (London: Kenny & Co., 1882), 8.
125. Sunday Lecture Society, *Fifteenth Annual Report*, 1884, 6–8.
126. "Correspondence. The Birmingham Sunday Lecture Society," *Birmingham Daily Post*, September 11, 1882: 4 (letter from Birmingham SLS secretary Thomas Rose); "The Birmingham Sunday Lecture Society," *Birmingham Daily Post*, March 26, 1882: 7 ("four quarters").
127. Sunday Lecture Society, *Twelfth Annual Report, October 1881* (London: Kenny & Co., 1881), 7–8.
128. Sunday Lecture Society, *Fifteenth Annual Report, October 1884* (London: Kenny & Co., 1884), 7 ("brilliant opening"); "The Tyneside Sunday Lecture Society," *Pall Mall Gazette*, February 5, 1885: 4 ("varied audiences and opinions" and "popularly known").
129. "Tyneside Sunday Lecture Society," *Newcastle Courant*, November 10, 1888: 5.
130. Sunday Lecture Society, *Sixteenth Annual Report, October 1885* (London: Kenny & Co., 1885), 8.
131. Sunday Lecture Society, *Eighteenth Annual Report, September* 1887 (London: Kenny & Co., 1887), 9 (Bradford); "Proposed Sunday Lecture Society," *Norwich Mercury*, October 17, 1891: 5 and October 24, 1891: 5.
132. Sunday Lecture Society, *Sixteenth Annual Report, October 1886* (London: Kenny & Co., 1886), 8 (Sunderland); Sunday Lecture Society, *Seventeenth Annual Report, October 1887* (London: Kenny & Co.), 8 (Liverpool); "Birmingham Sunday Lecture Society," *Birmingham Daily Post*, September 26, 1890: 7 ("union").
133. "Sunday Lecture Society. To The Editors of the Leeds Mercury," *Leeds Mercury*, October 21, 1892: 7 (letter from H. W. Hunter) and "Leeds Sunday Lecture Society. To the Editors of the Leeds Mercury," *Leeds Mercury*, November 8, 1892: 7 (letter from honorary secretary Henry Greenwood); "Yorkshire Echoes," *Yorkshire Evening Post*, November 28, 1892: 3–4 (Ball).

134. Lord Hobhouse, "Sunday Bill," *House of Lords Debate*, June 19, 1897, vol. 50 c. 689.
135. Lord Hobhouse, "Sunday Bill," *House of Lords Debate*, March 21, 1895, vol. 31 c. 1527.
136. See Sunday Lecture Society, *Twenty-First Annual Report, September, 1890* (London: Kenny & Co., 1890), 9, where Darlington described its "packed houses," and Sunday Lecture Society, *Twentieth Annual Report, September 1889* (London: Kenny & Co., 1889), 8, where Tyneside reported its interaction with the BAAS meeting.
137. "Birmingham Sunday Lecture Society," *Birmingham Daily Post*, September 26, 1890: 7.
138. John Wigley, *The Rise and Fall of the Victorian Sunday* (Manchester: Manchester University Press, 1980); Christopher Lane, "On the Victorian Afterlife of the 1781 Sunday Observance Act," in *BRANCH: Britain, Representation and Nineteenth-Century History*, ed. Dino Franco Felluga. Available online: https://branchcollective.org/ (accessed October 26, 2014); Amy Woodson-Boulton, *Transformative Beauty: Art Museums in Industrial Britain* (Stanford: Stanford University Press, 2012).
139. The Brighton Aquarium was found guilty of violating the act in 1875 in a case that continued to inspire caustic commentary sixty years later: "[The Aquarium] pleaded in its defence that this could not be deemed an entertainment as 17 bandsmen performed sacred music while the fish were fed." See "Common Informer," *House of Commons Debate*, November 6, 1934 (vol. 293 cc. 843–6; testimony of Sir Gerald Hurst).
140. Ernest G. Roberts, "Correspondence," *Leeds Mercury*, July 4, 1894 ("wanton and intolerant"); Lord Herschell, "Sunday Bill," *House of Lords Debate*, June 19, 1897, vol 50. col. 715 ("relic").
141. *Standard*, June 30, 1894: 2.
142. Wild, *Criticism*, 6.
143. *The Huddersfield Chronicle and West Yorkshire Advertiser*, June 7, 1894: 3 ("gloomy and stupid," letter from lecturer and dramatist Henry Arthur Jones).
144. "Museum Sunday. Letter to the Editor," *Leeds Mercury*, December 13, 1894: 3 (letter from Frederic Peake).
145. "Professor James Blackie on 'Christianity and Social Organization,'" *Scotsman*, December 6, 1886: 8 ("jokes or gestures"); "The Rev. W. Tuckwell on Church Reform," *Birmingham Daily Post*, February 8, 1886: 4 ("laughter … enthusiastic applause").
146. Hobhouse, "Sunday Bill," March 21, 1895.
147. Wild, *Criticism*, 7.
148. Hobhouse, "Sunday Bill," June 19, 1897.
149. "Leeds Sunday Lecture Society," *Leeds Mercury*, November 5, 1894: 2 (reporting a lecture by Dr. Andrew Wilson).
150. *Liverpool Mercury*, June 30, 1894: 4 (unsigned article).
151. Mark H. Judge, "Sunday Observance Legislation," *Westminster Review*, 148 (July 1897): 82.
152. Birt was a regular advertiser in the *Lecturers' Gazette* and the journal printed several of his lectures, usually spread out over a number of issues, as an inspiration to other lecturers (and, likely, to fill column space). See, for example, "Solar Spots" and "Comets," both appearing over several months in 1862.
153. Advertisements for these lectures ran monthly in the *Lecturers' Gazette*, usually on the first or second page, until ill health forced Kidd (1803–1867) to retire from

the platform. Kidd earned a living as a publisher and printer in London, often skirting the law in his early years as he reprinted works without attribution, but by mid-century his publishing work had become more careful. He was a self-taught ornithologist, opening and operating an aviary in the heart of the city, and producing several well-received essays on birds and insects. For coverage of his 1862 lecture, see "Chichester Mechanics' Institution," *ILG* (April 1862): 52–3. See also Rodrick, "Chatting up the Sciences."

154. Chichester Mechanics' Institution," *ILG* (April 1862): 53.
155. See, for example, "Institute Intelligence. Brixton," *ILG* (May 1879): 1771 (lectures by Miss Arabella Buckley).
156. "Local News," *Newcastle Courant*, October 7, 1887: 4.
157. "Local News," *Newcastle Courant*, October 7, 1887: 4.
158. Moulton will figure significantly in Chapter 5, as one of the figures linking the popular lecture to the emerging University Extension movement.
159. "Local News," *Newcastle Courant*, October 7, 1887: 4.
160. "Institutional Changes," *ILG* (November 1886): 2585.

Chapter 5

1. Thomas Huxley, "Preface," *Discourses, Biological and Geological* (London, 1894).
2. Sir Phillip Magnus, "Lectures and Lecturing. An Address to the Students of the Working Men's College, January 23, 1893," in *Educational Aims and Efforts, 1880–1910*, ed. Phillip Magnus (London: Longman Green, 1910), 246, 260–1.
3. George Bott, *Sponsored Talk. A History of the Keswick Lecture Society* (Keswick: The Society, 1968), 33–4. Keswick relied almost entirely on gratis lectures by local men until after the turn of the century.
4. Untitled, *Newcastle Courant*, December 7, 1895: 4.
5. "Popular Lectures," *Morpeth Herald*, November 5, 1898: 3.
6. Timmins, *Address, Delivered at the Annual Meeting of Members*, 12.
7. Heathorn, "'Let Us Remember that We, Too, Are English.'"
8. "Editorial," *Coventry Herald*, August 14, 1891; quoted in Brad Beaven and John Griffiths, "Urban Elites, Socialists and Notions of Citizenship in an Industrial Boomtown: Coventry, c. 1870–1914," *Labour History Review* 69, no. 1 (2004): 11.
9. Beaven and Griffiths, "Creating the Exemplary Citizen," 204–5 ("civic spirit" and "behavior"); Brad Beaven, *Visions of Empire: Patriotism, Popular Culture and the City, 1870–1939* (Manchester: Manchester University Press, 2012), 33, 209 ("sporting" and "local").
10. J. A. R. Pimlott, *Toynbee Hall: Fifty Years of Progress* (London: J. R. Dent, 1935); quoted in Beaven and Griffiths, "Creating the Exemplary Citizen," 210.
11. "Correspondence," *Leeds Mercury*, May 3, 1888; quoted in Beaven, *Visions of Empire*, 198–9.
12. YUMI, *Annual Report for 1890*, 32, 23 (remarks of Rev. S. F. Williams). The emergence of the library movement was rehearsed at the 1904 annual meeting by the Marquess of Ripon, then president of the Union; see YUMI, *Annual Report for 1904*, 51.
13. YUMI, *Annual Report for 1890*, 37–40 (remarks of Sir Joseph Pease, chair, at the annual dinner).

14. For a discussion of this language, see Meller, "Urban Renewal and Citizenship, 63–84.
15. Timmins, *Address, 1874*, 13–14 ("personal duty"); "King's Heath and Moseley Institute," *Birmingham Daily Post*, August 23, 1882: 4 ("sympathy," remarks of John Cole, vice president); "The Marquis of Lorne in Birmingham: Suburban Institutes Union," *Birmingham Daily Post*, October 6, 1886: 5 ("fellow-citizens"); Joseph Chamberlain, "The Work of Severn Street School," in *Mr. Chamberlain's Speeches, Volume 1*, ed. Charles W. Boyd (New York: Houghton Mifflin, 1914), 52 ("welfare and happiness").
16. Rachel Ablow, "Unsettling Sympathy," *Victorian Studies* 64, no. 4 (2022): 573.
17. John Henry Newman's 1854 "What Is a University?" was one of the most widely read but certainly not the only essay built around both sympathy and collision.
18. YUMI, *Annual Report for 1897*, 39 (remarks of J. Compton Rickett).
19. "H.," "A Working Man's View, *Oxford University Extension Gazette [OUEG]* 2 (1892): 123.
20. H. J. Mackinder and M. E. Sadler, *University Extension: Has It a Future?* (Oxford: Horace Hart, 1890), 3. Early overviews of the Extension movement by participants include R. D. Roberts, *Eighteen Years of University Extension* (Cambridge: Cambridge University Press, 1891); John Mackinder and Michael Sadler, *University Extension, Past, Present, and Future* (London: Cassall, 1891); and W. H. Draper, *University Extension 1873–1923* (Cambridge: Cambridge University Press, 1923). See also Kelly, *History of Adult Education in Great Britain*; N. A. Jepson, *The Beginnings of English University Adult Education* (Leeds: Michael Joseph, 1973); Brian Simon, *Education and the Labour Movement, 1870–1920* (London: Lawrence & Wishart, 1969). More recent work includes Bernard Jennings, *The University Extension Movement in Victorian and Edwardian England* (Hull: University of Hull, 1992), and Alexandra Lawrie, *The Beginnings of University English* (Oxford: Oxford University Press, 2014). An excellent historiographical overview of adult education can be found in Mark Freeman, "Adult Education History in Britain: Past, Present and Future (Part 1)," *Paedagogica Historica* 56, no. 3 (2020): 384–95.
21. Mackinder and Sadler, *University Extension, Past, Present and Future*, 125.
22. J. H. Muirhead, *A Liberal Education: An Address to the Students of Mason University College, Birmingham* (Birmingham: Cornish Bros., 1899), 7. For an overview of scholarship on liberal education in Britain, see Harold Silver, "'Things Change but Names Remain the Same': Higher Education Historiography 1975–2000," *History of Education* 35, no. 1 (2006): 121–40.
23. "H.," "A Working Man's View," *OUEG* 2 (1892): 123.
24. See Jennings, *The University Extension Movement in Victorian and Edwardian England*, 5–6, for the typical organization of these early courses. The percentage of students emerging from the initial lecture audience was always low, with about 20 percent enrolling and between 5 percent and 10 percent ultimately sitting for the final credential-granting examination.
25. "Notes on the Work," *OUEG* 3 (1893): 54 (commenting on an article in the *Saturday Review*, January 21, 1893).
26. "Scheme for a Citizens' College in a Large Town," *OUEG* 2, no. 18 (1892): 58.
27. Mackinder and Sadler, *University Extension, Past, Present and Future*, 5 ("living cultured teacher").
28. "Recreation in Ancoats," *OUEG* 4 (1893): 19. The Gilchrist Educational Trust was established in 1841 through an endowment from John Borthwick Gilchrist, FRSE, to provide support to higher education in a variety of forms, including lectures on

the sciences to working-class men. They began in 1865 after years of legal wrangling over the land in Australia that funded the trust. See "The Gilchrist Trust: Pioneer Work in Education," *Times Educational Supplement* no. 2 (October 4, 1910): 26. The importance of the contributions of the Gilchrist lectures to "fresh educational endeavour," particularly to Extension efforts in London, were highlighted in Gilchrist Educational Trust, *Pioneer Work in Education* (Cambridge, 1930), 12, 15.

29. George Horsley, *Darlington Lecture Association*, http://www.darlingtonlecture.org.uk/history.html (accessed November 19, 2020).
30. Midland Institute, *Annual Report* (1893), 14.
31. T. W. Haddon, "England. University Extension," *School and College* 1, no. 10 (1892): 616.
32. Lawrie, *The Beginnings of University English*, 6–7. Martyn Walker notes that within the YUMI alone, these included mechanics' institutions in Barnsley, Bradford, Cleckheaton, Doncaster, Dewsbury, Filey, Halifax, Harrogate, Hartlepool, Hebden Bridge, Heckmondwike, Huddersfield, Hull, Ilkley, Keighley, Leeds, Middlesbrough, Pontefract, Ripon, Rotherham, Scarborough, Sheffield, Shipley, Skipton, Sowerby Bridge, Stockton, Sunderland, Thirsk, Todmorden, Whitby, and York; Walker, *Development of the Mechanics' Institute Movement*, 54–6.
33. Mackinder and Sadler, *University Extension, Past, Present and Future*, 8–9.
34. Ibid., 14–15.
35. "Comments of By-standers," *OUEG* 4 (1894): 113 ("lecturing-bureau"); "The City Councils Technical Instruction Scheme," *Western Times*, March 16, 1891: 2 (Extension lecture given to Exeter City Council in the Congregational Schoolroom "to a fairly numerous audience").
36. Oscar Browning, "The University Extension Movement at Cambridge," *Science* (Friday, January 21, 1887): 61. Browning also lectured extensively about the movement in the United States.
37. "Arrangements for 1893. Spring," *OUEG* 3 (1893): 63–4.
38. Laura Stuart, "The Facts about University Extension," *The Nineteenth Century* (September 1894): 383, 386. Stuart was responding to critic Charles Whibley, who in the previous issue of the journal had suggested that the movement's emphasis on sympathy "implie[d] a corresponding aversion for thoroughness and method."
39. James Stuart, "Education by Lectures: A Paper Read at the Annual Meeting of the Leeds Ladies' Educational Association, April 26, 1871," *Cambridge Syndicate Report* ("think for themselves"); C. E. Mallet, "Report," *University Extension Journal* II: 87 ("lighter courses"), both quoted in Jepson, *Beginnings of English University Adult Education*, 288–300; Mackinder and Sadler, *University Extension, Past, Present and Future*, 3 ("emasculate the national mind"); YUMI, *Annual Report for 1897*, 31 (remarks of T. Williamson, Mayor of Ripon); John Henry Newman, "Preface," *The Idea of a University;* quoted in Dinah Birch, *Our Victorian Education* (London: Blackwell, 2008) ("real dignity in Knowledge"); P. H. J. H. Gosden and A. J. Taylor, eds., *Studies in the History of a University to Commemorate the Centenary of the University of Leeds 1874–1974* (Leeds: University of Leeds, 1975), 250 ("national interests," quoting Lord Frederick Cavendish, 1877).
40. "Mr. Ruskin on Lectures," *OUEG* 3 (1893): 75.
41. Mary R. Lacey, "Taking Notes at Lectures," *OUEG* 3 (1892): 14–15.
42. Ibid.
43. "Mr. Ruskin on Lectures," *OUEG* 3 (1893): 75.

44. "University Extension and County Council Grants," *OUEG* 4 (1894): 59 (Samuel Fielding and Robert Halstead, "Appeal to Co-operators").
45. "The Educational Value of Classes," *ILG* (November 1865): 395 (italics in original). This was the only editorial use of the word *caste* in the run of the journal.
46. R. G. Moulton, writing in *Education* September 1891; quoted in Jepson, *Beginnings of English University Adult Education*, 99.
47. See Sheila Rowbotham's classic account of extension student experience, "Travellers in a Strange Country: Responses of Working Class Students to the University Extension Movement 1873–1910," *History Workshop* 12 (1981): 62–95.
48. By the 1880s, "brain-labour" was perceived as enervating almost to the same degree as hard manual labor, and especially problematic for middle-class women who were entering universities and white-collar professions in increasing numbers; see, for example, Emily Pfeiffer, *Women and Work. Treating on the Relation to Health and Physical Development, of the Higher Education of Girls, and the Intellectual or More Systematised Effort of Women* (London: Trubner & Co., 1888). Worries about children now being "stuffed" with education were also rampant: Amelia Bonea, Melissa Dickson, Sally Shuttleworth, and Jennifer Wallis, *Anxious Times: Medicine and Modernity in Nineteenth-Century Britain* (Pittsburgh: University of Pittsburgh Press, 2019), chapter 5: "Knocking Some Sense into Them: Overpressure Debates and the Education of Mind and Body," 149–80. See also J. Mortimer Granville, "Worry," *The Nineteenth Century* 10, no. 55 (1881): 423–9, where he discusses the relationships between "over-work," "brain labour," "cram," and "worry," and compares a mind unprepared for sustained labor or uninspired by dull work to "an engine with the safety-valve locked, the steam-gauge falsified, the governing apparatus out of gear." He argues that worry, rather than overwork or frivolous reading, was the peril of the age (427–8). The fears linking reading to disease had a long history; see, for example, J. Kennaway, "Two Kinds of 'Literary Poison': Diseases of the Learned and Overstimulating Novels in Georgian Britain," *Literature and Medicine* 34, no. 2 (2016): 252–77.
49. Constance C. W. Naden, "Is the Increasing Predominance of Brain over Muscle Conducive to National Welfare?" *The Mason College Magazine* 4, no. 1 (April 1883): 86.
50. "Prince Krapotkine [sic] in Darlington," *Northern Echo*, March 10, 1890: 3 ("brain worker"); J. D. M., "Impressions of the Summer Meeting. From an Old Friend," *OUEG* 2 (1892): 121 ("brain-spinner").
51. "Letters to the Editor," *OUEG* 3 (1892): 9 (letter signed by M. E. Sadler).
52. Thomas Wright had argued two decades earlier that there was no actual link between higher education and higher pay for most in the working classes; see *Our New Masters* (London: Strahan & Co., 1873), 118.
53. "A Lancashire Man of Business on University Extension," *OUEG* 4 (1894): 84 (letter from T. H. Tregidga).
54. *The Halifax Sunday Lecture Society Minute Book*, November 16, 1901 (West Yorkshire Archive Service, Calderdale, MISC 6/106) [hereinafter *HSLS Minute Book*], Cooke's letter of November 14, 1901.
55. A. D. Hall, "An Adviser for Every Centre," *OUEG* 2 (1892): 32.
56. Robert Halstead, "An Appeal from a Working Man to Working Men Concerning University Teaching: A Paper Read at a Conference of University Extension Students and Others at the Co-operative Hall, Hebden Bridge, on Saturday, March 18th, 1893," *OUEG* 3 (1893): 109. Halstead was a fustian worker from Hebden Bridge and became

a powerful working-class voice within the extension movement; see Rowbotham, "Strangers."

57. Robert Halstead, "Are Workmen Interested in University Extension?" *OUEG* 3 (1893): 96.
58. See, for example, Graham Wallas, *University Extension Lectures: Syllabus of a Course of Lectures on the English Citizen Past and Present* (London: Co-operative Printing Society, Ltd., 1891) and City of Norwich Technical School, *Prospectus of Day Classes for Manual Instruction, Evening Classes for Artisans, Recreative Classes, Scholarships, and University Extension Lectures, 1895–96* (Norwich, 1896), 40, advertising a twelve-lecture series by Thomas Lawrence, LLD.
59. "Down with the Dons," *OUEG* 3 (1893): 88–9.
60. Ibid.
61. According to the 1908 *Oxford and Working-Class Education*, the WEA was a "federation" of over 1,000 existing bodies, including unions, cooperative societies, adult schools, university colleges, and 350 "Literary Societies, University Extension Centres, and Others." Workers' Education Association, *Oxford and Working-Class Education: Being the Report of a Joint Committee of the University and Working-Class Representatives on the Relation of the University to the Higher Education of Workpeople* (Oxford: Oxford University Press, 1908), 10. See the essays in Stephen K. Roberts, ed., *A Ministry of Enthusiasm: Centenary Essays on the Workers' Educational Association* (London: Pluto Press, 2003), especially Bernard Jennings, "The WEA: The Foundation and the Founder," 12–25, and Lawrence Goldman, "The First Students in the Workers' Educational Association: Individual Enlightenment and Collective Advance," 41–58, as well as the historiography in Silver, " 'Things Change but Names Remain the Same.'" See also Stuart Marriott, *A Backstairs to a Degree: Demands for an Open University in Late Victorian England* (Leeds: University of Leeds School of Continuing Education, 1981).
62. WEA, *Oxford and University Education*, 38–50.
63. Ibid., 61. Lawrence Goldman notes that the earliest WEA lectures, like the University Extension lectures, were often given to audiences "running into the hundreds," Goldman, "The First Students in the Workers' Education Association," 42.
64. WEA, *Oxford and University Education*, 59.
65. "News of the Midland Branches," *The Highway: Birmingham Supplement* 3, no. 4 (1910): 3. By 1911, the "Birmingham Supplement" had been renamed "The Midland Supplement."
66. "The Handsworth W. E. A. Winter Lectures," *The Highway: Midland Supplement* 5, no. 24 (1912): 3. (By 1912, the journal appeared biweekly rather than monthly.)
67. "The Caravan," *The Highway: A Monthly Journal of Education for the People* 2, no. 3 (1909): 1.
68. "Labour and Learning: The Citizen and the University," *The Highway. Birmingham Supplement* 2, no. 7 (1909): 3.
69. "An Old Member," "Halifax Mechanics' Institution," *Halifax Courier*, March 11, 1899: 9. For an analysis of the working-class administration of the mechanics' institute in the years after its 1831 founding, see Iwama, "Voluntary Societies and the Urban Local Community," 17–25.
70. *HSLS Minute Book*, November 28, 1895.
71. "A Sunday Lecture Society for Sheffield," *Sheffield Daily Telegraph*, November 5, 1895: 3 (letter from Henry Greenwood).

72. Gerald Christy took over the Lecture Agency, Ltd., established in 1879, in 1891. Based in London, it competed with and eventually replaced a number of individual agents who had represented the bigger names on the English circuit and in lecture tours to America. The largest agency in the United States at this time was Pond's; see Waller, *Writers, Readers, and Reputation*; J. B. Pond, *Eccentricities of Genius: Memories of Famous Men and Women of the Platform and the Stage* (New York: Dillingham Co., 1900); Paul Fatout, *Mark Twain on the Lecture Circuit* (Carbondale, IL: Southern Illinois University Press, 1969). Christy's main rival, the London-based Lecture League, established in 1908 under the direction of Frederick Thomasson, eventually represented a number of stars, including T. E. Lawrence; see Adam Gotch, "The Lecture League," *The Journal of the T. E. Lawrence Society* 25, no.1 (2016): 29–63.
73. Untitled, *Lichfield Mercury*, October 19, 1894: 5; *HSLS Minute Book*, July 11, 1904.
74. *HSLS Minute Book*, May 6, 1907; this fee did not include individual lecture fees.
75. *HSLS Minute Book*, July 14, 1903.
76. Horsley, *Darlington Lecture Association*.
77. "Chat of the Week," *Halifax Courier*, October 28, 1899: 11.
78. This letter was reproduced in the minutes of a special meeting called on October 23, 1899 and sent on October 24.
79. "Halifax Sunday Lecture Society. Mr. Fred Knock," *Halifax Courier*, January 21, 1899: 7 ("au fait," reporting on "the indefatigable entomologist"); HSLS *Minute Book*, June 1, 1905 (report of the 10th annual meeting).
80. J. Ernest Phythian, "The Arts as a Subject for Extension Teaching. A Paper Read at the Autumn Conference of the Lancashire and Cheshire Association for the Extension of University Teaching," *OUEG* 4 (1893): 23.
81. "The Sunday Lecture Society," *Halifax Courier*, September 23, 1899: 5. See note 96.
82. "Voyages in Cloudland," *Halifax Courier*, November 4, 1899: 9.
83. "Halifax Sunday Lecture Society," *Halifax Courier*, November 18, 1899: 4.
84. "Politics as Sunday Lectures," *Shields Daily Gazette*, October 12, 1885: 3; "'Egypt: A Plea of Honour,' Lecture by Mr. Wilfrid S. Blunt," *Newcastle Courant*, October 16, 1885: 7.
85. "Correspondence," *Yorkshire Post and Leeds Intelligencer*, March 7, 1902: 4. Lupton's lecture for the Leeds SLS, originally scheduled to take place in the local Co-operative Hall, was forcibly relocated to an outdoor space commonly used by the Salvation Army: "Pro-Boer Lock-Out at Castleford," *Yorkshire Post and Leeds Intelligencer*, March 10, 1902: 5. Other lecturers on the war were deliberately noncontroversial. Mrs. Philip Watts, whose husband was a navy contractor with the Newcastle Artillery, focused largely on the geography of the area and various feats of military engineering: "Jarrow Mechanics' Institute," *Jarrow Express*, March 7, 1902: 5. A Miss Friend delivered "some comical incidents" about the Siege of Mafeking in a "bright and amusing narrative," describing Baden-Powell as "writing a military despatch [sic] with his right hand and answering a dinner invitation with his left." "The Siege of Mafeking. Some Comical Incidents," *Tyrone Constitution*, February 15, 1901: 3.
86. "Richard G. Moulton," *Book News* (Philadelphia, May 1891); reprinted in *OUEG* 1 (1891): 118.
87. "Sunday Lecture Society," *Sunderland Daily Echo and Shipping Gazette*, January 23, 1893: 3 (reviewing Bennett Burleigh on "Campaigning in the Soudan"); "Sunday Lecture Society, *Birmingham Daily Post*, October 2, 1890: 3 (reviewing C. E. Mathews on "Scrambles in Rome"); "Mrs. Beerbohm Tree's Recital in Leeds," *Yorkshire Post and Leeds Intelligencer*, December 21, 1903: 6 ("modulated tones").

88. "A Plea for the Obvious," *Globe*, November 6, 1900: 1; "The Art of Happiness. Madame Sarah Grand," *Lancashire Evening Post*, November 6, 1900: 2.
89. A. R., "Shall Bedford Have a Sunday Lecture Society?" *Bedfordshire Times and Independent*, November 20, 1903: 6. The "northern society" was probably Leeds.
90. William M. Flinders Petrie was an archaeologist and Egyptologist, and the inaugural chair of the Edwards Professor of Egyptian Archaeology and Philology at University College London; his ideas about race hierarchy fed into contemporary eugenics arguments. Walter Crane was an artist and a book illustrator, both for children's books and for a variety of socialist publications. Karl Pearson was a mathematician and biostatistician, and as a social Darwinist was one of the early proponents of eugenics and race science. Francis Gotch was a neurophysiologist specializing in the electrical stimulation of the brain. Thomas Marshall was the president of the Leeds Phil.-&-Lit. from 1886 to 1889 and a longtime member; his lecture here was gratis. H. J. Palmer served as editor of the *Yorkshire Post* from 1899 to 1903; he was also a longtime member and also gave his lecture gratis. Henri (or Henry) Edward Berthon, a Paris native, taught at the King Edward School in Birmingham from 1890 to 1895 and then at University College, Nottingham, and University of Oxford; he was the author of several collections of French literature and volumes of French grammar. Albert Forbes Sieveking's popular *The Praise of Gardens: An Epitome of the Literature of the Garden-Art* appeared in 1899. Oliver Lodge was a physicist at University College, Liverpool, and became the first president of Birmingham University in 1900; he embraced spiritualism later in his life. Charles Hargrove was a Unitarian minister in Leeds for thirty-six years and was a member of a number of Leeds societies, including the Phil.-&-Lit., where he served as president in 1894–5; his lecture here was gratis. Edmund Gosse was a poet, literary critic, and lecturer in English literature at Cambridge. Israel Zangwill was a novelist and reformer associated with Jewish emancipation and Zionism. William Hancock was a longtime member of the society and delivered this lecture gratis. Henry Crowther was the curator of the society's museum. Leeds Philosophical and Literary Society, *The 80th Annual Report* (Leeds: By the Society, 1900).
91. *A Leaflet Promoting Lectures by Henry Crowther (born c. 1848 – 29 November 1937), Former Curator of Leeds Museum, Leeds, West Yorkshire, England*, n.d. Available online: https://commons.wikimedia.org/wiki/File:Henry_Crowther_(3).JPG (accessed June 24, 2023).
92. John Morley, *Studies in Literature* [1891]; quoted in Lawrie, *The Beginnings of University English*, 75.
93. Alfred Cort Haddon, Cambridge anthropologist and ethnologist, lectured here about his expedition to the Torres Straits. William Hall Griffin was a noted Browning scholar. William Martin Conway, an art critic, archaeologist, politician, and mountaineer, was a longtime member and, for two years, the president of the Alpine Club, and broke several records in his summits in Norway and in Tierra del Fuego; he became 1st Baron Conway of Allington in 1931. C. H. Bothamley was a well-known photographer and the author of the 1890 *Ilford Manual of Photography*, still in print. Sebastian Evans, a conservative politician, poet, and artist, was the editor of the *Birmingham Daily Gazette* 1867–70 and ran unsuccessfully for MP from Birmingham in 1868; he earned an LLD from Cambridge and began practicing law in 1873. Francis Bennett-Goldney was Evans's younger son, who took the surname of his maternal grandfather, a founder of the London Joint Stock Bank. Alfred Sidgwick was a classics scholar and liberal educationist, serving as lecturer

and officer of the Association for Promoting the Higher Education of Women at Oxford. William Henry Hadow was a composer and musicologist. Whitworth Wallis was the director of the Birmingham Museum and Art Gallery from its founding in 1885. John Mackenzie Bacon was a famous astronomer and aeronaut and played an important part in the expeditions to India and to North Carolina for the solar eclipses. Alexander Hill was Vice-Chancellor of the University of Cambridge at the time of this lecture; he was a member of a number of learned societies including the Royal College of Surgeons, and specialized in the activities of brain neurons. John Watson was a minister of the Free Church of Scotland and was best known for the stories of rural Scotland he published as Ian Maclaren. Sir James Crichton-Browne was a pioneer in psychiatry and was especially interested in brain injury and mental illness. Hugh Robert Mill was a geographer and meteorologist. Louis Compton Miall was a professor of biology, specializing in paleontology at University of Leeds and a past president of the Leeds Phil.-&-Lit.

94. This was also published as *The Praise of Gardens: An Epitome of the Literature of the Garden-Art* (London: Dent, 1899).
95. "The Winter Season in Birmingham," *Magazine of Music* (April 1891): 76.
96. Morley Roberts was an English novelist whose travels to Australia figured extensively in his fiction. His lecture here was "a disaster"; see p. 171. Eugene Arnold Dolmetsch was a musician and instrument-maker specializing in medieval and early modern music; he and his family appeared in concert across the kingdom. Arthur Smithells was a professor of chemistry at Leeds. Hugh Reginald Haweis, a London cleric, was the author of the bestseller *Music and Morals* and lectured regularly on music and on his past service under Giuseppe Garibaldi. Richard Kerr was a microscopist and the author of several books, including *Nature, Curious and Beautiful* and *Hidden Beauties of Nature*, published by the Religious Tract Society. Alfred Henry Fison, DSc, was a Fellow of the Royal Astronomical Society and spent twenty years lecturing in astronomy for the Oxford Extension Movement; he also served as secretary to the Gilchrist Trust. Charles Fry was an internationally acclaimed orator. Mary Kingsley was an ethnographer and one of the first non-missionary women to explore Africa. John Foster Fraser was a journalist who traveled the world on a bicycle; his 1899 book *Round the World on a Wheel* included several chapters on India and Burma. Haskett Smith was a travel writer and editor of the 1892 *Murray's Handbooks for Travellers to Syria and Palestine*. Frank Thomas Bullen was a writer who spent his youth at sea and produced a variety of essays and novels about his adventures. Madame Annie Grey was a singer who specialized in oratorio and, under the tutelage of Professor John Stuart Blackie, developed a well-respected repertoire of Scottish ballads. Arthur Diosy was the founder of the Japan Society of the United Kingdom. John Walter Gregory was a geologist and explorer.
97. "Bradford Mechanics' Institute," YUMI, *Annual Report for 1903*, 138.
98. See, for instance, the reports of the Conference of Women Workers in Bristol and the Conference of Women Workers at Leeds in the 1890s; "Conference of Women Workers," *The Englishwoman's Review. New Series* CCXVI (1893): 1–5; L. Marshall, "Conference of Women Workers at Leeds," *Charity Organisation Review* 10, no. 108 (1894): 7–9.
99. "The Women Lecturers' Association," *The Review of Reviews* (April 1893): 396; "Women Pioneer Lecturers," *OUEG* 3 (1893): 114; "Association of Women Pioneer Lecturers," *Englishwoman's Review* (1893): 112.

100. "Women Lecturers' Institute. To the Editor of 'The Nursing Record,'" *The Nursing Record and Hospital World*, November 16, 1895: 362.
101. "Sunday Recreation in Leeds. The Lord Mayor's Attitude," *Leeds Mercury*, November 16, 1903: 4.
102. The Lecture Agency, Ltd., *Concerning Popular Lectures* (London, 1911). The agency sent this pamphlet to committees of "Literary and Scientific Societies, Philosophical Institutions, Mechanics' Institutes, Lecture Associations, Y.M.C.A.'s, Colleges, Schools, Entrepreneurs, and Managers throughout the Country."
103. The wonders of the magic lantern were not without danger: The Newcastle Lit.-&-Phil. lost much of its library in a fire that was traced to lantern equipment improperly stored after the 100-year-anniversary conversazione, while a young boy was killed when he tripped on his way to an auditorium, carrying poorly packed gas cylinders for the evening's public lecture. "A Fiery Centenary," *OUEG* 3 (1893): 69 (Newcastle); untitled, *OUEG* 4 (1893): 30 (death).
104. T. C. Abbott, "Literary Societies and Civic Life," in Manchester Literary Club, *The Manchester Quarterly: A Journal of Literature and Art* XV (1896): 429–33 (paper read on February 3, 1896).
105. "Wanted: Subjects for Debate," *One and All: The Organ of the Adult School Movement* 1(1891): 122, 138.
106. Ladies' Debating Society, *Inaugural Address of the Session, 1882-3, Delivered on the 26th of October, 1882, by Mrs. H. W. Crosskey, President* (Birmingham: Cornish Bros., 1882), 11. See also Wood, *Debating Women*, especially chapter 2, "Women of Infinite Variety": The Ladies' Edinburgh Debating Society as an Intergenerational Argument Culture, 1865–1935," 53–102.
107. Ladies' Debating Society, *Session 1882-3. Third Annual Report* (Birmingham: Cornish Bros., 1883), 4–5.
108. Birmingham and Edgbaston Debating Society, *Report of Committee, Session 1895-6* (Birmingham: Cornish Bros., 1896), 7.

Conclusion

1. Richard Clarke, *Informal Adult Education between the Wars: The Curious Case of The Selborne Lecture Bureau* (London: University of London, 2005).
2. Traice, *Hand-book*, 7.
3. "Confessions of an Extension Lecturer," *All the Year Round* 43, no. 1041 (1888): 436.

Select Bibliography

Primary Sources

Periodicals

All the Year Round
Bedfordshire Times and Independent
Birmingham Daily Gazette
Birmingham Daily Post
Birmingham Mirror
Birmingham Mutual
Bradford Observer
British Controversialist
Buckingham Advertiser and Free Press
Chambers' Papers for the People
Charity Organisation Review
The City Jackdaw (Manchester)
The Englishwoman's Review
The Examiner
The Globe
The Graphic
Halifax Courier
The Highway: Midland Supplement
The Highway: A Monthly Journal of Education for the People
Huddersfield Chronicle [and West Yorkshire Advertiser]
The Illustrated London Magazine
Institute, and Lecturers' Gazette
International Journal of Ethics
Jarrow Express
Journal of the Society of Arts
Journal of the Statistical Society of London
Lancashire Evening Post
Leeds Mercury
Leeds Times
Lichfield Mercury
Literary World
Liverpool Mercury
The London Investigator: A Monthly Journal of Secularism
The London Quarterly Review
Magazine of Music

Manchester Courier [and Lancashire General Advertiser]
Manchester Examiner and Times
Manchester Guardian
Manchester Magazine: An Illustrated Northern Serial of Literature, Science, Art, and Social Progress
Manchester Quarterly: A Journal of Literature and Art
Manchester Review
Mason College Magazine
Monmouthshire Merlin and South Wales Advertiser
Monthly Literary and Scientific Lecturer
Morning Post
Morpeth Herald
New Zealander
Newcastle Courant
The Nineteenth Century
Northern Echo
Norwich Mercury
Nursing Record and Hospital World
One and All: The Organ of the Adult School Movement
Oxford University Extension Gazette
Pall Mall Gazette
Pitman's Popular Lecturer and Reader
Putnam's Magazine
Review of Reviews
School and College
Science
The Scotsman
Sheffield Daily Telegraph
Shields Daily Gazette
Shields Daily News
South Wales Daily News
Southern Literary Messenger
Sunderland Daily Echo and Shipping Gazette
Swindon Advertiser and North Wilts Chronicle
The Technologist, or Industrial Monthly: A Practical Journal for Manufacturers, Mechanics, and Builders
Times Educational Supplement
Tyrone Constitution
Western Times
Westminster Review
Working-Man's Friend, and Family Instructor
Yorkshire Post and Leeds Intelligencer

Reports and Transactions

Birmingham and Edgbaston Debating Society, *Annual Reports*
Birmingham and Midland Institute, *Annual Reports*

Halifax Sunday Lecture Society Minute Book, Yorkshire Archive Service, Calderdale (MISC 6/106)
House of Lords Debates
Ladies' Debating Society [Birmingham], *Annual Reports*
Leeds Mechanics' Institute, *Annual Reports*
Leeds Philosophical and Literary Society, *Annual Reports*
Northern Union of Mechanics' Institutions, *Annual Reports*
Proceedings of the Birmingham Philosophical Society
Sunday Lecture Society, *Annual Reports*
Transactions of the Manchester Geological Society
Transactions of the National Association for the Promotion of Social Science
Transactions of the Royal Historical Society
Yorkshire Union of Mechanics' Institutes, *Annual Reports*

Books and Articles

Adams, W. E. [William Edwin]. *Memoirs of a Social Atom*. New York: Augustus M. Kelley Publishers, 1968; originally published in 2 vols., 1903.

"Address by Samuel Ogden, Esq., J.P., President of the Athenaeum, in Celebration of the 50th Anniversary of the Foundation of the Institution." In *Manchester Athenaeum. Addresses 1835–1885*, 195–6. Manchester: For the Athenaeum, 1888.

An Act to Exempt from County, Borough, Parochial, and Other local Rates, Land and Buildings Occupied by Scientific or Literary Societies [1843] (6 & 7 Vict. c. 36).

An Act to Explain and Amend the Act for Exempting from Local Rates Land and Buildings Occupied by Scientific and Literary Societies [1857] (8 Vict. c. 35).

Arnold-Foster, H. O. *The Citizen Reader. For the Use of Schools*. London: Cassell, 1885.

Baines, Thomas. *History of the Commerce and Town of Liverpool, and of the Rise of Manufacturing Industry in the Adjoining Counties*. London: Longman, 1852.

Bernays, Albert James. *Household Chemistry; Or, Rudiments of the Science Applied to Every-day Life*. London: Samson Low, 1852.

Birmingham and Edgbaston Debating Society. *Report of Committee, Session 1895–6*. Birmingham: Cornish Bros., 1896.

"Birmingham and Midland Institute." *Ward and Lock's Pictorial Guide to Warwickshire*. London: Ward and Lock, 1883.

Birmingham Suburban and District Institutes Union. *An Address Delivered by the Most Honourable the Marquis of Lorne, KT, President, ... on October 5, 1886*. Birmingham: For the Union, 1886.

"Broadsides." Available online: http://www.bidsquare.com/online-auctions/potter-potter/broadside-for-lectures-on-electricity-galvanism-electro-magnetism-pneumatics-979079. Accessed July 21, 2020.

Campbell, George, 8th Duke of Argyll. "Address Delivered to the Members of the Glasgow Athenaeum, on the 21st January, 1851." In *The Importance of Literature to Men of Business: A Series of Addresses Delivered at Various Popular Institutions*, 253–78. London: John J. Griffin and Company, 1852.

Census of Great Britain, 1851. Education. England and Wales. Report and Tables. Presented to Both Houses of Parliament by Command of Her Majesty. London: E. Eyre and W. Spottiswoode, 1854.

Chamberlain, Joseph. "The Work of Severn Street School." In *Mr. Chamberlain's Speeches, Volume 1*, edited by Charles W. Boyd, 51–6. New York: Houghton Mifflin, 1914.
Chester, Harry. *Schools for Children and Institutes for Adults. An Address on National Education*. London: Longman, Green, 1860.
City of Norwich Technical School. *Prospectus of Day Classes for Manual Instruction, Evening Classes for Artisans, Recreative Classes, Scholarships, and University Extension Lectures, 1895–96*. Norwich: for the school, 1896.
Clarke, William J. *The Growth of the Suburban Institutes* (Birmingham: for the [Birmingham Suburban and District Institutes] Union, 1883 [reprinted from the *Birmingham Daily Mail*, November 17, 1883].
"Clubs, Reading Rooms, and Lecture Halls. (From the *Athenaeum*)." *Morning Post*, March 30, 1872: 7.
Cobbe, Frances Power. *Why Women Desire the Franchise*. London: National Society for Women's Suffrage, 1877.
"Common Informer," *House of Commons Debates*, November 6, 1934, vol. 293 cc. 843–6.
Common Informers Act, 14 & 15 (Geo. 6, c. 39).
Cooper, Thomas. *Eight Letters to the Young Men of the Working Classes*. London: F. Farrah, 1868.
Curzon, Frank. "List of Lectures." In Yorkshire Union of Mechanics' Institutes, *Annual Report for 1883*, appendix. Leeds: Goodall & Suddick, 1883.
Dale, R. W. "*A Sermon on the Tercentenary of the Birth of William Shakespeare, Preached at Stratford-on-Avon, on Sunday, April 24, 1864*. London: Hamilton, Adams, & Co., 1864.
Dawson, George. *An Address to the Eclectic Society of Birmingham, at Their First Public Meeting*. Birmingham: E. C. Osbourne, 1846.
De Fraine, John. *Autobiography: Or Forty Years of Public Lecturing Work, and Recollections of the Great and Good*. London: Bowers Brothers, 1900.
Dodd, J. P. *Lecture on the Best Means of Promoting the Intellectual Improvement of Youth. Delivered in the Lecture Room of the Literary and Philosophical Society of Newcastle, on September 26th, 1846*. London: Longman, Brown, Green, and Longmans, 1847.
Dodd, J. P. *Ten Letters on Self-Education, with Introduction and Notes*. Newcastle: Hamilton & Adams, 1856.
Duppa, B. F. *A Manual for Mechanics Institutions. Published under the Superintendence of the Society for the Diffusion of Useful Knowledge*. London: Longman, 1839.
Edwards, Edward. *Memoirs of Libraries, Including a Handbook of Library Economy, Vol. 1*. London: Trubnor & Co., 1859.
Faraday, Michael. *A Course of Six Lectures on the Chemical History of a Candle*, edited by W. Crookes. London: Griffin, Bohn & Co., 1861.
Greenbank, Thomas. *The British Orator: Comprising Observations on Vocal Gymnastics, Articulation, Melody, Modulation, Force, Time, and Gesture*. London: Simkin and Marshall, 1849.
Guy's Learner's Poetic Task-Book. London: R. Clay, 1849.
Handbook of Birmingham. Prepared for the Members of the British Association. Birmingham: Hall and English, 1886.
Herschel, J. F. W. "Address Delivered to the Subscribers to the Windsor and Eton Public Library, on the 29th January 1833." In *The Importance of Literature to Men of Business: A Series of Addresses Delivered at Various Popular Institutions*, 31–48. London: John J. Griffin and Company, 1852.

Hervey, Arthur. *A Suggestion for Supplying the Literary, Scientific, and Mechanics' Institutes of Great Britain and Ireland with Lecturers from the Universities.* Cambridge: Macmillan & Co., 1855.

Higginson, Edward. *Astro-Theology; or, The Religion of Astronomy: Four Lectures in Reference to the Controversy on the "Plurality of Worlds," as Lately Sustained between Sir David Brewster and an Essayist.* London: E. T. Whitfield, 1855.

Higinbotham, George. *Self-Education: A Lecture Delivered at the Brighton [Australia] Mechanics' Institute on Friday, August 8, 1862, Published by Request of the Committee.* Melbourne: Blundell and Ford, 1862.

Hole, James. *An Essay on the History and Management of Literary, Scientific, and Mechanics' Institutions: And Especially How Far They May Be Developed and Combined so as to Promote the Moral Well-Being and Industry of the Country.* London: Longman, Brown, 1853.

Holyoake, George Jacob. *Literary Institutions: Their Relation to Public Opinion.* London: J. Watson, 1854.

Hudson, James William. *History of Adult Education, in Which Is Comprised a Full and Complete History of the Mechanics' and Literary Institutions, Athenaeums, etc.* London: Longmans, 1851.

Huxley, Thomas. "Preface," *Discourses, Biological and Geological.* London: Macmillan and Co., 1894.

Huxley, Thomas. *Lay Sermons, Addresses, and Reviews.* London: Macmillan and Co., 1870.

Kitchin, G. *A Lecture on Lectures. Delivered before the Members of the Bradford Church of England Literary Institute.* London: Bell and Daldy, 1859.

Knight, John Joseph. "Isabella Glyn," *Oxford Dictionary of National Biography, 1885–1900, Volume 22.* Available online: https://en.wikisource.org/wiki/Glyn,_Isabella_Dallas[DNB00]. Accessed July 18, 2020.

Langford, John Alfred. *Modern Birmingham and Its Institutions, Vol. 2: A Chronicle of Local Events, from 1841 to 1871.* Birmingham: E. C. Osbourne, 1873.

A Leaflet Promoting Lectures by Henry Crowther (born c. 1848–29 November 1937), Former Curator of Leeds Museum, Leeds, West Yorkshire, England, n.d.. Available online: https://commons.wikimedia.org/wiki/File:Henry_Crowther_(3).JPG. Accessed June 24, 2023.

Literary and Scientific Institutions Act, 1854 (17 & 18 Vict. c. 112).

Mackenzie, Eneas. "Literary Institutions: Literary and Philosophical Society." *Historical Account of Newcastle-upon-Tyne Including the Borough of Gateshead,* 461–86. Newcastle-upon-Tyne, 1827. Available online: *British History Online* http://www.british-history.ac.uk/no-series/newcastle-historical-account/pp461–486. Accessed January 24, 2019.

Mackinder, H. J., and M. E. Sadler. *University Extension: Has It a Future?* Oxford: Horace Hart, 1890.

Magnus, Phillip. "Lectures and Lecturing. An address to the Students of the Working Men's College, January 23, 1893." In *Educational Aims and Efforts, 1880–1910,* edited by Phillip Magnus, 246–61. London: Longman Green, 1910.

"M. E." [Foster Barham Zincke]. *How Much Longer Are We to Continue Teaching Nothing More than Was Taught Two or Three Centuries Ago?* London: J. Hatchard & Son, 1850.

Manchester Athenaeum, *Addresses, 1835–1885, also, Report of Proceedings of the Meeting of the Members in Celebration of the 50th Anniversary of the Institution, October 28th, 1885.*

McCulloch, John Ramsay. *A Descriptive and Statistical Account of the British Empire: Exhibiting Its Extent, Physical Capacities, Population, Industry, and Civil and Religious Institutions, Volume 2*. London: Longmans, 1854.

Morley, John. *On Popular Culture. An Inaugural Address Delivered [to the Birmingham and Midland Institute] in the Town Hall, Birmingham, on the 5th of October, 1876*. London: Virtue, 1876, 4.

Muirhead, J. H. *A Liberal Education: An Address to the Students of Mason University College, Birmingham*. Birmingham: Cornish Bros., 1899.

Naylor, F. W. *Popular Libraries in Rural Districts*. London: Simkin, Marshall, & Co., 1855.

Pond, J. B. *Eccentricities of Genius: Memories of Famous Men and Women of the Platform and the Stage*. New York: Dillingham Co., 1900.

Pfeiffer, Emily. *Women and Work. Treating on the Relation to Health and Physical Development, of the Higher Education of Girls, and the Intellectual or More Systematised Effort of Women*. London: Trubner & Co., 1888.

Randall, Samuel Sidwell. *Mental and Moral Culture, and Popular Education, 2nd. edition*. New York: C. S. Francis & Co., 1855.

Reid, Hugo [as Roger Boswell]. *The Art of Conversation, Giving Hints, Suggestions, and Rules for Cultivating and Promoting Social Intercourse* (London: Cassell and Co., 1867; 1st. edition, 1862). In Andrew St. George, *The Descent of Manners: Etiquette, Rules and the Victorians*. London: Chatto and Windus, 1993.

Reid, Thomas Wemyss. *A Memoir of John Deakin Heaton, M.D., of Leeds*. London: Longman, Greens, 1883.

Report of the Proceedings Connected with the Grand Soirée of the Manchester Athenaeum, Held on Thursday, October 3rd, 1844: From the Manchester Guardian of Saturday, October 5th, 1844. Manchester: Cave and Sever, 1844.

Report of the Proceedings at the Eleventh Annual Soiree of the Blaydon and Stella Mechanics' Institution, Held in the Lecture Hall, Blaydon, on Monday, 31st August, 1857. Blaydon: Thomas Francis Moseley, 1857.

Roberts, R. D., *Eighteen Years of University Extension*. Cambridge: Cambridge University Press, 1891.

Rowton, Frederic. *The Debater: A New Theory of the Art of Speaking*. 2nd. edition. London: Longmans, Green, & Co., 1850.

Scott, Alexander John. *Self-Education: An Opening Lecture Delivered to the Members of the Salford Mechanics' Institution, on Wednesday Evening, January 11th, 1854*. Manchester: A. Ireland and Company, 1854.

Scott, Benjamin. *Practical Hints to Unpractised Lecturers to the Working Classes: Fourth Edition*. London: Q. P. Baron, 1858.

Seeley, J. R. *A Midland University: An Address Delivered [to the Midland Institute] in the Town Hall, Birmingham, on the 10th October, 1887*. Birmingham: Offices of the Journal, 1887, 6.

Smiles, Samuel. *Self-Help: With Illustrations of Character and Conduct*. London: John Murray, 1859.

Smith, Swire. *The Work of Mechanics' Institutes in Our Towns. A Paper Read at the Conference of the Delegates and Members of the Yorkshire Union of Mechanics' Institutes, 1877*. Leeds: Charles Goodall, 1877.

Society for the Encouragement of Arts, Manufactures, and Commerce, Union of Institutions. *List of Lecturers and Their Subjects, Together with a List of the Institutions in Union. Revised edition, 14 August 1854*. London: W. Trounce, 1854.

Society for the Encouragement of Arts, Manufactures, and Commerce, Union of Institutions. *List of Lecturers and Their Subjects, Together with a List of the Institutions in Union*. London: W. Trounce, 1862.
Society of Arts. *Subjects for Discussion Classes in Institutions*. London: W. Trounce, 1862.
St. Clair, George, ed. *Biographical Lectures by George Dawson, M. A*. London: Kegan Paul, Trench & Co., 1886.
Stevens, Thomas, and William Lewis Schactleben. *Across Asia on a Bicycle*. New York: Century Co., 1894.
Sunday Lecture Society. *Mr. W. Henry Domville's Report to the Preliminary Meeting Held at Freemasons' Tavern, on the 25th of November, 1869*. London: Kenny & Co., 1869.
Sunday Observance Act 1781 (21 Geo. 3. c. 49).
The History of Hartlepool. Hartlepool: Alfred Moore, 1844.
The Lecture Agency, Ltd. *Concerning Popular Lectures*. London: The Lecture Agency, Ltd., 1911.
Thompson, Henry. *Cremation: The Treatment of the Body after Death*. London: Henry S. King and Co., 1874.
Timmins, Samuel. *Address, Delivered at the Annual Meeting of Members, 12th January 1874 [at the Birmingham and Midland Institute]*. Birmingham: Offices of the Journal, 1874.
Timmins, Samuel. "Charles Cowden Clarke." *Oxford Dictionary of National Biography, 1885–1900, Volume 10*. Available online: https://en.wikisource.org/wiki/Dictionary_of _National_Biography,_1885-1900/Clarke,_Charles_Cowden. Accessed November 4, 2023.
Traice, W. H. J. *Hand-Book of Mechanics' Institutions, With Priced Catalogue of Books Suitable for Libraries*. 2d edition. London: Longman Green, 1863.
Vaughan, Robert. *The Age of Great Cities; Or, Modern Society Viewed in Its Relation to Intelligence, Morals, and Religion*. London: Jackson and Walford, 1843.
Wall, James. "Essay on Mechanics' Institutions." In *Prize Essays of the Northern Association of Literary, Mechanics', and Educational Institutions, 1857*, 1–18. Newcastle-on-Tyne: John Bell, 1858.
Wallas, Graham. *University Extension Lectures: Syllabus of a Course of Lectures on the English Citizen Past and Present*. London: Co-operative Printing Society, Ltd., 1891.
Watson, Robert Spence. *The History of the Literary and Philosophical Society of Newcastle-upon-Tyne (1793–1896)*. London: Walter Scott, Limited, 1897.
Wild, Arthur F. V. *A Criticism of the Second Report of the Select Committee of the House of Lords on the Lord's Day Act, 1781 (21 Geo. III c. 49), Appointed on Motion for the Second Reading of the Sunday Bill, 1895*. London: The Sunday Lecture Society, 1897.
Wilson, Wright. *The Life of George Dawson, MA, Glasgow, Being an Account of His Parentage and His Career as a Preacher, Lecturer, Municipal and Social Reformer, Politician and Journalist*. Birmingham: Percival Jones Ltd., 1905.
Women Workers. Papers Read at a Conference, Convened by the Birmingham Ladies' Union of Workers Among Women and Girls, In November, 1890. Birmingham: Lawrence and Company, 1891.
Workers' Education Association. *Oxford and Working-Class Education: Being the Report of a Joint Committee of the University and Working-Class Representatives on the Relation of the University to the Higher Education of Workpeople*. Oxford: Oxford University Press, 1908.
Wright, Thomas. *Our New Masters*. London: Strahan & Co., 1873.

Secondary Sources

Books and Articles

Ablow, Rachel. "Unsettling Sympathy." *Victorian Studies* 64, no. 4 (2022): 573–8.
Adams, Amanda. *Performing Authorship in the Nineteenth-Century Transatlantic Lecture Tour*. Aldershot: Ashgate, 2014.
Adelman, Juliana. *Communities of Science in Nineteenth-Century Ireland*. London: Pickering and Chatto, 2009.
Alberti, Samuel J. M. M. "Conversaziones and the Experience of Science in Victorian England." *Journal of Victorian Culture* 8, no. 2 (2003): 208–30.
Allan, D. G. C. "The Society of Arts and Government, 1754–1800: Public Encouragement of Arts, Manufactures, and Commerce in Eighteenth-Century England." *Eighteenth-Century Studies* 7, no. 4 (1974): 434–52.
Allen, Joan. *Rutherford's Ladder: The Making of Northumbria University 1871–1996*. Chicago: Northumbria University Press, 2005.
Altick, Richard. *The English Common Reader: A Social History of the Mass Reading Public, 1800–1900*. Chicago: University of Chicago Press, 1957; 2nd. edition, Ohio State University Press, 1998.
Ashplant, T. G. "London Working Men's Clubs, 1875–1914." In *Popular Culture and Class Conflict 1590–1914: Explorations in the History of Labour and Leisure*, edited by Eileen Yeo and Stephen Yeo, 241–70. Sussex: Harvester Press, 1981.
Baragwanath, Pam, and Ken James. *These Walls Speak Volumes: A History of Mechanics' Institutes in Australia*. Victoria: Ken James, 2015.
Barlow, Paul, and Colin Trodd, eds. *Governing Cultures: Art Institutions in Victorian London*. Aldershot: Ashgate Press, 2000.
Barton, Ruth. "Sunday Lecture Societies: Naturalistic Scientists, Unitarians, and Secularists Unite against Sabbatarian Legislation." In *Victorian Scientific Naturalism: Community, Identity, Continuity*, edited by Gowan Dawson and Bernard Lightman, 189–219. Chicago: University of Chicago Press, 2014.
Barton, Susan. "The Mechanics Institutes: Pioneers of Leisure and Excursion Travel." *Transactions of the Leicestershire Archaeological and Historical Society* LXVII (1993): 47–58.
Beaven, Brad. *Leisure, Citizenship and Working-Class Men in Britain, 1850–1945*. Manchester: Manchester University Press, 2005.
Beaven, Brad, and John Griffiths, "Creating the Exemplary Citizen: The Changing Notion of Citizenship in Britain 1870–1939." *Contemporary British History* 22, no. 2 (2008): 203–25.
Beaven, Brad, and John Griffiths. "Urban Elites, Socialists and Notions of Citizenship in an Industrial Boomtown: Coventry, c. 1870–1914." *Labour History Review* 69, no. 1 (2004): 3–18.
Bilston, Sarah, "'Your Vile Suburbs Can Offer Nothing but the Deadness of the Grave': The Stereotyping of Early Victorian Suburbia." *Victorian Literature and Culture* 41, no. 4 (2013): 621–42.
Birch, Dinah. *Our Victorian Education*. London: Blackwell, 2008.
Bishop, Nicola. *Lower-Middle-Class Nation: The White-Collar Worker in British Popular Culture*. London: Bloomsbury Academic Press, 2021.

Black, Alistair. "Lost Worlds of Culture: Victorian Libraries, Library History and Prospects for a History of Information." *Journal of Victorian Culture* 2, no. 1 (1997): 95–112.
Boase, George Clement. "Daniel Puseley." *Dictionary of National Biography, 1885–1900, Volume 47*. Available online: https://en.wikisource.org/wiki/Puseley,_Daniel_[DNB00]. Accessed July 21, 2020.
Bode, Carl. *The American Lyceum: Town Meeting of the Mind*. Carbondale: Southern Illinois University Press, 1956.
Bonea, Amelia, Melissa Dickson, Sally Shuttleworth, and Jennifer Wallis. *Anxious Times: Medicine and Modernity in Nineteenth-Century Britain*. Pittsburgh: University of Pittsburgh Press, 2019.
Bott, George. *Sponsored Talk. A History of the Keswick Lecture Society*. Keswick: The Society, 1968.
Bradley, Matthew, and Juliet John, eds. *Reading and the Victorians*. Farnham: Ashgate, 2015.
Briggs, Asa. *Victorian Cities*. London: Odhams Books, 1963.
Brock, Michael G., and Mark C. Curthoys, eds. *The History of the University of Oxford. Volumes 6 and 7: Nineteenth-Century*. Oxford: Oxford University Press, 2000.
Brown, Richard D. *The Strength of a People: The Idea of an Informed Citizenry in America 1650–1870*. Chapel Hill: University of North Carolina Press, 1996.
Bud, Robert, and Gerrylynn K. Roberts, *Science versus Practice: Chemistry in Victorian Britain*. Manchester: Manchester University Press, 1984.
Clark, Peter. *British Clubs and Societies 1580–1800: The Origins of an Associational World*. Oxford: Oxford University Press, 2000.
Clarke, Richard. *Informal Adult Education between the Wars: The Curious Case of The Selborne Lecture Bureau*. London: University of London, 2005.
Clifford, David, Elisabeth Wadge, Martin Willis, and Alex Warwick. *Repositioning Victorian Sciences: Shifting Centres in Nineteenth-Century Scientific Thinking*. New York: Anthem Press, 2006.
Collins, P. A. W. "Dickens and Adult Education." *British Journal of Educational Studies* 3, no. 2 (1955): 115–27.
Collins, Phillip. "'Agglomerating Dollars with Prodigious Rapidity': British Pioneers on the American Lecture Circuit." In *Victorian Literature and Society: Essays Presented to Richard D. Altick*, edited by James R. Kinkaid and Albert J. Kuhn, 2–29. Columbus, OH: Ohio State University Press, 1984.
Cross, Gary. *A Social History of Leisure Since 1600*. State College, PA: Venture Publishing, 1990.
Crowe, M. J. *The Extraterrestrial Life Debate, 1750–1900: The Idea of a Plurality of Worlds from Kant to Lowell*. Cambridge: Cambridge University Press, 1986; 2nd. edition, Dover Publications, 1999.
Cunliffe-Jones, Janet. "A Rare Phenomenon: A Woman's Contribution to 19th-Century Adult Education." *Journal of Educational Administration and History* 24, no. 1 (1992): 1–17.
Cunningham, Hugh. *Leisure in the Industrial Revolution*. London: Croom Helm, 1980.
Daunton, Martin. "Introduction." In *The Organisation of Knowledge in Victorian Britain*, 1–28. Oxford: Oxford University Press, 2005.
Davis, John. "Radical Clubs and London Politics, 1870–1900." In *Metropolis London: Histories and Representations Since 1800*, edited by David Feldman and Gareth Stedman Jones, 103–28. London: Routledge, 1989.

Dennis, R. *Cities in Modernity: Representations and Productions of Metropolitan Space, 1840–1930*. Cambridge: Cambridge University Press, 2008.
Dent, A. P. "The Union of Lancashire and Cheshire Institutes. An Outline of Its Functions and Work." *Journal of the Textile Institute Proceedings* 29, no. 7 (1938): 365–73.
Deslandes, Paul R. *Oxbridge Men: British Masculinity & the Undergraduate Experience, 1850–1920*. Bloomington, IN: Indiana University Press, 2005.
Doern, Kristen G. "Balfour, Clara Lucas." *Oxford Dictionary of National Biography* (online edition). https://doi.org/10.1093/ref:odnb/1183. Accessed September 23, 2004.
Draper, W. H. *University Extension 1873–1923*. Cambridge: Cambridge University Press, 1923.
Duffy, Séamus S. "'Treasures Open to the Wise': A Survey of Early Mechanics' Institutes and Similar Organisations." *Saothar* 15 (1990): 39–47.
Eley, Geoff. "Culture, Nation and Gender." In *Gendered Nations: Nationalisms and Gender Order in the Long Nineteenth Century*, edited by Ida Blom, Karen Hagemann, and Catherine Hall, 27–40. Oxford: Berg, 2000.
Ellis, Heather. "Elite Education and the Development of Mass Elementary Schooling in England, 1870–1930." In *Mass Education and the Limits of State Building, c. 1870–1930*, edited by Laurence Brockliss and Nicola Sheldon, 46–70. New York: Palgrave Macmillan, 2012.
Ellis, Heather. "Knowledge, Character and Professionalisation in Nineteenth-Century British Science." *History of Education* 43 no. 6 (2014): 777–92.
Everitt, Anthony. "Culture and Citizenship." In *Citizens: Towards a Citizenship Culture*, edited by Bernard Crick, 64–73. London: Blackwell, 2001.
Fatout, Paul. *Mark Twain on the Lecture Circuit*. Carbondale, IL: Southern Illinois University Press, 1969.
Feely, Catherine Clare. "Scissors-and-Paste Journalism." In *Dictionary of Nineteenth-Century Journalism in Great Britain and Ireland*, edited by Laurel Brake and Marysa Demoor, 561. London: Academia Press, 2009.
Fieldhouse, Roger. *A History of Modern British Adult Education*. Leicester, England: National Institute of Adult Continuing Education, 1996.
Fieldhouse, Roger. *The Workers' Educational Association: Aims and Achievements 1903–1977*. New York: Syracuse University, 1977.
Finnegan, Diarmud A. *Natural History Societies and Civic Culture in Victorian Scotland*. London: Pickering and Chatto, 2009.
Flint, Kate. *The Woman Reader 1837–1914*. Oxford: Oxford University Press, 1993.
Freeden, Michael. "Civil Society and the Good Citizen: Competing Conceptions of Citizenship in Twentieth-Century Britain." In *Civil Society in British History: Ideas, Identities, Institutions*, edited by Jose Harris, 276–81. Oxford: Oxford University Press, 2003.
Freeman, Mark. "Adult Education History in Britain: Past, Present and Future (Part 1)." *Paedagogica Historica* 56, no. 3 (2020): 384–95.
Fyfe, Aileen, and Bernard Lightman, "Science in the Marketplace: An Introduction." In *Science in the Marketplace: Nineteenth Century Sites and Experiences*, edited by Aileen Fyfe and Bernard Lightman, 1–19. Chicago: University of Chicago Press, 2007.
Garner, A. D. "The Society of Arts and the Mechanics' Institutes: The Co-ordination of Endeavour towards Scientific and Technical Education, 1851–54." *History of Education* 14, no. 4 (1985): 255–62.

Garnett, Richard. "Charles John Plumptre." *Dictionary of National Biography 1885–1900*, vol. 45. Available online at https://en.wikisource.org/wiki/Dictionary_of_National_Biography,_1885-1900/Plumptre,_Charles_John. Accessed August 9, 2022.

"George H. Snazelle." OperaScotland: Listings and Performance History. http://www.operascotland.org/person/3375/George-Snazelle. Accessed June 23, 2020.

Georgiou, Dion. "Leisure in London's Suburbs, 1880–1939." *London Journal*, 39, no. 3 (2014): 175–86.

Gerard, David E. "Subscription Libraries," in *Encyclopedia of Library and Information Science, Volume 29*, edited by Allen Kent, Harold Lancour, and Jay Elwood Daily, 205–21. New York: Marcel Dekker, 1980.

Gibson, Susannah. *The Spirit of Inquiry: How One Extraordinary Society Shaped Modern Science*. Oxford: Oxford University Press, 2019.

Gilbert, Pamela K. *Disease, Desire, and the Body in Victorian Women's Popular Novels*. Cambridge, MA: Cambridge University Press, 1997.

Gilchrist Educational Trust. *Pioneer Work in Education*. Cambridge: Cambridge University Press, 1930.

"The Gilchrist Trust: Pioneer Work in Education." *The Times Educational Supplement* no. 2 (1910): 26.

Gleadle, Kathryn. *Borderline Citizens: Women, Gender, and Political Culture in Britain 1815–1867*. Oxford: Oxford University Press, 2009.

Goldman, Lawrence. "The First Students in the Workers' Educational Association: Individual Enlightenment and Collective Advance." In *A Ministry of Enthusiasm: Centenary Essays on the Workers' Educational Association*, edited by Stephen K. Roberts, 41–58. London: Pluto Press, 2003.

Goldman, Lawrence, ed. *Welfare and Social Policy in Britain since 1870: Essays in Honour of Jose Harris*. Oxford: Oxford University Press, 2019.

Gosden, P. H. J. H., and A. J. Taylor, eds. *Studies in the History of a University to Commemorate the Centenary of the University of Leeds 1874–1974*. Leeds: University of Leeds, 1975.

Gotch, Adam. "The Lecture League." *Journal of the T. E. Lawrence Society* 25, no.1 (2016): 29–63.

Grant, Matthew. "Historicizing Citizenship in Post-War Britain." *Historical Journal* 59, no. 4 (2016): 1187–206.

Green, Andy. "Technical Education and State Formation in Nineteenth-Century England and France." *History of Education* 24, no. 2 (1995): 123–39.

Griest, Guinevere L. "A Victorian Leviathan: Mudie's Select Library." *Nineteenth-Century Fiction* 20, no. 2 (1965): 103–26.

Griffiths, John R. "Civic Communication in Britain: A Study of the *Municipal Journal c. 1893–1910*." *Journal of Urban History* 34, no. 5 (2008): 775–94.

Gunn, Simon, and Rachel Bell. *Middle Classes: Their Rise and Sprawl*. London: Weidenfeld and Nicolson, 2011.

Hall, Catherine, Keith McClelland, and Jane Rendall. *Defining the Victorian Nation: Class, Race, Gender and the Reform Act of 1867*. Cambridge: Cambridge University Press, 2000.

Harrison, Brian. "Civil Society by Accident? Paradoxes of Voluntarism and Pluralism in the Nineteenth and Twentieth Centuries." In *Civil Society in British History: Ideas, Identities, Institutions*, edited by Jose Harris, 79–96. Oxford: Oxford University Press, 2003.

Harrison, Brian. "Planning in Modern Britain: Its History and Dimensions." In *Welfare and Social Policy in Britain since 1870: Essays in Honour of Jose Harris*, edited by Lawrence Goldman, 79–102. Oxford: Oxford University Press, 2019.
Harrison, J. F. C. *Social Reform in Victorian Leeds: The Work of James Hole, 1820–1895*. Leeds: Thoresby Society, 1954.
Hartog, Philip Joseph. "Albert James Bernays." *Dictionary of National Biography, 1901 Supplement*. Available online: https://en.wikisource.org/wiki/Bernays,_Albert_James_[DNB01]. Accessed July 19, 2020.
Hays, J. N. "The London Lecturing Empire, 1800–1850," in *Metropolis and Province: Science in British Culture 1780–1850*, edited by Ian Inkster and Jack Morrell, 91–119. London: Hutchinson, 1983.
Heater, Derek. *Citizenship in Britain: A History*. Edinburgh: Edinburgh University Press, 2006.
Heathorn, Stephen. "'Let Us Remember that We, Too, Are English': Constructions of Citizenship and National Identity in English Elementary School Reading Books, 1880–1914." *Victorian Studies* 38 (1995): 395–428.
Hemming, John P. "The Mechanics' Institutes in the Lancashire and Yorkshire Textile Districts from 1850." *Journal of Educational Administration and History* 9, no. 1 (1977): 18–33.
Hewitt, Martin. "Aspects of Platform Culture in Nineteenth-Century Britain." *Nineteenth-Century Prose* 29, no.1 (2002): 1–34.
Hewitt, Martin. "Beyond Scientific Spectacle: Image and Word in Nineteenth-Century Popular Lecturing." In *Popular Exhibitions, Science and Showmanship, 1840–1910*, edited by Joe Kember, John Plunkett, and Jill A. Sullivan, 79–96. London: Pickering and Chatto, 2012.
Hewitt, Martin. "Confronting the Modern City: The Manchester Free Public Library, 1850–80." *Urban History* 27, no. 1 (2000): 62–88.
Hewitt, Martin. *The Emergence of Stability in the Industrial City: Manchester, 1832–67*. Aldershot: Scolar Press, 1996.
Hewitt, Martin. "Hole, James." *Oxford Dictionary of National Biography* (online edition). https://doi.org/10.1093/ref:odnb/94048. Accessed September 23, 2004.
Hewitt, Martin. "Popular Platform Religion: Arthur Mursell at the Free Trade Hall, 1856–65." *Manchester Region History Review* 10 (1996): 29–39.
Hewitt, Martin. "Preaching from the Platform." In *Oxford Handbook of The British Sermon 1689–1901*, edited by Keith A. Francis and William Gibson, 79–96. Oxford: Oxford University Press, 2012.
Hewitt, Martin. "Ralph Waldo Emerson, George Dawson, and the Control of the Lecture Platform in Mid-nineteenth Century Manchester." *Nineteenth-Century Prose* 25, no. 2 (1998): 1–25.
Heyck, T. W. *The Transformation of Intellectual Life in Victorian England*. London: St. Martin's Press, 1982.
Higgitt, Rebekah, and Charles W. J. Withers. "Science and Sociability: Women as Audience at the British Association for the Advancement of Science, 1831–1901." *Isis* 99, no. 1 (2008): 1–27.
Hobbs, Andrew. "Five Million Poems, or the Local Press as Poetry Publisher, 1800–1900." *Victorian Periodicals Review* 45, no. 4 (2012): 488–92.
Hodos, Jerome I. *Second Cities: Globalization and Local Politics in Manchester and Philadelphia*. Philadelphia, PA: Temple University Press, 2011.

Hoegaerts, Josephine. "Speaking Like Intelligent Men: Vocal Articulations of Authority and Identity in the House of Commons in the Nineteenth Century." *Radical History Review* 121 (January 2015): 123–44.

Howes, Anton. *Arts and Minds: How the Royal Society of Arts Changed a Nation*. Princeton, NJ: Princeton University Press, 2021.

Hudson, Derek, and Kenneth W. Luckhurst. *The Royal Society of Arts 1754–1954*. London: John Murray, 1954.

Hurt, J. S. "General Notes: Studies in the Societies Archives. Harry Chester: The Early Years." *Journal of the Royal Society of the Arts* 116, no. 5138 (1968): 156–9 ["The Early Years"]; 116, no. 5139 (1968): 262–4 ["The Middle Years"]; 116, no. 5140 (1968): 321–3 ["The Later Years"].

Inkster, Ian. "Culture, Institutions and Urbanity: The Itinerant Science Lecturer in Sheffield 1790–1850." In *Essays in the Social and Economic History of South Yorkshire*, edited by S. Pollard and C. Holmes, 218–32. Sheffield: South Yorkshire County Council, 1976.

Inkster, Ian. "Popularised Culture and Steam Intellect: A Case Study of Liverpool and Its Region, circa 1820–1850s." In *The Steam Intellect Societies: Essays on Culture, Education, and Industry circa 1820–1914*, edited by Ian Inkster, 44–59. Nottingham: University of Nottingham Press, 1985.

Inkster, Ian. "The Public Lecture as an Instrument of Science Education for Adults: The Case of Great Britain, c. 1750–1850." *Paedagogica Historica* 20, no. 1 (1980): 80–107.

Inkster, Ian. "Science and the Mechanics' Institutes, 1820–1850: The Case of Sheffield." *Annals of Science* 32 (1975): 451–74.

Inkster, Ian. "Science and Society in the Metropolis: Preliminary Examination of the Social and Institutional Context of the Askesian Society of London, 1796–1807." *Annals of Science* 34, no. 1 (1977): 1–32.

Inkster, Ian. "The Social Context of an Educational Movement: A Revisionist Approach to the English Mechanics' Institutes, 1820–850." *Oxford Review of Education* 2 (1976): 277–307.

Iwama, Toshihiko. "Voluntary Societies and the Urban Local Community: A Case Study of the Halifax Mechanics' Institution." *Family & Community History* 11, no. 1 (2008): 17–25.

Jennings, Bernard. *The University Extension Movement in Victorian and Edwardian England*. Hull: University of Hull, 1992.

Jennings, Bernard. "The WEA: The Foundation and the Founder." In *A Ministry of Enthusiasm: Centenary Essays on the Workers' Educational Association*, edited by Stephen K. Roberts, 12–25. London: Pluto Press, 2003.

Jepson, N. A. *The Beginnings of English University Adult Education*. Leeds: Michael Joseph, 1973.

Jones, Aled. "The *Dart* and the Damning of the Sylvan Stream: Journalism and Political Culture in the Late-Victorian City." In *Encounters in the Victorian Press: Editors, Authors, Readers*, edited by Laurel Brake and Julie F. Codell, 177–94. New York: Palgrave Macmillan, 2005.

Jones, H. S. "The Civic Moment in British Social Thought: Civil Society and the Ethics of Citizenship, c. 1880–1914." In *Welfare and Social Policy in Britain since 1870: Essays in Honour of Jose Harris*, edited by Lawrence Goldman, 29–43. Oxford: Oxford University Press, 2019.

Kargon, Robert H., *Science in Victorian Manchester: Enterprise and Expertise*. Baltimore: Johns Hopkins University Press: 1977; 2nd. edition. New Brunswick, NJ: Transaction Publishers, 2010.

Karpenko, Lara, and Shalyn Claggett, eds. *Strange Science: Investigating the Limits of Knowledge in the Victorian Age*. University of Michigan Press, 2017.

Kelly, Thomas. *George Birkbeck: Pioneer of Adult Education*. Liverpool: Liverpool University Press, 1957.

Kelly, Thomas. *A History of Public Libraries in Great Britain 1845–1975*. London: The Library Association, 1973.

Kelly, Thomas. "The Origin of Mechanics' Institutes." *British Journal of Educational Studies* 1, no.1 (1952): 17–27.

Kember, Joe. "The Lecture-Brokers: The Role of Impresarios and Agencies in the Global Anglophone Circuit for Lantern Lecturing, 1850–1920." *Early Popular Visual Culture* 17, nos. 3–4 (2019): 279–303.

Kennaway, J. "Two Kinds of 'Literary Poison': Diseases of the Learned and Overstimulating Novels in Georgian Britain." *Literature and Medicine* 34, no. 2 (2016): 252–77.

Kitson Clark, Edward. *A History of 100 Years of the Life of the Leeds Philosophical and Literary Society*. Leeds: Jowett and Sowry, 1924.

Kitson Clark, Edward, *Leeds Conversation Club, 1849–1939*. Leeds: Conversation Club, 1939.

Lampert, Sara. "Bringing Music to the Lyceumites: The Bureaus and the Transformation of Lyceum Entertainment." In *The Cosmopolitan Lyceum: Lecture Culture and the Globe in Nineteenth-Century America*, edited by Tom F. Wright, 67–89. Amherst: University of Massachusetts Press, 2013.

Lane, Christopher. "On the Victorian Afterlife of the 1781 Sunday Observance Act," *BRANCH: Britain, Representation and Nineteenth-Century History,* edited by Dino Franco Felluga. Available online: https://branchcollective.org/. Accessed October 26, 2014.

Laqueur, Thomas. *Religion and Respectability: Sunday Schools and Working Class Culture, 1780–1850*. New Haven, CT: Yale University Press, 1976.

Laurent, John. "Science, Society and Politics in Late Nineteenth-Century England: A Further Look at Mechanics' Institutes." *Social Studies of Science* 14, no. 4 (1984): 585–619.

Lawrie, Alexandra. *The Beginnings of University English*. Oxford: Oxford University Press, 2014.

Lawton, Robert. "An Age of Great Cities." *The Town Planning Review* 43, no. 3 (1972): 199–224.

Leaney, Enda. "'Evanescent Impressions': Public Lectures and the Popularization of Science in Ireland, 1770–1860." *Eire-Ireland* 43, nos. 3–4 (Fall/Winter 2008): 157–82.

Lees, Andrew. *Cities Perceived: Urban Society in European and American Thought, 1820–1940*. New York: Columbia University Press, 1985.

Lightman, Bernard. "*Knowledge* Confronts *Nature*: Richard Proctor and Popular Science Periodicals." In *Culture and Science in the Nineteenth-Century Media*, edited by Louise Henson, Geoffrey Cantor, Gowan Dawson, Richard Noakes, Sally Shuttleworth, and Jonathan R. Topham, 199–210. Aldershot: Ashgate Publishing, 2004.

Lightman, Bernard. "Lecturing in the Spatial Economy of Science." In *Science in the Marketplace: Nineteenth Century Sites and Experiences*, edited by Aileen Fyfe and Bernard Lightman, 97–132. Chicago: University of Chicago Press, 2007.

Lowden, Bronwyn. *Mechanics' Institutes, Schools of Arts, Athenaeums, etc.: An Australian Checklist – 3rd. Edition*. Donvale, Australia: Lowden Publishing Co., 2010.

Lowe, Eugenia. "The Concept of Citizenship in Twentieth-Century Britain: Analysing Contexts of Development." In *Reforming the Constitution: Debates in Twentieth-Century Britain*, edited by Peter Catterall, Wolfram, and Ulrike Walton-Jordan, 179–99. London: Frank Cass, 2000.

Lowerson, J. R. "Baines, Sir Edward." *Oxford Dictionary of National Biography* (online edition). https://doi.org/10.1093/ref:odnb/1090 Accessed September 23, 2004.

Lubenow, William C. *"Only Connect": Learned Societies in Nineteenth-Century Britain*. Woodbridge: Boydell Press, 2015.

Martin, Robert Bernard. "Kemble, Frances Anne [Fanny]." *Oxford Dictionary of National Biography* (online edition). https://doi.org/10.1093/ref:odnb/15318. Accessed November 4, 2023.

Marriott, Stuart. *A Backstairs to a Degree: Demands for an Open University in Late Victorian England*. Leeds: University of Leeds School of Continuing Education, 1981.

Marshall, T. H. *Citizenship and Social Class and Other Essays*. Cambridge: Cambridge University Press, 1950.

McConnell, Anita. "Reid, Hugo." *Oxford Dictionary of National Biography* (online edition). https://doi.org/10.1093/ref:odnb/23329. Accessed September 23, 2004.

Meller, Helen. "Urban Renewal and Citizenship: The Quality of Life in British Cities, 1890–1990." *Urban History* 22, no.1 (1995): 63–84.

Meller, Helen. "Women and Citizenship: Gender and the Built Environment in British Cities 1870–1939." In *Cities of Ideas: Civil Society and Urban Governance in Britain, 1800–2000. Essays in Honour of David Reeder*, edited by Robert Colls and Richard Rodger, 231–57. Aldershot: Ashgate Publishing, 2004.

"Meltham Mills Mechanics' Institute." Available online: https://huddersfield.exposed/wiki/Meltham_Mills_Mechanics%27_Institute. Accessed July 21, 2020.

Miskell, Louise. "Meeting Places: The Scientific Congress and the Host Town in the South-West of England, 1836–1877." *Urban History* 39, no. 2 (2012): 246–62.

Morgan, James. *A Short History of the Birmingham Sunday Lecture Society*. Birmingham: Allday, 1917.

Morgan, Simon. *A Victorian Woman's Place: Public Culture in the Nineteenth Century*. London: Tauris Academic Studies, 2007.

Morris, R. J. *Class, Sect and Party: The Making of the British Middle Class: Leeds, 1820–1850*. Manchester, UK: Manchester University Press, 1990.

Morris, R. J. "Middle-Class Culture, 1700–1914." In *A History of Modern Leeds*, edited by Derek Fraser, 200–22. Manchester University Press, 1980.

Morrison-Low, A. D. "Brewster, Sir David (1781–1868)." In *Oxford Dictionary of National Biography* (online edition). (Oxford University Press, 2004). Available online: https://doi:10.1093/ref:odnb/3371. Accessed November 4, 2023.

Moses, Julia. "The Reluctant Planner: T. H. Marshall and Political Thought in British Social Policy." In *Welfare and Social Policy in Britain since 1870: Essays in Honour of Jose Harris*, edited by Lawrence Goldman, 127–6. Oxford: Oxford University Press, 2019.

Naylor, Simon. "The Field, the Museum and the Lecture Hall: The Spaces of Natural History in Victorian Cornwall." *Transactions of the Institute of British Geographers (NS)* 27 (2002): 494–513.

Neswald, Elizabeth. "Science, Sociability and the Improvement of Ireland: The Galway Mechanics' Institute, 1826–51." *British Journal for the History of Science* 39, no. 4 (2006): 503–34.

O'Day, Rosemary. "Women and Education in Nineteenth-Century England." In *Women, Scholarship and Criticism: Gender and Knowledge c 1780–1900*, edited by Joan Bellamy, Ann Laurence, and Gill Perry, 91–109. Manchester : Manchester University Press, 2000.

O'Reilly, Carole A. "Professional Identity and Social Capital: The Personal Networks of Victorian Popular Journalists." (2019). Available online: http://usir.salford.ac.uk/id/eprint/48332/. Accessed September 23, 2019.

Parker, Julia. *Citizenship, Work and Welfare: Searching for the Good Society*. New York: St. Martin's Press, 1998.

Pattie, Charles, Patrick Seyd, and Paul Whiteley. *Citizenship in Britain: Values, Participation and Democracy*. Cambridge: Cambridge University Press, 2004.

Perry, Adele. *On the Edge of Empire: Gender, Race, and the Making of British Columbia, 1849–1871*. Toronto: University of Toronto Press, 2001.

Ray, Angela G. "How Cosmopolitan Was the Lyceum, Anyway?" In *The Cosmopolitan Lyceum: Lecture Culture and the Globe in Nineteenth-Century America*, edited by Tom F. Wright, 23–41. Amherst: University of Massachusetts Press, 2013.

Ray, Angela G. *The Lyceum and Public Culture in the Nineteenth-Century United States*. East Lansing, MI: Michigan State University Press, 2005.

Reid, John S. "Faraday's 'Advice to a Lecturer.'" University of Aberdeen Natural Philosophy Collection (2017). Available online: https://homepages.abdn.ac.uk/npmuseum/article/Faraday'sAdvice.pdf. Accessed July 2, 2020.

Roberts, Evan. "The Peripatetic Career of Wherahiko Rawei: Maori Culture on the Global Chautauqua Circuit, 1893–1927." In *The Cosmopolitan Lyceum: Lecture Culture and the Globe in Nineteenth-Century America*, edited by Tom F. Wright, 203–20. Amherst: University of Massachusetts Press, 2013.

Roberts, Lewis. "Trafficking in Literary Authority: Mudie's Select Library and the Commodification of the Victorian Novel." *Victorian Literature and Culture* 34, no. 1 (March 2006): 1–25.

Robinson, J. Jeffrey. *Social Control and the Education of Adults in the Nineteenth and Early Twentieth Centuries: The Role of Religion, Natural Law, Science and Useful Knowledge in Curbing Licentiousness, Promoting Moral Rescue and Averting Working-Class Dissent*. Boca Raton, FL: BrownWalker Press, 2013.

Roderick, G. W., and M. D. Stephens. *Education and Industry in the Nineteenth Century: The English Disease?* London: Longman, 1978.

Rodrick, Anne B. "Chatting up the Sciences: The Mid-Victorian 'Lecture-Gossip.'" *Victorian Review* 49, no. 2 forthcoming.

Rodrick, Anne B. "Melodrama and Natural Science: Reading the 'Greenwich Murder' in the Mid-Century Periodical Press." *Victorian Periodicals Review* 50, no.1 (2017): 66–99.

Rodrick, Anne B. *Self-Help and Civic Culture: Citizenship in Victorian Birmingham*. Surrey: Ashgate, 2004.

Rooney, Paul Raphael, and Anna Gasperini, eds. *Media and Print Culture Consumption in Nineteenth-Century Britain: The Victorian Reading Experience*. London: Palgrave Macmillan, 2016.

Rowbotham, Sheila. "Travellers in a Strange Country: Responses of Working Class Students to the University Extension Movement 1873–1910." *History Workshop* 12 (1981): 62–95.

Royle, Edward. "Mechanics' Institutes and the Working Classes, 1840–1860," *The Historical Journal* 14, no. 2 (1971): 305–21.
Schroeder, Janice. "Speaking Volumes: Victorian Feminism and the Appeal of Public Discussion." *Nineteenth-Century Contexts* 25, no. 2 (2003): 97–117.
Scott, Donald M. "The Popular Lecture and the Creation of a Public in Mid-Nineteenth-Century America." *Journal of American History* 66, no. 4 (1980): 781–809.
Scott, Donald. "The Profession that Vanished: Public Lecturing in Mid-Nineteenth-Century America," in *Professions and Professional Ideologies in America*, edited by Gerald L. Geison, 12–28. Chapel Hill: University of North Carolina Press, 1983.
Scott, Peter. "The Reform of English Higher Education: Universities in Global, National and Regional Contexts." *Cambridge Journal of Regions, Economy and Society* 7 (2014): 217–31.
Shapin, Steven, and Barry Barnes. "Science, Nature and Control: Interpreting Mechanics' Institutes." *Social Studies of Science* 7, no. 1 (1977): 31–74.
Silver, Harold. "'Things Change but Names Remain the Same': Higher Education Historiography 1975–2000." *History of Education* 35, no. 1 (2006): 121–40.
Simon, Brian. "Education and Citizenship in England." In *The State and Educational Change: Essays in the History of Education and Pedagogy*, edited by Brian Simon, 75–83. London: Lawrence & Wishart, 1994.
Simon, Brian. *Education and the Labour Movement, 1870–1920*. London: Lawrence & Wishart, 1969.
Sinha, Mrinalini, "Britishness, Clubbability, and the Colonial Public Sphere: The Genealogy of an Imperial Institution in Colonial India." *Journal of British Studies* 40, no. 4 (2001): 489–521.
Small, Helen. "Dickens and a Pathology of the Mid-Victorian Reading Public," in *The Practice and Representation of Reading in England*, edited by James Raven, Helen Small, and Naomi Tadmor, 263–90. Cambridge: Cambridge University Press, 1996.
Snell, K. D. M. "The Sunday-School Movement in England and Wales: Child Labour, Denominational Control and Working-Class Culture." *Past and Present* 164 (1969): 122–68.
Sutcliffe, Marcella Pellegrino. "The Origins of the 'Two Cultures' Debate in the Adult Education Movement: The Case of the Working Men's College c. 1854–1914." *History of Education* 43, no. 2 (2014): 141–59.
Tannen, Deborah. *The Argument Culture: Moving from Debate to Dialogue*. New York: Random House, 1998.
Taylor, R. V. "Barnett Blake." In *Supplement to the Biographia Leodiensis; or, Biographical Sketches of the Worthies of Leeds and Neighbourhood*, 611–14. London: Simkin and Marshall, 1867.
Thomas, R. A. "The Mechanics' Institutes of the Home Counties, c. 1825–70. Part 1." *The Vocational Aspect of Education* 31, no. 79 (1979): 67–72.
Thomas, R. A. "The Mechanics' Institutes of the Home Counties, c. 1825–70, Part 2." *The Vocational Aspect of Education* 31, no. 80 (1979): 103–8.
Thompson, F. M. L., ed. *The Rise of Suburbia*. Leicester University Press, 1982.
Tinniswood, Adrian. *The Royal Society and the Invention of Modern Science*. New York: Basic Books, 2019.
Traice, W. H. J. *Hand-Book of Mechanics' Institutions, With Priced Catalogue of Books Suitable for Libraries*. 2d edition. London: Longman Green, 1863.
Turner, C. M. "Political, Religious, and Occupational Support in the Early Mechanics' Institutes." *The Vocational Aspect of Secondary and Further Education*, 20, no. 45 (1968): 65–70.

Turner, C. M. "Sociological Approaches to the History of Education." *British Journal of Educational Studies* 17, no. 2 (1969): 146–65.
Tylecote, Mabel. *The Mechanics' Institutes of Lancashire and Yorkshire before 1851.* Manchester: Manchester University Press, 1957.
Tylecote, Mabel. "The Manchester Mechanics' Institution, 1824–50." In *Artisan to Graduate: Essays to Commemorate the Foundation in 1824 of the Manchester Mechanics' Institution, Now in 1974 the University of Manchester Institute of Science and Technology,* edited by D. S. L. Cardwell, 55–86. Manchester: Manchester University Press, 1974.
Vincent, A., and R. Plant. *Philosophy, Politics and Citizenship: The Life and Thought of the British Idealists.* Oxford: Blackwell, 1984.
Vogrinčič, Ana. "The Novel-Reading Panic in 18th Century England: An Outline of an Early Moral Media Panic." *Medijska istraživanja* 14, no. 2 (2008): 103–24.
Wach, Howard M. "Culture and the Middle Classes: Popular Knowledge in Industrial Manchester." *Journal of British Studies* 27, no. 4 (1988): 375–404.
Wade, Charles. *The Lucid Expression of Thought: The Birmingham and Edgbaston Debating Society, 1846–2006.* Redditch: Brewin Books, 2007.
Walker, Martyn. *The Development of the Mechanics' Institute Movement in Britain and Beyond.* London: Routledge, 2017.
Walker, Martyn. "'The Yorkshire Union Has Grown to the Most Extensive Educational Confederation in the Kingdom': The Growth and Distribution of the Yorkshire Union of Mechanics' Institutes, 1838–1890." *The Australian Library Journal* 62, no. 2 (2013): 134–9.
Waller, Philip. *Writers, Readers, and Reputations: Literary Life in Britain 1870–1918.* Oxford: Oxford University Press, 2006.
Walton-Jordan, Ulrike, and Jutta Schwarzkopf. "Transforming Relations of Gender: The Feminist Project of Societal Reform in Turn-of-the-Century Britain." In *Reforming the Constitution,* edited by Peter Catterall, Wolfram Kaiser, and Ulrike Walton-Jordan, 158–78. London: Routledge, 2000.
Waterhouse, Rachel E. *The Birmingham and Midland Institute, 1854–1954.* Birmingham: Council of the Birmingham and Midland Institute, 1954.
Weisz, George. "The Anatomy of University Reform 1863–1914." *Historical Reflections/Réflexions Historiques* 7, no. 2–3 (1980): 363–79.
White, Alan. "Class, Culture, and Control: The Sheffield Athenaeum Movement and the Middle Class 1847–64." In *The Culture of Capital: Art, Power, and the Nineteenth-Century Middle Class,* edited by Janet Wolff and John Seed, 83–115. Manchester: Manchester University Press, 1988.
Wigley, John. *The Rise and Fall of the Victorian Sunday.* Manchester: Manchester University Press, 1980.
Wilson, Arline. "'The Florence of the North'? The Civic Culture of Liverpool in the Early 19th Century." In *Gender, Civic Culture and Consumerism: Middle-Class Identity in Britain, 1800–1940,* edited by Alan Kidd and David Nicholls, 34–46. Manchester: Manchester University Press, 1999.
Wolff, Michael. "The British Controversialist and Impartial Inquirer, 1850–1872: A Pearl from the Golden Stream." In *The Victorian Periodical Press: Samplings and Soundings,* edited by Joanne Shattock and Michael Wolff, 367–92. Toronto: University of Toronto Press, 1982.

Wolff, Michael. "The British Controversialist and Literary Magazine: Devoted to the Impartial and Deliberate Discussion of Important Questions in Religion, Philosophy, History, Politics, Social Economy, Etc., and to the Promotion of Self-Culture and General Education." *Victorian Periodicals Newsletter* 1, no. 2 (June 1968): 27–45.

Wood, Carly S. *Debating Women: Gender, Education, and Spaces for Argument, 1835–1945*. East Lansing, MI: Michigan State University Press, 2018.

Wood, Henry Trueman. *A History of The Royal Society of Arts*. London: John Murray, 1913.

Woods, Alan. "The Mechanics' Institutes of North-East Lancashire 1851–89: A Comparative Study." *The Vocational Aspect of Education*, 29, no. 72 (1977): 37–44.

Woodson-Boulton, Amy. *Transformative Beauty: Art Museums in Industrial Britain*. Stanford: Stanford University Press, 2012.

Wright, Susannah. "Citizenship, Moral Education and the English Elementary School." In *Mass Education and the Limits of State Building, c. 1870–1930*, edited by Laurence Brockliss and Nicola Sheldon, 21–43. New York: Palgrave Macmillan, 2012.

Wright, Tom F. *Lecturing the Atlantic: Speech, Print, and an Anglo-American Commons 1830–1870*. Oxford: Oxford University Press, 2017.

Wright, Tom F. "The Results of Locomotion: Bayard Taylor and the Travel Lecture in the Mid-Nineteenth-Century United States." *Studies in Travel Writing* 14, no. 2 (2010): 111–34.

Wright, W. H. K. *West-Country Poets: Their Lives and Works*. London: E. Stock, 1896.

Yeandle, Peter. *Citizenship, Nation, Empire: The Politics of History Teaching in England, 1870–1930*. Manchester: Manchester University Press, 2015.

Yeo, Richard. "Reading Encyclopedias: Science and the Organization of Knowledge in British Dictionaries of Arts and Sciences, 1730–1850." *Isis* 82, no. 1 (1991): 24–49.

Yeo, Richard. "Whewell, William (1794–1866)". *Oxford Dictionary of National Biography* (online edition). https://doi.org/10.1093/ref:odnb/29200. Accessed November 4, 2024.

Zarefsky, David. "What Does an Argument Culture Look Like?" *Informal Logic* 29, no. 3 (2009): 296–308.

Zboray, Ronald J., and Mary Saracino Zboray. *Literary Dollars and Social Sense: A People's History of the Mass Market Book*. New York: Routledge, 2005.

Dissertations

Cherches, Peter. "Star Course: Popular Lectures and the Marketing of Celebrity in 19th Century America." PhD dissertation, New York University, 1997.

Flexner, Janet. "The London Mechanics' Institution: Social and Cultural Foundations 1823–1830." PhD dissertation, University College London, 2014.

Martin, Janette Lisa. "Popular Political Oratory and Itinerant Lecturing in Yorkshire and the North East in the Age of Chartism, 1837–1860." PhD dissertation, Department of History, University of York, 2010.

Sims, Jana Hilda. "Mechanics' Institutes in Sussex and Hampshire, 1825–1875." PhD dissertation, University of London, 2010.

Stockdale, C. "Mechanics' Institutes in Northumberland and Durham." PhD dissertation, University of Durham, 1993.

Walker, Martyn. "'Solid and Practical Education Within Reach of the Humblest Means': The Growth and Development of the Yorkshire Union of Mechanics' Institutes, 1838–1891." PhD dissertation, University of Huddersfield, 2010.

Watson, Douglas Robert. "'The Road to Learning': Re-evaluating the Mechanics' Institute Movement." PhD dissertation, University of Plymouth, 2018.

Watson, Michael Ian. "Adult Education in North Lancashire in the Second Quarter of the Nineteenth Century." PhD dissertation, University of London Institute of Education, 1988.

Website

"Fanny Kemble," *History of American Women* (website). Available online: https://www.womenhistoryblog.com/2011/08/fanny-kemble.html. Accessed November 4, 2023.

Index

adult education 4, 14, 18, 20, 43, 54, 87, 155, 159, 166, 178, 180–1
Alton Mechanics' Institute 79, 87
American lyceum system 10, 13, 33, 135, 151, 170
argument culture 4, 102. *See also* debate
arts
    as extension programming 163
    galleries 66, 68
    (*see also* lecture topics; performance)
Association of Women Pioneer Lecturers 178
athletics 53–4, 59

Baines, Edward 20, 55, 65, 73, 89, 198 n.51
Baring, William Bingham, Lord Ashburton 21, 28, 30, 61
Barking Mutual Improvement Society 85
Barnet Institute 84, 87
Barnsley Mechanics' Institute and Literary Society 83, 89
Basingstoke Mechanics' Institute 22, 88
Battersea Literary and Scientific Institution 130
Battle Mechanics' Institution 85
"*be* and *do*" 113, 131, 166
Birkbeck Literary and Scientific Institution 43
Birmingham 3, 74, 113, 134, 135, 140, 146
Birmingham Amateur Orchestral Society 140, 149, 177
Birmingham and Edgbaston Debating Society 67, 102, 105
Birmingham and Midland Institute 21, 45, 66–71, 80, 82, 84–6, 88–9, 98, 100, 118, 134, 138, 146–7, 149, 151–2, 154, 158, 163, 173–4, 177
Birmingham and Suburban Institute Union 134
Birmingham Polytechnic Institution 83–5, 95–6

Birmingham Sunday Lecture Series 139–41, 146–7, 151, 158. *See also* Sunday Evening Meetings for the People
"Black Board Lectures" 118
Blackburn Literary, Scientific, and Mechanics' Institution 48, 86
Blake, Barnett 30, 33, 48, 50, 52, 61, 83, 107, 122, 152, 157, 202 n.114
book clubs 43
Booth, James 33, 62, 71
Bradford 3, 82
Bradford Mechanics' Institution 38, 49–50, 84, 95, 97, 173, 175, 177–8
Bradford Sunday Lecture Series 140–1
"brain-work" 164–6
Brechin Mechanics' Institute 1, 83
Brewster, David 108–11, 222 n.89
Bristol Sunday Lecture Society 143
British Association for the Advancement of Science 141
British Controversialist and Impartial Inquirer 74, 101–5, 108–10, 112–13, 141
Bromley Literary Institute 86
Bury St. Edmunds Athenaeum 22, 38, 51, 89

caste 9–10, 57, 62, 67, 116–17, 129, 131, 159, 161, 164–6
categories of debates 104–5
categories of lectures 76
Chelmsford Literary and Mechanics' Institution 83
"chemistry of the breakfast table" 30, 78–80
Chester, Harry 4, 22, 28, 35, 45, 51–4, 56, 60, 112, 129, 157, 160, 189 n.15
Christianity 76, 83, 103, 108–11, 135. *See also* "Plurality of Worlds"
Christy's Lecture Agency (Lecture Agency, Ltd.) 169–71, 173, 175–6, 178–9
citizenship 6–9, 129, 162, 165, 180–1, 189 n.19

citizenship for children 159
citizenship via literature 130, 159
as extension programming 166
(*see also* participatory citizenship; sympathy)
civic culture institutions 5, 45–71
civic spirit 160, 179–80
clergy 35, 91–3, 96–7, 123, 131, 135
"clubbability" 15, 117, 121, 150
"collision of mind with mind" 161, 168
common informer 142
Concerning Popular Lectures 179
conservatism 13, 135, 162
consumer good, lectures as 16, 53, 155, 159, 179
controversy 13, 52, 102–10, 132
  value of 102
conversaziones 9–10, 15, 18
courses of lectures 24, 74, 78, 99
credentialing 42, 61, 70, 91, 99, 112, 115, 121–2, 157–8, 178. See also Lecturers' Association
Crimea 32, 51, 59, 65, 105
Croydon Scientific and Literary Institution 55, 78, 84–5, 86–9, 95, 97–8
cultural competence 9–10, 15–17, 20, 22–3, 43, 109
current events 5, 50–1, 69, 73. *See also* categories of lectures; debate topics; lecture topics; newspaper rooms

Darlington Lecture Association 163, 169
Darlington Mechanics' Institution 47, 86, 87
day schools 43, 63–4, 67
debate 73, 101–7
  debating clubs 53, 133
  general topics 104–6
  as requirement of citizenship 103
debate topics
  current events 104
  democracy 106
  economics 104, 106
  education 104
  Elizabeth I 110, 112
  ethics 104, 106
  ethnography 104
  foreign affairs 104

history 104, 106
law 106
literature 104, 106
national progress 104
Oliver Cromwell 106
philosophy 104, 106, 111
political economy 104, 106
politics 104
psychology 106
religion 104
science 104
social sciences 104
spiritualism 105
The Debater 102, 106
democracy 26
Department of Science and Art examinations 117
Domville, W. Henry 135, 137

education. *See* elementary education; day schools; lecture topics; primary schools; higher education; secondary schools
educationists 26, 98, 113, 130–1, 157, 166, 182
Education Act of 1870 24, 61, 117, 130, 159, 182
elementary education 65, 117, 130, 131, 154, 159, 161. *See also* primary schools
empire 5, 8, 65, 71, 129, 159, 172. *See also* debate topics; lecture topics
entertainment 14, 20, 24, 48, 62, 70, 112, 115, 151, 152. *See also* spectacle
  education and 2, 16, 25, 28–31, 104, 116–18, 142, 154
"entertainments" 118, 124–9, 133, 146, 149, 178
esprit de corps 55, 122
evening classes 18–19, 64, 66–7, 117
examinations by Society of Arts 43, 45, 61–2, 64, 78, 112, 117

Farnham Young Men's Association 78, 86, 88
Federation of Sunday Societies 142
fees
  charged by lecturers 16, 31–2, 34, 36, 42, 91, 121, 123, 137, 169, 175

memberships 20, 58, 62, 170
subscriptions 16, 33, 46, 67, 96–7, 99, 101, 137, 204 n.10
tickets 16, 46, 67, 99, 137, 162, 170
finances, institute 20, 30, 31, 34, 46–8, 54, 60, 136–7, 140, 171. *See also* fees; fundraising
franchise 6, 9, 129, 159–60
fundraising 47, 64–5. *See also* finances

games 53–4, 59
General Union of Literary, Scientific, and Mechanics' Institutes ("Institutions in Union") 21–3, 53, 113
generational conflict 57–60
Gilchrist Trust 181
Gilfillan, George 91
Glasgow Athenaeum 51, 123
Glasgow Sunday Society 140
Gosport and Alverstoke Literary and Scientific Institution 83, 86
"gossips" 118, 145–6. *See also* humor; oratory
gratuitous lecturers 32–36, 92, 100, 123, 171. *See also* voluntaryism; fees

Halifax Mechanics' Institute 50, 92, 102
Halifax Sunday Lecture Society 158, 165, 168–74, 177
Handsworth Workers' Education Association 167
Handsworth Working Men's Association 167
Harborne and Edgbaston Institute 134, 146–7, 151–2, 154
Hartley Institute 98–101
Hastings Mechanics' Institute 62, 82, 85–6, 88, 92, 95–7
higher education 10, 14, 25, 62, 116, 161–2, 164, 167, 182
Highgate Literary and Scientific Society 35
history 28, 67, 69, 70, 73, 129. *See also* debate topics; lecture topics
as extension programming 163
Hole, James 4, 19–20, 34–5, 54, 57, 63, 67, 74, 79
Holyoake, George Jacob 48
Huddersfield Institute 127, 128, 132

Huddersfield Mechanics' Institution 27, 61, 79
Hudson, James 4, 18–20, 22, 51, 54, 57, 67, 74, 78, 104, 118, 196 n.34
humor 76, 127–8, 146, 149, 153. *See also* "gossips"; categories of lectures
Huxley, Thomas Henry 11, 108, 134–5
hybrid lecture model 66–71, 135, 161

industrialization 3, 23
"institute men" 115, 122, 125, 129–31, 135, 151, 158
institute secretaries 25–6, 31–3, 46, 49, 91, 93–5, 106, 120–1, 123
Institute, and Lecturer's Gazette 11, 115, 119–20, 123–4, 127, 128–9, 132
advertisements by lecturers in 119–20, 122, 124–8, 145, 149, 152
Institutions in Union. *See* General Union of Literary, Scientific, and Mechanics' Institutes
itinerant lecturers 16–17

Journal of the Society of Arts 10, 14, 20, 23, 26, 42–3, 47, 70, 73, 76, 93, 95, 102, 104, 108, 112, 119, 136, 143, 152, 191 n.1
juvenile lectures 63–4, 99

Kelvedon Literary Institution 22
Keswick Lecture Society 158
King's Heath Institute 134
Kingston Mechanics' Institute 87
knowledge-based culture (defined) 2–6

Labour College movement 166
laboratories 66
"lady lecturers" 122, 125, 178
Langford, John Alfred 67–72, 112, 151, 160, 214 n.149
lecture agencies 1, 121, 170. *See also* Christy's Lecture Agency
Lecture Agency Ltd. *See* Christy's Lecture Agency
Lecture Association 136, 138, 178
Lecture League 183
lecture topics
Abyssinia 88, 175
Algeria 88, 153

Alps 88–9
anatomy 17, 76, 150
Anglo-Saxons 40–1, 85
anthropology 76, 99, 150
applied sciences 75–6, 80, 96
archaeology 76, 85, 86, 99, 128
architecture 100, 164
Arctic exploration 88–9, 170
arts 11, 43, 73, 95, 98, 99, 100, 130–1, 133, 135, 138, 150, 153–4, 168, 171, 177. *See also* performance
Assyria 86
astronomy 75, 104, 108–9, 128, 149, 177
Australia 22, 28, 71, 89, 98
ballooning 100, 138, 177
biography 23, 30, 69, 75, 76, 82, 84, 85, 86, 99, 128, 150
Boer War 172
Bolivia 100
botany 17, 24, 75, 145, 170, 181
Canada 88
chemistry 17, 24–5, 61, 68, 75–6, 99–100, 149, 177. *See also* "Chemistry of the Breakfast Table"
China 71, 79, 119
Christianity 24, 142
Crystal Palace 91
current events 71, 75–6, 84–9, 97, 124, 133, 146, 150
domestic economy 4, 43
domestic morality 25, 76, 83–4, 95, 127
education 76, 84
Egypt 86, 138, 172–3
empire 76, 79, 86–7, 98, 171. *See also individual countries* as lecture topics
ethnography 76, 99, 128
foreign affairs 76, 87, 89, 146
geography 75–6, 99, 129
geology 17, 24, 67, 70, 75, 76, 99–100, 104, 109, 111, 138, 152
George Stephenson 61, 75, 86
government 76
great reptiles 90, 98
Greece 177
health 4, 9, 71, 76, 84, 86
history 1, 11, 23, 30, 35, 40, 61–2, 64, 66, 76, 84–5, 114, 135, 138, 149, 150–1, 168, 171
hygiene 71

Iceland 138
India 22, 61, 71, 79, 89, 91, 118, 175, 177
Italy 88, 173
Japan 118, 169–70
Jamaica 169
Jerusalem 88
John Franklin, death of 89
John Howard, prison reformer 86
law 149
linguistics 76, 82
literature 35, 46, 62, 64, 66–70, 95–101, 128, 133, 150–1, 168, 171, 176–7
mathematics 66–7, 76, 99
mental science 76
mesmerism 76
meteorology 76, 145, 177
Morocco 153
mountaineering 177
music 11, 34–5, 64, 74–6, 95–8, 131. *See also* performance
national progress 76, 84, 86
natural history 4, 15, 23, 30, 75, 101
New Zealand 71, 88, 98, 153, 170
Nineveh 86
Norway 88, 153
Oliver Cromwell 29, 68, 71, 84–5
oratory 76, 82, 99, 127
paleontology 76, 1
Palestine 88
Peru 100, 175
philosophy 64, 76, 135, 138, 149, 150, 168, 170
phonetics 82
photography 83
phrenology 76, 100
physics 25, 68, 75, 76, 99–100, 111, 150, 175
physiognomy 76
physiology 67, 76, 78, 150
poetry 76, 82, 93–4, 100, 106, 124, 128, 131
political economy 1, 84
politics 20, 52, 60, 84
prison reform 86–7
psychiatry 76
psychology 76, 152
religion as lecture topic 76, 104, 138, 150
sanitary science 76, 86

science 15–19, 25, 70, 73–4, 78, 95–8, 101, 127–8, 130, 133, 135–8, 143, 149, 151–2, 168, 171, 176. *See also individual sciences* as lecture topics
self-improvement 76, 83
Sepoy Mutiny 89
Shakespeare 39, 40, 82, 100, 106, 174
social science 76, 78, 84–9, 95, 97
sociology 168
spiritualism 76
Switzerland 100, 167
theology 16, 17, 35, 52, 60, 108–9
travel 11, 35, 61, 62, 76, 87, 100, 133, 146, 153, 165, 171, 175–6, 178
Tudors 84, 106, 112
United States Civil War 89, 105
watchmaking 80
zoology 76, 149–50
lecturers, individual
Allport, D. W. 170
Andre, P. H. 89
Applebee, James Kay 83, 98, 124
Armbruster, Carl 153
Aveling, Edward 137
Aveling, Thomas W. 88
Bachhoffner, George H. 90
Bacon, John M. 171–2, 174, 177
Bacon, Thomas 88
Baines, F. E. 88
Balfour, Clara Lucas 1, 30, 36–42, 82, 84, 86, 91, 95–8, 127–8, 203 n.144
Ball, Robert S. 127–8, 137, 141, 149–51, 163
Bankes, George 82
Barkas, T. P. 149
Barker, George 97
Barr, Archibald 152
Barrett, W. F. 127, 149
Barry, Alfred 84
Bateman, J. F. 88
Bateson, Vaughan 175
Bayliss, Wyke 153
Beke, Charles T. 88, 99
Belcher, Edward 89
Bellew, J. M. 101, 127
Belloc, Hilaire 179
Bennett, Georgiana 84, 96
Bennett, John 80
Bennett-Goldney, F. 174

Benson, H. L. P. 169
Bernays, Albert James 79
Berthon, H. E. 173
Bertram, Charles 151
Bickersteth, Robert, Bishop of Ripon 86
Birt, William Radcliffe 96, 145–6
Blackburn, Henry 88, 153
Blackie, James S. 138, 142
Blackwell, Elizabeth 137
Blanc, Louis 1, 90
Bleadon, Julia 83
Blencoe, R. W. 87
Blockley, John Sanders 92
Blunt, Wilfred Scawen 172
Bothamley, C. H. 154, 174, 177
Bradley, Edith 178
Bristowe, J. S. 138
Brocklehurst, J. D. 83
Brown, Hugh Stowell 98, 100, 102
Bruce, John Collingswood 149
Buckland, George 97
Buckmaster, J. C. 28, 130
Bullen, Frank T. 174
Burn, Robert Scott 86
Burnett, David 92
Carlisle, H. H. 86
Carpenter, Joseph Edwards 83
Carpenter, W. B. 138, 150
Carpenter, William Lant 140, 152
Case, George 83
Chamberlain, A. B. 153
Chamberlain, J. H. 100
Chapman, F. W. 88
Chatterton, Frederick 83, 93, 96, 125
Christmas, Henry 121–2
Churchill, Winston 179
Clarke, Charles Cowden 82, 95–6, 216 n.15
Clayton, D'Arcy 175
Clayton, John 94
Clifford, W. K. 150
Cobbold, T. Spencer 138, 150
Conder, G. W. 97
Conway, Martin 174, 177
Conway, Moncure D. 150
Cooke, J. H. 165
Coutt, J. 89
Cox, Annie 83
Crane, Walter 173, 175

Crichton-Browne, James 149, 154, 174, 177
Crocker, Grace Jean 175
Crosskey, Henry 131, 134
Crowther, Henry 149, 173, 175
Curzon, Frank 118, 131, 151–3, 157, 224 n.13
D'Orsey, J. D. 82
Dallinger, William Henry 149, 153, 175
Daniel, J. C. 85, 98
Dawkins, Boyd 169
Dawson, George 1, 36–42, 56, 67, 69, 82, 84–5, 91, 95–100, 102, 107, 127–8, 149
De Fraine, John 124
Dickens, Charles 16, 96
Dickens, Charles, Jr. 179
Diosy, Arthur 11, 169–70, 174
Disraeli, Benjamin 58–9
Dodwell, Robert 82
Dolmetsch, Arnold 171, 174
Doyle, Arthur Conan 179
Dresser, Christopher L. 100
Du Chaillu, Paul 90
Dudgeon, Robert Ellis 139
Duppa, B. F. 49
Dyke, Colvil 134
Ebsworth, Joseph Woodfall 97
Eddison, John Edwin 149
Edney, John 91
Egerton, Grace 83
Ellaby, J. N. 152
Ellis, Robert 83
Evans, Sebastian 67, 100, 174, 177
Faraday, Michael 25, 94
Fawcett, Joshua 97
Fawcett, Millicent Garrett 150
Finch, Arthur Elley 138
Fishbourne, J. C. 82
Fison, Alfred H. 171, 174, 177
Fletcher, A. W. 170
Flinders Petrie, W. M. 173, 175–6
Foster, Michael 78
Francis, Adolphus 98
Fraser, John Foster 171, 175, 177–8
French, Percy 175
Froude, James Anthony 84, 99
Froy, W. N. 85
Fry, Charles 174

Gaston, E. Page 177
Ghosh, Sarath Kumar 175
Glaisher, James 65, 100–1, 138
Gleeson, J. 175
Glyn, Isabella 82
Gosse, Edmund 31, 153, 173, 175–6
Gosse, Philip Henry 101
Gotch, Francis 173
Grand, Sarah 169, 172
Greenbank, Thomas King 99–100
Greenwood, Henry 168
Gregory, J. W. 97, 174, 177
Grey, Annie 171, 174
Griffin, W. Hall 174
Griffiths, H. 90
Grossmith, George 1, 36–42, 91, 97–8, 102, 127–8
Grossmith, George Jr. 175, 178
Grundy, C. H. 134, 175
Haddon, A. C. 174
Hall, Robert 87
Hall, Spencer T. 30, 100
Halstead, Robert 165
Hancock, William 173, 175
Hargrove, Charles 173, 175
Harris, George 85
Hatchard, T. G. 86
Haweis, Hugh Reginald 141, 171–2, 174
Hawkins, Benjamin Waterhouse 97, 101
Heaton, Herbert 167
Heaton, John Deakin 82
Hepworth, Thomas Craddock 169–70
Herbert-Jones, W. 170
Herschel, John 108
Hewins, Thomas 151
Hibbert, Henry 175
Hicks, Thomas 169, 170
Higginson, Edward 82, 108–10
Higinbotham, George 75
Hill, Alexander 174, 177
Hill, Arthur C. 175
Hilsop, Gordon 167
Hincks, Thomas 82, 99
Hjaltalin, Jon A. 138
Hobhouse, Arthur 142
Hodgson, William Ballantyne 68, 86
Hopkins, Thomas 74
How, Harry 170
Hunt, Robert 94, 102

Irving, Henry 169
Jones, Thomas Rymer 75
Just, John 75
Kemble, Fanny (Mrs. Butler) 82, 216 n.17
Kendall, Harriet 152, 153, 169
Kerr, Richard 174, 177
Kidd, William 145–6
King, D. W. 97
Kingsford, Anna 150
Kingsley, Mary 171, 174
Kinkel, Johann Gottfried 75, 98
Kitchin, G. W. 116
Kropotkin, Pyotr 162
Lambert, Frederick 175
Lancaster, W. J. 151
Lankester, Edwin 31, 42, 80, 91, 101
Leatham, Edward Aldham 87
LeGalliene, Richard 162
Lodge, Oliver J. 173, 175–6
Lord, John 96
Lubbock, John 80, 101, 127
Lupton, Arnold 172
Lupton, Sydney 149
Macdonald, George 127
Malden, B. J. 127, 134, 152
Marshall, Thomas 173, 175
Martin, Horace 85
Martineau, R. F. 151
Mascall, Elizabeth 83
Mascall, Mary 83
Matesdorf, T. 153
McKensie, Charles 90
Merz, John Theodore 149
Miall, Louis Compton 149, 174
Miles, William 153, 175
Mill, Hugh Robert 174
Miller, Florence Fenwick 132, 137–8
Mills, Alexander 177
Milnes, R. Monckton 87
Moffatt, Graham 175
Moffatt, Kate 175
Montefiore, Arthur 169–70
Morgan-Browne, H. 175
Morley, John 176
Morris, William 134, 141, 162, 169
Morse, T. D. C. 84
Moss, D. C. 84
Moulton, Richard Green 149, 164

Newman, John Henry 108
Nicholls, John Ashton 45
Nichols, Arthur 150
North, Frederick, MP 88, 97
O'Rell, Max 134, 142, 151, 169, 170
O'Shea, John Augustus 118
Ormbe, Elizabeth 150
Owen, Robert 100
Pakington, John 21, 45, 69
Palmer, H. J. 173, 175
Parkyn, Ernest Albert 149
Pauer, Ernst 149
Peake, Frederic 142
Pearsall, Thomas John 95
Pearse, H. H. 146
Pearson, Karl 137, 173, 175
Pendleton, J. 170
Pepper, John Henry 31, 95, 96, 101, 133
Phillips, Henry 96, 98
Phillips, John 75
Phythian, J. Ernest 171
Plumptre, Charles John 92, 121, 128–9, 138, 225 n.30
Poulton, Edward Bagnall 149, 152
Proctor, Richard A. 127–8, 149
Puseley, Daniel 98
Rawnsley, Hardwicke D. 158
Rea, William 76, 149
Reid, Henry 142
Rhys Davids, T. W. 150
Rice, Harry 175
Richardson, Benjamin 150
Richardson, W. 97
Roberts, Morley 171, 174
Roberts, R. W. 177
Robertson, J. W.
Roscoe, Henry 141, 162
Rowlandson, Michael J. 89
Rowton, Frederic 102, 104, 106
Rowton, Walter 98, 124–5, 128, 132, 151
Ruskin, John 123–4, 128, 164
Ryan, John 79
Seaton, Rose 127
Sedgwick, Adam 95, 108
Seeley, H. G. 138, 149
Seeley, John Robert 149
Shackleton, Ernest 179
Shaw, Hudson 162
Shuttleworth, H. C. 139

Sicard, Clara 122
Siddons, Sarah 151
Sidgwick, Alfred 174
Sidgwick, Arthur 153
Sieveking, Albert Forbes 173–4, 177
Sinclair, William 87, 95
Smith, C. L. 89
Smith, G. H. 168
Smith, Haskett 170, 175, 178
Smith, W. Wyke 87
Smithells, Arthur 171, 174, 177
Snazelle, C. H. 11, 151, 191 n.30
Snow, J. D. 87
Solger, Reinhold 96
Spark, William 95
Stanley, Henry 65, 134, 151, 169, 179
Stevens, Thomas 118
Stocqueler, J. H. 91
Stuart, James 161
Stuart, Lizzy 83
Stubbs, William 169–70
Swan, Joseph Wilson 149
Sydney, Edwin 89
Symonds, John Addington 137
Theobald, William 89
Thorpe, T. E. 149
Till, W. 100
Timmins, Samuel 67, 100, 151
Topham, James Tell 92, 125
Toulmin Smith, Joshua
Trevelyan, George 151
Tuckwell, William 131, 134, 142, 151, 153
Tyler, Moses Coit 127–8
Vardy, A. R. 153
Villiers, Frederick 146, 169, 170
Vincent, Henry 84, 87, 94
Wallace, Alfred Russel 99
Wallace, Robert 170
Wallis, Whitworth 11, 149, 151–2, 153, 169, 171, 174, 177
Ward, Marshall 154
Ward, Mary Elizabeth (Mrs. Humphrey Ward) 169
Watson, Alex 175
Watson, John ("Ian Maclaren") 174
Wells, Samuel 175
Westmacot, Percy 99
Wheeler, Edmund 96, 98, 127, 128

Wicksteed, Charles 95
Wilde, Oscar 134, 151
Wilson, Andrew 149–50, 165, 169, 170
Wilson, John 175
Womersley, C. J. 97
Wood, Theodore 175
Wotherspoon, George 150
Wray, W. F. ("Kuklos") 175, 178
Wykeham, Martin C. 86
Yates, Edmund 87, 91
Young, Basil 86, 124–5, 127, 128
Zangwill, Israel 171, 173, 174–6
Zerffi, G. G. 43, 138, 150
Lecturers' Association 120–1, 128, 133–4, 149–50, 155, 159. *See also* Lecture Association
Leeds 3, 18, 63–6, 74, 82, 113, 135, 140, 146
Leeds Mechanics' Institute and Literary Society 21–2
Leeds Mechanics' Institution 22, 55, 63–6, 83, 87, 88, 95–6, 152–3
Leeds Philosophical and Literary Society 63–6, 68, 80, 82, 86–9, 95, 98–9, 103, 118, 134, 146, 149, 152–3, 173, 175, 177
Leeds Sunday Lecture Society 141–3, 150
Leeds Young Men's Association 83
leisure 2, 5, 14, 15, 28, 53, 55, 58, 87, 116, 134, 159, 181. *See also* recreation
    dangers of 4, 56
Lewes Mechanics' Institution 87
libraries
    institute libraries 4–5, 18–19, 47–53, 55, 66, 118, 133, 160
    public libraries 3, 161 (*see also* reading rooms)
"List of Lecturers" (*Journal of the Society of Arts*) 74, 83, 89–91, 98, 152
Literary and Educational Year-book 74, 89–91
Literary and Scientific Institution Act 46
literature 23, 25. *See also* lecture topics; debate topics
    as extension programming 163
    books as institute offering 22, 48–52, 73–4, 76, 82
    dangers of 49–50, 161
    popular literature 28, 161, 164

literary readings 82, 98, 106, 129. *See also* penny readings
Liverpool 3, 19, 98
Liverpool Sunday Society 140-1, 143
localism 43, 62, 68-9, 98
London 2-3, 48, 82, 85, 133
Lords' Day Observance Society 142, 157

Mackinder, Halford 173
magicians 119, 146
Magnus, Phillip 157
Manchester 3, 74, 113, 135, 140
Manchester (Ancoats) Sunday Lecture Series 140-1, 162
Manchester Athenaeum 17, 24, 45-8, 51, 54, 58, 74, 103
Manchester Mechanics' Institution 18, 54, 56, 59-60, 68, 74, 94
"manner" of speaking, critiques of 94
mechanics' institutions 17-22, 26, 29, 78. *See also* specific organizations
Midland Institute. *See* Birmingham and Midland Institute
modernity 3, 5, 180
modernization 3, 7, 159, 181
MOOCs 182
Moulton, Richard Green 149, 164
Mossley Mechanics' Institute 79
museums 4, 18, 47, 53-4, 63, 65-7, 136
music 28, 48, 54, 68, 128
  performances 20, 53, 59, 62, 83, 119, 124, 127, 133, 146-7, 150, 152-4, 171, 176-7

National Association for the Provision of Social Sciences (NAPSS) 61, 131
National Sunday League 139
Newcastle 3, 79, 82, 85, 94, 100, 140, 146
Newcastle Literary and Philosophical Society 17, 22-3, 30, 76, 80-2, 84, 94-5, 98, 99-100, 118, 140, 146-7, 149, 150-1, 158, 162, 172
Newcastle Sunday Lecture Series 140, 150
Newland Young Men's Mutual Improvement Society 83
Newport (Wales) Athenaeum and Mechanics' Institute 47, 83, 84, 98
Newport Pagnell Literary and Scientific Institute 127-8

newspaper rooms 50-2, 66-7
Northern Union of Literary and Mechanics' Institutions 92, 118
Norwich Sunday Lecture Society 141, 143
Nottingham Mechanics' Institution 50, 79, 82, 85, 87

Oldham Mechanics' Institute 29
orators 119, 129
oratory 129, 137, 149, 154, 177. *See also* "gossips"; humor
Owens College, Manchester 26
Oxford University Extension 124

"pack of knowledge" 28, 30, 131, 150, 154, 180, 182
Papers for the People 29
participatory citizenship 10, 11, 27, 30, 43, 45, 55, 57, 59, 70, 113, 117-18, 131, 154, 159-60, 180-1
participatory culture 9, 27, 59, 116
patriotism 63-6, 146, 159-62
penny readings 43, 128-9. *See also* literary readings
periodicals (provided by institutes) 49-51, 55, 60, 162. *See also* reading rooms
performance, critiques of 83, 149, 151. *See also* art; music; theatricals
Pitman's Popular Lecturer 75
"plurality of worlds" 107-12
Plymouth Mechanics' Institute 85, 152, 153
politics
  as a banned topic at institutes 53, 60, 103
  (*see also* debate topics; lecture topics)
primary schools 61, 68, 117-18, 159
Primrose Society 160
professionalization of popular lecturing 17, 115-55, 171, 182
Public Libraries Act 118

questions from audience 122, 141

reading rooms 4, 18-19, 47, 48-52, 73, 118, 133, 160
recreation 30, 52-5, 133
  intellectual recreation 61
  rational recreation 10, 52, 130, 186 n.14
Redditch Literary and Scientific Institute 46, 87

Redhill Institution 82, 85
refreshments 53
Reid, Hugo 23–4, 26, 29, 57, 93, 199 n.64
religion
  as banned subject at institutes 20, 103
  (*see also* debate topics; lecture topics; Sabbatarianism)
reviews of lectures in newspapers 123, 138–9, 171–2. *See also* performance, critiques of

Sabbatarianism 136–7, 139, 140, 142
Sadler, Michael 173
Salisbury Literary and Scientific Institution 79, 84
"sappers and miners" 34–5, 93, 116, 137, 157, 177–8, 180
science
  as extension programming 163
  (*see also* debate topics; lecture topics)
Scientific Societies Acts 46
scissors-and-paste reporting 2, 9, 172
Scottish Secular Union (Edinburgh) 139
secondary education 24, 61, 116–17, 130, 154, 160. *See also* technical education, higher education
Selbourne Society 181
self-improvement 4, 11, 17–22, 27, 33, 57, 86, 102, 103, 109, 139, 154, 157, 160. *See also* lecture categories; topics of lectures
Shakespeare 4, 54, 70–1, 174. *See also* lecture topics
Sherborne Literary Society 79
Simpson, Alfred 152
Simpson, Joseph 11, 115, 119–24, 128–30, 132–3, 149–52, 154–5, 157, 158–9, 164, 179, 223 n.3
Smiles, Samuel 8, 27, 86, 129
social sciences
  as extension programming 163
  (*see also* categories of debates; categories of lectures)
Society of Arts 4, 10, 14, 18, 21–3, 25, 29, 31, 32, 45–6, 67, 102, 107, 117, 134
soirees 10, 15, 20, 47, 66–7
Solly, Henry 52
Southport Town Hall Literary Lectures 127–128

spectacle (in lectures) 16, 97, 125, 136, 143, 145, 154
suburban institutes 11, 119, 133–4, 173
Sudbury Literary Institution 56, 85
suffrage 9, 70, 87, 159–60
Sunday Evenings for the People 139
Sunday Lecture Societies 135–9, 158. *See also specific cities*
Sunday Lecture Society (London) 11, 31, 42, 48, 76, 115, 135–9, 141, 146, 150–1, 158, 168
Sunday Observance Act 136, 142–3, 229 n.103
Sunderland Sunday Lecture Society 141
sympathy in/as citizenship 159–61, 173

technical education 23, 61, 62, 130, 160, 175
TED talks 182
theatricals 48, 59, 62, 133, 150, 152, 154
1851 census 18, 22
1867 Reform Act 26, 159
Traice, W. H. J. 21, 23, 25, 30, 33–4, 43, 49, 95, 198 n.52
trends in lecture topics by period
  1850–1871 76–113
  1871–1914 112–13, 143–55, 172–8
Tyneside Sunday Lecture Series 140–1

Ulverston Mechanics' Institute 84, 98, 100
Union of Institutions 14, 18, 29, 31, 33, 42, 45, 67, 107
university extension movement 11, 155, 161–6, 178–9
  funding 162, 166
urbanization 3

ventriloquism 92, 134
"*viva voce*" 112
voluntaryism 9, 33–6, 45. *See also* gratuitous lecturers

Wakefield Mechanics' Institute 84, 87, 90, 95, 98, 152, 153
war correspondents 118, 138, 146
Watson, Robert Spence 76, 100, 149
Whewell, William 107–11, 222 n.89
Women Lecturers' Association 178

Women Lecturers' Institute 178
Workers' Education Association 11,
 155, 166
 1908 Report 166–7
Working Men's Clubs 52
working men's colleges 61

Working Men's Educational Union 29
Wright, Thomas 99, 165

Yorkshire Union of Mechanics' Institutes
 18, 31–3, 48, 56, 60–3, 73–4, 83, 92,
 117, 129, 136, 160

www.ingramcontent.com/pod-product-compliance
Lightning Source LLC
Chambersburg PA
CBHW071813300426
44116CB00009B/1292